D0026678

TE DUE

Oxford Studies in the History of Art and Architecture

General Editors   Francis Haskell · Charles Mitchell · John Shearman

JAMES TISSOT

MICHAEL WENTWORTH

CLARENDON PRESS · OXFORD

1984

UNIVERSITY OF TOLEDO LIBRARIES

Oxford University Press, Walton Street, Oxford OX2 6DP

London Glasgow New York Toronto
Delhi Bombay Calcutta Madras Karachi
Kuala Lumpur Singapore Hong Kong Tokyo
Nairobi Dar es Salaam Cape Town
Melbourne Auckland

and associated companies in
Beirut Berlin Ibadan Mexico City Nicosia

Oxford is a trade mark of Oxford University Press

Published in the United States
by Oxford University Press, New York

© Michael Wentworth 1984

All rights reserved. No part of this publication may be reproduced,
stored in a retrieval system, or transmitted, in any form or by any means,
electronic, mechanical, photocopying, recording, or otherwise, without
the prior permission of Oxford University Press

British Library Cataloguing in Publication Data
Wentworth, Michael
James Tissot.
(Oxford studies in the history of art & architecture)
1. Tissot, James
I. Title.
759.4   ND553.T6
ISBN 0-19-817364-4

Library of Congress Cataloging in Publication Data
Wentworth, Michael.
James Tissot.
(Oxford studies in the history of art and architecture)
Bibliography: p.
Includes index.
1. Tissot, James Jacques Joseph, 1836–1902.
I. Title.   II. Series.
ND553.T6A4 1984   759.4   83–12196
ISBN 0-19-817364-4

Typeset by Hope Services, Abingdon.
Text printed at the
University Press, Oxford.
Plates printed by
BAS Printers Ltd, Over Wallop, Hampshire.

ND
553
.T6A4
1984

Preface and Acknowledgements

I have read, and sometimes written, about Tissot for twenty years. Those years have seen the development of an attitude towards French painting in the second half of the nineteenth century radically different from that prevailing when this study was begun, and Tissot, a shadowy ghost from a discredited past, has emerged into the limelight as a fit subject for scholarly research, as a painter again worthy of the attention of major museums, and as that corrodent of aesthetic values and civilized life, an *investment*. The reader of these pages will soon discover that I am not without reservations about much of what has happened. The desire to enlarge our understanding of nineteenth-century painting with a disinterested reconsideration of the Academy as well as its now-triumphant victims is only to be praised, but this admirable endeavour too often degenerates into something less proportionate. Fraught with dangerous confusions, it can only distort our sense of historic significance and our aesthetic values, ultimately compromising our own standards and the standing of those who truly deserve the designation of greatness. For that reason, perhaps, I have taken what may seem unnecessary pains to keep Tissot in perspective. I have tried to do him full justice and still avoid the superlatives which give the literature of rediscovery an air of sanctimony that would be amusing were it not dangerous, and I will doubtless be accused of benighted pessimism in this euphoric new world of artistic reviviscence.

When I began to study Tissot, hardly anyone thought him significant, and few found him interesting. My aberration was rarer in those innocent days, but even then I differed from the general opinion only in finding him interesting. Increased knowledge of his strange artistic character, his complex position in the art of his time, and his pictures themselves has long since proved his abiding fascination. My aim, however, is neither to rescue his battered reputation nor to equip him with an importance to which he has no claim in his own time or in ours. If I compare him freely to his greater contemporaries, it is a juxtaposition intended to demonstrate similarities or differences, but not to suggest equality of talent or historical significance. On his own merits, Tissot is one of the few truly interesting artists of the *juste milieu*. As a painter he was able, intelligent, and aware. He was concerned with the problems of his art, and if his concern too often took second place to the desire to manufacture commercial *objets de luxe*, his failure and our loss can still be read in the rare quality of his best pictures.

His art was compromised, but it was not barren. He was sympathetic to a great deal of painting more advanced than his own—an attitude uncommon enough among his peers to appear almost a virtue—and if, as Degas suggested of someone else, sympathy was inspired by a desire to pick the artistic pockets of the avant-garde, there was also acknowledgement of interaction of a more positive nature. Tissot repays study with greater understanding of his century and genuine if inter-mittent aesthetic pleasure. I have attempted to evaluate an artist not of the first rank within a particular context and in a manner suitable to his gifts and qualities. If this study succeeds, its success lies not only in the clarification of his individual accomplishment, but also in helping to point up the quite different accomplish-ments of his peers.

The remarkable course in nineteenth-century draughtsmanship given by Charles S. Chetham at the University of Michigan in 1962 gave me my first oppor-tunity to study Tissot under the guidance of a knowledgeable teacher, and to write about him for the catalogue of the exhibition *A Generation of Draughtsmen*, which was among the first to consider the artists of the Academy *vis-à-vis* the masters of Impressionism. I am grateful to him for his encouragement then, and for his kindness over the years. In 1968, I was invited to take part in the *Tissot Retrospective Exhibition* organized by the Rhode Island School of Design and the Art Gallery of Ontario. It gave me the opportunity to give order to information I had accumulated and to augment it with that gathered by the other authors of the catalogue, Henri Zerner and David S. Brooke. Our work together informs this study in the most fundamental way. Henri Zerner's introduction to the catalogue remains central to any understanding of Tissot: its ideas and insights can perhaps be elaborated upon, they can hardly be enlarged. In 1978, the Minneapolis Institute of Arts mounted the first exhibition of Tissot's complete prints, and I am grateful to Samuel Sachs, II, Director, and to John W. Ittmann, Curator of Prints, for their invitation to undertake the *catalogue raisonné* which accompanied the exhibition. For their help in the preparation of the catalogue, I remain grateful to Harold Peterson, Director of Publications, and to Nancy Akre and Dorothy Pamer Sinha, who served as editors. Some early drafts of the present study were written at the same time, and I can only thank them for their help in keeping both projects moving forward at once.

It is impossible to thank all the people who have given generously of their time and knowledge over the years, as this study gradually evolved. I can only hope that my oversights will be taken as a flaw of memory rather than a lack of gratitude, and be accordingly forgiven. Among Tissot scholars, Jane, Lady Abdy has been a generous and unfailing source of information and encouragement: her interest has added immensely to many aspects of this study. Chūji Ikegami generously shared his discoveries about Tissot's appointment as drawing master to Prince Akitake with me before its publication and also obtained the photograph of the Prince's portrait which is included here. Willard E. Misfeldt has contributed greatly to Tissot scholarship, and although I often differ from his aesthetic assessment of Tissot, my quite different conclusions in no way affect my admiration for his work or my debt to it. The late Marita Ross, an enterprising London journalist, was hardly a Tissot scholar in the technical sense, but she discovered the identity of Mrs Newton, writing about her with great verve, and she preserved the family photographs which have been of inestimable value to later scholars, putting us doubly in her debt. Ian Thomson, who is writing about Tissot as a religious artist, has been informative and generous. Hugh Gourley, Jeremy Maas, and Graham Reynolds have written about Tissot with great insight. It is also a pleasure to pay tribute to the two authors who served as my earliest introduction to Tissot. The late James Laver's *Vulgar Society*, despite its biographical errors, remains as evocative and stylish a study as even Tissot could have wished, and his kindness at the time of the 1968 *Tissot Retrospective Exhibition* was of great benefit. Sir Sacheverell Sitwell's writing on Tissot in *Narrative Pictures* captures the tart, elusive flavour of Tissot's painting with unsurpassed grace and has provided a model of insight and beauty.

When this book was already in the press, I was privileged to read the manuscript of Malcolm Warner's book on Tissot, which is a work of great perception and delightful wit. Gert Schiff's remarkable study of Tissot's illustrations to the Old Testament—works themselves long in storage—for the catalogue of the splendid exhibition at the Jewish Museum in New York in 1982 also appeared too late for me to take advantage of its many insights: it must be cited, however, as absolutely essential for an understanding of Tissot's last works. It has fortunately proved possible to include references to both books in the bibliography.

Crucial to future Tissot studies will be the three albums of photographs which Tissot himself kept as a record of his own work, and which have recently reappeared. Exhibited—and tantalizingly described in the catalogue—at his Dudley Gallery exhibition in 1882, the albums figured among Tissot material with a provenance of the château de Buillon which was sold at Sotheby's, Monte Carlo, in June 1982, almost exactly a hundred years after their last public appearance. Rediscovered when most of these pages were already in proof, it has proved possible only to test my assumptions about unlocated works against the evidence of this new material, and in some few cases to take advantages of the photographs themselves to reproduce unlocated pictures. Although the album photographs have sometimes suffered slight damage, and are not always of ideal quality for reproduction, their documentary value clearly outweighs their defects. The albums themselves are now in a private collection in the United States and in the near future are to serve as the basis of a catalogue raisonné of Tissot's paintings.

The study of Tissot must be predicated in great part on the work of scholars writing on his friends and contemporaries, and I am indebted to those scholars whose names are to be found in the bibliography and notes. In some cases, it is necessary to add personal gratitude to professional thanks. The late Professors Jacob Rosenberg and Benjamin Rowland must be mentioned as much for their kindness as for the examples of scholarship they set. Agnes Mongan has been inimitable as a scholar and irreplaceable as a friend. Christopher Lloyd, of the Ashmolean Museum, Oxford, Geneviève Lacambre, of the Musée d'Orsay, Paris, and Theodore Reff, of Columbia University, have taken an interest in this study for which I am most grateful, and Marjorie B. Cohn, of the Fogg Art Museum Department of Conservation, has shared technical insights and offered her encouragement for many years. I am also grateful to Ronald Pickvance, of Glasgow University, who has often brought my attention to material I might otherwise have missed, and has offered valuable suggestions about the scope of this book, and to Guy Sainty, of Stair–Sainty, Fine Arts, Ltd., New York, who has shared his insights (the identification of Emma Dobigny in *Le Goûter* is his), and his enthusiasm for Tissot, with great generosity.

I am indebted to the libraries which have made so much of the work for this study a pleasure. The Harvard University Libraries have been the mainstay of my research. At the Fogg Museum Library, I am grateful to William Frietag, Librarian, Mary Ward, Librarian Emeritus, and to Richard Simpson and Brian Tynemouth for their helpfulness, and at the Houghton Library, to Eleanor M. Garvey, Curator of Printing and Graphic Arts, and the staff of the Reading Room. At the Boston Athenaeum, I am indebted to Rodney M. Armstrong, Director, for his kindness, and to Sally Pierce for her tireless assistance in my quest of nineteenth-century periodicals. At the Boston Public Library, I am grateful to the staff of the Fine Arts Reading Room, to Sinclair H. Hitchings, Keeper of Prints, and to Earl R. Taylor, Department of Rare Books and Manuscripts, who helped with the compilation of material for appendix VI, for their kindness. I am also indebted to the staffs of the Bibliothèque-Nationale, Paris, the Frick Reference Library and the Metropolitan Museum Library, New York, the New England Historic Genealogical Society Library, Boston, and the Victoria and Albert Museum Library and the Witt Library of the Courtauld Institute, London.

I am indebted to the collectors, curators, and dealers who have generously given permission to reproduce works in their possession and have often gone to considerable difficulty to obtain photographs for me. In every case, I have attempted to trace both current owner and copyright holder of the photographs, and where I have been unable to do so, I apologize for the omission. For their help with photographs and permissions, I am particularly grateful to the Marquis of Bristol; Adeline Cacan de Bissy, Conservateur, Musée du Petit Palais; Peter Cannon-Brookes, Keeper of Art, the National Museum of Wales; Robert Cashey, the Shepherd Gallery; Margaret Christian, Christie's; Fionah Creigh, Sotheby's Belgravia; Derek FitzGerald, Christie's, London; Sir John Geilgud; Richard Green,

The Richard Green Galleries; Gregory Hedburg, Curator of Painting, the Minneapolis Institute of Arts; Robert Isaacson; Marcus Linell, Sotheby's Belgravia; Jeremy Maas, the Maas Gallery; Roy Miles, Roy Miles Fine Paintings; the Marquis de Miramon; Jean-Marie Moulin, Conservateur, Musée National du Château de Compiegne; Gabriel M. Naughton, Thomas Agnew and Sons; Ronald P. Nolan, Secretary, the National Gallery of Victoria; Vincent Price; Liberty Reese, Stair–Sainty Fine Arts Ltd.; Joseph Rishel, Curator of European Painting, the Philadelphia Museum of Art; Polly J. Sartori, Department of Painting, the Metropolitan Museum of Art; Herman Shickman, The Shickman Gallery; Maria-Christina Wittgenstein, Sotheby Parke-Bernet; Tamsyn Woolcombe, Sotheby's Belgravia; Jeffrey Wortman, The Shickman Gallery; and Baronne van Yperzele de Strihou, Curator of the Royal Collection at Brussels. I am also grateful to B. T. Batsford Ltd. and Constable and Co. for their permission to reproduce now unlocated pictures from their publications, and to Suzanne Stohlman, Michael Nedzweski, and Rick Stafford of the Fogg Museum Photographic Service for their assistance.

I am grateful to Professor Jean Seznec for reading an early draft of my manuscript and bringing it to the attention of Oxford University Press. The manuscript was typed by Jane Nussbaum with patience and accuracy. The late Marianna Barzun read early chapters as they were typed, and Jacques Barzun was kind enough to make suggestions concerning technical and literary problems. The late Alice Lowell read the manuscript and encouraged my writing with the wisdom and generosity which long endeared her to her friends. Annella Brown, Peter See, Arthur McCabe, and Richard and Leslie Sheehan took an interest in my work and gave valuable advice on many points. Ellen Faulke and Laura Miknyocki kindly assisted with the development of this study; Doris and Frederick Bensen offered their hospitality as some of it was written; and Ruth and Herbert Schimmel watched over its development with benevolence. Elaine Loeffler and Elsbeth Dusenbury generously checked references for me in Europe and America when I was unable to do so myself. Elyse Salignac Rushford helped me with the translation of certain troublesome French texts and shared her unrivalled memories of a Paris childhood at the turn of the century as the daughter of one of the most admired artists at the Opéra-Comique. Her reminiscences of Sarah Bernhardt, who knew Tissot, of Réjane, whose portrait he painted, and of Widor, who played at the dedication of his colossal Christ, have given them a reality they otherwise never could have had for me. The late Patricia Smallwood Blaine often discussed this book with me; her rare sense of history and vibrant wit added greatly to my own concept of it as it evolved. It is perhaps my greatest regret that she did not see its completion. George Gravert encouraged my work with unlimited patience and total understanding; that it reached its conclusion is due in great part to his belief that it would, and I am very grateful to him.

I am grateful to all the officers of Oxford University Press for their help, but especially to John Bell, whose patience and kindness have made every aspect of the production of this book an absolute pleasure. I am also indebted to Frances Whistler, whose editing has made her on occasion virtually a collaborator.

If I have so far failed to name my friends Eugenia Parry Janis and David S. Brooke, it is from the desire to give my thanks an emphasis of position. Eugenia Janis and I have talked about Tissot and the nineteenth century for twenty years, and I am grateful to her for those conversations, for her generous response to each draft of this manuscript, and for her perceptive criticism. David Brooke and I met because of Tissot in 1965, and since that time his ideas, criticism, and wit have brought—and kept—much material in focus for me as my writing progressed. His generosity and enthusiasm for this project have added immeasurably to the pleasure I have taken in it. I would like to dedicate this book to them, to George Gravert, and to my parents.

Contents

List of Plates

Unless otherwise indicated, all works are by James Tissot. Dimensions give height before width.

COLOUR

MONOCHROME

1866). Oil on canvas, 116.84 × 73.66 cm.; signed and dated lower left: *J. J. Tissot / 1865*. Southampton Art Gallery

33. *Le Confessional*, c.1866. Water-colour replica of the 1866 Salon picture acquired by George A. Lucas for William T. Walters in February 1867, 24.13 × 14.29 cm.; signed lower left: *J. Tissot*. The Walters Art Gallery, Baltimore

34. Alfred Stevens (1823–1906), *Les Rameaux*, c.1862 (replica of an unlocated painting exhib. Salon of 1863). Oil on panel, 34.29 × 26.04 cm. The Walters Art Gallery, Baltimore

35. *Jeune Femme chantant à l'orgue* (exhib. Salon of 1867). Whereabouts unknown; reproduced from a Goupil photograph in the Bibliothèque-Nationale, Paris

36. *Self-Portrait*, c.1865. Oil on panel, 49.85 × 30.16 cm.; signed lower right: *James Tissot*. The California Palace of the Legion of Honor, San Francisco, Mildred Anna Williams Collection

37. Edgar Degas (1834–1917), *James Tissot dans un atelier d'artiste*, c.1868. Oil on canvas, 151.45 × 111.76 cm. The Metropolitan Museum of Art, New York, Rogers Fund

38. *The Family of the Marquis de Miramon on the Terrace of the Château de Paulhac*, 1866 (exhib. Cercle de l'Union Artistique, 1866). Oil on canvas, 180.34 × 220.35 cm.; signed and dated lower left: *J. J. Tissot / 1866*. The Marquis de Miramon, Paulhac

39. *Le Cercle de la rue Royale*, 1868. Oil on canvas, 215.9 × 330.2 cm.; signed and dated lower right: *James Tissot 1868*. Private Collection, Paris

40. *The Marquise de Miramon, née Thérèse Feuillant (1840–1912)*, 1866 (exhib. *Exposition Universelle* 1867). Oil on canvas, 127.64 × 75.57 cm.; signed and dated lower right: *J. J. Tissot / 1867*. The Marquis de Miramon, Paulhac

41. *Eugène Coppens de Fontenay*, 1867. Oil on canvas, 69.85 × 39.05 cm.; signed and dated lower right: *J. J. Tissot / Avril 1867*. The Philadelphia Museum of Art, Wilstach Collection

42. *Portrait de femme* (*Rêverie*), ?1867. Oil on canvas, 41.28 × 27.31 cm.; signed and dated indistinctly left centre: *J. J. Tissot / 6(?7)*. Private Collection, Paris (formerly Alphonse Kann, Saint-Germain-en-Laye)

43. *Déjeuner sur l'herbe*, c.1865–8. Oil on canvas, 30.48 × 52.07 cm.; signed lower right: *J. J. Tissot*. Whereabouts unknown

44. *La Terrasse du Jeu de Paume*, c.1867. Oil on canvas, 48.26 × 68.58 cm.; Whereabouts unknown; photograph courtesy of Sotheby's Belgravia

45. *La Retraite dans le jardin des Tuileries*, 1867 (exhib. Salon of 1868). Whereabouts unknown; reproduced from a Bingham photograph in the Bibliothèque-Nationale, Paris

46. Study of a zouave drummer for *La Retraite dans le jardin des Tuileries*, c.1867. Oil on board, 40.64 × 19.37 cm.; signed and inscribed lower left: *Jousef / Ben Moustapha / 3ième Bataillon / J. Tissot*. Photograph courtesy of the H. Shickman Gallery, New York

47. *L'Armoire*, 1867. Oil on canvas, 114.3 × 63.5 cm.; signed and dated lower right: *J. J. Tissot / 1867*. Private Collection, New York

48. *Le Gôuter*, 1869. Oil on canvas, 56.62 × 39.05 cm.; formerly signed and dated lower left: *J. J. Tissot / 1869* (slight damage to the area of the signature was formerly over-painted and a new signature and date added which has since been removed, although it appears in the present reproduction: a Goupil photograph of 1869 records the original signature). Stair–Sainty Fine Arts, Ltd., New York.

49. Stevens, *Fleurs d'automne*, 1867 (exhib. *Exposition Universelle* 1867). Oil on canvas, 74.93 × 55.25 cm. Musées Royaux des Beaux-Arts de Belgique, Brussels

50. *Rêverie*, 1869. Oil on canvas, 33.02 × 41.91 cm.; signed upper right: *J. J. Tissot* and dated upper left: *1869*. Pennsylvania Academy of the Fine Arts, Philadelphia. Bequest of Henry C. Gibson

51. *Une veuve*, 1868 (exhib. Salon of 1869). Whereabouts unknown; reproduced from the

I. James Tissot

*The original quality in any man of imagination is imagery. It is a thing like
the landscapes of his dreams; the sort of world he would wish to make or
in which he would wish to wander; the strange flora and fauna of his own
secret planet; the sort of thing he likes to think about. This general atmosphere, and pattern or structure of growth, governs all his creations however
varied; and because he can in this sense create a world, he is in this sense
a creator; the image of God.*

G. K. Chesterton, *Robert Louis Stevenson* (1928).

THE last decade has seen a serious and widespread reappraisal of the painters of
the nineteenth century. As contemporary taste grows more eclectic, artists who
were until recently dismissed and forgotten have made sensational come-backs in
the sale-room, have once again been given pride of place in the galleries of major
museums, and have been treated to the full barrage of scholarly apparatus in
academic institutions. This enthusiasm has created a problem only now becoming
apparent, for we are faced with the necessity of creating a new methodology and
a new set of standards for the study of artists of marginal aesthetic and historical
importance. The intoxication of rediscovery has led to exhibitions and monographs in which artists of dubious talent are treated by galleries, museums, and
scholars with the reverence formerly reserved for the masters. Yet, if these
exhibitions and monographs have proved anything, they have proved the basic
soundness of history's judgements: after the shouting stops, these artists remain
remarkably as we found them, with their technical accomplishment, their narrative fascination—and their often remarkable silliness, or worse, dullness—neither
diminished nor enlarged. A number of artists of importance, or at least of interest
and charm, have also been given a well-deserved new lease of life. If the treasure-
hunt has not been an unmixed blessing, the tedium of second-rate exhibitions
and the unctuous prose of rediscovery are prices low enough to pay for a greater
good, for this trend points up something more than the miscellaneous skills of
individual artists; it shows the necessity of writing once again the history of a
period until recently considered written with finality.

The real importance of such history lies in its usefulness to the present, but
perhaps less as a factual lesson than as the means of redefining attitudes and

formulating culture. It is easy, and indeed sufficient, to write on Tissot in purely historical terms, for such reconsideration can only cast new light on qualities too long undervalued and neglected. It is more difficult to write about him in aesthetic terms, but the result is more rewarding. Tissot is a minor master with a number of interesting ideas and real technical skill, but nothing will ever make him an artist of the first rank. In accepting his limitations, his gifts can be seen with greater clarity and his individuality appreciated on its own terms.

Too much writing about Tissot has been from a single point of view. The drama and romance of his personal life in juxtaposition with the social heights his pictures seem to scale have tempted writers to dwell with breathless curiosity on biographical irregularities and doting snobbishness on the subjects of his work. There is a certain justification for this approach, for his life, more than many, is of critical importance for an understanding of his art. Told to avoid the biographical fallacy, in Tissot we are faced with what might truly be called the biographical necessity. For him, art was an extension of life, and life, in its turn, became an extension of art; the world he created in his pictures is autobiographical in intent and can serve to reconstruct his life. That romantic idealization gives them the air of a society novel (and later that of a church homily) does not obscure the quality of the diary about them, for it was with the same guises of perfection that he sought to dress his life.

An understanding of this autobiographical bias is essential, but it must be kept in its place. The important thing about Tissot is not that he led a confused personal life or that he mirrored smart society on canvas; it is his qualities as an artist pure and simple, and the insight those qualities can give us about him and about the art of his time. Ruskin once referred to Tissot's canvases as 'mere coloured photographs of vulgar society'.[1] But for Ruskin's derogatory 'mere', Tissot might not have been offended by the remark, for he seems consciously to have sought a non-committal quality in his work then considered characteristic of the camera. His method was suited to his aims, and his skill was great. It was admired at the time, and it is admirable still, but his interest no longer lies in the accuracy of his record; it is found in the subtle distortions he imposed upon reality. His failure at making 'mere coloured photographs' has become their surest guarantee against oblivion.

The great artist nearly always changes our vision and creates a fundamentally new way of seeing. Often radically different from what it succeeds, this vision frightens and alienates the public; and the history of nineteenth-century painting can be written in the series of shocks which punctuate the development of modernism. The historical importance of a painter like Tissot lies in his function as a kind of bridge. Enough of a true artist to appreciate and understand, in a limited

---

[1]   J. Ruskin, *Fors Clavigera*, repr. *Works*, vii, 161.

way, a new kind of vision, but also enough of a conservative to be shocked by it in its pure form, he was yet able to apply advanced ideas to traditional forms. As a result, his pictures were at once exciting and palatable to a large public, and he was able to become the disseminator of advanced concepts on a popular level. In this way, for example, the subjects of Courbet's most scandalous pictures or the radical ideas of Japanese composition were combined with the perfectly familiar— and perfectly respectable—narrative content and high finish required by the Salon, in a manner which helped make advanced seeing part of everyday experience as the uncompromising approach of Manet, Whistler, or Degas never could. In his assimilation of new vision and his application of it in a sensitive but not controversial way, Tissot is clearly ideal. He mirrors nearly every important artistic development of the second half of the nineteenth century in a way which permits its study in conservative popular form, and his parallels are precise as well as intelligent. His chameleon skill was often remarked by friends and, perhaps more often, enemies, in his own time.

But this is hardly enough. More important, Tissot was able to give these borrowed elements an unmistakably individual interpretation. Beyond cataloguing the artistic movements of his time, his canvases evoke the personality of their creator, and it is Tissot's own personality which gives his pictures their unfailing style. His autobiographical canvases conform to the pattern of their ideal world as faithfully as those of Degas or Whistler to theirs, and without a confusion of quality it is possible to say that a picture by Tissot is as easily identifiable, and for the same reason.

This sharp sense of individuality sets Tissot's pictures apart from the canvases of his peers, and assures them a life beyond the mere accuracy which might otherwise have dated them as hopelessly as a page from an illustrated magazine. This resolute accuracy gives him a secure and honourable place as a *peintre des modes*, offering a fascinating secondary theme for any study of his work, but the *peintre des modes* must give way in importance to the *peintre des moeurs*, for no small part of his gift lies in his brilliance as a narrative painter.

If Tissot had not been acutely aware of the changing artistic currents of his time and responsive enough to assimilate them with intelligence, it is likely that he would be forgotten today by all but the most determined admirers of the academic tradition. Had the shallow historicism of his Leysian beginnings perpetuated itself across the decades into the mediocrity of the Bible illustrations, his career might be of interest for the social and philosophical questions it posed, but hardly for its aesthetic significance. The modern world interposed itself between Tissot and that fate in the early 1860s. Brought to the subject by the example of friends and the insistence of a triumphant middle class that its pleasures be documented by its painters, Tissot began his evolution as a *peintre de la vie moderne*. The nineteenth century redefined and broadened subjects of modern life inherited from the rococo in terms of its own realities: the dandy and the 'modern' beauty replaced Cytherean pilgrims as the heroes and heroines of an art of pleasure that had moved from the bosquets of the *fête champêtre* to the boulevards, cafés, Salons, and parks of the city.

This happy meeting of artistic subject-matter and contemporary life in the sixties created a generation of *peintres-flâneurs* whose attitudes would create Impressionism and change the course of modern painting. The streets were the source of subjects, and artists took to them in quest of an ideal. The attempt to capture what was called 'modern sentiment', a blend of modern emotion, modern setting, and modern beauty, would become the search for perfection. Beneath a purposefully dispassionate surface, deep emotion and careful reasoning would govern every aspect of their study. Tissot most clearly approached the ideal in his early London picture *Waiting for the Train (Willesden Junction)* (pl. 98): with its sense of casual encounter and modern beauty—a stranger glimpsed in the crowd—and its modern setting (the railroad was often considered the epitome of civilization), it is a clear nineteenth-century answer to the *Embarquement pour Cythère*.

Painters as diverse as Tissot, Alfred Stevens, Manet, and Renoir were all the inheritors of the rococo tradition; each in his own way was temperamentally suited to translate the sheen of flesh and the pleasures of the *fête galante* into middle-class terms without the loss of spaciousness and grace. Stevens's *La Dame en rose* (pl. 58), Manet's *La Musique dans le jardin des Tuileries* (pl. 105), and Renoir's *Le Moulin de la Galette* (1876; Louvre) each look to the eighteenth century in an emulation and homage of an entirely personal kind. In works like *Still on Top* and *Holyday* (pls. 109 and 123), Tissot also shows himself capable of such mellifluous eighteenth-century balance, and indeed casts his *fêtes champêtres* with such conviction in terms of the Victorian plutocracy that one cannot fail to wonder if satire is not also present in these Watteaus *chez* St. John's Wood. Tissot's vision of paradise is always beset by doubt. A mass of contradictions, reservations, pessimism, and ironic detachment, he was too much of his century to admit to an untroubled vision of pleasure. Only for a brief moment in the late seventies when love dissolved anxiety did Eden become artistically viable. More often, man exists in a world which may reflect his feelings, as in *A Passing Storm* (pl. 116), but only those of his own alienation and indifference. His English masterpiece, *The Ball on Shipboard* (pl. 102) is as ravishing a *fête champêtre* as anything in eighteenth-century painting, but beneath the glassy surface of its perfection a total lack of human interplay and an equal absence of any real sense of pleasure hints that the world—for Tissot, at least—had indeed lost something of Tallyrand's sweetness of life. For Tissot, the pleasures of the rich are fraught with a sadness and tension which even their glittering surfaces cannot disguise. Pleasure and parade have become the pretexts which fill the empty hours of a class with plenty of leisure and no real responsibilities, and Tissot is at pains to suggest the wearisome quality of the treadmill beneath the brilliant round of pleasure—the sense of emptiness, tension, and loneliness at the centre of the crowd. To a very real degree, Tissot knew the ways of such society with the subtle understanding of an insider, although by temperament he preferred to stand somewhat apart, and its *longueurs* were as familiar to him as its surface homogeneity and its harmonious face. *The Ball on Shipboard*, despite its quality of casual observation and its subject-matter, is neither a snapshot of social life nor a carefree record of pleasure. In its hallucinatory perfection it is a summation, and an abstraction, of what it represents. Its means are essential to its end: composed with a formal deliberation rare in his work and painted with a command that is total, design and execution only throw its psychological fragmentation into sharper relief.

The *Ball on Shipboard* is like a sumptuous dress rehearsal for the series *La Femme à Paris* which Tissot completed some ten years later, for in this series Tissot attempted a monumental summary of his aesthetic as a painter of society. Society itself is now clearly seen as ritual. Self-conscious, and with a hostile consciousness of the viewer, the stilted forms and stylized expressions of *La Femme à Paris* are archetypic rather than particular, and Tissot's tart humour, always present in some degree in his work (pl. 88), comes vividly into its own to flavour these comedies with an ironic detachment entirely personal.

The fifteen pictures of the series are Tissot's last great statement as a painter of modern life. In many ways, they still await rediscovery—too many remain unlocated, and they demand an exhaustive study of their position in the art of their time, which is complex. Too often, they are considered in terms of Impressionism and denigrated as monstrous anachronisms. They are both more and less. If they do in truth owe much to Impressionism, they owe as much to Leys and to English painting. And if they are obsolete, their very obsolescence somehow serves to propel them forward into the world of Seurat and Vuillard where their formal structure and sense of ritual appear quite comfortably at home.

La Femme à Paris was a failure when it was exhibited, but whether Tissot considered it as such had already become an academic question. Work on the last picture in the series, *Musique sacrée* (whereabouts unknown) had taken him into Parisian churches to seek local colour, and the shock brought him full circle to his beginnings as a quasi-religious painter. His return to the church avoided the questions raised by *La Femme à Paris* in artistic if not personal terms, but it was an answer common enough among world-weary reprobates at the height of the Catholic Revival. The popular triumph of the Bible illustrations belongs as much to the history of religion as the history of art.

Like Degas, Tissot was essentially an artist of ideas, of human psychology defined by gesture, and human relations described by space. Close association in the 1860s made their aesthetic philosophy develop along parallel lines and a similarity of temperament made for a superficial resemblance in their pictures. When Tissot went to London, his work veered sharply in the direction of narrative, but until 1885 there are often numerous points of comparison. Yet Tissot's artistic personality was quite different. More than Degas, he attempted to tie psychological exploration to an art of pleasure. As a result, he tended towards an aesthetic *faire joli* which was of little interest to Degas, towards a different kind of subject-matter and a 'higher' class of people. Yet to the narrow world of Parisian soubrettes and French widows, and later to the daughters of British plutocrats, he brought a refined and subtle sense of dramatic possibility.

For modern taste, much of Tissot's individuality and appeal resides in his masterful manipulation of the various elements of his narrative. Retaining the high finish expected at the Salon and the Academy, he focused his real gifts on the subtle elaboration of dramatic content. Rejecting the 'subjectlessness' of Impressionism, as philosophically difficult for the nineteenth century to comprehend as a lack of finish, he was equally careful to avoid the paralysing overstatement of his academic contemporaries, and his pictures cannot be read in the same manner. He always preferred breadth of interpretation and *double entendre*: feelings and situations are never explicit. Late in his career, Tissot told Alfred de Lostalot that he had always avoided descriptive titles as much as possible; the titles of his pictures were 'not intended to express anything'.[2] Reticence and wit are his pictures' greatest charm. The subject is indicated, but it is never laboured, and, as with successful plays, everything is made to contribute directly to the whole.

Tissot's cast of characters is always extremely limited, although it changes from period to period and always suggests a strong element of self-projection. Drawn to alienation and estrangement, his protagonists are often socially anomalous, at a tangent to the society to which they belong. Widows, widowers, and orphans are set apart by mourning (pls. 48, 122, 138 and 180); young women by abstraction (pl. 99), anxiety (pl. 52), and failing strength (pl. 100). Young people struggle with romantic difficulties (pl. 124), or misalliance (pls. 178 and 185), and even twin sisters find themselves uncomfortable rivals (pl. 137).

Like his protagonists, Tissot's dramaturgy is circumscribed. He favoured situations which had in common reticence, imbalance, and latent tension. Typical of his subjects are lovers' quarrels (pl. 97), partings (pl. 76), convalescence (pl. 113), boredom (pl. 77), romantic choice (pl. 115), and travel (pl. 147).

Drama is played out in the ambiguous tension of works like *Bad News* or the *Calcutta* (pls. 78 and 124) in a language of gesture, the direction of eyes and the turn of a head. Single figures are imbued with a like atmosphere; *L'Escalier* and *A Convalescent* (pls. 52 and 99) are charged with the anticipatory gaze of one young woman and the vacuous lack of energy of the other. Often, an atmosphere

---

[2] A. de Lostalot, 'James Tissot', *Society of French Aquarellistes*, p. 381.

heavy with an almost narcotic sensuality hints at obsession at odds with subject. The *double entendre* of *Boarding the Yacht* (pl. 88) is a case in point, but even the seemingly innocent domesticity of a work like *Croquet* (pl. 142) has a sexual edge which it is impossible to ignore.

Psychological state is made concomitant with setting. In *Les Adieux* (pl. 76), the column separating the lovers makes their parting tangible; in *London Visitors* (pl. 106), the chill monumental architecture points up the Parian sensuality of the hostile protagonist. Weather and season serve similar purposes, and psychological states are contrasted with faded hopes (pl. 114) or equated with passing storms (pl. 116). Tissot always used such backgrounds to promote dramatic intent. They give energy and dimension to the central image as they continually redirect attention to it. Setting, weather, and season describe aspects and emotions; all heighten and activate feeling.

This circular construction gives his pictures powerful psychological impact. In their neurotic intensity and ambiguous situation they become the embodiments of fable and romance, for if simplification makes character one-dimensional, it also makes it larger than life. As obvious images of self-projection, in which Tissot directs the action and takes all the parts, his pictures' success must ultimately be measured in terms of his own troubled psychology. In 1890, Edmond de Goncourt described the essence of his contradictory being. As vivid as one of Tissot's narratives, his portrait can stand beside them to serve as a foil for, if not an explanation of, his art:

Tissot, cet être complexe, mâtiné de mysticisme et de roublardise, cet intelligent laborieux en dépit de son crâne inintelligent et de ses yeux de merlan cuit, ce passionné, trouvant tous les deux ou trois ans un nouveau appassionnement avec lequel il contracte un nouveau petit bail de sa vie.[3]

[3] E. and J. de Goncourt, *Journal: mémoires de la vie littéraire*, iii, 1112.

II. Le Jeune Homme Moyen-Âge

Si quelqu'un doit finir la cathédrale de Cologne, ce sera M. Tissot.

Émile Chantrel, 'Salon de 1863'.

THE most complete contemporary account we have of Tissot's antecedents and childhood is contained in an article by George Bastard which was published in the *Revue de Bretagne* in 1906.[1] Although it appeared four years after the artist's death, a letter from Tissot reproduced in the text attests to the acquaintance of biographer and subject, and the article itself has the marks of having been based on first-hand information: its anecdotes and ambiguities have the ring of truth. Obviously, the story Bastard tells of Tissot's schoolboy preference for sliding on the waxed parquet of the Musée de Nantes in high-spirited neglect of the works of art is a personal reminiscence of Tissot's, and genealogical details have all the proud vagueness of family tradition.[2] Whatever its factual veracity, the article is of singular interest, for it undoubtedly records what Tissot himself remembered and believed.[3]

According to Bastard, the Tissot family was Italian in origin, claiming descent from an Alessandro Tizzone, or Tizzoni, who lived at Vercelli in the eleventh century. The family established a number of branches in France, adopting the French variations Tizzo, Tisso, and Tissot, of the Italian Tizzone, the *tizzone*, or *tison*, a burning brand, being their ancient coat of arms.[4] The painter's ancestors

---

[1] G. Bastard, 'James Tissot', *Revue de Bretagne*, 253–78. Unless otherwise cited, genealogical data and material on Tissot's life prior to his departure for Paris are based on Bastard, pp. 253–7.

[2] For the first, 'il passait le majeure partie de son temps à essayer des patins à roulettes sur le parquet ciré du musée', p. 256; for the second, an ancestor 'géographe du roi d'Espagne au temps de Velasquez', p. 253. Credence is given to this unlikely-sounding claim by the fact that the Franche-Comté remained a part of the Spanish Empire until 1667. As a French province, it remained intact until the Revolution, after which it was divided into three *départements*, the Doubs, the Jura, and Haute-Saône. The Tissot family lived in the area which became the Doubs.

[3] Bastard's account corresponds in its major outlines with biographical research by Willard E. Misfeldt which is based in part on the study of municipal records at Nantes and on an unpublished Tissot genealogy by Gerard de Gournay: see W. Misfeldt, *James Tissot: A Bio-Critical Study*, pp. 11–14, 238.

[4] The Tizzone arms are blazoned 'trois tisons, sable allumés de gueules, en bande, sur argent' (Théodore de Renesse, *Dictionnaire des figures héraldiques*, 7 vols. (Brussels: Société Belge de Librairie, 1903), vii, 43). None of the French Tissots appear to have used this coat: the arms of the Tissots in the Franche-Comté were 'd'azur au sautoir engrêlé d'or, chargé d'un cœur du champ' (J.-B. Rietstep, *Armorial général*, 2 vols. (Gouda: G.B.

in the Franche-Comté descended from a Claude Tissot, several times mayor of Pontarlier, who was granted a fief there in 1532 and was released from salt taxes the following year in return for an embassy undertaken for Charles V to the Swiss Confederation.[5] One of Claude Tissot's descendants removed from Pontarlier to Trevillars at the beginning of the seventeenth century, and for the next two hundred years the family lived as minor *noblesse de campagne*, supplying *seigneurs* and dignitaries of local distinction to Trevillars and Mèche, little mountain villages close to the Swiss border, with fortified châteaux and low chalets which Bastard likens to the settings of Erckmann-Chatrian's *L'Ami Fritz*.

Marcel-Théodore Tissot, the artist's father, was born at Trevillars on 15 February 1807, the son of Joseph-Marie Tissot and Marie-Catherine Beck. Trevillars, however, could not contain his ambition, and in his early twenties he left home, presumably to improve his fortune—another product of the restlessness and social change which marked the years following Waterloo. After travelling in Flanders and Brittany, he settled at Nantes and went into business as a wholesale *marchand de nouveautés*,[6] an occupation interesting enough in view of his son's later preoccupation with the minute delineation of modish *toilettes*, and one which initiated the artist from birth in the mysteries of fashionable dress. In a biographical article written to mark the painter's election to the Société d'Aquarellistes Français in 1883, Alfred de Lostalot says that the elder Tissot was an avid amateur conchologist. His mania had an exclusivity which 'left him no tenderness towards the fine arts' and robbed his son's artistic success of any value in his eyes.[7] In 1832, Marcel Tissot married Marie Durand, a young woman said to have been brought up, like the heroine of one of Balzac's *Scènes de la vie de province*, 'dans des principes très religieux et des sentiments tout à fait royalistes' by a family 'austère et pieuse, ruinée par la Révolution'.[8] Mlle Durand had also made her way

van Goor, 1884–7), ii, 916), and the arms of Tissot de Pontarlier, those of the painter's family, appear to have been differenced by replacing the original charge with 'une rose d'azur' (Roger de Lurion, *Nobiliarie de Franche-Comté*, p. 552).

[5] Lurion, p. 552. Claude Tissot was also the ancestor of the family which established itself nearby at Orgelet in the seventeenth century and took the name Tissot de Mérona in 1745 when Pierre-François Tissot, a successful lawyer, bought the seigniory of Mérona. In other lines of descent, the family established protestant branches in Switzerland and Holland.

[6] Municipal Records, Nantes, cited in Misfeldt, p. 13. As a wholesale linen-draper in a port city, Marcel Tissot doubtless based much of his business on import–export trade. For a discussion of linen-draping, one of the most profitable trades in the

nineteenth century, see anon., *The Book of English Trades* (London: Richard Phillips, 1818), pp. 226–31.

[7] Lostalot, 'Tissot', p. 370. An unlocated still life which is dated 1866 is composed principally of specimen shells (accompanied by books, one of them Japanese, a couple of small Egyptian antiquities, and a globe), and may well have been intended by the painter as a tribute for his father.

[8] Bastard, p. 254. Bastard's statements concerning Marie Durand were doubtless based on family tradition but are not otherwise documented; they seem plausible enough for a family of royalist sympathies in the area around the Vendée at the time of the Revolution. Misfeldt, p. 14, on the basis of de Gournay, establishes her as the daughter of a veterinary surgeon whose family came to Nantes from Mayenne at the time of the Revolution. She was born at Nantes in 1802 and died at Buillon in 1861.

in trade, and Bastard speaks of her as a successful *fabricante de chapeaux* whose wares were exported to the Antilles. Four sons were born of the union: Marcel-Affricani (1835–77), Jacques-Joseph (1836–1902), Albert-François (1838–40), and Oliver-Humbert (1840–69).[9] Ambition, acumen, and piety brought their rewards, and Marcel Tissot was able to return to the Doubs in 1845 with fortune sufficient to buy the château de Buillon, and with it, doubtless, that *position sociale* so eagerly sought by the rising bourgeoisie of the reign of Louis-Philippe.[10]

Bastard makes an interesting summary of Tissot's inheritance from his parents: 'fils d'un Franc-Comtois et d'une Bretonne, il hérita de l'esprit positif de son père et du caractère mystique de sa mère.'[11] The appraisal is accurate, if a trifle facile, and personal enough to make one wonder whether Tissot himself suggested it. The son of a Franc-Comtois, a people most often associated with those qualities ascribed to the Swiss, and a Bretonne, in whose Celtic imagination religion merged fluidly with melancholy and mysticism, Tissot was always to hold the practicality of his father and the piety of his mother in uneasy, if effective, alliance.

Jacques-Joseph Tissot, who would later call himself James, was born at Nantes on 15 October 1836, in the family house, the maison de Guiny in the rue Basse-Grande, close to the house where the Duchesse de Berry had been arrested, and facing the château where Anne of Brittany was born.[12] His first twelve years were spent against a background of the port at the height of the great age of sail. Ships from all over the world lay berthed in the heart of the town, and the sight of tall-masted vessels at the quais was a part of everyday life. James Laver has pointed out that it must have been as a child that Tissot acquired the knowledge of ships and their rigging that he demonstrates with such spellbinding ease in his English shipboard pictures, a kind of familiarity never gained in adult life, being the sole result of early acquaintance and enthusiasm.[13]

In addition to the wonders of the port, Nantes also possessed a well-preserved and newly-appreciated architectural heritage from the Middle Ages. For over a decade, Baron Taylor's encyclopaedic *Voyages pittoresques et romantiques dans l'ancienne France* had been recording monuments which were once again a source of national pride, and at Nantes relics of the medieval past still had all the accessible,

[9] Bastard, p. 254, and Misfeldt, p. 238, for birth and death rates.

[10] Misfeldt, p. 15, for the year of purchase. The château de Buillon, near Besançon, was built in the eighteenth century on the ruins of a suppressed abbey and was sometimes called by its old name, a confusion that led to the tale that Tissot had taken holy orders in his old age. The estate passed to the painter as his father's sole living heir in 1888, and on his death in 1902 it went to his niece, Jeanne Tissot, who died there unmarried in 1964. The estate and the contents of the château, derelict, but preserved as much as possible by Mlle Tissot as her uncle had left it, were sold at auction in 1964.

[11] Bastard, p. 255.

[12] Bastard, p. 255. By 1840, the family had moved nearby to the quai d'Orléans (Municipal Records, Nantes, cited in Misfeldt, p. 14).

[13] J. Laver, *Vulgar Society*, p. 6.

neglected charm which his volumes record.[14] Doubtless Tissot had a familiarity with the town equal to his knowledge of the shipping and the port.

In 1848, after what must have been a thoroughly religious upbringing, Tissot was sent to the Jesuit *collège* at Brugelette, in Flanders, and then, perhaps because he was by his own admission an indifferent scholar, to Vannes, about sixty miles from Nantes, in Brittany, and then to Dôle, in Normandy, before returning to Nantes for his *rhétorique et philosophie*. In response to biographical questions from Alfred de Lostalot in 1883, Tissot wrote:

I do not think there was ever such a lazybones as I. . . . I am one of those rare specimens of pupils who had to pass three times through the examination for the third class. But on the other hand my desk was a perfect museum. Everything was to be seen there, drawings, sculpture, architecture; a gothic belfry in wood, with an octagonal dome, a spire, bell-turrets, etc.[15]

A similar account is found in Bastard, who also calls attention to Tissot's precocious interest in drawing: 'l'amour du dessin le préoccupa beaucoup plus. Ses heures de classe s'écoulaient à illustrer ses livres de vignettes, à historier ses cahiers d'arabesques . . .'.[16] Both biographers remark on Tissot's youthful fascination with the gothic, and it is not surprising that the gloomy solitude of the Flemish and Breton towns where he was educated, towns which also preserved the medieval fabric of their past, turned his thoughts to the art and architecture of the Middle Ages.

According to Bastard, it was architecture which first attracted Tissot. Returning to Nantes, and faced with the necessity of choosing a profession, he considered architecture as a career and is said to have spent his time drawing the details of gothic buildings, the designs of antique furniture, and decorative bric-à-brac. Had he persevered, Tissot might well have joined Viollet-le-Duc in the Second Empire 'medievalization' of gothic France. Instead, he decided to become a painter. Beginning to think seriously of a career as an artist at the age of seventeen, his decision was surely the result of natural inclination and gradual evolution. Bastard tells us only that 'il s'adonna enfin à la peinture, justifiant par là le dicton que: "lorsqu'un talent se produit, on peut en retrouver sa trace dans la lignée ancestrale," car il avait eu dans sa famille un parent, élève de Groos.'[17] If the remark sheds little light on immediate circumstances, it at least suggests a laconic temperament which persisted.

Tissot's decision set in motion that familiar nineteenth-century drama which has as its most famous curtain-line Alexander Cassatt's explosive response to his daughter: 'An artist! I would almost rather see you dead.' Marcel Tissot, with his lack of 'tenderness' towards the fine arts, disavowed natural inclination and insisted on a career more surely rewarding. Paternal opposition stiffened the

[14] Taylor's volumes on Nantes and Brittany were published in 1845–6. It seems likely that Tissot was familiar with them.

[15] Lostalot, 'Tissot', p. 370.

[16] Bastard, p. 255.

[17] Bastard, p. 256. Presumably Gerard de Groos, an engraver at Antwerp in the seventeenth century.

young man's resolve, and Bastard says that Tissot began his career without sympathy or assistance from his father: 'Aussi, lui signifia-t-il un jour, ne désirant pas, disait-il, l'encourager dans cette voie ... d'illusions, qu'il aurait à se tirer d'affaire tout seul s'il voulait persister. Cette résolution décida de la vie artistique de James, qui préféra quitter la maison paternelle.'[18] But his wife's intercession soon eroded Marcel Tissot's intransigence, for Mme Tissot had encouraged her son's resolve from the beginning, and it seems unlikely that the young artist's ties with his family were actually strained to the breaking-point. According to Lostalot, the circumstances were, in fact, far less dramatic: 'It seems probable that Tissot had no great trouble in overcoming the objections of his father, for we find him again at the age of twenty sitting quietly before an easel in the studio of Lamothe.'[19] Unfortunately, we do not know what compromises were, or were not, reached. But whatever the conditions, Jacques-Joseph Tissot went to Paris to become a painter.

He arrived there, at the age of twenty, late in 1856 or early in 1857, and his presence in the city is first recorded at the end of January when he registered for permission to copy at the Louvre.[20] Mme Tissot is said by Bastard to have entrusted her son to Jules-Élie Delaunay, a Nantais painter of her acquaintance, for guidance in Paris,[21] and it may well have been at Delaunay's suggestion that Tissot enrolled as a pupil in the studios of two of his own former teachers, Hippolyte Flandrin and Louis Lamothe, Lyonnais painters who had come to Paris together to study with Ingres. It is difficult to suggest an exact sequence, but Tissot probably began his studies with Flandrin, in whose studio he remained only briefly, or possibly with both artists at once, and then continued his studies with Lamothe alone. In any case, the majority of Tissot's artistic education was unquestionably with Lamothe.[22]

As early as 1883, and perhaps with Tissot's knowledge, Lostalot dismissed Lamothe with scant praise: 'Lamothe? We hardly know where to look for Lamothe

---

[18] Bastard, p. 257.

[19] Lostalot, 'Tissot', p. 371.

[20] Bastard, p. 257, says he left for Paris at the age of twenty, about 1856. The main source of information about Tissot's early addresses in Paris is contained in the files of registrations for permission to copy at the Louvre and the Bibliothèque-Nationale which are transcribed in T. Reff, 'Copyists in the Louvre', *Art Bulletin*, 557-8: registration, 26 January 1857, 41 rue Monsieur-le-Prince (Louvre, carte des permissions, no. 63); 13 April 1858, 10 rue Racine (Louvre, carte no. 218); 16 October 1858, 60 rue Saint-Louis (Cabinet des Estampes, register no. 2266); 14 February 1863, and 22 August 1865, 39 rue Bonaparte (Louvre, cartes d'artistes, nos. 265 and 245). The catalogue of the Salon of 1859 gives his address as 60 rue Saint-Louis; those for 1861-7

as rue Bonaparte. In 1867 or 1868, Tissot moved to a house he had built at 64 avenue de l'Impératrice where he lived until he fled to England in 1871 (catalogues of the Salon, 1868-70). He kept the house, and probably returned to it more often than has previously been suggested during the years he lived in England: the catalogue of the Salon of 1876 gives both his address in London and that in the avenue du Bois de Boulogne (the former avenue de l'Impératrice), and it became his residence again after he left London in 1882.

[21] Bastard, p. 257.

[22] Lostalot, 'Tissot', p. 372. The catalogues of the Salons of 1859 and 1861 list him as a pupil of Flandrin and Lamothe; those for 1863 and 1864 as a pupil of Lamothe, after which all reference to his training is dropped.

today. Assuredly he was a bad painter. True, he had received the instructions of Ingres, and perhaps he was wise enough to hand them on to others.'[23] His judgement is too harsh, whatever truth there may be in the evaluation. Lamothe was a highly competent painter, sometimes even a moving and poetic one, and his influence can hardly have been as baleful as Lostalot suggests. As a teacher, 'cet excellent professeur, baigné dans cette atmosphère ingresque',[24] must have in fact been a sympathetic and understanding guide for his students, and he was clearly able to pass on the priceless technical skills which were the legacy of Ingres. It is perhaps telling enough that Degas, Lamothe's most illustrious pupil, is said to have sought advice from his old teacher long after he left the studio.[25] Henri Lerolle, one of his later pupils, made what is the most gentle, yet ultimately the most just, appraisal of his teacher, 'un pauvre homme voué au malheur':

Il fut élève d'Ingres en même temps que Flandrin. Il avait un dessin noble et incisif qu'il tenait de son maître et qui était bien au-dessus du dessin mou et raboté de Flandrin. Seulement sa nature timide et sa misère l'ont empêché de se montrer autant qu'il l'aurait dû . . . et toute sa vie se passa à l'ombre de Flandrin à qui il était bien supérieur. Il est vrai que Ingres disait quelquefois pour l'encourager: 'quand je serais mort vous me remplacerez': mais Ingres vécut longtemps.[26]

One cannot but wonder whether it was a turn of character in Lamothe—sickly, disappointed, and melancholy—which helped to bring out the strain of melancholy we find in both Tissot and Degas. In any case, the accuracy and refinement of Tissot's basically unexceptional draughtsmanship and execution, as well as the technical complexity of the compositional problems his solves with such ease, can be traced in great part to Lamothe's rigorous academic training. This solid underlying structure gives Tissot's work formal qualities which sometimes falter but are never entirely lost.

For his part, Tissot appears to have been a model student. His docility, or, more likely, his desire to succeed, is said to have been so great that he submitted to Lamothe's teaching without question or complaint. Under Lamothe's guidance, he studied the Italian primitives at the Louvre—an unexpected taste which Ingres had passed on to pupils. This indigenous school of pre-Raphaelites is typified at mid-century by the work of Flandrin and Lamothe in a number of Parisian churches. Tissot would use their work as models for his first pictures, and somewhat later a trip to Italy augmented this taste with firsthand study of the early Florentine and Venetian masters. Lamothe was far less sympathetic to the early northern schools, but despite his opposition they remained of central interest to Tissot and he turned to them for inspiration in his first independent works,

[23] Lostalot, 'Tissot', p. 371.
[24] Henri Lerolle, quoted in P.-A. Lemoisne, *Degas et son œuvre*, i, 11.
[25] Henri Herz, *Degas* (Paris: Alcan, 1920), cited in R.H. Ives Gammell, *The Shop-Talk of Edgar Degas* (Boston: University Press, 1961), p. 8.
[26] Lemoisne, i, 11.

filtering his passion for the Flemish and German masters through the medium of Henri Leys. He also studied the antique, which left no trace in his work beyond a few pictures painted twenty years later of tourists in the classical galleries at the Louvre (pls. 193–5), and copied the works of Ingres (pl. 28). Bastard makes a point of remarking on Tissot's lifelong admiration for Poussin, a taste he shared with Degas, and one not surprising in a painter trained in the tradition of Ingres, although not easy to discover in his work.[27]

Lamothe's training was intended to develop Tissot's natural gifts—giving him a thorough knowledge of his craft and grounding him in the basic principles of his art—in order to prepare him for acceptance at the École Impériale des Beaux-Arts and, ultimately, the Salon, for without the approbation of those august institutions there was little hope of critical, popular, or official advancement in nineteenth-century France. As Jacques Lethève has suggested, the royal road to success in artistic France began at the Beaux-Arts and led by way of the Salon, it was fondly believed, to immortality.[28] Tissot, however, appears to have spent less time at the Beaux-Arts than its curriculum demanded. Paying lip-service to its status and using its facilities to his own advantage, he may never have seriously intended to stand for any of its prizes, and there is little trace of him in its records.[29] His art was never that of the *grandes machins* favoured by state patronage, a fact he surely recognized instinctively from the beginning, and although he cleverly courted official recognition and public notoriety with works like *Le Retour de l'enfant prodigue* and *Les Deux Sœurs* (Pls. 14 and 29), he quickly turned to cabinet pictures, at first medieval but soon modern, which were fashionable with the picture-buying public. In any case, his talent seems to have taken a high finish rather quickly, and three years after arriving in Paris he took the essential, and precocious, step of putting himself before the public at the Salon of 1859.

During these years, Tissot's traditional academic training was balanced by association with artists of more independent viewpoint. Brought into contact with the most advanced currents of artistic thought, at first probably as much by chance as by inclination, Tissot's essentially conservative approach was quickly tempered by an infatuation with the avant-garde which persists in his work. It is the attempted resolution of these contradictory sources, or perhaps the exploitation of them, which becomes the basis of his picture-making throughout his

[27] Material on Tissot's curriculum in Lamothe's studio and his artistic interests at the time are based on Bastard, pp. 257–8.

[28] Material on the *École des Beaux-Arts* is based on C. H. Stranahan. *A History of French Painting from its Earliest to its Latest Practice*, chap. VII, and J. Lethève, *Daily Life of French Artists in the Nineteenth Century*, chap. II.

[29] The Registre Matricole de l'École des Beaux-Arts, Paris, vol. XXIII, no. 4341, cited in Misfeldt, p. 30, contains three documents, a birth certificate submitted 25 February 1857, as proof of French citizenship; a declaration by Lamothe of Tissot's competence to stand for the *concours aux places* dated 9 March 1857; and a declaration by Lamothe of Tissot's competence to stand for the *concours au Grand-Prix de Peinture* dated 4 April 1857.

life, explaining at once many of the problems and much of the intensity inherent in his *œuvre*.

James McNeill Whistler must have been one of Tissot's first acquaintances in Paris, for they are said to have met in 1857 while both were copying Ingres's *Roger délivrant Angélique* at the Luxembourg.[30] They remained friends until the time of the Whistler–Ruskin trial in 1877 when Tissot declined to testify on Whistler's behalf. It was a fortunate meeting for Tissot, for it brought him into contact with a number of other artists. It may well have been through Whistler that Tissot had met Fantin-Latour, Legros, Bracquemond, and perhaps even Courbet. Whistler also had a number of American and English friends in Paris— George Lucas, Thomas Armstrong, Edward Poynter and George du Maurier among them—and Tissot must also have come in contact with them.[31] Giving way to the general Anglomania of the Second Empire, if not the more immediate prompting of his English-speaking friends, Tissot was inspired to Anglicize his name to James at this time.[32]

Ignoring almost all formal instruction, Whistler already looked to the most advanced trends in contemporary painting for inspiration. His work was greatly influenced by Courbet, at this time, and doubtless the traces of Courbet's style we find in Tissot's early work can be traced to Whistler's enthusiastic propagandizing. The immediate influence of Whistler's own work on Tissot was small, but its lesson took root and was to have a marked effect. If there is little obvious connection between the intimate subject-matter and low key of Whistler's *Au piano* (1858–9; The Taft Museum, Cincinnati), rejected at the Salon of 1859, and Tissot's academic *machins* cluttered with brilliant gothic bric-à-brac, the parallels soon became apparent. In the opinion of many, the relationship between the work of the two was often only too clear. When Whistler sent his *Symphony in White No. 3* (1865–7; Barber Institute of Fine Arts, University of Birmingham) to Paris in 1867, Fantin-Latour reported to him that Tissot was 'comme un fou de ce tableau, il en sautait de joie', and warned that Tissot and Alfred Stevens would imitate it.[33] What might have been youthful homage in the sixties became a bad habit in the seventies. Writing to his mother from Venice in 1880, Whistler described his pastels of the city, adding sharply: 'Tissot I daresay will try his hand

---

[30] E. R. and J. Pennell, *The Life of James Mc-Neill Whistler*, i, 73. Ingres's *Angélique* remained at the Luxembourg until 1874, so Tissot's registration at the Louvre in 1857 cannot have been for this purpose. Whistler's copy, dated 1857, is in a private collection in New York; Tissot's has not been located.

[31] Whistler met Fantin-Latour at the Louvre in 1858; he introduced him to a number of French artists, Courbet among them; he must also have met Bracquemond and the artists of the etching revival at the printer Delâtre's, who took the impressions of

his *French Set* the same year; Lucas later acquired Tissot's water-colour after *Le Confessional* (pl. 33) for William T. Walters; du Maurier left an unflattering portrait of Whistler at this time in the original version of *Trilby* in 1894.

[32] Lostalot, 'Tissot', pp. 372–3. Tissot was calling himself James by 1859, by which name he is listed in the catalogue of the Salon; he also signed a number of his pictures at this time with the Latin *Jacobus* in emulation of the early northern masters.

[33] Pennell, i, 185.

at once'.[34] The stimulation of new influences also became a necessary element in Tissot's development, perhaps a part of his repeated attempt to reconcile disparate sources, or, as the Goncourts suggest, simply to gain another little hold on life.

The most important friendship Tissot formed at this time, personally as well as artistically, was with Degas. They may have met at Lamothe's some time after April 1859, for although Degas had left the studio before Tissot enrolled and had spent much of his time between 1856 and 1859 in Italy, he probably visited his former teacher after his return to Paris. Alternatively, they may also have been introduced by Élie Delaunay, a friend of Degas as well as Mme Tissot, who had met Degas at the École des Beaux-Arts in 1855. The recognition of Degas's pre-eminent position in the art of his time has tended to obscure the fact that he and Tissot developed along remarkably similar lines in the 1860s, and that there was a great amount of technical and philosophical give-and-take between them which was of immense value to both. Beneath the different surfaces of their work is an aesthetic which springs from a common source, developed through personal interaction and shared experience. Often, to understand something of one is to understand the other better. Their ultimate personal and artistic divergence, the former about 1895 and the latter far earlier, was inevitable in view of their gifts, ambitions, and personalities. In our time it has consigned Tissot to oblivion and Degas to fame, but in the 1860s their positions were almost the reverse, as Tissot made his way as a consistently successful Salon painter and Degas met with repeated official rejection.

Tissot must also have met Manet at this time. There at first appears to have been little common aesthetic ground between them, but by the seventies there were a number of Tissot's major works which would have been philosophically impossible without Manet's example, as is the case with *Hush!* (Pl. 103); and in the eighties a growing aesthetic *faire joli* sometimes brings them close in spirit if not always in artistic quality. They also seem to have been temperamentally somewhat alike, probably more so than Tissot and Degas, and took pleasure in one another's company over a long period. Each was always ambitious for official recognition and fashionable success, a trait in both which infuriated Degas, and each was an accomplished *boulevardier* and an avid *coureur de femmes*. They remained friends until Manet's death in 1883, keeping in touch during Tissot's London years and even travelling to Venice together at mid-decade, and Tissot was able to demonstrate a loyalty unusual for him when he contributed to the subscription organized by Monet in 1889 to offer the *Olympia* to the Louvre.[35]

By the middle sixties, Tissot was poised between two distinct, if overlapping,

---

[34] Letter in the Whistler Collection, University of Glasgow, quoted in A. Staley, *From Realism to Symbolism: Whistler and His World*, p. 133.

[35] É. Moreau-Nélaton, *Manet raconté par lui-même*, ii, 111.

groups. Part of a circle which included advanced painters like Monet, Renoir, Berthe Morisot, and Fantin-Latour, as well as Whistler, Degas, and Manet, he was also the familiar of conservatives like Meissonier, Heilbuth, Gérôme, and Alfred Stevens.[36] By that time, he was adept at combining such diverse models in his work, using the audacities of the avant-garde to give a piquant gloss of modernism to his otherwise academic canvases.

Virtually nothing is known of Tissot's life in Paris in the 1850s beyond the documentation of official records and later biographical material, so it is of great interest to have one friendship which casts a personal light and gives some sense of individual colour to these years. Tissot met Alphonse Daudet when he took a studio above him in the rue Bonaparte in 1859 or 1860,[37] and Daudet recalled the time in a fictionalized autobiography published in 1877, *Le Petit Chose*. Unfortunately, Daudet does not include a character identifiable as Tissot, but his descriptive passages are richly evocative of student life in the rue Bonaparte. Daudet and Tissot had lost sight of one another by the time Tissot went to England, but met again after Tissot's return to Paris in 1882. According to Bastard, the reunion was the natural occasion for reminiscence, and he gives a fictionalized dialogue which may well have been based on a recollection of it by Tissot:

Puis, le cours de la conversation s'élargit en entraînant une foule d'idées qui se pressaient quand Daudet, songeant aux vitraux d'église dont Tissot avait reçu la commande, dans son modeste atelier de la rue Bonaparte, s'adressant au croyant illuminé, épris de fabuleux et de surnaturel, s'écria dans un accès de boutade:

—Ah! mon cher, vous avez une cathédrale dans la tête. Elle est grande grande . . . Mais elle est vide!

—Pas si vide que vous pensez, répliqua Tissot, car elle est parfumée d'encens et remplie de songes merveilleux![38]

As Tissot prepared his first independent works for exhibition, he did so very much under the influence of Lamothe and Flandrin, enamoured of liturgical

---

[36] It is not known whether Tissot knew Monet and Renoir; Berthe Morisot was to visit him in London; Gérôme and Stevens were friends of Degas; Bastard, pp. 260–1 remarks on his friendships with Meissonier and Heilbuth.

[37] Bastard, p. 258. The friendship is documented by a drawing of Daudet made at this time which Tissot presented to Mme Daudet in March, 1883 (Musée Alphonse Daudet, Fontvieille). He also made a water-colour portrait of Mme Daudet with her children in 1890 on the white vellum binding by Pierson for the presentation copy of her *Enfants et mères* (Paris: Lemerre, 1889) in the Goncourt collection (*Bibliothèque des Goncourt*: I.

Livres modernes (*ouvrages ornés du portrait des auteurs*), Hôtel Drouot, Paris, 29 March–3 April 1897, lot 7, bought by Lucien Daudet for 450 francs, present whereabouts unknown). Other friendships outside the visual arts are suggested by a drawing of the composer A.-E. Chabrier dated 9 October 1861 (repro., *Revue des beaux-arts de France*, II (December–January 1942–3), 65), and the dedication of a poem to Tissot in 1861 by André Lemoyne, the librarian of the École des Arts Décoratifs and a minor poet of distinction (see M. Wentworth, *James Tissot: Catalogue Raisonné of his Prints*, no. 3).

[38] Bastard, p. 259.

pomp and ceremony, devout, and deeply under the spell of the Middle Ages. If these pictures offer no reflection of the revolution in the arts which was taking place around him, they were none the less a most accurate summary of his first twenty-three years.

Tissot had five works accepted for exhibition at the Salon of 1859. Unfortunately, four of the five pictures are unlocated, but judging from the single work known today and from contemporary photographs and reviews, it is possible to form a clear idea of his Salon début.

Two of the lost works were the designs for stained-glass windows mentioned by Bastard: *Saint Jacques-le-Majeur et Saint Bernard* and *Saint Marcel et Saint Oliver*,[39] paired figures of saints, their names inscribed in Latin on their haloes, standing on promontories against a neutral ground of pale sky, with broad river landscapes stretching out behind them which barely fill the lower part of the canvas. A somewhat studied iconographical scheme included the name-saints of the painter and his two living brothers, while the fourth, Saint Bernard of Clairvaux, was the founder of the Cistercian order which had built the abbey at Buillon where the Tissot country house stood, and although the ultimate purpose of the windows is not known, it is difficult not to connect them in some way with a family chapel Mme Tissot built at Buillon at this time.[40] The formal sources of the windows seem more certain. Paul Mantz called attention to the influence of Flandrin in the delicate treatment of the heads,[41] and certainly the work Flandrin was doing in Parisian churches at this time was their immediate inspiration, as was similar work by Lamothe.[42] Like the work of Flandrin and Lamothe, Tissot's are doubtless the spiritual descendants of Ingres's designs for the Chapelle de Saint-Fernand at Neuilly and the Chapelle-Royale at Dreux, where portraits of the Orléans family appear superimposed on hieratic figures of their name-saints.[43] To point up a purposeful archaic quality, the designs were executed in *peinture à la cire*, a difficult encaustic process which enjoyed a

---

[39] Salon of 1859, nos. 2870 and 2871.

[40] According to Misfeldt, pp. 31–2, who also comments on the iconography of the designs, the chapel at Buillon does not contain stained-glass windows which can be associated with Tissot's designs: it therefore seems most likely that the designs were in fact studio exercises done for Lamothe. Bénézit states without documentary reference that they were destined for a church at Nantes (E. Bénézit, *Dictionnaire critique et documentaire des peintres, sculpteurs, dessinateurs et graveurs*, Nouvelle Édition (Paris: Grund, 1956), viii, 325).

[41] P. Mantz, 'Salon de 1859', *Gazette des beaux-arts*, p. 272.

[42] Flandrin decorated the churches of Saint Séverin, Saint Germain-des-Prés, and Saint Vincent de Paul; Lamothe decorated Saint Clothilde and Saint François-Xavier as well as Saint Irénée de Lyon and the Chapelle Pastrée at Marseilles.

[43] The *Duc d'Orléans as St. Fernandus and Marie-Amélie de Bourbon as St. Amelia* of 1842 (repro., R. Rosenblum, *Ingres*, figs. 32 and 33) are typical. Without Tissot's works, it is impossible to draw conclusions, but it would not be surprising if his works continued the impossible stylistic problem Rosenblum points out, in which two visual moods—iconic stiffness and nineteenth-century specificity—confront one another across an unbridgeable stylistic gulf.

limited popularity in France with artists of pre-Raphaelite inclination for works of a religious nature.[44] Lamothe had used the medium extensively in the churches he decorated and also exhibited two *peintures à la cire* at the Salon of 1859.

Two other lost works were portraits: *Mme T . . .* and *Mlle H. de S . . .*,[45] described by Louis Jourdan, with a sense of discovery, as 'violets, half-hidden by the grass': 'M. James Tissot a exposé deux petits portraits imperceptibles: l'un d'une belle jeune fille; l'autre d'une dame dans la splendeur de sa maturité. C'est d'une excessive finesse de tons; le modèle est ferme et sobre, le dessin est correct.'[46] Maurice Aubert thought them to be ·'remarquables par de sérieuses qualités où l'on reconnaît les fortes traditions d'un grand maître',[47] but one would be hard pressed to find any of those qualities present in a marked degree in the single picture of the five known today, *Promenade dans la neige* (Pl. 1).[48] Although Paul Mantz found its archaicism piquant enough to write that Tissot should have been born in the era of the illuminated missal, Zacharie Astruc tartly suggested that such student exercises might better remain in the studio.[49]

Technically, the paint is thin and transparent, showing the top grain of the canvas in many places as if it had been repeatedly scraped and reworked, while in other parts, especially the white highlights of snow and linen, it is thick and opaque, lying uncomfortably over the transparent surface. The drawing is hardly convincing, where it is not actually clumsy. Colour, too, is tentative, with a grey-brown tonality scarcely broken by the hard local colour of a yellow sunset and a red stomacher. Struggle is everywhere evident.

Whatever its artistic qualities, *Promenade dans la neige* is of the greatest iconographical interest. Prophetically, at the very beginning of his career, it introduces an aspect of psychological tension and of mood, a use of weather, season, and setting to point up a central theme, which would continue to form the narrative basis of his best pictures. Its subject is a lovers' quarrel, and wintry emotion was given an explicit parallel with the season by a quatrain which was inscribed on the original frame:

[44] Generally used to give permanent results under drastic conditions, as in church frescos, dry pigment is mixed with melted beeswax and resin. The work is completed by a burning-in which fuses pigment and support and is then polished, giving the surface a dull, durable sheen. Tissot's use of the medium was obviously experimental and had no practical necessity. For encaustic, see Ralph Mayer, *The Artist's Handbook of Materials and Techniques* (New York: Viking, 1957), pp. 334–9.

[45] Salon of 1859, nos. 2873 and 2874. The portrait of *Mme T. . .* is in all likelihood the portrait of Mme Tissot which Bastard, p. 260, and Lostalot, 'Tissot', p. 371, refer to as Tissot's first exhibited work. Bastard, however, gives the date of exhibition as 1857 rather than 1859, probably incorrectly, so the identification of the present work remains slightly problematical. He also states, p. 278, that the portrait, which Tissot had kept, was retained by the family when the contents of his studio were sold in 1903.

[46] L. Jourdan, *Salon de 1859*, pp. 46–7.

[47] M. Aubert, *Souvenirs du Salon de 1859*, p. 233.

[48] Salon of 1859, no. 2872.

[49] Mantz, 'Salon de 1859', p. 272, and Z. Astruc, *Les Quatorze Stations du Salon*, p. 22.

> April, lui, gracieux, doux, courtois, et plaisant,
> Celui fleur, force amour et beauté de nature,
> Décembre vint, adieu fleurs, baisers d'amour pure,
> Car neige couvre aussi ces deux coeurs à présent.[50]

Reinforced by literary allusion, the little picture takes on new interest. Later, such narrative equations will be made in purely visual terms, but *Promenade dans la neige* stands as the progenitor of a splendidly theatrical line, the ancestor of pictures like *The Letter* and *A Passing Storm* (Pls. 114 and 116).

Promenade dans la neige also introduces a more immediate aspect of Tissot's work, not long lasting, but of consuming intensity: fascination with the Middle Ages. Standing at the end of a long tradition, his medieval pictures are a surprisingly rich and intelligent synthesis of influences, and despite their position at the close of a worn-out genre, they have an unexpected vitality and life, sometimes even intensity and passion.

In France, interest in the Middle Ages, usually associated with Romanticism and the generation of Delacroix, actually extended back into the eighteenth century. The anti-Christian violence of the Revolution severed what might otherwise have been a tradition as unbroken as that of England and Germany, but in the Napoleonic era, at least after the Concordat of 1801 had restored the church to its former position, subjects associated with the Christianity of the Middle Ages began to reappear, a part of the style called the *genre troubadour*. In these pictures, there was a conscious attempt to recreate a pictorial manner appropriate to their subject, and painters took up the clarity of detail and miniature scale which they rediscovered in the paintings and illuminated manuscripts which were their inspiration. The domestic aspects of the Middle Ages were most attractive to them, and there was an attempt to include as much precise information as possible about the furniture, costume, and decoration of the period in their works which makes them the medieval equivalents of the neo-classic attempt by David and his followers to reconstruct classical antiquity.[51] But if the *genre troubadour* reintroduced Christian motifs, the traditional Christian themes of the Middle Ages— the Virgin and Child or the Crucifixion—became elements in the historical recreation of a world in which the faith these symbols represented was real. No longer sufficient in themselves as objects of devotion and belief, they become part of a sentimental attempt to recapture lost innocence which is often not without an aspect of quiet desperation. In a world from which absolute faith had long been absent, this retrospective approach becomes what Robert Rosenblum

---

[50] Astruc, pp. 22–3.
[51] For medievalism in French painting, see essays by Frederick J. Cummings, 'Painting Under Louis XVI', and Robert Rosenblum, 'Painting Under Napoleon' and 'Painting During the Bourbon Restoration', in Rosenberg, *French Painting 1774–1830: The Age of Revolution*.

perceptively calls 'spectator Christianity',[52] and the pictures it inspired cease to be religious objects, becoming merely theatrical re-creations of faith. This approach had enormous consequences in the nineteenth century, and is the key to much of its religious painting. It will apply not only to Tissot's *Faust* pictures, but also to his Bible illustrations of the eighties and nineties as well. As Rosenblum points out, it is an attitude which persists, and he discovers it in works like Gauguin's pictures of Breton peasants worshiping at their rustic Calvarys,[53] pictures that bear a strange family resemblance to Tissot's *Faust* in their approach, for both are the direct descendants of an attitude introduced at the beginning of the century.

In the 1820s, interest in the Middle Ages, fired by new influences, took a new direction. Romanticism, disillusioned and pessimistic at the deception of the Napoleonic myth, turned to the dark side of medieval life and to the suffering of an ignorant humanity reduced to animal terror and despair in a world no longer protected by faith. The 'waning' Middle Ages, the period of social *malaise* and the *danse macabre*, replaced the high gothic domesticity and romance of the *genre troubadour* and became the centre of interest, setting the individual against overpowering forces of intolerance, oppression, and superstition. This new direction found its most powerful expression in Victor Hugo's *Notre-Dame de Paris* in 1831,[54] and its portrayal of the Middle Ages was to have tremendous consequences in French art. At the same time, it crystallized an approach to the actual monuments from the Middle Ages, endowing them with an evil force of their own. To the dim legends of a northern past which Mme de Staël's *De l'Allemagne* had introduced to France in 1813, English authors of gothic romances—Sir Walter Scott, Anne Radcliffe, and 'Monk' Lewis—added a *frisson* of horror, giving the very buildings of the Middle Ages a brooding, nocturnal malignancy which is still a part of them in the popular imagination. By the 1820s, Baron Taylor's *Voyages pittoresques* had begun to combine this literary fashion with an accurate recording of France's medieval heritage, setting monuments, cathedrals, and ruins within the context of popular legend and historic anecdote, and helping to create not only a widespread interest in the preservation of what remained, but also an attitude of tremendous and lasting influence.

By the 1850s, the craze for the Middle Ages had waned. Michelet, writing in 1855, found his earlier judgement of the gothic in the second volume of his history to have been blindly enthusiastic: 'Mon trop aveugle enthousiasme s'explique par un mot; nous devinons, et nous avions la fièvre de la divination.'[55]

---

[52] Rosenblum, 'Painting During the Bourbon Restoration', in Rosenberg, *French Painting*, p. 170.

[53] Ibid.

[54] For a study of this medievalism, see Patricia A. Ward, *The Medievalism of Victor Hugo* ('The Pennsylvania State University Studies No. 39', University Park and London: Pennsylvania State University Press, 1975).

[55] Jules Michelet, Introduction, *Histoire de France* (Paris: Hachette, 1855), p. clv.

When Tissot began to paint his medieval pictures, they were already part of an exhausted tradition, although in their combination of the 'spectator Christianity' of the *genre troubadour* and the dark mood of Hugo's malevolent architectural personification there is a decidedly personal element. Tissot's first works are reactionary exercises in the fashionable genre of his youth, and this is not surprising, for it is common enough for a young artist to look to familiar models in his first efforts. Tissot grew up in medieval cities at a time when medievalism was both modish and avant-garde, and he drew with real inventiveness on a rich tradition sympathetic to his particular gifts and experience. Unfortunately, when he began, French painting was already concerned with the expression of truths more immediate and personal than the historical evocation of the past. Tissot began his career, as his critics were to tell him repeatedly in the next five years, in a cul-de-sac.

The central works of this medieval period are a group of paintings related to Goethe's *Faust*. The pictures cannot be thought of as a series, or even as a narrative sequence, since they have neither uniform size nor chronological progression. They deal with situations in *Faust* which appealed to Tissot, and in every case, interest centres on the feelings, or at least the figure, of a well-dressed and lethargic Marguerite.

At present, seven *Faust* pictures are known, in some cases through contemporary Bingham or Goupil photographs. In narrative order, they are: *Le Rencontre de Faust et de Marguerite* (Pl. 2),[56] *Faust et Marguerite au jardin* (Pl. I),[57] *Marguerite à la fontaine* (Pl. 4),[58] *Marguerite au rempart* (Pl. 8), *Marguerite à l'office* (Pl. 5),[59] and two versions of *Marguerite à l'église* (Pls. 6 and 7).[60]

Goethe's *Faust* was one of the most popular and influential books of the century, and in France it provided a theme which was to be played with seemingly endless variations. *Faust* is essentially a book of ideas, and it is ideas rather than narrative which give it meaning and greatness. It cannot be said that the essence of *Faust* lends itself to visual representation, but this appears to have been hardly noticed, or not to have mattered, for from the beginning French interest centred squarely on the romantic and supernatural aspects of the narrative, using them as excuses for sentimental piety and the *schauerromantik*. Fundamentally changed, *Faust* became what Gounod's operatic version—certainly the seminal expression of the genre—has so crushingly been called, 'a bedroom drama played outside the gates of heaven'.[61]

[56] Salon of 1861, no. 2972.
[57] Salon of 1861, no. 2970.
[58] There is a water-colour version of the painting in the Louvre (RF 16095).
[59] Salon of 1861, no. 2971.
[60] Pl. 6 was exhibited at the Goupil Gallery in Paris in 1860 (see E. Saglio, 'Exposition de tableaux modernes dans la Galerie Goupil', *Gazette des beaux-arts*, pp. 51–2.)
[61] Wallace Brockway and Herbert Weinstock, *The World of Opera* (New York: Modern Library, 1966), p. 259.

Stripped of psychological and philosophical pretensions, *Faust* became a staple of popular narrative and was acted, sung, danced, and mimed with astonishing regularity.[62] Welcomed by the *théâtre de merveilleux*, Faust and Marguerite played out their destiny against a background of supernatural spectacles, transformation scenes, and sputtering Bengal lights.[63] This *merveilleux* found equal favour with artists, and Romantic lithographers like Jazet, the Johannot brothers, Lemud, Boulanger, and Doré did very well reading *Faust*, 'la lanterne sourde d'Anne Radcliffe à la main'.[64] Chifflart, another *Faust* specialist, exhibited two drawings of this kind at the Salon of 1859, *Faust au combat* and *Faust au sabbat*, which Baudelaire found very much to his taste, especially the latter in which Marguerite, 'a long, sinister, unforgettable figure, floats in mid-air and stands out in relief, like a pang of remorse, upon the immense, pale disk of the moon'.[65]

Indeed, in France only Marguerite seems to have been able to hold her own against the supernatural. Her character proved endlessly fascinating, and more often than not she forms the centre of interest in French versions of the story.[66] She owes remarkably little to Goethe; his peasant Gretchen, the glass through which we read human error and divine forgiveness writ large, is equipped with a fluent piety and social distinction far removed from the original. Instead, she descends from French prototypes which are simply fitted into Goethe's narrative. The general conception of her character is closer to Esmerelda in *Notre-Dame*, a one-dimensional, fixed personality who fulfils the symbolic function of her fate, or to Alice in Meyerbeer's *Robert le Diable*, a cardboard figure of a peasant girl whose limpid piety saves Robert from the fate of Faust,[67] than to Goethe's tormented *vraisemblable*.

Marguerite had not escaped the attentions of French painters. By the time Tissot exhibited his first *Faust* pictures, Léon LaGrange could only suggest that if he insisted on his obsolete 'genre résurrectionniste', he might at least have the decency to leave 'la pauvre Marguerite, éternelle et banale victime des peintres de notre temps', in peace.[68] Previously, Ary Scheffer had made a specialty of Marguerite and the *Faust* legend. At the Salon of 1831, his *Faust au cabinet* and *Marguerite au rouet* had such success that his name was linked inseparably with

---

[62] For the operatic settings of *Faust*, see Félix Clement and Pierre Larousse, *Dictionnaire lyrique, ou histoire des operas* (Paris: Administration du Grande Dictionnaire Universal, n.d.), p. 274–5.

[63] For *Faust* in the popular theatre, see Marian Hannah Winter, *Le Théâtre du merveilleux* (Paris: Perrin, 1962), p. 150.

[64] Théophile Gautier, preface, *Dessins de Victor Hugo*, repr. *Œuvres complètes*, ed. Jean Massin, 18 vols. (Paris: Club français de livre, 1967–70), xviii, 3, quoted in Patricia Ward, op. cit., p. 1.

[65] C. Baudelaire, 'Salon of 1859', *Art in Paris*, p. 184.

[66] For a discussion of *Marguerite à la française*, see Paul de Saint-Victor, 'Les Femmes de Goethe: la Marguerite et la Frédérique', *L'Artiste*, 9 (January 1870), 5–19.

[67] Alice is also the direct prototype of Marguerite in Barbur and Carrée's libretto for Gounod's *Faust*.

[68] L. LaGrange, 'Salon de 1861', *Gazette des beaux-arts*, p. 346.

that of Goethe. In his *Salon of 1846*, Baudelaire considered that the vogue for Scheffer's murky canvases, which he thought looked like pictures by Delaroche that had been left out in the rain, was due entirely to respect for the memory of Goethe, the homage of 'aesthetic ladies who revenge themselves on the curse of their sex by indulging in religious music'.[69] In his review of the same Salon for *La Presse*, Théophile Gautier found Scheffer more to his taste, remarking that Marguerite belonged to him almost as much as to Goethe himself.[70] Before moving on to specialize in Monique and Mignon, the 'painter of Marguerite' could indeed have claimed a propriety right-by-number, and in his many canvases, a prim, Nazarine-looking young woman moves through a scenario of temptation and torment with the deft practicality of a German housewife.[71]

Only Delacroix seems to have achieved a real degree of fidelity to the original, and his subtle interpretation is alone said to have pleased the poet.[72] In concept, Tissot's *Faust* is decidedly and typically French, and it would be misleading to consider it, as one must with Delacroix, in relation to the original. It should be thought of as part of an evolving conception which had long since become essentially French. By the time Tissot came to treat the subject, in the late 1850s, there could be little question of direct quotation: *Faust à la française* had become a part of common cultural stock and offered a series of images as familiar as quotations from the Bible. Confronted with the first of Tissot's *Faust* pictures at the Salon of 1861, there was surely justification for Hector de Callias's remark that Tissot might at least have troubled to read *Faust*.[73]

More decidedly original was Tissot's choice of a formal source. There were abundant French models for this 'genre résurrectionniste'. A provocatively archaic style had been practised by Ingres himself during the years of the Restoration, and the vibrant, studied colour and porcelain surfaces of his 'gothic' pictures had found a ready following. Gérôme and Delaroche come immediately to mind, and Tissot himself had copied Ingres's *Roger délivrant Angélique* soon after he arrived in Paris. Placed beside Tissot's medieval pictures, one sees that the obsessive qualities of the *Roger*, its wilful archaizing, suspended action, and sense of anguished silence, had not been lost on the young artist, and even the wilting pose of the Angelica would seem to echo faintly in some of Tissot's Marguerites.

For immediate inspiration Tissot turned to northern painting in the person of the Belgian Henri Leys. The importance of Leys as a painter has been eclipsed,

[69] Baudelaire, *Art in Paris*, p. 99.

[70] Ibid., n. 2.

[71] Tissot was probably familiar with the entire range of Scheffer's *Faust* paintings since seven of them had been included in an important retrospective of 1859: see the *Catalogue des œuvres de Ary Scheffer exposées au profit de l'Association des œuvres des Artistes Peintres, Sculpteurs, Architectes, et Dessinateurs*, Paris, May 1959, nos. 23, 27, 28, 30, 38, 90, and 92.

[72] See Ulrich Finke, 'Eugene Delacroix's Illustrations to Goethe's Faust', in Finke, *French 19th Century Painting and Literature* (New York: Harper and Row, 1972), pp. 341–6.

[73] H. de Callias, 'Salon de 1861', *L'Artiste*, p. 29.

but in his own time he was a remarkably vital force in contemporary art. An idea of his influence can be felt in a letter from Vincent van Gogh to his brother Theo in 1883, for van Gogh puts Leys in the perspective of his own time and gives him a vivid immediacy he has lost for us today:

You know one of the pictures I think most beautiful of all is the 'Walk on the Ramparts' by Leys. That style, however, is not the fashion nowadays, but the sentiment in it has something eternal; one may have different conceptions of reality, or nature, and yet find again, even now, what was more generally sought after and felt in Leys' time than now.[74]

Leys sought to be the resuscitator of a national art, and his importance for an artist like van Gogh lay in his expression of a profound national consciousness. At the time when the Pre-Raphaelite movement was beginning in London, Leys took a similar step at Antwerp, giving his archaic revolution a decidedly national character by its exclusive use of early northern models and subjects. His recreations of historic national events and indigenous genre in the stylistic tradition of early northern painting struck a deeply responsive chord in a society newly oriented to national feeling and the historic past, and earned him a position 'plus titre en Belgique que jamais Raphael ne la fut à Rome'.[75]

For Tissot, as Henri Zerner has pointed out,[76] Leys' appeal must have been quite the opposite. For him, the use of a tradition other than his own could only be for its superficial elements of picturesqueness, quaintness of costume, bric-à-brac, and for the very sense of estrangement it created. At a time when many of his contemporaries, including close friends, were consciously making reference to the art of the past in order to establish the *Frenchness* of their art and their place in their own tradition,[77] Tissot turned instead to the art of the north. To some extent, this distinction represents the sum of past influence: with his northern upbringing, Tissot doubtless felt far closer to northern painting and the national school Leys was founding in Belgium than did Parisians like Manet and Degas, but his decision also carried the full weight of deliberate choice. He was to remain tenaciously faithful to it for several years in the face of repeated critical attack.

Whatever his reasons, Tissot's choice now appears as astute in terms of its understanding of personal temperament and individual artistic needs as it does culturally anomalous. The tradition of the *genre troubadour* was as acutely conscious of historical exactitude as Leys ever thought of being, but its subject-matter,

---

[74] V. van Gogh, *Letters*, ii, 39. In another letter to Theo, concerning a trip to Amsterdam (ii, 439), van Gogh says 'probably the first thing I shall do there will be to go and see the pictures by Leys in his *dining hall*.' There are numerous other references to both Leys and Tissot in the correspondence.

[75] J. Castagnary, 'Salon de 1868', *Salons*, i, 298.

[76] Henri Zerner, Introduction, in Brooke, Wentworth, Zerner, *Tissot*, no page number.

[77] Manet's relationship to French art has been the subject of special study: see Michael Fried, 'Manet's Sources: Aspects of his Art, 1859–1865', *Art Forum*, 7, no. 7 (March 1969), 28–82.

focused on aristocratic pageantry, and its pictorial method, based on the style of Fouquet and the fifteenth-century manuscript, was too brittle, too small-scale, and too jewel-like for Tissot's immediate needs. The still, monumental quality he discovered in Leys, with his large-scale figures immobile beneath the weight of their dignity and his unrelieved tone of high moral purpose, was precisely what Tissot sought for his own pictures. It is unlikely that he could have found a more sympathetic model.

By 1855, Leys had fully mastered his archaic style, and the three works he sent to the *Exposition Universelle* in Paris that year were full of northern medieval feeling.[78] They won him one of the two *grandes médailles d'or* awarded to foreigners, and a loyal French following. Although French critics continued to be disconcerted by Leys' manner, the question of pastiche in his hybrid pictures was generally resolved in his favour because his style was based on what was considered to be a valid personal, as well as national, impulse. In other words, Leys was original. A discussion by Théophile Gautier at the time of the *Exposition Universelle* is typical of the general approach:

Est-ce donc là, dira la critique, un peintre original? Ses toiles ont un air archaïque et rappellent les anciennes peintures des maîtres flamands et hollandais, ou plutôt allemands. S'il est permis de ressembler à quelqu'un, c'est sans doute à son père, et M. Leys est dans ce cas: chez lui il n'y a pas imitation, mais similitude de tempérament et de race; c'est un peintre de seizième siècle venu deux cents ans plus tard; voilà tout. Les âmes n'ont pas toujours l'âge de leur apparition dans le monde. M. Leys est un élève de Wolgemuth ou d'Albert Dürer qui ne s'est produit que de nos jours, par une des ces combinaisons mystérieuses qui ne sont pas si rares qu'on le pense, et dont on pourrait citer maints exemples.[79]

A great part of Leys' success at home and abroad can be traced to the fact that his pictures were in fact far less primitive than was thought at the time. Essentially a Romantic painter whose impasto technique and warm colour was influenced by his lifelong admiration of Delacroix, he always avoided the hard and dry effects which had met with such prejudice in the first half of the century. As Gerald Reitlinger has pointed out, this critical and popular attitude towards early painting and its imitators was not complicated: since the painters of Raphael's day had learned to paint closer to nature than ever before, why trouble about those who did not possess the advantage? Although in France the school of David had discovered a marked affinity with quattrocento painting, and Vivant Denon had collected early Italian paintings assiduously for the Louvre, the taste essentially disappeared with the Empire. Ingres's works in the *genre troubadour* are in fact

---

[78] The three works were (361) *Les Trentaines de Berthal de Haze* of 1855; (362) *La Promenade de Faust hors des murs* of 1854 (pl. 3); and (363) *Le Nouvel An en Flandre* of 1853.

[79] T. Gautier, *Les Beaux-Arts en Europe: 1855*, pp. 210–11. For a discussion of Leys' position in France, see P. Mantz, 'Artistes contemporains: M. Henri Leys', *Gazette des beaux-arts*, pp. 297–317.

far closer to the primitives than any of Leys', and far more revolutionary in their archaicism. Reitlinger also points out that prejudice against the primitive masters was less intense in the north, regional patriotism and ancestor-worship having created a taste for them as early as the eighteenth century, which had only been intensified by the long struggle against French domination between 1792 and 1815.[80] Leys' hybrid manner was entirely suited to its time, and could hardly have failed to meet with quick sympathy and a ready market.

For the nineteenth century, Leys realized the past with the forcefulness of a contemporary. With a remarkably beautiful facture, the product of the same tradition that produced Alfred Stevens and Alma-Tadema, an exacting truthfulness of observation, and a rare sense of colour,[81] Leys re-created the world of the northern past in a way considered suitable to it. Reproducing the 'errors' he found in an artist like Cranach, he filled his canvases with false perspectives and drained them of atmosphere. In doing so, he carried the attempt of the *genre troubadour* to find an archaic technique and scale suitable to its subject one step further. The quality of the spectator is swallowed up in the process of becoming: Leys is not an imitator; he is a medieval artist, as Gautier says: 'M. Leys n'était pas un imitateur, mais un semblable.'[82]

This feeling about Leys is extremely important in understanding contemporary critical reaction to Tissot's Leysian works, for where Leys is praised, Tissot is damned for what today appears to be exactly the same thing. To modern eyes, the works of the two are nearly interchangeable in their wilful archaism; but to the nineteenth century Leys was both the heir and the creator of a national consciousness and style, a *semblable*, where Tissot, in copying him without such philosophical underpinnings, is simply a *pasticheur*. It was as such that the critics generally considered him:

Au voleur! au voleur! pourrait crier M. Leys devant le peinture de M. Tissot; il m'a pris mon individualité, ma peau, comme un larron de nuit emporte un vêtement laissé sur une chaise. —A cela M. Tissot répondrait qu'il a beaucoup étudié Van Eyck, Albert Dürer, Lucas Cranach, Wolgemuth, Martin Schongauer, Holbein, et les vieux maîtres allemands, comme l'a fait M. Leys luimême. —Acceptons cette réponse pour valable, car il y a beaucoup de talent chez M. Tissot, et le pastiche poussé à ce point de perfection vaut presque une œuvre originale.[83]

Without doubt, Tissot studied the early northern masters, as Gautier has him reply, but the young painter, 'Jacobus Tissot, s'il vous plait',[84] most certainly

[80] G. Reitlinger, *The Economics of Taste*, ii. 119–20, 129.

[81] Maxime du Camp, for example, found Leys superior to all contemporary French painters in his 'qualités de facture et de vérité observée' (M. du Camp, *Les Beaux-Arts a l'Exposition Universelle* p. 316); Mantz found that the colour of the *Trentaines de Bertal de Haze* to be 'd'ailleurs parfait, et,

on peut le dire éloquent, dans sa gamme sérieuse' (Mantz, 'Artistes contemporains: M. Henri Leys', p. 306).

[82] Gautier, *Les Beaux-Arts en Europe: 1855*, p. 214.

[83] T. Gautier, *Abécédaire du Salon de 1861*, p. 338.

[84] Mantz, 'Salon de 1859', p. 272.

looked as closely as Leys at any primitive and cast the fruits of his study very much in the manner of the 'Van Eyck of the nineteenth century'. Leys inspired an avalanche of teutonic antiquarianism in his follower, and Tissot's sometimes halting but none the less remarkably skilful works are as energetic as they are derivative in their homage. According to Lostalot, admiration prompted Tissot to visit Leys at Amsterdam in 1859.[85] If emulation was his motive, Tissot's time was well spent, for where the *Promenade dans la neige* (Pl. 1) of 1858 is as tentative in its Leysian mannerisms as it is in technique, the works which followed his visit not only demonstrate a mastery of the most personal of Leys' idiosyncrasies but quote directly from his work. Even the most cursory comparison of Tissot's pictures with those of Leys makes his debt immediately clear.

It seems certain, for example, that Tissot saw Leys' *Martin Luther enfant chantant dans les rues d'Eisenach* (Pl. 9)[86] of 1859 still in the studio, for the figure of the girl seated at the centre of the composition is repeated in two of Tissot's *Faust* pictures, *Marguerite à l'église* and *Marguerite au rempart* (Pls. 7 and 8), although Tissot gives Leys' truthful simplicity and northern indifference to conventional beauty a gloss of Parisian affectation and chic quite absent in the original. Apparently even Leys' protestant subject attracted Tissot, who also painted a Luther picture soon after (Pl. 10).

If he had not seen it before, it is possible that Tissot now saw Leys' *La Promenade hors des murs* (Pl. 3) of 1854, one of the works exhibited at the *Exposition Universelle* of 1855, which was then in the royal collection. Its subject from *Faust* was duplicated in his own *Le Rencontre de Faust et de Marguerite* (Pl. 2) the next year, and the picture reads like a studio reconstruction of the Leys from which narrative impulse, if not life itself, has been completely drained. Tissot's Faust and Marguerite are remarkably close in feelings to Leys' protagonists, and surely it is not far-fetched to rediscover the family at the right of Leys' picture posing uncomfortably at the left of Tissot's, or the man sitting cross-legged at the centre of the Leys in a similar position in the Tissot.

If these direct quotations demonstrate the degree as well as the nature of Tissot's infatuation, equally important was the general delight in archaism and medieval bric-à-brac which Tissot found in his mentor. From Leys also came an archaic flattening of space, with the ground plane tipped forward in imitation of the early masters, and the 'primitive' emphasis on each separate object without regard for compositional or narrative importance, or for the effects of aerial perspective. Throughout his career, Tissot was to be castigated for his disregard of atmospheric effects and his inability to subordinate detail. Considering these

---

[85] Lostalot, 'Tissot', p. 372. Although the visit has been doubted because Lostalot alone makes reference to it, visual evidence strongly supports the assumption.

[86] A study by Leys for the figure of the girl is reproduced in C. Cook, *Art and Artists of Our Time*, iii, 309.

early works, one can but wonder how much of that later failure was inherent and how much was indelibly ingrained from these early exercises in primitivism.

The composition of *Martin Luther chantant dans les rues d'Eisenach* and *La Promenade hors des murs* are typical of a design Leys favoured with repetitive exclusiveness at this time, and it is repeated in several of Tissot's *Faust* pictures. In Leys, a roughly parallel spatial recession is interrupted near the frontal plane by a wall or screen which serves to isolate and enclose the principal figures, while above, deeper space opens out which gives amplitude and genre interest as well as spatial contrast. Clearly seen in *La Promenade hors des murs*, it is duplicated in a work like *Faust et Marguerite au jardin* (Pl. I). Leys uses this formal device in a direct way to confine and focus psychological and narrative interest within a narrow foreground, giving a kind of key to the relative importance of figures which composition and technical treatment ignore. For Tissot, it quickly becomes a narrative device more subtle and complex. In *Marguerite à l'office* (Pl. 5), the choir screen not only focuses attention on Marguerite, it makes her spiritual isolation a tangible fact, as does the pillar in a picture of the same date now called *Martin Luther's Doubts* (Pl. 10). Tissot continued to use this device in widely divergent contexts throughout his career: in *Les Adieux* (Pl. 76), where a fence becomes the symbol of unwanted separation, or in the sophisticated narrative of *L'Escalier* (Pl. 52), in which a glass wall creates a feeling of anticipation and anxiety that is ineffably compelling.

Technically, Leys was also a model, although Tissot did not abandon the lessons he had learned from Lamothe and soon combined his Leysian mannerisms with an interest in the somewhat similar methods of Courbet. Leys generally treated the broad elements of his pictures with the creamy pigment and open brushwork of his Romantic training. Details, like the pattern of costume, are laid on with glaze and scumble over the thicker ground. Compositionally, this use of contrasted areas of broad, waxen paint with thinner, generally brighter detail lends itself to a spotting of elements across the flattened, shallow surface to give interest and emphasis as required. In a work like the unlocated *Marguerite à l'église* (Pl. 6), the extreme treatment of the right side of the canvas carries this tendency to the point of abstraction, with random details of hatchment, wall painting, and architecture destroying a sense of spatial continuity. Within the essentially realistic aesthetic of these works, this abstract quality must have originally had a more intensely 'primitive' effect than it does to eyes long accustomed to the flattened picture plane, for modern impulse is to read it as abstract rather than as archaic and hierarchical. One has recourse to van Gogh once again to discover the effect these pictures created in their own time. Describing a stained-glass window to his brother, he is put in mind of Leys and Tissot:

There is a painted window which I think is superb—very, very curious. A beach, a green sea with a castle on the rocks, a sparkling blue sky of the most beautiful tones of blue, greenish, whitish, deeper, higher of tone. An enormous three-master, quaint and phantasmal, stands out against the sky, diffusion everywhere, light in the dark, dark in the light. In the blue figure of the Holy Virgin, bright yellow, white, orange. Higher up the window reappears dark green, with black, with fiery red. Well—do you remember it? It is very beautiful, and Leys would certainly have fallen in love with it, or James Tissot in his old style.[87]

Leys had a profound and lasting effect on Tissot's development. With the *Faust* pictures, Tissot became an accomplished painter of history, skilled in the construction of a historical setting, if sometimes less happy in creating a powerful narrative to dominate his *mise-en-scène*. Leys taught Tissot the value of verisimilitude and careful documentation in his historical dramas as the catalysts of both narrative and meaning, if not also as ends in themselves, and when Tissot began to paint subjects from modern life his training proved of incalculable worth. The attitudes and techniques of the history painter give later pictures of modern life an authority they could have gained in no other way. Leysian genre prepared Tissot admirably for what he would do best.

As a painter, Leys was always deeply concerned with the content of his art. High ideals and noble sentiments give his work a measured gravity which can move even when the subject itself has become obscure. His narratives of the conflict between private happiness and public duty or the spiritual confrontations of faith are often phrased with a truthful simplicity which transcends their forgotten historical subjects. Tissot chose to begin his career as a painter of similar moral subjects, touching twice on the Bible itself, and the question of meaning remains central to any understanding of him as a painter.

Even when Tissot consciously decided against such meaning in his work, this Leysian bias—kept potent by personal temperament—provided the solid stratum on which he built his most successful pictures of modern life. The narrative of *L'Escalier* (Pl. 52) gains immeasurably by its descent from *Martin Luther's Doubts* (Pl. 10). A kind of moral conviction separates it from the flaccid genre to which many of his contemporaries subscribed, and allows Tissot to glide past the jarring trivialities, voyeurism, and cold humour which mark so much French painting of the time. Later, the commonplaces of *The Last Evening* (Pl. 84), treated with all the documentary passion and moral seriousness Leys would have brought to a historical subject, take on an importance and meaning greater than their subject would otherwise allow. Ultimately, Tissot himself would answer the question of meaning in his work with the illustrations to the Bible.

But as important as anything Tissot discovered in Leys was a brooding sense of alienation and disjunction among the figures in his work. This quality alone might well have struck a responsive chord in Tissot and made him a devoted follower. Drained of movement, mute and passionless in their isolation, and

[87]   van Gogh, *Letters*, iii, 647, no. 443.

locked in the tilted, claustrophobic space of their archaic composition, they are the figures in a tableau vivant which is within an ace of becoming lifeless wax-work. As often as not, it is only the eyes of the protagonists which serve to animate the whole: within the gelatinous atmosphere, they dart and flicker, or glaze in stupefaction, the only quick things able to describe psychological states and complex relationships. The introspective and strangely vacant girl at the centre of *Luther chantant dans les rues d'Eisenach* which served as a physical model for Tissot could as easily be the psychological pattern for his Marguerites; but more important, the construction of the picture, with its insistence on the total isolation of each figure, has the psychological disjunction which becomes a constant in Tissot's work. Already obvious in *Le Rencontre de Faust et de Marguerite* (Pl. 2), it is no less apparent years later in *The Ball on Shipboard* (Pl. 102) or *La Plus Jolie Femme de Paris* (Pl. 182).

The disjunctive pair in Leys' *La Déclaration* (Pl. 11), painted just as Tissot began to move away from Leysian genre, might well serve as the paradigm for Tissot's debt to this painter. Again and again, Tissot will freeze emotion in precisely the same manner as some action or event—here, a declaration of love, but more often in his work a parting or a quarrel—paralyses emotional response. *Les Adieux* (Pl. 76) offers exactly the same dilemma of interpretation for us as for the departing gentleman: his bold gesture of farewell through the iron railing and his ardently questioning gaze are met only with eyes which flutter downward and a gesture impossible to read—like the abstracted toying with a glove in *La Déclaration*—as an indication of feeling or emotional response. Later, the same stricken lassitude and impenetrable stare we find in *La Déclaration* are again the response to the passionate questions posed by *The Last Evening* or *The Captain and the Mate* (Pls. 84 and III); they are still to be found, transformed somewhat but clearly recognizable, in many of the pictures Tissot painted of himself with Mrs Newton (Pls. 118 and 119); and it is not perhaps unreasonable to discover traces of them in pictures from *La Femme à Paris*, in which the viewer himself is forced to read the equivocal stares of *La Mondaine* or *Les Femmes de sport* (Pls. 185 and 188). In Tissot's enthusiastic assumption of Leys' mannerisms, it should never be forgotten that he also found a tremendously sympathetic model for the narrative tone of his pictures. The trappings of medievalism fall away, formal qualities evolve and change; but the spirit of alienation that Tissot discovered in Leys remains a constant in his work until the end.

Of the *Faust* pictures, *Le Rencontre de Faust et de Marguerite* (Pl. 2) is the earliest and most directly Leysian. It had the singular good fortune to attract the attention of the comte de Nieuwerkerke, who arranged for its acquisition by the State for the Musée du Luxembourg before its exhibition at the Salon of 1861, a rare honour for a young artist who had not yet received a medal.[88]

[88] Bastard, p. 260. The painting was purchased 17 July 1860, by the state for the Musée du

Although Tissot's progress in the year since *Promenade dans la neige* is clear, *Le Rencontre de Faust et de Marguerite* still reaches for effects beyond its grasp. Fragmented formally and as a narrative, the effectiveness it might otherwise have is dissipated in a lifeless uniformity of mood disturbed only by an occasional triviality. Every figure seems paralysed within the gelatine atmosphere, petrified in the attitudes of models who have posed too long. Faust's gesture of greeting and Marguerite's unfortunate expression retain a trace of life, but it is a trace that makes the frozen attitudes of the others seem preferable. Indeed, it is only the child on the stairs, rubbing the balustrade in a surfeit of boredom, and the miserable child in its festive dress by the tree, who engage what little sympathy we have for the actors in this faltering drama.

Although the airless atmosphere, clearly a 'jour d'atelier',[89] was criticized at the time, the unrelated collection of Leysian figures, posed separately in the studio and assembled on the canvas, appears to have escaped notice, as did its dependence on *La Promenade hors des murs*. Doubtless, its approach is conditioned by Tissot's still imperfect skill in the composition and execution of a complicated figure group, but even so there is a wilful disjunction which was clearly intended. Where Leys has a strength of purpose that unifies discursive visual elements, Tissot appears to take pleasure in the fragmentation of narrative and formal qualities to a point beyond understanding or repair. If this curiously static effect reflects the early masters, or at least their Leysian counterparts, Leys' naturalism is also everywhere apparent. The rigorous, abstract vision and pure intellectual line that Ingres brought to his gothic works is hardly discernible in the indiscriminate literal descriptiveness of Tissot's approach. In colour alone, *Le Rencontre de Faust et de Marguerite* departs from its Leysian models. Leys' colour, based on that of the Dutch school and influenced by Delacroix, was warm, robust, and sober; in his paintings 'les sonorités puissantes sont celles des orgues'.[90] Tissot turned instead to the hard, brilliant colour—studied and acrid in its use of secondary and tertiary combinations—that distinguishes the *genre troubadour*. With its harsh violets, apple greens, teal blues, cold yellows, and bluish crimsons, *Le Rencontre* clearly looks to the 'gothic' Ingres for inspiration. In this aspect, if no other, Tissot betrays his training in the studio of Lamothe and his place in the neo-classic tradition. If *Le Rencontre*, despite the obvious talent it displays, is overpowered by its arch mannerisms it remains, despite its flaws, an image with the power to capture and hold the imagination.

Among Tissot's *Faust* pictures, the three versions of Marguerite in church have the most formal and narrative interest (Pls. 5, 6, and 7). In each, the drooping

Luxembourg for 5,000 francs and was delivered to the Dépôt de l'État on 25 July 1863. G. Lacambre, *Le Musée du Luxembourg en 1874*, p. 172, no. 226.

[89] LaGrange, 'Salon de 1861', p. 346.
[90] G. Vanzype, *Henri Leys*, p. 62.

cadence of Marguerite's figure is set against a grid of church architecture which gives its lyric flow great formal emphasis. The archaic conceit which grants equal importance to each element creates an intriguing spatial displacement, giving the clumsy, inflexible backgrounds an expressive quality which reinforces the troubled psychology of the figures. Random, if carefully chosen, elements of the composition interweave in sharp focus with the figures themselves, assuming equal importance, and the eye, moving without pause from one element to another, duplicates the sharp contrast between the troubled restlessness of Marguerite's thoughts and the terrible physical lassitude they have created.

Such psychological tension is created with formal solutions of surprising boldness. Empty space and physical barriers are used to suggest inner torment and spiritual isolation. In the unlocated *Marguerite à l'église* (Pl. 6), the positive spiritual force of the family on the left, rapt and unified in prayer, confronts its negative in the figure of Marguerite across the void at the centre of the picture. Her crisis of faith, expressed in the attitude of the sinner seated on the ground like a madonna of humility, contrasts with the plentitude of belief across the empty church, separating from it like oil from water. The same formula is less successfully repeated in the other version of the picture (Pl. 7), although it is compensated by a greater lyricism of mood, and it is made physical in the *Marguerite à l'office* (Pl. 5), where Marguerite is divided from the devout by a choir screen.

In all of these pictures, the choice of detail contributes powerfully to their psychological effectiveness. Images of judgement and death surround and threaten the desperate sinner: crucifixions, Last Judgements, ex-votos of the dead Christ without a single note of serenity or hope. The setting itself becomes the embodiment of judgement and damnation as well as the personification of Marguerite's tormented soul. Nearly as successful, if quite different in mood, is the *Faust et Marguerite au jardin* (Pl. I), which also makes narrative concomitant with setting, equating the blooming trees and narcissi with the feelings of Faust and Marguerite. Fortunately, they also soften what is one of Tissot's most expansive flights of medieval erudition.[91]

Less successful are those pictures where narrative is not underscored by setting. The affecting figure of Marguerite, which Tissot adapted from Leys for his *Marguerite au rempart* (Pl. 8), is without such support, and its potential dissipates in a welter of architectural detail. In *Marguerite à la fontaine* (Pl. 4), the neurotic intensity of the superbly realized figure is once again insufficient, and too unlike in its linear approach, to dominate or even relate convincingly to the Courbet-like landscape, worked with a palette knife, on which it appears to be pasted.

---

[91] The well-head at the right of the picture, for example, is taken from one in the courtyard of the Musée de Cluny.

Critical reception of Tissot's Leysian works was not particularly favourable. The question of pastiche remained a central issue, and while it was generally conceded that Tissot had remarkable talent and a bright future, critics were at one in telling him that he might spend his time to better advantage than as an adroit *pasticheur* in a worn-out genre. Reviewing the Salon of 1861, Hector de Callias took accurate measure of Tissot's archaism, perceptively linking him not only with Leys, but with Millais, the English Pre-Raphaelites, and the painters of the *genre troubadour*. He was quite aware of that aspect of archaism which made it seem avant-garde to Tissot and other painters *en Leys* whose naïveté was merely a provocative pose:

M. Tissot a beaucoup de talent, mais il s'imagine peut-être qu'il a inventé le préraphaélisme après M. Millais, et après M. Leys, et après je ne sais plus déjà quel peintre du temps de l'Empire. Quel progrès, que de ramener l'art à ses procédés élémentaires et primitifs! M. Tissot sera probablement depassé dans cette voie: les gamins de l'Académie libre des inscriptions et belles lettres seront pour lui de redoutables concurrents. Il semble vraiment croire qu'un pastiche d'après Alfred Dürer est moins pastiche qu'un pastiche d'après Raphael.[92]

If talent was acknowledged, difficulties did not escape notice. Tissot's drawing was never exceptional, and it could be quite faulty indeed:

Si vous déshabillez le *Faust au jardin*, de M. Tissot, vous aurez sous les yeux un monstre, dont les bras démesurément longs s'emmanchent en pleine poitrine, dont les jambes non moins démesurées sortent on ne sait d'où. La *Marguerite à l'office* cache aussi sous son manteau un bras dont il lui serait difficile de justifier l'origine.[93]

Nor did they fail to notice hard local colour, an absence of aerial perspective, and a total inability to subordinate detail which forced narrative meaning, if not all trace of life itself, to give up the ghost in competition with archaeological bric-à-brac. The veiled narrative of *Marguerite à l'église* (Pl. 6) also sent the public running to their catalogues for elucidation, perhaps for the first, but certainly not the last, time, and Saglio's complaint will sound like a leitmotif throughout Tissot's career:

Ils sont peints d'une couleur énergique, mais dure, les liaisons manquent entre les tons, les ombres sont noires; tous les détails sont curieusement étudiés, mais ils le sont trop également, et en revanche les figures ne sont pas assez; tout vient en avant dans son principal tableau et occupe les yeux à la fois, et ce qui arrête le moins les regards, ce sont les têtes, trop peu dessinées et peintes; enfin la vie (je ne dis même pas le drame) est absente de cette composition, empruntée au theâtre allemand: on ne devinerait jamais, sans le secours du catalogue, qu'elle représente *Marguerite à l'église*.[94]

---

[92] Callias, 'Salon de 1861', p. 29.
[93] LaGrange, 'Salon de 1861', p. 346.

[94] E. Saglio, 'Exposition de tableaux modernes dans la Galerie Goupil', pp. 51–2.

Most of all, critics resented Tissot's 'sujets retrospectives', what Castagnary called a 'goût de bibelot'[95] which had been propagated by Romanticism: 'Mais comment M. Tissot ne s'aperçoit-il pas qu'il va trop avant dans le domaine de l'érudition pure? L'élément humain disparaît dans ces résurrections qui trahissent l'effort, et qui ne sont pas après tout que l'apothéose de la curiosité et le triomphe du bric-à-brac.'[96]

For modern taste, Tissot's *Faust* pictures are of great interest as a revelation of personality. They draw almost entirely on tradition, but their combination of elements makes them unique in their reflection of character and milieu. The precise archaeological correctness which was the heritage of the *genre troubadour* is given the psychological edge we find in the Middle Ages as conceived by Victor Hugo, where the tangible symbols of a faith no longer absolute are endowed with a malevolence of their own. The symbols which surround Tissot's Marguerite call up no visions of Christian sentiment and piety. They are a menace and a threat, blighted and reproachful ghosts from a world which has been lost. This feeling sets Tissot's *Faust* pictures apart from their contemporaries, for the official sanctity of the Second Empire insisted on a Christianity more optimistic if hardly less equivocal.[97] There is an urgency and individual accent in these narratives which suggests the most personal of statements. An energy of feeling lies beneath their listless surfaces which gives them the tension and life they would otherwise lack. There is always what appears to be a strong element of self-projection in Tissot's work, and lacking biographical information, one can only guess what personal crisis led him to these images of despair.

The loss of faith is also the subject of a picture dated 1860 and now called *Martin Luther's Doubts* (Pl. 10), which was published in a Bingham photograph in 1861 as *Les Vêpres*. If, as Misfeldt suggests,[98] *Les Vêpres* is in fact the lost *Pendant l'office* from the Salon of 1861,[99] its debt to Leys is narrative as well as stylistic. On the basis of physical resemblance, the picture almost certainly makes reference to Luther, and by inference to his crisis of faith, although his name does not appear to have been associated with the picture before 1868, and we do not know if it was then with Tissot's consent.[100] As a Luther picture, it springs from the same impulse that made Marguerite brooding in church the subject of three canvases. Exhibited at the Salon with *Marguerite à l'office* (Pl. 5), its position as a narrative and compositional pendant must have been immediately clear.

[95] Castagnary, 'Salon de 1868', *Salons*, i, 300.

[96] P. Mantz, 'Salon de 1863', *Gazette des beaux-arts*, p. 506.

[97] For comparison, see, for example, Robert Rosenblum's discussion of Ingres's *Joan of Arc at the Coronation of Charles VII* of 1854 in *Ingres*, pp. 160–3.

[98] Misfeldt, p. 44.

[99] Salon of 1861, no. 2969.

[100] The picture was exhibited at Leeds in 1868 as *Young Luther in Church*, the property of Charles Waring (A. Graves, *A Century of Loan Exhibitions*, iii, 1315), and was sold anonymously in 1886 as *Luther's Misgivings, in the manner of Leys* (G. Redford, *Art Sales*, ii, 210).

Tissot's Leysian pictures have been harshly judged when not passed over in silence. Dismissed as pastiche and denigrated for their patent faults, they are easily separated from the later representations of 'vulgar society' with which his name was soon associated, and conveniently ignored. Like the Bible illustrations of the nineties, they do not fit the twentieth-century concept of Tissot as a *peintre des mœurs.* Yet at the end of the nineteenth century, Tissot's pictures of modern life were themselves dismissed, repudiated by their creator and lost in the tidal wave of admiration that greeted his illustrations to the Bible. In 1900, Tissot was thought of as a religious painter, and it is not difficult to consider him as just that today—a religious painter who indulged in fashionable genre—although it necessitates relegating what is now considered much of his best work to a secondary position. Religious works probably make up the larger part of his *œuvre* in number if not quality, and his genre pictures themselves sometimes hint at religion. In the 1860s, his fashionables more than once found themselves in church, and in the 1870s, biblical parables jostled modern genre. Indeed, throughout his life a somewhat unpleasant moralizing tone and a desire to preach is never far beneath the surface. There is a lesson to be learned from his *Faust*, a lesson which predicts the mammoth proselytization of the Tissot Bible.

A number of pictures not related to the *Faust* group also developed out of Tissot's Leysian manner. An unmistakable moralizing note was sounded by one of the earliest, exhibited at the Salon of 1861: *Voie des fleurs, voie des pleurs* (Pl. 12)[101] was accompanied in the catalogue by the Latin funeral tag *penetrantes in interiora mortis*, and appears to be the only instance where Tissot matched his medieval style with a genuine medieval subject. The *danse des morts* had found a responsive audience in the plague-torn Europe of the fifteenth century: in Tissot's hands, however, it can only be considered an academic exercise in historical iconography.[102]

> Their days on worldliness depend,
> And pleasure, sought voluptuously:
> Suddenly they to hell descend,
> Where joy is turned to misery.[103]

[101] Salon of 1861, no. 2973. The painting at Providence, which is dated 1860, can be identified with the Salon picture on the basis of an engraving after it which was published in *L'Artiste*, 1, no. 8 (15 April 1862) following p. 184. A study for the picture or an earlier version of it, dated 1859, which omits some figures and places others in a different order, was sold at Christie's, London, 28 January 1972, lot 91 (repro., *An Allegory of the Transience of Life*, oil on canvas, 31.75 × 97.79 cm.).

[102] For the numerous late fifteenth- and early sixteenth-century *danse macabre* woodcut series, see Arthur M. Hind, *An Introduction to the History of the Woodcut*, 2 vols. (New York: Dover, 1963), i, 243, 366; ii, 644–8. Tissot's immediate inspiration is perhaps suggested by Gautier (*Abécédaire*, p. 338), who likens the picture to the *danse des morts* in the cemetary at Basle, a city close to the Tissot country house at Buillon and a source which Tissot may well have known since childhood.

[103] Werner L. Gundersheimer, introd., *The Dance of Death by Hans Holbein the Younger: A Complete Facsimile of the Original 1538 Edition* (New York: Dover Publications, 1971), p. 139.

Théophile Gautier admired the picture greatly and explained its complex iconography at length in his review of the Salon:

En tête, la Mort, déguisée en joueuse de vielle, tourne la manivelle de son instrument avec un geste extravagamment anguleux; deux joueurs de cornemuse l'accompagnent, pressant du coude leur outre enflée; ensuit vient un couple amoureux dont les bouches rieuses se cherchent pour le baiser; ivres d'amour et de jeunesse, ils ne voient pas la sinistre musicienne qui gambade ironiquement devant eux. —Un seigneur couronné de laurier et magnifiquement vêtu arrive derrière, dansant avec une belle fille en tenant une autre à son bras.

La marche continue par un vieillard aux allures cacochymes dont la femme encore jeune laisse prendre un baiser sur sa main par un élégant cavalier qui la suit. En dehors de la file, l'enfant, que personne ne surveille, traîne un petit chariot. Plus loin gesticule un homme désespéré et montrant le poing au ciel. Un cadavre sanglant, étalé en travers la route, barre le chemin au cortège; mais un groupe d'ivrognes titubants l'enjambe avec insouciance. Un vieux, à cause de son or, épouse une jeune fille qui se résigne à cet hymen monstrueux. Une courtisane demi-nue s'avance poursuivie par la Luxure sénile agitant à ses oreilles, d'une main décharnée, des bourses pleines de ducats. —La Mort ferme la marche, comme elle l'ouvrait. Son accoutrement est des plus bizarres: elle porte une cuirasse; ses tibias flottent dans des bottes à chaudron; un cercueil la coiffe, pendant derrière elle comme la queue d'une cagoule. Au rebord extrême du coteau, aimable petit détail qu'il ne faut pas oublier, apparaissent deux pieds d'homme assassiné, dont le corps gît sur l'autre revers.

Au premier plan, parmi les pierres, les broussailles et les flaques d'eau, on démêle de petits squelettes d'enfant sacrifiés au Moloch du libertinage.[104]

Despite its medieval trappings, *Voie des fleurs* also makes pointed reference to contemporary painting and personal concerns. The corpse over which the mercenaries stumble is quoted directly from that of Julius Caesar in Gérôme's immensely popular Salon picture of 1859, *Ave Caesar, morituri te salutant* (whereabouts unknown), a tribute which would have been immediately apparent to the Salon public.[105] The figure at the centre, described by Gautier as 'un homme désespéré', who appears revolted by the scene around him, is surely a self-portrait, and thus Tissot's moralizing once again takes on personal focus as he repeats the lesson of *Faust*: 'path of flowers, way of tears'.

In style, *Voie des fleurs* relies less heavily on Leys than do the *Faust* pictures, turning without intermediary to the works of German and Swiss artists of the late fifteenth and early sixteenth centuries for stimulus, as the subject itself turns directly to the Middle Ages. The small-scale figures in their fantastic costumes, painted mainly in shades of red and purple, and silhouetted against a colourless sky to make the most of their heraldic outline, do capture something of the spirit of their models, despite an unmistakably nineteenth-century flavour.

---

[104] Gautier, *Abécédaire*, pp. 339–40.
[105] Pointed out by Zerner in the 'Introduction' to Brooke, Wentworth, Zerner, *Tissot*, no page number; Gérôme's *César mort* was formerly in the Corcoran Gallery, Washington, DC and is now unlocated.

At the Salon of 1861, its clever iconography and jewelled brilliance enjoyed real popularity and attracted a great deal of critical attention. Gautier devoted nearly three pages to it in his review, ending his appreciation with a paean to its medieval spirit:

Les lanières, les lambrequins et les déchiquetures en barbe d'écrivisse du vieux costume alle-mand, voltigent sous le pinceau de l'artiste d'une façon si farouche, si héraldique, si moyen-âge, que les personnages semblent sortir d'un vitrage suisse ou d'un jeu de tarots; mais quelle finesse de couleur, quelle curiosité de détail, quelle intimité de sentiment gothique![106]

And LaGrange, although he found little to admire in Tissot's 'genre résurrection-niste', admitted that 'la silhouette intitulée *Voie des fleurs, voie des pleurs* est une ballade pleine d'humeur', and even Degas, who was not himself immune to the charms of the Middle Ages at this time, found it interesting enough to make a rapid copy from memory in one of his notebooks.[107]

The three pictures Tissot sent to the Salon of 1863 were also medieval in costume and moralistic in tone. With a single exception, they were the last works of an archaic nature he was to exhibit there, for by the next year he had turned his attention to modern genre and henceforth it was primarily as a *peintre de la vie moderne* that he chose to be known. As if to mark his renunciation of this painting *en Leys*, the three pictures were so wilfully crammed with archaeological bric-à-brac that they make what had gone before appear chaste by comparison.

Le Départ du fiancé (Pl. 13)[108] is spiritually the last of the *Faust* pictures. Marguerite's splendid Teutonic wardrobe makes its final appearance on the mute heroine of the drama, and the frozen narrative has a feeling of anguish and alie-nation which links it directly to earlier works. Like *Martin Luther's Doubts*, its subject is ostensibly protestant, for this family goes into exile, giving up what appears to have been considerable earthly goods as well as their daughter's happi-ness, in order to maintain their faith, the victims of religious intolerance.[109] If the narrative is opaque, it is given personal focus in the manner of *Voie des fleurs*, for the young man about to be separated from his betrothed is once again almost certainly a self-portrait.

The unlocated picture appears to have contributed little new to its Leysian genre beyond a landscape which opens out to offer new possibilities for medieval 'error'. If anything, if drifts subtly away from Leys and into mannerisms which suggest a new interest in the *genre troubadour*. By this time, critics considered Tissot's hard colour, lack of aerial perspective, and difficulties with anatomy as normal, enumerating them by rote and tagging their remarks with the now familiar invitation to abandon the Middle Ages:

[106]   Ibid., pp. 340–1.
[107]   LaGrange, 'Salon de 1861', p. 346. T. Reff, *The Notebooks of Edgar Degas*, Nb. 18, p. 109, reproduces Degas's copy.

[108]   Salon of 1863, no. 1802.
[109]   Suggested in E. Strahan, *Modern French Art*, p. 50.

Les objects, de tons mats et ternes, ressemblent aux pièces mal ajustées d'une mosaïque, et puis, quelle singulière disposition! Au milieu du tableau 'Départ du fiancé,' un long jeune homme, habillé de rouge, tient embrassée la femme dont il va bientôt se séparer. Ces deux acteurs principaux, nous les critiquerons pas, bien que leurs mains, par exemple, soient très défectueuses. Mais quel est ce caniche en bois, dressé sur de petits morceaux de carton découpé? Et ce tout petit chasseur qui tire dans le lointain sur un tout petit cerf? Homme et gibier, ne les prendrait-on pas pour des joujoux d'enfants? Décidément, la tentative de M. Tissot est malheureuse; qu'il laisse le moyen-âge et soit de son époque; avec son talent il ne peut qu'y gagner.[110]

Le Retour de l'enfant prodigue (Pl. 14),[111] again 'dry, lustreless, and mosaic-like', is conceived in a kind of super-Leysian manner, and its display of bric-à-brac is far more important than its subject. Although Tissot turns to the Bible for his text, its pious lesson of error and forgiveness, the *voie des fleurs* with a happy ending, is extinguished by the elaboration of the picture's staging. Previous works had a historical reason for medieval costume, but *Le Retour de l'enfant prodigue* is medieval entirely at pleasure. This desire to exploit picturesque detail and give narrative added bite through a clever disjunction of subject and setting appealed to Tissot, and he returned to it in the ambitious series of the early 1880s which takes the same text, setting it as a series of modern genre pictures (Pls. 154–7). The recurrence of the subject in his work suggests that it had an importance and meaning for him greater than its almost incidental first appearance might suggest.

The unbridled archaism of *Le Retour de l'enfant prodigue* at last put critics completely out of patience with Tissot's 'gothic' mannerisms. Hector de Callias, who thought Tissot talented but had no sympathy for what he considered the ridiculous pretence of his aesthetic pose, had already pointed out a gulf between appearance and actuality in the school of Leys which robbed it of any real artistic significance: 'M. Tissot et les autres peintres en Leys se font naïfs à plaiser et ne sont pas au fond aussi naïfs qu'ils en ont l'air. Ce sont des peintres d'esprit qui se donnent des airs bêtes.'[112] Reviewing *Le Retour* in 1863, he invited Tissot to 'regarder le calendrier' and humorously declined further notice until he did so: 'M. Tissot est tellement lancé à la poursuite d'Holbein, que personne ne songe à la suivre. Bon voyage! Quand il aura fait assez d'archéologie, quand il lui prendra fantaisie de revenir a la peinture, nous ferons comme le père de l'enfant prodigue, qu'il a exposé cette année; nous tuerons le veau gras, et nous lui pardonnerons'.[113]

Although based on careful and quite accomplished studies from life (Pl. 15), the operatic, if wooden, gestures of *Le Retour de l'enfant prodigue* brought Tissot to the attention of the cartoonists as well as the critics, suggesting that his works were now popular enough to come in for their share of Parisian wit and

---

[110] C. Gueullette, *Les Peintres de genre au Salon de 1863*, pp. 49–50.
[111] Salon of 1863, no. 1803. The picture was also exhibited at the Royal Society of British Artists in 1864, no. 259, where it was priced at £320.
[112] Mantz, 'Salon de 1863', p. 506.
[113] H. de Callias, 'Salon de 1863', *L'Artiste*, p. 238.

abuse. In his *Salon de 1863*, Cham offers an engagingly skinny prodigal who begs a 'papa' of wonderful anatomical distortion and exaggerated medieval dress 'de ne plus se laisser faire par M. Tissot qui le rend ridicule'.[114] The picture was among the first Tissot exhibited abroad, sending it to the Society of British Artists in London in 1864, but English critics were hardly more enthusiastic. The *Athenaeum* found it 'affected, false, and artificial', and thought it strange 'that a man who is so powerful an observer of character should condescend to imitate so *bizarre* a school of painters as that of ancient Flanders'.[115]

Its companion at the Salon, *Le Départ de l'enfant prodigue à Venise* (Pl. 16),[116] documents a brief shift in influences if not a change of direction. A trip to Italy, during which he visited Milan, Florence, and Venice, but not Rome, brought him under the spell of the early Italian masters. Bastard makes reference to the trip, which he says took place after Tissot had completed his *Faust* pictures, and Lemoisne reproduces a letter written by Tissot to Degas from Venice which is dated the eighteenth of September, but without a year, although it seems likely that the trip took place in 1862.[117]

Like Degas, Tissot was deeply struck by the Italian primitives:

Je suis dans les Carpaccio et je n'en sors pas. Quel cœur avait cet artiste, la manière dont il reproduit cette vie de Sainte Ursule est ce qu'il y a de plus touchant — il faut voir la noblesse des adieux du fiancé, du même qui rend compte, d'une mission de mariage — des gens qui assistent aux présentations des ambassadeurs, du départ, du retour . . . c'est admirable — je ne vous parle pas des autres peintres, vous les connaissez plus ou moins à Paris. A Bonifazio, un tableau, *le Mauvais Riche*, qui est admirable — l'*Assomption* du Titien m'a laissé froid — le Tintoret de Saint-Marc piquant une tête m'a bien étonné — Mais Andrea Mantegna, Bellini m'ont ravi. Comme Bellini devait aimer l'intimité d'une femme, ses têtes de vierge sont admirables de suavité et d'humanité'.[118]

---

[114] Cham (Noé, comte de), *Cham au Salon de 1863: deuxième promenade*, no page number.

[115] *Athenaeum* (9 April 1864), p. 513. Tissot sent a second unlocated picture to the Society and exhibited at the Academy for the first time; see below, n. 125.

[116] Salon of 1863, no. 1804.

[117] Bastard, p. 260, Lemoisne, i, 230–1, n. 45. In the letter, Tissot mentions Degas's *Sémiramis construisant une ville* (L. 82; Louvre, Paris) of 1861 in a manner which suggests its completion, says that he will have 'tout juste le temps pour le 3e tableau', presumably for the Salon of 1863, and speaks of meeting 'M. Schwiter, un baron très aimable, qui montre Venise et se met à votre disposition, lui et sa gondole avec beaucoup d'affabilité.' Louis de Schwiter, the subject of a portrait by Delacroix of 1827 which later belonged to Degas and is now in the National Gallery, London, was to have met Delacroix in Italy in the late summer of 1862, although the latter was unable to join him for reasons of health (see André Joubin, pub., *Correspondance générale d'Eugène Delacroix*, 5 vols. and Supplement (Paris, Plon, 1936–8), vi, 332–4. Brooke, 'Chronology', in Brooke, Wentworth, Zerner, *Tissot*, also dates the trip 1862. Misfeldt, p. 51, on the basis of Tissot's allusion to *Sémiramis*, dates the trip 1861. Reff suggests that Tissot was in Italy in the late 1850s, on the basis of references to him in the memoirs of Telemaco Signorini, *Caricaturisti e Caricaturati al Caffè "Michelangiolo"*, pp. 77 and 121, and to drawings in Degas's note-books (Reff, *Degas Notebooks*, Nb. 12, p. 58 and Nb. 13, p. 26). Signorini's memoirs, which were not published until many years later, may well telescope events, and suggest only that Tissot was in Florence sometime after 1855, while Degas's caricatures are perhaps too slight, despite the intriguing resemblance of Nb. 13, p. 26, for conclusive identification. If Tissot was in Italy before 1862 we have no definite proof of it.

[118] Lemoisne, i, 230–1, n. 45.

While in Venice, Tissot began work on *Le Départ de l'enfant prodigue à Venise*, an elaborate pastiche in the linear, high-keyed manner of Carpaccio's *St. Ursula and the Prince taking leave of Their Parents* in the Scuola di Sant'Orsola: 'J'ai composé quelque chose, cela vous plaira-t-il, je l'espère, je metterai le moins de caractère possible, vous m'entendez, c'est le départ de l'enfant prodigue à Venise, un peu pedant . . . mais si on pensait toujours aux expositions, que ferait-on?'[119] Tissot indeed seems to have put as little of his own artistic character as possible into this Second Empire Carpaccio. Its ineloquent drama is clearly intended to duplicate the stately reserve of its models, and it is probably not by chance that it offers the greatest possible contrast to its pendant at the Salon (Pl. 14). With *Le Départ*, Tissot's enthusiasm for the Renaissance vanished without a trace, the product of temporary impressions rather than artistic commitment. It is unique in his work, and proved to be the last attempt he made at a *grande machin* for the Salon. Although he continued to think 'toujours aux expositions', henceforth he sought to attract public attention with subjects from modern life like *Les Deux Sœurs* (Pl. 29).

A number of drawings from Tissot's Italian trip are equally pedantic in their desire to duplicate the effects of late fifteenth- and early sixteenth-century silverpoint drawings. There are studies for *Le Départ* which clearly essay the look of early Renaissance drawings while short-cutting their difficult technique with modern graphite (Pl. 17);[120] and the same means served with perhaps greater suitability for studies after the masters like a group of heads taken from Botticelli's *Adoration of the Magi* in the Uffizi.[121]

Although Tissot sent only one more medieval picture to the Salon (Pl. 20), where it kept company with his Pre-Raphaelite *Le Printemps* in 1865, he continued to paint them until almost the end of the decade. The last of them may well merge chronologically with the works in Directoire costume which he began about 1868.[122]

The shift away from Leysian models which is suggested by these Salon pictures is completed in these works from the middle of the decade. The naturalistic, if somnolent, figures which Tissot created for the *Faust* pictures, imbued with the

[119] Lemoisne, i, 231, n. 45. Lostalot, pp. 374–5 describes the picture as 'very light in tone, of a quiet harmony notwithstanding its brightness'.

[120] Two other drawings are known for *Le Départ*: a compositional study for the entire picture in pen and brush in brown ink over pencil, 15.24 × 31.75 cm., and a study of the prodigal in graphite heightened with white on grey paper, 23.97 × 25.08 cm. (both in the collection of the Metropolitan Museum, New York).

[121] Repro., Brooke, Wentworth, Zerner, *Tissot*, no. 41. One of a group of Italian studies broken up and sold by M. P. Prouté et ses fils, Paris, in 1964, which are said to have been given to the grandfather of the previous owner by Tissot. It is not known whether the three studies for *Le Départ* mentioned above were part of this lot.

[122] Pl. 21, which is probably one of the last of Tissot's sixteenth-century costume pieces, uses for the first time a river setting which afterwards appears in some of the Directoire costume pictures of 1868–70. Given his penchant for working in groups of pictures which use consistent settings, the two sets of pictures may well abut chronologically.

grave sobriety and heightened physical presence which Leys brought to his work, are now completely transformed. Taking the direction suggested by *Voie des fleurs*, figures grow smaller in relation to the ground, becoming doll-like and highly animated. Awakening life is answered by a new kind of narrative in which the moral dilemmas posed by Goethe and the Bible give way to the impulsive historical adventure and romance of Alexandre Dumas or Victor Hugo.

Stylistically, Tissot also found new models, and these vivid little scenes from sixteenth-century novels owe more to the *genre troubadour* than to Leys and northern painting. With its lively sense of anecdote, miniaturist brilliance, and delight in shimmering atmosphere, a picture like *Promenade sur les remparts* (Pl. 18) of 1864 invites comparison with Gérôme rather than Leys, and suggests that Tissot had looked carefully at a work like his *Louis XIV et Molière* (Pl. 19) at the Salon of 1863.

Promenade sur les remparts turns its back on moral significance. Narrative now revolves around the sly-looking girl giving her suitor a bold, if furtive, glance which has a worldliness purposefully at odds with the innocent delicacy of the pale spring landscape. She grasps opportunity in a manner far removed from the passive modesty of Marguerite, and the trivial vulgarity of the little comedy looks forward to the Directoire pictures which brought the decade to a close. The costumes are medieval, but the emotions are straight out of the Bouffes-Parisiens.

As with Tissot's *Faust*, these pictures are given a kind of continuity by a repetition of protagonists and costumes from one painting to the next. If the emotional control suggested by the self-possessed heroine of *Promenade sur les remparts* is far removed from the mute and passive Marguerite, in other pictures the heroine also becomes a victim. Thrust resentfully into the centre of action, she becomes an object of aggression and violent crime.

Tentative d'enlèvement (Pl. 20),[123] exhibited at the Salon of 1865, is a storybook anachronism more eccentric than any Gérôme. Thinly painted, with a rare luminosity and great delicacy of execution, its breath-taking treatment, dazzling 'false' perspectives, and swashbuckling narrative performed by animated dolls cast a spell to which even critics of its archaic manner were not entirely immune. Set beside Tissot's modern genre picture *Le Printemps* at the Salon, to most critics the *Tentative d'enlèvement* represented little more than an unfortunate return to an earlier manner, despite its technical perfection and potent charm. Paul Mantz, delighted that Tissot, 'longtemps enfermé dans le magasin de curiositiés de l'archaïsme', had at last begun to paint subjects from modern life, regretted the

---

[123] Salon of 1865, no. 2075. The work can definitely be identified as the picture exhibited at the Salon, on the basis of a description by Thoré: 'Sur une terrasse qui domine une ville, deux gentilshommes se disputent à l'épée une donzelle qui s'effare et appelle du secours' (T. Thoré, *Salons*, ii, 201). *Le Rendez-vous*, exhibited at the Exposition Universelle of 1867, uses the same setting and two main characters: it is, if anything, more mannered and balletic than the *Tentative*.

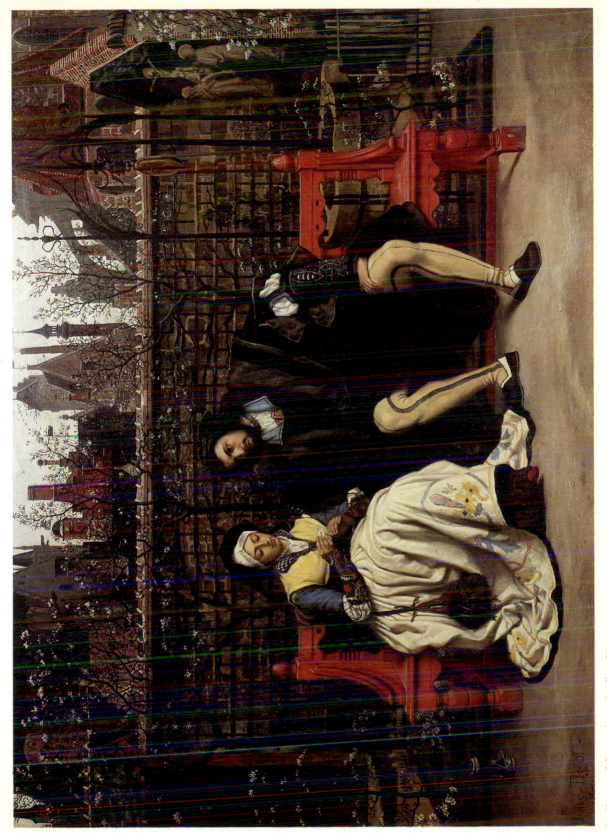

I. *Faust et Marguerite au jardin*, 1861.

lapse represented by what he grudgingly described as a 'jolie scène d'un roman du XVIe siècle', remarking that he liked Tissot better when 'il peint ce qu'il a vu, ce qu'il a senti'; Félix Jahyer admired its originality and execution, but thought that Tissot could only gain by changing his 'tendencies'; and Thoré, who had praised Tissot's first pictures of modern life, described it with regret as 'un ressouvenir de sa première manière moyen-âge qu'il paraissait avoir abandonné pour chercher sincèrement des effets naturels.'[124]

The violence suggested in the *Tentative* is exposed in another picture of the same subject, probably of a somewhat later date, for which no contemporary title has been preserved (Pl. 21). In no other known picture does Tissot take a subject of such aggression, and there is an almost sensual delight in the baroque despair of the women ambushed and dragged from their travelling carriage.[125] Speculation on prototypes suggests that Tissot may already have been familiar with some of the eighteenth-century prints which would shortly provide the subjects and mood for several of his Directoire pictures. A rococo *L'Enlèvement nocturne* (Bocher 20), engraved by Nicolas Ponce after Pierre-Antoine Baudouin (1723–69), for example, is remarkably, if perhaps coincidentally, similar, not only in its operatic emotion and staging, but also in its ambiguous confusion of sensual pleasure and physical violence in the painter's response. Claude Souviron perceptively links the present work with Degas's *Les Malheurs de la ville d'Orléans* (L. 124; Louvre, Paris), which was exhibited at the Salon of 1865, although with understandable confusion he identifies it with the *Tentative d'enlèvement*, which was shown the same year.[126] Considering its probable date of 1865–7, it can also be thought of with Degas's *Intérieur* (*Le Viol*) (L. 348; Henry P. McIlhenny, Philadelphia) of 1868–70, a work in which Tissot is known to have taken an active interest.[127] Each picture can only lead to speculation on the estrangement and hostility it suggests. But whatever each picture's personal and no doubt largely unconscious meaning, both painters soon began the transmutation of open physical aggression into the intangible psychological tension that underlies their most effective pictures of modern life.

Not all of Tissot's sixteenth-century costume pieces are of such violence. A picture from the middle of the decade now called *Sur la plage* (Pl. 22) makes its effect more quietly. Unfinished, its incompleteness makes it particularly attractive

---

[124] P. Mantz, 'Salon de 1865', *Gazette des beaux-arts*, p. 11; F. Jahyer, *Salon de 1865*, p. 137; and Thoré, 'Salon de 1865', *Salons*, ii. 200–1.

[125] Two unlocated pictures with what appear to be similar sixteenth-century subjects were exhibited in London in 1864: *At the Break of Day*, Royal Academy, no. 408, described as 'a snow-covered street in a medieval town by night, with a duellist or assassin making his way from the wayside cross before which his victim or antagonist is lying dead'

(*The Times* 11 May 1864, p. 5); and *The Elopement*, Royal Society of British Artists, no. 11, described as 'an exceedingly effective study of night, with thin snow on the ground' (*Athenaeum*, (9 April 1864), p. 513.

[126] Cited in J.-M. Moulin, *et al.*, *The Second Empire: Art in France Under Napoleon III*, no. VI–106, p. 355.

[127] See T. Reff, 'Degas's "Tableau de Genre",' *Art Bulletin*, pp. 316–37.

to modern taste, and its refined scale of colour—pale ochre and pink set against grey-green—gives it delicacy and openness. The same restraint is found in the subtle investigation of expectation and anxiety in the group which waits on the shore, and there is a real attempt to animate historical genre with a more empirical emotion and spirit. But picturesqueness limits an incisive exploration of psychology. About 1863, Tissot must have come to this conclusion himself, if he was not brought to it by the example of his friends or the chorus of advice from his critics, and the Salon of 1864 saw his emergence as a painter of modern life.

III. Modern Sentiment

Nos créations industrielles et artistiques peuvent périr, nos mœurs et nos costumes peuvent tomber dans l'oubli, un tableau de M. Tissot suffira aux archéologues de l'avenir pour reconstituer notre époque.

Élie Roy, 'Salon de 1869'.

TISSOT came to the painting of modern life by way of the portrait. The demands of likeness, individual psychology, and milieu seem to have suggested alternatives and answers to the problems inherent in historical genre, and he was not slow to realize the advantage in exchanging a literary painting which had to be understood as well as seen for one of more immediate sensibility and visual appeal. His development closely parallels that of Degas at this time and doubtless partook of mutual influence and exchange. Both reflect the tremendous shift in aesthetic theory which was to make everyday life their chosen subject and the definition of modern sentiment—the fleeting, transitory beauty of the age, its fashions, temperament, and emotions—their narrative aim.[1] With his first modest portraits, Tissot began to move away from the limitations of archaism towards the subtle and complex records of modern life which are his greatest and most lasting achievements.

According to Bastard, Tissot had gone to Paris without financial assistance from his father, and supported himself by making portrait drawings of hotel housekeepers and maids in the neighbourhood at forty francs apiece.[2] If so, the products of his industry are unknown today, having disappeared with their anonymous sitters, ephemeral souvenirs probably now unidentifiable if by chance preserved. Unlocated also are the two little circular *portraits d'initiaux* which he sent to the Salon of 1859, a child in profile, *Mlle H. de S . . .* , and *Mme T . . .*, probably a portrait of his mother, which Louis Jourdan thought notable for delicacy of tone, sober modelling, and accurate drawing, but Astruc found to be without special character, 'peintures d'élève' deriving all too clearly from Flandrin and Robert Fleury, 'honnête et patient jusqu'à l'ennui'.[3]

---

[1] For a recent study of this shift and a discussion of the complicated definitions of 'modernity' in the nineteenth century, see A.C. Hanson, *Manet and the Modern Tradition*, pp. 3–36.

[2] Bastard, p. 258.

[3] For the portraits, see chap. II, n. 45; Jourdan, *Salon de 1859*, pp. 46–7; Astruc, *Les Quatorze Stations du Salon*, p. 22.

The character of these works is preserved in the handful of portrait drawings and etchings which remain from the time: drawings of Alphonse Daudet and A.-E. Chabrier, and etchings of a child, a priest, two unidentified women, and Degas.[4] All are extremely modest in concept and scale. Avoiding contact with the viewer, the sitters seem introspective, if not sometimes hostile, immersed in private reveries of their own. The majority convey a singular impression of alienation and unhappiness which links them directly to the brooding figures of the *Faust* pictures and surely springs as much from Tissot's own state of mind as from the personalities of his sitters.

Another of the prints, an accomplished portrait of an unknown young woman (Pl. 23), is the most psychologically open of the group and can be related to a new relaxation which appears in Tissot's work about 1861. It is also clearly felt in one of the pictures Tissot sent to the Salon that year, *Mlle M. P . . . ,*[5] which Gautier alone seems to have noticed among the Leysian productions it accompanied, citing it in a single line as being of 'une expression si féminine et si indéfinissable'.[6] It is quite possible that the picture now called *A Girl in Black* (Pl. 24) is the work exhibited at the Salon; if not, it is of the same date and is doubtless very similar in feeling. This eccentric portrait, surely not a commissioned work, owes the better part of its *indéfinissabilité* to Courbet, whose work at this time was filled with just such expressions of equivocal femininity, and Tissot's enjoyment of physical fleshiness and torpid sensuality has an evocative richness and corporeality worthy of Courbet himself. *A Girl in Black* clearly owes more than a little to Courbet's *Les Demoiselles des bords de la Seine* (Pl. 25), a debt later still more explicit in works like the unlocated *Le Printemps*, and *La Confidence* (Pls. 30 and 31). It demonstrates the degree to which Tissot's Leysian archaism was given physical tangibility by a careful study of Courbet's realism, and also suggests that Tissot was attracted by Courbet's subject-matter as well as his style. Courbet's 'young ladies' were clearly of a less decorous class of female, and the *Demoiselles* had been found as shocking an affront to manners as to morals when it was exhibited at the Salon of 1857.[7] With what must have been conscious purpose, Tissot took subjects of a similar moral colour, and although their impact was watered down in translation, his pictures were also found guilty of mild offences against propriety. Needless to say, it did nothing to harm his growing popularity.

Mlle L. L . . . (Pl. 26),[8] the portrait Tissot sent to the Salon of 1864, is of key

[4] For the drawings, see chap. II, n. 37; for the etchings, see Wentworth, *Catalogue Raisonné of Prints*, nos. 1–5.

[5] Salon of 1861, no. 2974. Misfeldt, p. 59, also associates the picture with Pl. 24.

[6] Gautier, *Abécédaire*, p. 342.

[7] For a recent study of the effects of Courbet's pictures on the public, see Patricia Mainardi, 'Gustave Courbet's Second Scandal: "Les Demoiselles du Village",' *Arts Magazine*, 53, no. 5 (January 1979), 95–103.

[8] Salon of 1864, no. 1841. Now generally called *Jeune Femme en veste rouge*. There is a pencil study of the figure in the Louvre (RF 24316).

importance in his development. An extremely beautiful work in itself, resolving formal problems of great difficulty, it marks his real emancipation from the limits of Leysian costume genre and begins a process of self-recognition and a growing understanding of his particular gifts as an artist. Every element of the composition is calculated for its formal and psychological effect with remarkable assurance and subtlety. The pose of the model[9] is reminiscent of the Marguerites in the *Faust* pictures, but it has a welcoming amplititude quite unlike the alienated introspection of the earlier works. For the first time, the sitter makes direct, uncomplicated, and relaxed contact with the viewer. Her pose, like the general tone of fashionable refinement, may well owe something to Courbet, and indeed there is a plausible connection with the lavish bourgeois elegance of a work like his large *Mme Mathilde Cuoq* (Pl. 27), a picture Tissot may have seen exhibited in Courbet's studio.[10]

An even clearer prototype is to be found in Ingres's *Mme de Senonnes*, a picture which Tissot had copied in the Musée de Nantes (Pl. 28).[11] Indeed, it could be said that *Mlle L. L . . .* is a simple reworking of the elements Tissot found in Ingres. Analogies are immediately obvious, and if Ingres's incisive reading of character and tautly inevitable design are blurred by Tissot's discursive approach, the sophistication and understanding with which he handles similar formal elements remain impressive in its homage. Like Ingres, he is particularly successful in the creation of an atmosphere of indolent luxury. An almost imperceptible note of vulgarity is perhaps a less attractive addition, but it gives agreeable bite to what otherwise would be a strangely passive picture.

As Tissot entered his first period of independent activity in the 1860s, he did so in the company of Manet, Fantin-Latour, Whistler, and Degas. In his preoccupations with modern life, Courbet, and perhaps photography,[12] he touched

[9] An unlocated half-length portrait of the same young woman seated in an armchair is dated November 1863—three months before the Louvre picture—and is very close in feeling; it clearly served as a kind of trial-run for the more ambitious full-length portrait. The fact that the same woman also appears in *Les Deux Soeurs* in 1864 also suggests the professional model rather than the paying sitter. The title of the painting was doubtless purposefully misleading in an attempt to attract portrait commissions: if so, it was entirely successful, for within a short time Tissot was a popular society portrait painter. The same young woman appears yet again as the central figure in what is probably the most anomalous of Tissot's pictures of the sixties, a circular canvas representing three nude nymphs (one a child seated on a roebuck *à la* Courbet) pursued by a satyr brandishing a tambourine.

[10] Astruc, *Les Quatorze Stations du Salon*, pp.

389f., speaks of the portrait which was exhibited in Courbet's studio after the painter had lost patience with the demands of the sitter and her family and had finished it for his own pleasure; it seems possible that Tissot saw the picture there. For the portrait, until recently incorrectly called Marie Crocq rather than Mathilde Cuoq, see the entry by Hélène Toussaint in Alan Bowness, Marie Thérèse de Forges, Michel Laclotte, and Hélène Toussaint, *Gustave Courbet* (London: Arts Council of Great Britain, 1978), no. 52.

[11] Acquired by the Musée de Nantes in 1835, it is probable that Tissot copied the picture before coming to Paris in 1856. If so, it is the earliest work known by him today. Bastard, p. 257, speaks of such pre-1865 copies without giving specific examples.

[12] Although a later use of photographs as a compositional aid is known, there is no documentation of Tissot's use of them at this time. Degas,

on common interests which resulted in paintings of some superficial similarity. In many ways, *Mlle L. L . . .* could have been painted by Degas, for it is unlike his work more in temperament than in conception, and it certainly fulfils his dictum to 'faire des portraits des gens dans des attitudes familières et typiques, surtout donner à leur figure le même choix d'expression qu'on donner à leur corps'.[13] Only Degas's psychological and visual precision are lacking in Tissot's more tentative and generalized approach.

Mlle L. L . . . is enriched to surfeit with details which suggest both personality and milieu. The iconographic scheme is equally subtle in its assumption—common in the arts in the nineteenth century—that one's possessions also reflect one's morality, as is often the case with the portraits of Degas or the novels of Henry James.[14] The archaeological approach of Tissot's Leysian pictures is applied to the documentation of modern life, but with a shift in focus to the study of personality and the delineation of contemporary feeling it takes on new clarity and point.

Every element is chosen to give definition and resonance to the young woman who is so much at home among them. The use of the Ingresque device of a mirror behind the sitter, here reflecting an open door, extends the extremely shallow pictorial space, sets up an ambiguous relationship which makes the viewer part of the painted space, and predicates psychological involvement. The little salon with its delicate wallpaper, the Louis XV *fauteuil* heedlessly piled with books and a portfolio, the birdcage, and the photograph stuck carelessly in the mirror all contribute to an image feminine and intellectual, an image which caused Thoré to wonder if the lady 'a peut-être des bas bleus câchés sous les longues draperies de son jupon noir' and LaGrange to remark that neither the lady's *toilette*, fashionable if slightly boyish with its crimson *caraco à l'Impératrice*, nor her *meubles de fantaisie* 'n'exhalent plus le parfum sain de la famille' in a picture whose 'premier mérite consiste dans la sincerité du sentiment moderne'.[15]

---

however, is known to have taken some interest in photographic sources at this time, and it seems likely that Tissot did also. The presence of a photograph in *Mlle L. L . . .*, a *carte de visite* of a child wearing what appears to be a Leysian costume, might support the assumption, and the use of the mirror behind the figure is a device as common in contemporary photographic portraits as it is in Ingres.

[13] Reff, *Degas Notebooks*, Nb. 23, pp. 46–7.

[14] See, for example, the discussion between Isabel Archer and Madame Merle in *The Portrait of a Lady* (London: Oxford University Press, 1954), p. 216, where Madame Merle says: 'What shall we call our "self?" Where does it begin? Where does it end? It overflows into everything that belongs to us—and then it flows back again. I know a large part of myself is in the clothes I choose to wear. I've a great respect for *things!* One's self—for other people —is one's expression of one's self; and one's house, one's furniture, one's garments, the books one reads, the company one keeps—these things are all expressive.'

[15] Thoré, 'Salon de 1865', *Salons*, ii, 102; La-Grange, 'Le Salon de 1864', *Gazette des beaux-arts*, p. 525. The costume itself was decidedly fashionable: from the day of the marriage of the Empress Eugénie, 'the Spanish love of colour and contrast ruled French taste in dress . . . reds of every kind, solferino, marengo, sang de boeuf, and so forth, enough to drive all the bulls in Andalusia into madness, were constantly invented and greedily

The composition, which already shows a marked taste for the cutting of form by the edges of the canvas and an overlapping of elements within a shallow ground,[16] has an interest and animation greater than that of the amiable but passive young woman at its centre. The elegant and nonchalant figure surrounded by clues to its own character has an effect not at all unlike that which Degas was to find appropriate when he painted Tissot's portrait in 1868.[17] With unfailing psychological insight, Degas uses a composition which echoes Tissot's own to frame a disturbing portrait of the man himself.

In *Mlle L. L . . .* , there is a growing concern for the problems of aerial perspective which can also be noticed in Tissot's later medieval subject pictures like *Promenade sur les remparts* (Pl. 18). But despite a delicate harmony of tone and pattern in *Mlle L. L . . .* , colour continues to trouble, for there is no principle which unifies its treatment. Refined and slightly acrid in its juxtaposition of greens, violets, pinks, and yellows with the black and red of the costume, the overall effect remains vaguely reminiscent of the *genre troubadour*, colourful rather than coloured, and local tints still take precedence over any unifying tonal approach. In his review of the picture at the Salon, Thoré pointed out, not for the last time, that 'la vraie qualité du coloriste n'est pas tant la valeur du ton local que dans la relation des valeurs elles-mêmes'.[18] It was a lesson Tissot never really learned, and a failure which was continually brought to his attention throughout his career.

Colour was the central issue in Tissot's other Salon picture in 1864, *Les Deux Sœurs; portrait* (Pl. 29),[19] a large exhibition picture which received wide popular and critical attention, effectively overshadowing the less obvious but perhaps more durable charms of *Mlle L. L . . .* . The two young women in white summer dresses standing beside a pond gained a mild notoriety, suitable to their bland charm, because of the green reflections on faces and dresses, earning the ironic sobriquet 'les dames vertes'[20] from a public which had works like Manet's *Christ aux anges* and *Le Toréador mort* to really amuse it that year.

Thoré devoted considerable space to *Les Deux Sœurs* in his review of the Salon, finding that 'sa couleur étrange, mais parfaitement vraie, choque les yeux habitués aux couleurs conventionelles des peintres favoris'. He suggested that it would suffice for a bourgeoisie 'tellement habitué à une fausse nature' to pass

purchased'. They were worn with *señorita* jackets 'which embued their wearers with a sort of daring, boyish, hoydenish air, a touch of boldness and independence that was occasionally more than fascinating'. O. Uzanne, *Fashion in Paris*, pp. 129, 134.

[16] It is possible that this represents a very early use of elements to be found in Japanese prints.

[17] L. 175. For a discussion of the formal and psychological implications of the picture, see T. Reff, 'The Pictures Within Degas's Pictures', *Metropolitan Museum Journal*, pp. 133–40.

[18] Thoré, 'Salon de 1864', *Salons*, ii, 102.

[19] Salon of 1864, no. 1860.

[20] After the title of Georges Sand's novel. Somewhat later, Tissot himself refers to Millais's *Eve of Saint Agnes* as 'la dame verte de Millais' in a letter to Degas (Reff, 'Degas' "Tableau de Genre",' p. 332).

through the Tuileries Gardens on leaving the Salon to observe, 'sous la voûte des hautes maronniers touffus, le ton particulieur des ombres, que se reflètent en vert pâle sur les promeneurs et glancent de vert toutes les couleurs de leurs vêtements, surtout les couleurs claires, plus sensibles à l'ombre que les foncées'. This is 'la nature vraie', and he recognized its accurate duplication in the picture.[21]

Others found 'la nature vraie' much less to their taste. Edmond About, for example, found only that 'l'atmosphère de son grand tableau est d'un vert opaque qui rapelle un peu l'eau croupie'.[22] But truth to nature or ditch water, it is certain that Tissot was trying to find a solution to the real difficulties he had in meeting the conflicting demands of local colour and aerial perspective. *Les Deux Sœurs* is the first full-scale example of what soon became his standard solution: everything is allowed to slide into a greenish-grey tonality—justified by the setting—which serves to bind the discursive elements of local colour together. Within the overall tonality he establishes, local colour no longer need be observed in relation to every other colour, but only as a decorative accent which can be improvised according to the necessities of the total composition. By changing its basic function within the picture, Tissot was able to deal with colour more successfully on his own terms, and at least give the appearance of having bridged the gap between local colour and aerial perspective. It was a common method in the nineteenth century—Alfred Stevens always used it with great brilliance—and Tissot relied on it in one form or another throughout his career. In England, the chalky grey of what were often called his 'black and white' pictures revealed the same proclivities, and *The Ball on Shipboard* (Pl. 102) would reiterate both the problem and the solution of *Les Deux Sœurs*.

Despite its politely unorthodox colour, *Les Deux Sœurs* pleased with its vacuous air of good breeding. Equally far from the brutality of realism and the vulgarity of the society portrait, it was found to be the very pattern of aristocratic propriety and high-toned simplicity:

Ici, l'on ne saurait appliquer à M. Tissot le reproche, assez juste souvent, qu'on adresse aux réalistes, de peindre des sujets grossiers ou de vilains types, car la jeune femme est un modèle d'élégance, de noblesse, et de simplicité. Sa tête nue est sérieuse et pensive; ses mains délicates sont finement dessinées et son ajustement est d'un goût irréprochable. On ne pourrait désirer qu'une couleur plus tendre au chapeau noir pendu par un ruban à son bras gauche. Elle est debout et presque de profil, dans une pose modeste et digne, sans aucune affectation maniérée. Ah! que nous sommes loin des portraits à la mode, avec leurs airs prétentieux et leurs brillants atours![23]

[21] Thoré, 'Salon de 1864', *Salons*, ii, 100, 101.
[22] E. About, *Salon de 1864*, p. 291.

[23] Thoré, 'Salon de 1864', *Salons*, ii, 101–2.

Stylistically, the derivation of *Les Deux Sœurs* appears remarkably complex. Firmly set upon the foundation of naturalism which had developed out of his Leysian manner and the lesson of Courbet, whose *Demoiselles des bords de la Seine* was clearly its immediate inspiration (although he has scoured it of even a hint of impropriety), a new *appassionnement* can be detected in an evocation of mood which he had recently discovered in the work of the English Pre-Raphaelites. Whistler, who had settled in London in 1859, returned to Paris to work for a time in 1861. In England, he had come under the influence of the Pre-Raphaelite painters Millais and Rossetti, and during the winter of 1861–2 he demonstrated the degree of his enthusiasm in *The White Girl*, (National Gallery of Art, Washington, DC) a portrait of his mistress Joanna Heffernan which was painted in his studio in the Boulevard des Batignolles.[24] The picture, rejected at the Royal Academy in 1862 and at the Salon of 1863, was exhibited at the Salon des Refusés in 1863. It created a sensation comparable to that of Manet's *Déjeuner sur l'herbe* and was to have a far-reaching influence on French painting in the ·1860s.

The idea which grew up later that Whistler was artistically isolated in England because of his advanced aesthetic theories is largely false, mainly fostered by his own later remarks. In fact, his position with regard to the English avant-garde was probably more dependent than has sometimes been suggested. Indeed, the evocation of 'mood' which Millais sought at the expense of 'subject', and Rossetti's concept of art as decoration, were to have a profound and lasting influence on his work.[25] As early as 1855, Millais had said that he intended his painting *Autumn Leaves* (Pl. 91) to be 'full of beauty and without subject',[26] and he continued to refine the concept in works like *The Vale of Rest* (1858; Tate Gallery) and *Spring (Apple Blossoms)* (1859; Lady Lever Art Gallery, Port Sunlight), both of which Whistler and Fantin admired at the Royal Academy of 1859, and *The Eve of Saint Agnes* (1863; H.M. Queen Elizabeth the Queen Mother), which Tissot and Degas looked to as a model for their own works.[27] The influence of Millais was quickly apparent in Whistler's painting, beginning perhaps with *Alone With the Tide* (1861; Wadsworth Atheneum, Hartford), where the pensive mood of the figure is equated with the landscape as it is in a work like *The Vale of Rest* but not in contemporary French painting (although Tissot's own *Promenade dans la*

---

[24] As David Brooke has pointed out (oral communication), this must have been Tissot's first encounter with a Pre-Raphaelite 'stunner', those mistress–model cult-figures whose obsessive images are central to Pre-Raphaelite iconography, an obsession later echoed in Tissot's recording of Kathleen Newton.

[25] For Whistler's position in regard to the Pre-Raphaelites, see A. Grieve, 'Whistler and the Pre-Raphaelites', *Art Quarterly*, 34 (Summer 1971), 219–28.

[26] Quoted in the *Catalogue of the Millais Exhibition* (Walker Art Gallery, Liverpool, 1967), p. 41.

[27] See Reff, 'Degas's "Tableau de Genre" ' for a discussion of the influence of Millais on Tissot and Degas.

neige (Pl. 1) offers a somewhat tentative exception, and suggests a natural predisposition to this kind of narrative). Millais's influence is even clearer in *The White Girl*. Whistler was rapidly moving away from the realist influence of Courbet, and the pale palette, the elongated canvas, and the spiritual intensity of *The White Girl* announce his emancipation. Whistler maintained that *The White Girl* was simply an exercise in colour, but he must have been well aware of the suggestive overtones which the ambiguous subject and intensive mood give to the work, and its kinship with Millais is patent. With its psychological isolation, indefinable subject, and troubled eroticism, *The White Girl* came as a revelation of Pre-Raphaelite aesthetic ideas to French painters, and its impact reverberates in many brooding images of the sixties.[28] In *Les Deux Sœurs*, Tissot pays his own timid homage to it.

When *Les Deux Sœurs* was exhibited, the naturalistic effects of filtered and reflected light were widely noticed—effects which Tissot was always to find particularly attractive—and the debt of the picture to Courbet was tacitly acknowledged, but the psychological disjunction and ambiguous mood of the canvas, surely intended like Millais's *Autumn Leaves* to be a picture 'full of beauty and without subject', escaped notice, probably because it was not yet clearly defined. The oversight was corrected the next year when the reliance of Tissot's *Le Printemps* on Millais's picture of the same name was widely remarked.

Another source for the complex iconography of *Les Deux Sœurs* is to be found in the fashion plate, a form of popular imagery which proliferated in the women's magazines of the sixties. Its conventions offered an immediate precedent for the presentation of artificially posed figures in an outdoor setting, the elaborate unfurling of costume, and a lack of psychological interaction which many painters, the incipient Impressionists not least among them, were to find extremely attractive. Certainly an artist of the period who was involved in a type of figure painting which used fashionable costume was conscious, directly or indirectly, of the products of the medium in relation to his own work. Chronologically, Tissot appears to have been among the first to make use of such conventions.[29]

The Salon of 1865 found Tissot still more deeply under the hybrid influence

---

[28] Staley, *From Realism to Symbolism*, p. 22, discusses the influence of *The White Girl* in France and gives Manet's portraits of Berthe Morisot in *Le Balcon* (Louvre) and *Le Repos* (Museum of Art, Rhode Island School of Design) as examples.

[29] For a discussion of the role of the fashion-plate in the art of the sixties, see M. Roskill, 'Early Impressionism and the Fashion Plate'; for a discussion of the convention of such paintings of the figure in outdoor settings as developed by the Impressionists, see K. Champa, *Studies in Early Impressionism*, pp. 44–5. Champa suggests that Renoir's *Lise Holding a Parasol* (Salon of 1868,

Folkwang Museum, Essen) has its prototype in the conventions of English portrait painting, a source which seems equally likely in the case of Tissot's *Les Deux Sœurs*. It might also be suggested that the *Lise Holding a Parasol*, with its monumental scale and close study of outdoor light, may also have *Les Deux Sœurs* as a now forgotten prototype. Painted two years after the success of Tissot's picture at the Salon, the large scale and traditional elegance of the *Lise*, as well as its interest in the effects of filtered light, may recall Tissot's picture, if not in aesthetic emulation, at least in the hope of duplicating the elements of its success.

of Courbet and Millais. *Le Printemps*[30] (Pl. 30) seems to have relied equally on Courbet's *Demoiselles des bords de la Seine* for its naturalistic subject and handling and on Millais's *Spring (Apple Blossoms)* for its equivocal mood and unusual season.[31] For Thoré, *Le Printemps* duplicated the sensation of *Les Deux Sœurs* with its stunning Pre-Raphaelite *féerie printanière*:

Cette année, M. Tissot provoque encore l'étonnement du publique timide, avec une scène de *Printemps* où les pommiers fleuris tachettent de leurs bouquets toute la toile. En Angleterre, M. Millais a osé plusieurs fois ces féeries printanières, auxquelles l'école classique ne nous a point habitués. Les tableaux du printemps sont très-rares, même chez nos excellents pay sagistes actuels.[32]

In his review of the Salon, Paul Mantz gave Thoré's passing reference to Millais sharp and malicious focus:

M. Tissot a traduit en français une peinture du préraphaélite M. Millais, que nous avons vue à Londres en 1862, et qui nous a frappé: *Apple Blossoms*, disait le catalogue. En effet, c'étaient les mêmes pommiers avec leur neige rosée, et ce même gazon vert où jouaient de jeunes filles en fraîches toilettes de printemps. L'idée, malgré ces deux éditions, reste nouvelle, et nous voudrions que le public s'intéressât peu à peu aux audaces de M. Tissot.[33]

Obviously, a great part of the interest in *Le Printemps* came from its choice of an unusual subject. Like *Les Deux Sœurs*, it made its effect on a single note. It seems, however, to have been something of a hasty production, unless Mantz confused a purposeful lack of finish, for he found it carelessly executed and noted again the old failure to subordinate detail and the old trouble with atmosphere and colour:

Malheureusement, dans son tableau du Printemps, les figures sont d'un dessin très-lâché et très sommaire: M. Tissot peint des robes, des chapeaux, des châles, mais il ne met rien dessous; les notes rouges, chantant sur des fonds verts, le ravissent; il se plaît au contraste des blancs et des noirs. Nous aimons aussi ces jolies batailles de la couleur, mais à une condition, c'est qu'elles exprimeront quelque chose.[34]

A third picture, exhibited two years later at the Salon of 1867, continues this naturalist Pre-Raphaelitism, although by this time Tissot had also come under the influence of Alfred Stevens, whose approach is clearly felt in the treatment of the

---

[30] Salon of 1865, no. 2074. The picture was also exhibited in London the following year at Ernest Gambart's annual French Exhibition in Pall Mall; see J. Maas, *Gambart*, p. 191.

[31] Tissot doubtless knew Courbet's *Demoiselles* from the Salon of 1857; it is more difficult to establish his obvious familiarity with Millais's *Spring*, which was first exhibited at the Royal Academy in 1859. Had he visited London then, it seems likely that some reference to his trip would be preserved.

It is more likely that he first saw *Spring* at the International Exhibition in 1862, which also included one of his own works, although that trip cannot be documented either. The dependence noted by Thoré and Mantz surely relies on direct contact with the original rather than photographic or engraved reproductions.

[32] Thoré, 'Salon de 1865', *Salons*, ii, 200.

[33] Mantz, 'Salon de 1865', p. 12.

[34] Ibid.

figures and the thread of narrative implied by the title. *La Confidence* (Pl. 31)[35] once again looks to Courbet's *Demoiselles* for its narrative impetus, modified again for social propriety,[36] and to Millais for its poetic vagueness of mood. The painting was the subject of an extended discussion by Philip Gilbert Hamerton in his *Painting in France* of 1869, where he describes it as being typical of modernism and modern sentiment, and as such directly opposed to the spirit of classicism in its rejection of simplicity, feeling, and form. With justice, he calls *La Confidence* a 'picture of petticoats and parasols', noting that although the place is perhaps suitable for revelations, the costumes are scarcely suitable for the place, and then excuses himself for talking about dresses, 'for nothing in the picture can for one moment contend with them in importance'. In the entangled draperies and all but impossible poses he finds a desire to satisfy a predilection in the modern mind for intricacy and the unusual which had replaced, 'serious artistic aim' with 'needless, or even dangerous excess'.[37] Hammerton points to what is perhaps the central problem of these pictures: their unnatural quality. With neither naturalistic realism nor ritualistic vagueness of subject, they are neither genre nor symbolist and end by being vaguely annoying in their lack of clarity and purpose. These few pictures represent Tissot's Pre-Raphaelitism at its height, but it is clear that Pre-Raphaelite vision had not been taken over wholesale in the way Leys' archaism had been. What Tissot discovered in the Pre-Raphaelites of estrangement and brooding disjunction can only have reinforced what he had already found in Leys. In attempting to combine the intangibility of mood which attracted him in this English painting with the full-blooded reality of Courbet, he created a compelling but ultimately untenable style, and the result was always an uneasy marriage of influences.

Curiosity about the Pre-Raphaelites in France in the 1860s has not yet been thoroughly studied and documented. Both Tissot and Degas took a lively interest in the Pre-Raphaelite painters, Millais especially, and their enthusiasm is hinted at in Tissot's reference to Millais's *Eve of Saint Agnes* as a model for Degas's *Intérieur*. In a letter to Tissot which dates from the early seventies, Degas makes clear what Tissot must have sought in his Pre-Raphaelite works with their combination of Courbet and Millais:

---

[35] Salon of 1867, no. 1469. At the *Exposition Universelle* of 1867, Tissot exhibited two works, *Le Rendez-vous* (no. 588, unlocated) and *Portrait de Mme la marquise de M* . . . (no. 589; Pl. 40).

[36] A modification which was successful but not without difficulties of its own: if Courbet's 'ladies' could loll on a river-bank with impunity, ladies of quality clearly could not. The unsuitability of their choice of setting for a talk was found objectionable,

and after the decorum of *Les Deux Sœurs*, their eccentric behaviour appeared underbred. Cham, who made a caricature of the picture for his 'Salon', thought they looked like 'two tipsy women on a spree put off at the sight of a stream' and added 'Que dira le faubourg Saint-Germain???' (*Cham au Salon de 1867*, no page number).

[37] P.G. Hamerton, *Painting in France After the Decline of Classicism*, pp. 54–5.

Remember the art of Le Nain and all medieval France. Our race will have something simple and bold to offer, the naturalist movement will draw in a manner worthy of the great schools and then its strength will be recognized. The English art that appeals so much to us often seems to be exploiting some trick. We can do that better than they and be just as strong.[38]

Certainly, much Pre-Raphaelite painting could be said to exploit some 'trick' of mood, season, or setting, and this exploitation, in combination with what Tissot may have intended to be a 'bold and simple' naturalism, could serve as an accurate summary of these pictures. Their combination of elements served admirably to bring him to the attention of the public as an advanced yet respectable artist. Large in scale and mildly shocking in effect, they were clearly designed to attract attention in exhibitions where paintings had to be calculated to stand out from legions of enormous works to catch the eye of a public which came to the Salon 'as they would to a pantomime or a circus'.[39]

The Salon of 1866 saw another sleight of hand by the Goncourt's 'peintre plagiarie', and a new *appassionnement*. Veering away from the 'peintures des effets' of the Pre-Raphaelites, Tissot now began to give his canvases new narrative probability. Falling under the spell of Alfred Stevens's sumptuous and highly popular pictures, Tissot adopted his genre.[40] Stevens's fame had grown tremendously in the sixties, reaching its dazzling apogee at the *Exposition Universelle* in 1867, and Tissot doubtless was aware of the artistic and financial possibilities of the demand Stevens had created for genre pictures of stylish women in contemporary settings. No intrusive moralizing tone is ever allowed to mar the placid surface of Stevens's narrative or his delight in the sheen of beauty as an end in itself. In dresses that are a veritable index of the age, miracles fresh from the House of Worth, Stevens's women read letters, daydream, or admire chic bibelots from the Far East (Pl. 58). If emotion is allowed to intrude, it is only in playful *bouderie*, nostalgic regrets *en souvenir*, or in the mild sadness of friends' parting and the commemoration of Holy Days—occasions on which sensual beauty is given added charm and promise by melancholy overtones. Painted with a mellifluous technique and a sense of colour that made him the envy and despair of fellow artists, and with a sensibility and turn of subject that gave his pictures potent charm, Stevens enjoyed a rare popularity with artists and public alike.

He had discovered the key to his genre in the traditions of eighteenth-century painting. The painters of the rococo age offered him ideal models for the portrayal of modern sentiment and the cult of women. Unlike his predecessors, however, he

---

[38] E. Degas, *Letters*, pp. 30–1.

[39] Hippolyte Taine, *Paris-Guide* (Paris: Lacroix, 1867), i, 849.

[40] For a recent study of Stevens which contains an extensive bibliography, see the exhibition catalogue by W. A. Coles, *Alfred Stevens*; for Stevens at the *Exposition Universelle*, see P. Mitchell, 'The Success of Alfred Stevens at the Exposition Universelle of 1867', p. 263; for Stevens and the traditions of eighteenth-century painting, see C. Duncan, *The Pursuit of Pleasure*, pp. 106–8.

offers a less overtly sensual femininity. Even when he paints the courtesan, her specifically sexual function is discreetly ignored, and he always inclines more to the everyday life of the *haute bourgeoise* for his subjects. That Second Empire army of *'vespasiennes'* with their strident luxury and dazzling vulgarity, hair coloured 'red like a cow's tail and curled like a lap-dog's',[41] is absent, but Cornelias with their jewels abound, and young ladies who go to church and revere their parents with all the modest decorum the Faubourg Saint-Germain could require.

In Stevens, Tissot found a model ideally suited to his particular gifts and temperament. Courbet's influence was always constrained by Tissot's cooler sensuality and lesser stature as an artist, but Stevens offered obvious and immediately useful examples. Although Tissot remained untouched by Stevens's technique, Stevens's genre led him to the refinement of a kind of narrative which had attracted him from the beginning. Tissot had always been interested in a careful description of impeccable costume—certainly his Marguerite need look to the condition of her soul rather than that of her wardrobe—and the inchoate narratives of the *Faust* pictures suggest a search for an iconography that is evocative without being descriptive or literary. Stevens's approach seems to have given Tissot the key, for in his work at this time we can recognize a clearly individual narrative voice for the first time. Using Stevens as a point of departure, Tissot at once began to transmute his essentially bland genre into the intense and flexible aesthetic of his own drama—tart, ironic, brooding, and entirely personal.

Tissot's debt to Stevens was clear in the works he sent to the Salon of 1866. Thoré thought *Le Confessional* (Pl. 32),[42] of which there is a particularly accomplished watercolour replica (Pl. 33),[43] to be one of the most charming works of the year although 'un peu trop peut-être dans le genre d'Alfred Stevens'[44] and of less interest than the more individual *Les Deux Sœurs* of 1864. Something of the artificial quality of that picture is preserved in the artful manner in which the young woman, whom Thoré found very distinguished, grasps the back of the prie-dieu, but it has a narrative probability which can be traced to Stevens. The handkerchief which she holds is mildly suggestive of a melancholy declaration, and the prayer book and gloves stuck into the muff are a particularly apt summary of the fashionable churchiness which informs the picture. Stevens was a master of such restrained and sentimental piety, as a work like *Les Rameaux* (Pl. 34) suggests, but he maintains an unaffected simplicity of gesture and an uncomplicated narrative which Tissot did not choose to emulate.[45]

[41] Quoted in Sacheverell Sitwell, *For Want of the Golden City* (New York: The John Day Company, 1973), p. 356, without source.

[42] Salon of 1866, no. 1844.

[43] The water-colour was acquired from the artist by George A. Lucas for William T. Walters in February 1867. Lucas probably met Tissot through Whistler.

[44] Thoré, 'Salon de 1866', *Salons*, ii, 312.

[45] The original version of *Les Rameaux* was exhibited at the Salon of 1863 and again at the *Exposition Universelle* of 1867 with great success.

Jeune Femme chantant à l'orgue (Pl. 35),[46] the last of Tissot's church pictures
of the 1860s, was exhibited at the Salon the following year. With it, he seems to
have lost interest in the depiction of religious sentiment of even such doubtful
sincerity, for twenty years. It is a remarkably important work in his *œuvre*, however, for its subject and probably its composition was used again for the last
picture in the series *La Femme à Paris*, the unlocated *Musique sacrée*, and it was
the latter picture which induced the celebrated spiritual crisis which led to Tissot's
return to the church and his decision to devote his life to illustrating the Bible.
Both pictures represented a fashionable woman singing a duet with a nun in the
organ loft of a church, a practice afterwards banned by the Archbishop of Paris
as being more competitive than devotional, for which reason it doubtless attracted
Tissot's attention in the first place, the subject having exactly the ironic twist he
seems to have enjoyed.

The particular combination of elements in these pictures invites comparison
with the works representing Marguerite in church from the *Faust* pictures, and
certainly there is a correspondence in their combination of elaborate costume
and religious setting if not religious sentiment. But in the later works, any feeling
of apathy or misery is dispersed in a polite and superficial observation of forms,
and there is no hint of spiritual confrontation or religious crisis. Tissot does not
attempt the slightest insight into character, nor does he try to educate, or elevate,
the spirit, and settings are used simply to give zest and flavour to these fashion-
plate images. If they tell us anything, works like *Jeune Femme chantant à l'orgue*
suggest how the crisis of faith postulated by the religious young provincial in
works like *Martin Luther's Doubts* (Pl. 10) was solved by the successful young
Parisian artist and man-about-town of the Second Empire.

By the middle of the decade, Tissot was beyond question a popular and
successful painter. Honourable mention at the Salon of 1861 and the purchase
of *Le Rencontre de Faust et de Marguerite* for the Luxembourg the same year
were followed by a medal at the Salon of 1866 which made him *hors concours*,
free to exhibit without submitting his works for the approval of the jury, and
financial success had followed close upon official recognition. Modern genre had
proved more popular than Leysian medievalism. Bastard says that in 1863, the

Unlocated, it is reproduced in Coles, *Stevens*, p. 20.
The Walters version which is dated by Coles *c.*1862
has a number of minor variations. Stevens treated
religious sentiment with still greater reverence in
another work of the same date, *In Memoriam*
*c.*1862; (Museum of Fine Arts, Boston) which
depicts a young woman in black lighting a taper in
a church while another muses with a prayer-book
in her lap.

[46] Salon of 1867, no. 1468. A description of
the picture in Cook, *Art and Artists of Our Time*,
i, 158-9, as an example of Tissot's early work,
distinguishes it from the later *Musique sacrée* with
which it has understandably been confused (as by
Laver, *Vulgar Society*, p. 10). The style of the
costume, clearly of the late sixties, and the smaller
size of the canvas, make it impossible for it to have
been part of the later series *La Femme à Paris*.

year Tissot turned to modern life as a subject, he was more than 100,000 francs in debt, but that by 1865 he was earning 70,000 francs a year.[47]

In 1866, Tissot gave tangible proof of his artistic success. Acquiring a lot at 64, avenue de l'Impératrice, Baron Haussmann's magnificent new street running between the place d'Étoile and the Bois de Boulogne, he built a house with a large studio and was in residence by 1868. Doubtless the house, which is no longer standing, was worthy of its fashionable location and its gaudy age. Prophetically enough, Zola described the area as being English in appearance, with the irregular architecture of the private houses, their lawns behind green fences running along the pavements, and the Arc de Triomphe white against the sooty horizon.[48]

At the heart of the house was the studio, a room so daringly à la mode that it was soon written up in the newspapers: 'La dernière [originalité] qui doit être signalée est l'ouverture de l'atelier japonais d'un jeune peintre assez richement doté par la fortune pour s'offrir un petit hôtel dans les Champs-Elysées'.[49] Other rooms are doubtless depicted in Tissot's canvases after 1868 and are typical of the riotous confusion of periods, continents, and modern comforts which marked Second Empire taste, or the lack of it. Bastard says that the life Tissot lived there was of the most decorous and reserved simplicity: 'Point de fêtes ni de réceptions, toutefois, dans son habitation du Bois; il en redoutait autant l'éclat que le bruit. Rien que des réunions intimes, où les mêmes amis se retrouvaient en petit comité. Degas, Meissonier, Heilbuth firent parti de ce cénacle.'[50]

Although Champfleury adds 'les princes et princesses' to Bastard's list, they were no doubt sitters and collectors rather than intimates, and Tissot never seems to have sought any particular social lustre of that kind. He must have used his *hôtel*, as Bastard suggests and his pictures confirm, as a gathering place for friends, a setting for beautiful women, and a place to arrange his growing collections.[51]

---

[47] Bastard, p. 260. As a point of comparison, Meissonier, said to have been the most highly paid painter of his era, reputedly earned 150,000 francs a year at this time. A letter from Tissot to a collector now in the Musée de Gray suggests that his fees were extremely high: 'Monsieur, plusieurs propositions me sont faites par des amateurs sérieux pour m'acheter mes tableaux. Si j'ai attendu jusqu'aujourd 'hui pour me décider, c'était pour mieux choisir les galeries òu mes tableaux devront être placés en lieux honorables ... J'ai fait quelques concessions. Je vous en fait (sic) part. Voici jusqu'òu je puis descendre: Marquerite à l'église, 5.500 fr.; Rencontre de Faust, 6.500 fr.; Marguerite au jardin, 5.000 fr.; Danse Macabre, 5.000 fr.; Pendant l'office, 9.000 fr.' (A.-P. de Mirimonde, *Catalogue de Musée Baron Martin A. Gray* (Gray: Musée Baron Martin, 1959), s.v. 'Tissot', n. 1).
[48] In the opening pages of *La Curée* (1871).

[49] Jules Champfleury, 'La Mode des Japoniai-series', *La Vie parisienne* (21 November 1869), repr., Lacambre, *Le Réalisme*, p. 143. The creation of Tissot's Japanese studio can probably be linked to the sale of Japanese objects and architectural elements which took place after the close of the *Exposition Universelle* of 1867 in 1868, although Chūji Ikegame's discovery of Tissot's appointment as drawing master to Prince Akitake offers the attractive alternative that they were a gift from the Prince; see below, n. 69.
[50] Bastard, pp. 260–1.
[51] Tissot's activities as a collector have not been documented. By the end of his life, he had owned—and apparently sold—works by Manet, Degas, and Pissarro: only furniture, bric-à-brac, and a few decorative prints were sold in addition to his own work and the contents of his studio in the Vente Tissot in 1903, which was made up of the furnishings of the

Tissot made no attempt to turn his studio into a rendezvous for smart society, and the pattern was duplicated when he was in England in the 1870s. In London, there were never those afternoons 'at home' like Alma-Tadema's 'Tuesdays' which made his studio a bohemian drawing-room for artistic duchesses. This was due in large part to the socially unacceptable nature of Tissot's relationship with Mrs Newton, but it seems to have been a deep-rooted natural preference as well. Life in St. John's Wood was to be elaborate and perhaps a little pretentious, but it was unshakably domestic. After Tissot's return to Paris in 1882, when he was again fashionable after the success of the Bible illustrations, their nature made it necessary for the *hôtel* in the avenue du Bois (the new name of the avenue de l'Impératrice) to take on the character of a church, or at least that of a medium's establishment, and the visits of sitters for portraits seem to have alternated with spiritualist materializations.

An unfinished self-portrait from the middle sixties shows the successful historian of modern life and a cosmopolitan, if perhaps neurotic, *boulevardier* (Pl. 36). It invites comparison with Degas's roughly contemporary portrait (Pl. 37), an image rather less suggestive of amused tolerance and psychological stability.[52]

By the middle of the decade, the success of works like *Mlle L. L. . .* and *Les Deux Sœurs* had made Tissot a popular society portrait painter. Principal commissions at this time not only demonstrate how far behind he had left drawings of maids at forty francs apiece, but also a now truly remarkable skill at solving the most complicated artistic problems. In 1865, Tissot received a commission for major family portraits from the marquis de Miramon. The most important, a large group portrait of the marquis, his wife, and their two eldest children grouped *à l'anglaise* on a terrace (Pl. 38) was exhibited at the Cercle de l'Union Artistique in 1866:

house in the avenue de l'Impératrice, and the Vente Jeanne Tissot which dispersed the contents of the château de Buillon in 1964 consisted of similar articles, including the works by her uncle which she had inherited. Tissot's purchase of Manet's *Blue Venice* (1865; Shelburne Museum, Shelburne, Vermont) and his sale of a picture Degas had given him, probably *Chevaux dans la prairie* (L. 289, *c.*1871; formerly Durand-Ruel, Paris), are discussed elsewhere in the text; the Pissarro in his collection cannot at present be identified. All that is known is that it was this work that Pissarro submitted unsuccessfully to the Royal Academy in 1871, as is made clear in a letter to Théodore Duret from the painter, dated 17 January 1881: 'En 70 [*sic*] j'avais envoyé avec Monet à l'exposition de l'*Academy*, nous avons été mis à la porte avec ensemble, c'était le tableau appartenant actuellement à Tissot . . .' (Janine Bailly-Herzberg, *Correspondance de Camille Pissarro* (Paris, Presses Universitaires de France, 1980), I:145). When Tissot acquired the picture is not known, although it was probably in 1871 or shortly before. Its presence in his collection suggests that he was familiar with Pissarro's London work, a supposition put forth by the present author in 'Energized Punctuality', *Worcester Art Museum Journal*, p. 19. I am indebted to Ronald Pickvance for bringing the Pissarro letter to my attention.

[52] For the formal and psychological implications, see Reff, 'The Pictures Within Degas's Pictures', pp. 133–40.

M. Tissot a essayé des grandes proportions pour un portrait de famille. M. le marquis de M . . . , sa femme et ses deux enfants se groupent assez naturellement sur la terrasse d'un parc. La jeune femme est charmante, son bébé dans ses bras. L'autre enfant existe trop peu. En général, la peinture manque de solidité. Elle se réduit presque à un camaïeu grisâtre qu'interrompent sans l'échauffer, quelques touches vives, insuffisantes pour créer des rapports de tons soutenus.[53]

For all its inventiveness, the picture clearly owes a great deal to the study of Degas's *La Famille Bellelli* (L. 79, 1858–60; Louvre).[54] The figure of Léon de Miramon with his leg tucked under him as he turns in his chair unquestionably comes directly from the figure of Julie Bellelli, and the frieze-like composition also probably originates in the Degas. But Tissot replaces the tragic nobility of the Bellellis with a stylish *gentilesse* less compelling but doubtless more attractive to the sitters. In the strangely arbitrary choice of season alone do we find an iconographical note which seems entirely personal. The autumn trees and the dead and drifting leaves on the terrace give a poignant and haunting quality to this otherwise luxurious image of Second Empire life, which lingers in the mind.

Yet Tissot as usual transmutes the elements he borrows into the totality of a remarkably personal statement, and few of his contemporaries would have been both willing and able to create an image as satisfying in artistic and social terms alike. If he offers few of the human insights in which the Bellelli portrait abounds, such layers of meaning would have been unsuitable and surely unwelcome, and he does preserve the Miramons from the vacuousness of the society portrait with the skill and accuracy of his documentation of their appearances and their world. His grey-green tonality is more felicitous than is sometimes the case, and his decorative touches of colour are unusually discreet. Its close tone, shallow pace, and reluctance to emphasize three-dimensional modelling give the picture formal unity and great style.

The marquis de Miramon was a member of a club housed in the rue Royale in Gabriel's splendid buildings on the place de la Concorde, and when some of his members decided to have a group portrait painted in 1868, it was no doubt his satisfaction with Tissot's pictures for him which led to the commission of what is probably Tissot's masterpiece, *Le Cercle de la rue Royale* (Pl. 39).[55]

[53] L. LaGrange, 'Exposition de l'Union Artistique', *Gazette des beaux-arts*, p. 400.

[54] Degas paid particular attention to the pose of Julie Bellelli, which is studied in a sketch *à l'essence* (L. 69; Bliss Collection, Dumbarton Oaks, Washington, DC) as well as a number of drawings; Tissot seems to have altered the Bellelli composition as much to accommodate the different ages of the sitters as to give psychological insight or aesthetic variation.

[55] Each sitter contributed 1,000 francs towards the artist's fee, and lots were drawn to decide ownership with baron Hottinguer the winner. From left to right, the sitters are: comte Alfred de la Tour-Maubourg, the marquis de Lau, comte Étienne de Ganay, comte J. de Rochechouart, C. Vansittart, the marquis R. de Miramon, baron Hottinguer, the marquis de Ganay, Gaston de Saint-Maurice, the prince de Polignac, the marquis de Gallifet, and Charles Haas. Reviewing the Royal Academy of 1868, Philippe Burty remarked on the rarity of such club portraits in France although they were commonplace in England ('Exposition de la Royal Academy', *Gazette des beaux-arts*, pp. 62–3).

Twelve men are set in a long frieze against a screen of foliage and architectural detail which opens out at the left to the place de la Concorde under a bright, cloudy spring sky, while the top half of the canvas is given over to a dazzling perspective view down Gabriel's colonnade. In its division into two parts, an enclosed lower half that opens out to embrace a wide view over the heads of the sitters, the *Cercle* is reminiscent of the compositional formulas developed in pictures like *Faust et Marguerite au jardin* (Pl. I), but freed of medieval conceits and rendered with an atmospheric openness that is nearly unique in his work, it becomes a device of compelling visual interest.

Beginning with the figure of Charles Haas, who steps out of the doorway on the right and surveys the scene, the eye is carried by the glance of several sitters across the composition to the figure of the comte de la Tour-Maubourg who sits on the balustrade in idle contemplation of the square and is then turned and carried back across by the look of the marquis de Lau who faces inward towards the door. The figures themselves, with their variety of casual poses, have the quality of arrested motion. Although less unrelated psychologically than in many earlier works, or with a narrative probability which makes disjunction less apparent, Tissot's sitters seem to be holding their poses for an early camera. It is not known how Tissot set about composing this complex work or whether he used photography as an aid. It seems more than likely that the camera was called into service to supplement individual sessions with the sitters and to record architectural detail. This quality of arrested motion is present in many pictures painted in the sixties. It is integral to works like Monet's *Women in a Garden* (1866–7; Louvre) and Bazille's *Family Portrait on a Terrace near Montpellier* (1868; Louvre), and can be traced in great part to the widespread interest artists took in photography. Particularly telling in this respect is the vignette of a trotting carriage horse and two moving pedestrians seen through the balustrade in the *Cercle*. Arrested in their passage, they are remarkably similar in treatment to other such figures in urban views like Renoir's *Pont des Arts* (1867; The Norton Simon Foundation, Los Angeles) or Manet's *Exposition Universelle* (1867; National Gallery, Oslo).

More than a series of carte-de-visite photographs, although doubtless inspired by them, the *Cercle* points up individual character with telling poses carefully integrated within the formal structure of the composition. Tissot was always a remarkably good portraitist of men, and his characterization of them is sharper and better-flavoured than that of his often generalized and flattering portraits of women. It is unfortunate that he did not have occasion to paint men more often.

Genre detail in the *Cercle* is also handled with an assurance and brio astonishing in its formal and psychological aptness. The disordered paraphernalia of a men's club—a seeming confusion of newspapers, hats, gloves, and discarded cigarettes—is fitted into the strict composition, giving a refreshing informality to its rigorous structure. Tissot's attention to detail also gives an almost hallucinatory feeling of time and place. The Louis XVI–Impératrice furniture covered in apple green *toile de perse*, the deep fringes on the red *voyeuses*, the rubber plants towering over the hedge, silent reminders of the South American exoticism still in vogue at the Tuileries: all are redolent of the *décor de la vie* of the Second Empire. In retrospect, even the unexpected perspective of Gabriel's eighteenth-century building as a setting for nineteenth-century life has a disconcerting and strangely provocative quality.

The remarkable power of *Le Cercle de la rue Royale* to conjure up the world of the Second Empire has often been noted. Proust, who used Charles Haas as the model for Swann, refers to it in that light in *A la recherche du temps perdu*.[56] In the large picture, Tissot's meticulous documentation and subtle iconography combine seamlessly with the demands of the portrait to distil the very essence of 'the poetry of modern life', and what can surely be called one of the abiding images of the age.

Equally evocative is another of the family commissions offered by the marquis de Miramon, a portrait of his wife which was painted in her rooms at the château de Paulhac and exhibited the next year at the *Exposition Universelle* of 1867 (Pl. 40).[57] Like the family group, the picture suggests comparison with the work of Degas, although in this case it seems that Tissot provided a remarkable and hitherto unsuspected prototype for the pastel portrait Degas made of his sister in their father's drawing room which is generally dated 1869 (L. 255; formerly Mme David-Weill, Paris).[58] Tissot uses familiar setting and typical gesture to define character in the most precise manner. Mme de Miramon's possessions, a *mélange* of rococo furniture and Japanese bric-à-brac, the height of fashion in 1867, and her costume, a rose-coloured 'Watteau' dress caped *à la pèlerine* and caught with a lace scarf and a cross at the throat, indicate character as dexterously as her fragile, highly-strung gesture and haughty turn of the head. One also senses contrast beyond the affinity of sitter and setting, and perhaps a subtle hint of psychological comment by the artist himself. The cheerfully stony assurance of the eighteenth-century bust on the chimney-piece is in marked contrast to the tenseness of the marquise, whose taut good looks and charged carriage are all the more readily identifiable, by comparison, as the ideal 'modern' beauty of the Second Empire. What might be considered a purely historic or social contrast is also made to suggest that the cool assurance of the young woman is more vulnerable than it might at first appear. It is a suggestion elaborated in turn by the still

[56] Marcel Proust, *A la recherche du temps perdu*, vol. iii, *Le Côté de Guermantes* (Paris: La Pleiade, 1955–6), p. 200.

[57] *Exposition Universelle*, 1867, no. 589. I am indebted to the marquis de Miramon for information about the portrait.

[58] For a discussion of Degas's portrait of Mme Morbilli, see Reff, 'The Pictures Within Degas's Pictures', pp. 140–3. His interpretation has provided the most subtle of models for my own study.

life of needlework on the Louis XVI stool behind her with its own story of domestic pleasure and family life.

A small portrait of *Eugène Coppens de Fontenay* (Pl. 41), repeating the genre approach of the *Cercle* and the composition of *The Marquise de Miramon*, represents the more usual scale of Tissot's portrait commissions at this time, and is representative of a number of as yet unlocated works. Once again, a profusion of details—the expensive, vaguely rococo ornaments which had become the necessary background for the rich—points up the social position of the wonderfully self-satisfied young man with his yellow gloves. Tissot was also a popular portraitist of children. One ambitious group of four siblings lolling amid a jumble of toys, which is unlocated but probably dates from 1868, establishes a pattern often to be reiterated in St. John's Wood (see Pl. IV). He always wisely preferred to paint conversation pieces rather than pure portraits, and they form a significant and rewarding part of his work with their generally high quality and fresh, inventive approach. Most of them seem to have engaged both his artistic attention and his human sympathy in a way other works sometimes do not, and as a result they are aesthetic objects and social documents of great charm.

Another little portrait from this time, now often understandably called *Rêverie* (Pl. 42), offers a more private aspect of Tissot's gifts as a portraitist. With great sympathy and discretion, he probes psychology and creates mood with a delicacy which needs no recourse to dramatic effects.

A series of genre pictures from this time, often left in an unfinished state, suggest an attempt on Tissot's part to find new subjects: an important oil sketch, *Déjeuner sur l'herbe* (Pl. 43). and nursemaids and their charges in an unfinished *Terrasse du Jeu de Paume* (Pl. 44). In both, one rediscovers a penchant for using grandiose settings for scenes of everyday life which may have grown out of work on the *Cercle*. The combination reappears during Tissot's English years when Trafalgar Square and the terraces of Regent's Park are used for the same purpose, and again in the eighties when the galleries of the Louvre are used as the settings for a number of pictures (Pls. 106, 153, 193, and 194).

One of the monumental statuary groups in the Tuileries Gardens sets the stage for what is probably the most important of Tissot's genre pictures from this time. *La Retraite dans le jardin des Tuileries* (Pl. 45)[59] combines the military genre which grew out of the Napoleonic legend with everyday life in a way which suggests that the lesson of Manet's *Musique aux Tuileries* (Pl. 105) had not been lost on Tissot.[60] Near the pavillon de Marsan, a group of children and nursemaids

---

[59] Salon of 1868, no. 2390. The picture was bought by the princesse Mathilde from the Salon (see *La Collection de S.A.I. Madame la Princesse Mathilde* (Paris: Galerie Georges Petit, 17–21 May 1904), lot. 205.

[60] A relationship suggested by H. Zerner, 'James Tissot', *L'Œil*, p. 22.

gather to watch the preparations for sounding the evening *retraite* by four military drummers, three in the bearskins of the hussars, the fourth in the uniform of a zouave, while in the foreground an errant pug scatters a group of pigeons. The melancholy, sickly grace of the November evening was particularly remarked:

M. Tissot, habitué aux longs plis et aux lingeries diaphanes des vêtements féminins au moyen âge, n'a point transigé avec les rudesses de l'uniforme de ses tambours qui se préparent, dans le jardin des Tuileries, à battre la *Retraite*. Mais soit calcul, soit hasard, il a éclairé son groupe du demi-jour d'une soirée de novembre, dont les ramures dépouillées des arbres, se découpant sur un ciel grisâtre, accusent la froideur et la mélancolie. Cet effet crépusculaire, qui va bien du reste au talent laborieusement inquiet de M. Tissot, donne une certaine grâce maladive à ses groupes d'enfants et atténue ce que les silhouettes de soldats présenteraient de rigide et d'anguleux.[61]

The *Retraite* is of special interest because it adds to our knowledge of Tissot's working methods. The recent appearance of a small oil study for the figure of the zouave drummer (Pl. 46), identified with the name and regiment of the sitter, points up Tissot's dependence on specific models and his reliance on traditional methods of composing his works from carefully studied drawings and oil sketches. Drawings for individual figures are not uncommon (see, for example, Pls. 15, 53, and 85), and there are a number of oil sketches for entire compositions (see, for example, Pls. 43, 134, 135, and 150). Unfinished works like the *Terrasse du Jeu de Paume* (Pl. 44) give a good idea of a work in progress, and so it is possible to reconstruct Tissot's working method, a method hardly surprising in view of his traditional training and his desire to create works of a finish acceptable at the Salon. Tissot's technique became more and more personal throughout the sixties, taking on an overall finish which can make even Gérôme look almost painterly in comparison, and it sets him completely apart from the qualities sought by friends like Manet and Degas. By the end of the decade, he had abandoned the enamel surfaces of his early works, the legacy of his training by a pupil of Ingres, and had developed a system of small brush-strokes and a use of dry pigment which gives his work a completely personal flavour. His careful technique had served him well in his historical reconstructions, giving a heightened conviction to the genre, but it proved to be somewhat less successful in the painting of modern life, bringing his canvases perhaps too close to a literal descriptiveness that becomes almost their entire *raison d'être*. Tissot was never more than superficially involved with advanced aesthetic research, perhaps never deeply involved with the problems of painting on any level beyond the development of a manual dexterity sufficient to the needs of meticulous rendering of the visible world. But laborious intelligence and aesthetic *appassionnements* made him continually alive to outside

[61]   J. Grangedor, 'Salon de 1868', *Gazette des beaux-arts*, p. 14.

developments and often brought him to incorporate useful aspects of them in his work, transformed and made unrecognizable by his essentially literary concept of painting and his unshakeable interest in technical finish. The gulf between Tissot and advanced painting is patent in his sketch for a *Déjeuner sur l'herbe* (Pl. 43). Comparison with similar works by the Impressionists—Monet's sketch for a picture of the same title (1866; Pushkin Museum, Moscow), for example—only points up Tissot's fundamentally academic technical approach, and the strangely allegorical feeling of Tissot's catalogue of earthly delights finds no parallel in Monet's uncomplicated record of a moment. Tissot remains a literary painter even at his most impressionistic, and although certain free sketches painted in London can be reminiscent of Whistler (Pl. 134) or Manet (Pl. 135), there is little attempt in the sixties to capture such purely painterly qualities.

Tissot painted other narrative pictures in the manner of the *Retraite* in the late 1860s, but the majority are in the genre of Stevens, and Tissot's record of fashion-plate beauty continued to be the theme for increasingly personal variations. *L'Armoire* (Pl. 47) is contemporary with works like *La Confidence* and *Le Confessionnal* (Pls. 31 and 32) and is as clearly part of the same impulse in its unabashed display of dress as in its pointed avoidance of narrative. What may represent an attempt to enlarge Stevens's genre is seen in the strange *Les Patineurs (lac de Longchamp)* (1869; unlocated) which offers a souvenir of the Second Empire craze for ice skating in the Bois near Tissot's house, although a Goupil photograph of the picture in the Bibliothèque-Nationale suggests an even greater airlessness than usual in this not-quite-successful attempt to capture rapid movement. *Les Patineurs* gives considerable credence to Réné Menard's remark at the end of the decade that 'M. Tissot continue, avec l'esprit et le talent qu'on lui connait, sa lutte acharnée contre la perspective aérienne'.[62]

Also dependent on Stevens is a picture, issued in a Goupil photograph of 1869 with the title *Le Gôuter*, which appears to have entered the collection of William H. Vanderbilt in New York soon after it was painted (Pl. 48). It is in all likelihood a simple variation of Stevens' *Fleurs d'automne* (Pl. 49), which was admired at the *Exposition Universelle* of 1867 for its colour harmonies of black and grey, its intimate sentiment, and its creation of mood without recourse to anecdote. Tissot gathers the same elements, but perhaps misses something of the poetic resonance, making of them a genre picture with a mildly amusing narrative in which a plump blonde, surely intended to represent a young widow, raises her solitary glass. He also attempts something of the close colour of *Fleurs d'automne*, but his brown and russet palette, set off with a stripe of green plants seen through the door of a conservatory, also departs somewhat from the essence of its model. Tissot was more interested in narrative than Stevens, and the individuality of *Le Gôuter* lies

[62] R. Ménard, 'Salon de 1870', *Gazette des beaux-arts*, p. 39. The picture is dated 1869.

neither in its poetry nor its colour. Its effectiveness is based on a series of carefully placed clues from which it is almost possible to construct a little domestic
drama. The lady with red-rimmed eyes (who may be the popular Parisian model
Emma Dobigny), alone with her afternoon nip, has a story to tell: that it engages
our attention so effectively is no small tribute to Tissot's consummate skill as a
narrative painter. A closely related picture of the same year, now called *Rêverie*
(Pl. 50), is made up of the same vague but suggestive elements. It seems likely
that a narrative key was provided for these pictures by what may have been the
most ambitious of them, *Une veuve* (Pl. 51), which was exhibited at the Salon
of 1869.[63] Élie Roy, put in mind of Alphonse Karr's remark to another 'veuve
facile à consoler', 'vous porterez le deuil, le noir va bien aux blondes', considered
the picture in *L'Artiste*:

Rien de plus simple comme sujet, rien de plus compliqué comme exécution. Tout ce que notre
luxe hétérogène peut entasser de bizarreries élégantes: siéges en jonc tressé, corbeilles, jardi-
nières, tabourets, tout cela est rendu, détaillé comme pour un inventaire, avec une perfection
désespérante, car par un oubli complet de la perspective aérienne et des effets de plein air,
aucun objet n'est à sa place.[64]

The fashionable—and clearly restive—widow, immured in the country by the
tedious proprieties of mourning, with only her mother-in-law (or mother) and
daughter for company, is almost surely intended as a modern-dress illustration of
the fable *Le Jeune Veuve* from the *Fables* of La Fontaine; such grief as she could
muster has given way to amorous musing long before the date of its official
termination. Her dreamy expression is carefully contrasted with the fidgeting of
the child and the placid contentment of the old lady, and the drift of her thoughts
is given clear expression by the copy of Bouchardon's *Cupid Stringing his Bow*
in the garden behind the arbor. With its elaborate staging and cynical parody of
the classics, *Une veuve* can hardly have failed to delight its Parisian audience, its
'desperate perfection' of technique, relentless and arid, only heightening the
pleasure for many. Bereavement was a theme to which Tissot was to return in
both his English work and *La Femme à Paris*. *The Widower* and *Orphan* (Pls. 122
and 138) date from his years in London, but the most direct debt to *Une veuve*
can be seen in *Quiet* (Pl. 169) which again juxtaposes the bored child and the
abstracted adult, though here without the theme of mourning. When he does
return to this subject in *La Femme à Paris*, however, it takes on a very different
complexion: *Sans dot*, though superficially similar, reveals the hopeless future of
a dowerless orphan, rather than the complacent anticipation of a rich widow.
More important, the jaded wit of *Une veuve* is replaced by a narrative tone of
sympathy which sets the two pictures worlds apart.

[63] Salon of 1869, no. 2269. Stevens had exhibited a picture of the same title at the Salon of
1861, and pretty widows are to be found in his
work throughout the decade.

[64] E. Roy, 'Salon de 1869', *L'Artiste*, pp. 81–2.

Bereavement of another kind was the subject of the water-colour *Mélancolie* exhibited at the Salon of 1868, and now unlocated: what is undoubtedly the principal version in oil is known.[65] Garden sculpture again gives focus to the emotional state of the protagonist, an unhappy young woman whose pose echoes that of a statue as she sits head in hand beside a pond, amid fallen autumn leaves, and guarded by a belligerent pug. This pug appears in a number of pictures at this time, as other dogs will later, echoing or commenting on the moods of its mistress (see, for example, Pls. 50 and 67). Tissot uses these dogs with an anthropomorphism which Ouida was to bring to its only too obvious conclusion the next year in *Puck: The Autobiography of a Dog*, whose canine author remarks that 'for viewing life,—all its cogs, and wheel, and springs,—there is nothing so well as to be a lady's pet dog'.[66]

L'Escalier (Pl. 52) is perhaps the most successful of Tissot's pictures of modern life in the sixties. It is a work of the most subtle innuendo, a narrative with context but without plot, full of unexplained psychological tensions. The anticipatory gaze of the young woman as she looks with repressed anxiety through the leaded glass screen into what is undoubtedly the drawing-room of Tissot's house creates a feeling of expectation neurotic in its intensity. The pose of the young woman is heightened with carefully chosen details which add to its suggestiveness. Comparison with a preparatory drawing for the figure (Pl. 53) shows a shift from a simple recording of costume and pose towards a heightened narrative intent, for in the unfinished work the woman leans forward in a far more expectant way and is given a letter and some books to hold, while the tightened fingers of her other hand are shown in a more dramatic position, alterations which become the telling, if unco-operative, signposts of a story. The glass-walled setting itself acts within the narrative to create a feeling of separation. In early works like *Marguerite à l'office* (Pl. 5), a physical barrier becomes the exact iconographical equivalent of Marguerite's psychological state, but in *L'Escalier* its use is less obvious and more sophisticated, creating an indefinable and contradictory barrier to the figure confronting its luminous transparency.

Whistler's *The White Girl* and the possible influence of Millais's *Eve of Saint Agnes* have been suggested as sources for the brooding, highly charged mood of *L'Escalier*, as has the extreme sensitivity of both Tissot and Degas at this time to even the smallest pictorial elements in the creation of narrative and atmosphere— a response matched by a close attention to formal composition which is admirably

---

[65] Salon of 1868, no. 3337. The oil version was sold at Sotheby's, 15 March 1967, lot 103 (as *Chagrin d'Amour*), and is reproduced in the catalogue.

[66] Ouida (Louise de la Rame), *Puck*, 2 vols. (Leipzig: Tauchnitz, 1870), i, 11. For a study of the traditional symbolism of the dog as it evolved in eighteenth-century French painting, doubtless Tissot's immediate source of inspiration for the use of an animal to point up the theme of a picture, see Donald Posner, *Watteau: A Lady at her Toilette* ('Art in Context', New York: Viking, 1973), chap. 6, 'The Lady and her Dog', pp. 77–83.

demonstrated in the present work.[67] Indeed, it is in a work like *L'Escalier* that Tissot comes closest to matching his narrative skill with true concern for the problems of pictorial representation in the 1860s.

The most stylistically pervasive and in many ways problematical of Tissot's *appassionnements* in the sixties was Japanese art. Its influence was iconographic at first, but grew increasingly stylistic and was to have a lasting effect on his work. Recent studies have charted the discovery and dissemination of Japanese art in Paris at this time, and with this added knowledge of the sources and development of *japonisme*, Tissot's own position has emerged with new clarity.[68]

Tissot's pre-eminence as an early *japoniste* has probably been obscured more by the superficiality of his understanding than by the passage of time, but at the end of the 1860s his position must have appeared unassailable. In 1868, the painter of fashionable *japonaiseries* and the collector of Japanese objects was given what must have amounted to quasi-divine status in social if not aesthetic terms when he was appointed *gwa-gaku*, or drawing master, to Prince Akitake, younger brother of the last Tokugawa shōgun, who was in Paris as the titular head of the Japanese Imperial Commission to the *Exposition Universelle* of 1867. Tissot's appointment, one of a number clearly intended to prepare the fourteen-year-old prince for a role in the wider diplomacy envisaged by the Edo Government, lasted from March to October 1868. His duties must have been in great part symbolic, but several visits to his studio are recorded in the diaries of the prince and his suite, and what appears to have been a happy association was commemorated by a water-colour portrait of the prince dated 27 September, 1868 (Pl. 54). Prince Akitake visited the avenue de l'Impératrice for the last time on 30 September, and may well have carried his portrait away with him as a parting gift. Mounted in green and gold silk as a hanging scroll, it remained forgotten in the Tokugawa collections at Mito for over a hundred years.[69]

It is probable that Felix Bracquemond introduced Japanese art to Paris when he discovered a copy of Hokusai's *Manga*, a book of woodcut studies of animals,

[67] In Reff, 'Degas's "Tableau de Genre",' pp. 332–7.

[68] See G. Weisberg, '*Japonisme*: Early Sources and the French Printmaker 1852–1882', in G. Weisberg *et al.*, *Japonisme*, in which old confusions concerning the Parisian shops selling Japanese goods in the sixties are clarified.

[69] Tissot's appointment, like the existence of the portrait, was discovered by Chūji Ikegami of Kobe University during the study of Japanese records relating to the Imperial Commission to the *Exposition Universelle* when he associated the phonetic rendering chisō with *Tissot*. His discovery was the subject of the paper 'James Tissot: maître de dessin du Prince Akitake' read at an international symposium on *Japonisme* in Tokyo in December 1979, and is included in the English translation in the published papers of the symposium. In an earlier form, it appeared in Japanese as an appendix to the catalogue of the exhibition *Ukiyo-e Prints and the Impressionist Painters: Meeting of East and West* (Tokyo: Committee for the Year 2001, 1979), pp. 178–83, which accompanied the symposium. I am indebted to Professor Ikegami for allowing me to use his information before its appearance in the West and for obtaining a photograph of the water-colour for reproduction.

flowers, landscapes, and figures, at the shop of the printer Auguste Delâtre in 1856. By the time of the *Exposition Universelle* in 1867, Japanese art had become a fashionable mania, and there were a number of shops which sold Japanese objects. The first of these appears to have been Descell's *A l'Empire Chinois* which stocked Japanese goods as early as the 1850s; it was followed in 1862 by the famous Mme Desoye's, herself called 'la japonaise', in the rue de Rivoli. These shops were of central importance as meeting-places for early *japonistes*. Manet, the Goncourts, Jacquemart, Degas, Burty, and Tissot are known to have frequented Mme Desoye's and doubtless they all made the rounds of similar shops which proliferated in the wake of the *Exposition Universelle*.

Tissot does not appear to have exhibited a work of *japoniste* character until 1869, but his enthusiasm for the Orient can be documented far earlier. He was in fact one of the earliest *japonistes*, and by 1864 was already known for his collection of Japanese art as well as his 'Japanese' pictures. In a letter dated 12 November 1864, Dante Gabriel Rossetti wrote to his mother of a visit he had paid to a shop, surely that of Mme Desoye, which his brother William had already visited, where Tissot's avid collecting and *japoniste* pictures were described with admiration by the proprietress: 'I have bought very little—only four Japanese books . . . I went to his Japanese shop, but found all the costumes were being snapped up by a French artist, Tissot, who it seems is doing three Japanese pictures, which the mistress of the shop described to me as the three wonders of the world, evidently in her opinion quite throwing Whistler into the shade.'[70]

It is likely that the *Japonaise au bain* (Pl. 55), which is dated 1864, is one of the pictures Rossetti heard described in such glowing terms. Although Japanese woodcuts of women at the bath undoubtedly suggested its subject, which brings the prints of Kiyonaga or Shigemasa immediately to mind, they clearly suggested little in terms of design, for Tissot's approach remains doggedly Western in its insistence on three-dimensional modelling, spatial recession, and cast shadow.

---

[70] D.G. Rossetti, *Letters*, ii, 524. Rossetti's reference to Tissot as a collector of Japanese art and a painter of *japonaiseries* is the earliest known; in the later 1860s, he is also cited as an early *japoniste* in Zacharie Astruc, 'Le Japon chez nous', *L'Etendard* (26 May 1868), p. 2, where he is included as 'le gothique Tissot' in a list of early *japonistes*; and in J. Champfleury, 'La Mode des japoniaiseries', *La Vie parisienne*, which is quoted in the present text. Champfleury also makes indirect reference to him as a collector of Japanese art in *Les Chats* when he reproduces, opposite p. 154, a 'Groupe de chats, caprice japonaise' which is identified, p. 329, as 'tiré de la collection de M. James Tissot'. Tissot's position as an early *japoniste* is also cited in 1878 in E. Chesneau, 'Exposition Universelle: le Japon à Paris', *Gazette des beaux-arts*, p. 387, where he is included in an extensive list of early *japonistes*, and p. 396, where he makes reference to the influence of Japanese art on his English pictures: in a list of the qualities of Japanese art assimilated by various artists, he ascribes to Tissot 'des hardiesses et même des étrangetés de composition comme en ses belles *Promenades sur la Tamise*.' For modern treatments of Tissot's *japonisme*, see principally Weisberg, *et al.*, *Japonisme*, pp. 10–11, 43; the introduction and relevant catalogue entries in Wentworth, *Catalogue Raisonné of Prints*; and Wentworth, 'Tissot and Japonisme', the text of a paper read at the symposium *Ukiyo-e Prints and the Impressionist Painters* in Tokyo, December 1979, published in the collected papers of the symposium.

There is nothing Japanese about the picture *except* its subject. Everything else, its large scale, opulently worked surfaces, and determined naturalism—to say nothing of its suggestive eroticism—demonstrates the impact of Courbet on Tissot's work in the early sixties. Once again, Courbet's *Demoiselles des bords de la Seine* (Pl. 25) is Tissot's aesthetic and spiritual prototype, and the *Japonaise au bain* is far closer to its artistic approach and provocative *déshabille* than to the abstract and emotionally distant bathers he would have discovered in the prints of the *ukiyo-e*. Tissot's *japonaise*, with her unmistakable Western features and bold stare, is clearly a near relative of the errant *demoiselles* who has augmented her ripe charms with an adventitious kimono and what appears to be a large selection of goods from Mme Desoye's exotic stock in the rue de Rivoli. As a result, Western naturalism and Western feature give what might otherwise be merely an amusing studio exercise a strangely prurient air, and the *Japonaise* hovers uncomfortably between the unintentionally silly and the unsuccessfully pornographic.

Yet this strangely attractive *japonaiserie* picture is hardly careless in its approach to its unfamiliar subject. It has nothing about it of the playfulness of eighteenth century *chinoiserie*; indeed, it is scientifically precise in its documentation of Japanese objects and its attempt to reconstruct a daily life Tissot had never known. Removed from his first-hand experience in space rather than time, its fundamental approach remains essentially Leysian.

As Tissot began his rapid emergence as a painter of modern life, the pattern of his *japonaiseries* changed completely. Whistler's *japonaiseries* obviously suggested the direction Tissot took in *Jeune Femme tenant des objets japonais* (Pl. 56), which must date from close to the middle of the decade, or at least after *La Princesse du pays de la porcelaine* (Pl. 57) was exhibited at the Salon of 1865, for it is a direct quotation of the formula Whistler had developed in his Japanese subject pictures. In both pictures, a young woman wearing one of the kimonos the two painters fought over at Mme Desoye's admires Japanese objects from the artist's collection, but the differences between the two works are more instructive than the obvious similarities. Whistler's models are Europeans wearing kimonos, but Tissot now essays a more anthropological method, for it seems certain that the model who posed for the *Jeune Femme tenant des objets japonais* has been supplied with a head taken from a Japanese doll. Where Whistler attempts to establish a new relationship between figure and background derived from study of the Japanese print, Tissot's conservatory points to little more than a delight in Japanese art as an ingredient of fashionable taste, or perhaps the lingering memory of the Cathay of Boucher's *chinoiseries*, where mandarins take their ease in the green shade of the bamboo and palm. But if Whistler's understanding of Japanese design was lost on Tissot, the superficial charm of *La Princesse du pays de la porcelaine* offered alternative enough to the archaeological erudition of the *Japonaise au bain* and probably gave him the hint he needed for the modern dress *japonaiseries* at the end of the decade, which are his most attractive as well as his most original contributions to the genre.

It is not coincidental that Tissot's first *japonaiseries* were painted at the time he began his subjects from modern life, for *japonisme* and *modernité* were to become nearly synonymous among painters of high life by the end of the decade. Alfred Stevens equated the two when he described Japanese art as 'un puissant élément de modernité',[71] undoubtedly making reference more to smart taste than advanced aesthetics; and as with Stevens, the appearance of Japanese objects in Tissot's pictures proves their chic rather than their artistic involvement with the principles of Japanese design. Stevens used oriental objects and costumes to give an air of fashionable currency to their owners: *La Dame en rose* (Pl. 58) is perhaps his first, and makes its point with great charm. Although its *bibelot exotique* is Indian and not Japanese, it is easy enough to recognize it as a prototype for Tissot's *japonaiseries* at the end of the decade.

Jeunes Femmes regardant des objets japonais (Pl. II),[72] Tissot's only *japonaiserie* exhibited at the Salon, is one of three known versions of the subject (Pl. 59 and unlocated). Élie Roy described the picture as 'ethnographic' in his review of the Salon when he remarked, 'nos créations industrielles et artistiques peuvent périr, nos mœurs et nos costumes peuvent tomber dans l'oubli, un tableau de M. Tissot suffit aux archéologues de l'avenir pour reconstituer notre époque'.[73] As Roy predicted, the Leysian approach of the *Jeunes Femmes regardant des objets japonais* has provided a remarkable document. Its jumble of objects reflects the proliferation of periods and continents which is the hall-mark of Second Empire taste, although even at the time Tissot's lavish hand with his treasures made the critic Frédéric Borgella muse '*Jeunes femmes regardant des objets japonais* ou des objets japonais regardant des jeunes femmes' before deciding that it came to the same thing in the end, like a Chinese puzzle, 'c'est tout un: matière de chinoiserie!'[74]

The same sentiment was voiced by Champfleury, himself an enthusiastic *japoniste*, who was already tired of a vogue which had made Japanese art into a fashionable cliché. In a sarcastic article published in *La Vie parisienne* in 1868, he made fun of the narratives Tissot had made popular—amorous little dramas in which arch soubrettes flirt with Japanese bronzes—which had been appropriated by fifty other painters. Beginning his article with a description of Tissot's 'Japanese' studio, which he describes dubiously as 'un signe du temps' in the

[71] A. Stevens, *Impressions sur la peinture*, no. ii, repr., C. Lemonnier, *Alfred Stevens et son œuvre*, p. 44.

[72] Salon of 1869, no. 2270. The assumption that the picture repr. pl. II is the version exhibited at the Salon is based on the evidence of a Goupil photograph in a series which generally, if not always, recorded exhibited pictures.

[73] Roy, 'Salon de 1869', p. 82.

[74] L. Auvray, 'Salon de 1869', *Revue artistique et Littéraire*, pp. 11–12, quoting Frédéric Borgella in *Le Globe*, 4 June 1869.

manner of Prudhomme, he makes fun of Tissot's aesthetic, which he found super-ficial, and his narrative, which he found trivial:

Déjà même de prétendus peintres de la vie élégante nous fatiguent de leurs cabinets japonais, de leurs fleurs japonaises de leurs laques et de leurs bronzes japonais qui prennent la place prin-cipale sur la toile et jouent un rôle bien autrement considérable que les personnages.

En avons-nous déjà assez vu de ces soubrettes élégantes qui, cachant un billet dans la main, se préparent à entrer dans la pièce voisine où de nombreuses précautions doivent être prises pour la remise du billet doux . . . Ce petit drame amoureux m'intéresse. Il y a sans doute un jaloux dans la chambre à côté. La jaloux est une mandragore japonaise en bronze qui fait vis-à-vis à des fleurs japonaises. Il paraît que la mandragore ne doit point avoir connaissance du billet.

Les amateurs trouvent ce drame ravissant, et l'achètent quelques billets de mille au peintre de la vie élégante.[75]

In truth, Tissot's *japonaiseries* were clearly contrived to display his collections, and by 1870 his fame as a painter had to compete with his reputation as a collector and guide to the latest fashionable novelties. Two unlocated still-life paintings attest the collector's passion. In one, which would seem to date from 1866, Tissot attempts a summary of his artistic preoccupations not unlike that Degas would essay a year or two later when he painted his portrait (Pl. 37): on the marble top of a Louis XV commode, and set against the doors of an ebony cabinet inlaid with the mother-of-pearl figure of a German mercenary, the rococo and the medieval give pride of place to a Japanese polychrome figure of a crane, a large *cloisonné* vase, and a lacquer ink box. In the other, close-in date to 1869, a Japanese doll in a plaid kimono has been tossed carelessly on to a console. Guarded by a grimacing Foo-Dog, its chalk features are mirrored in the polished surface of the table. This delight in the superficial sheen on his porcelains and silks doubtless did much to keep him from seeing beyond the exotic qualities of Japanese art to the possibilities it offered for the rendering of modern life with a new vividness and style. Throughout the sixties, his *japonisme* remains *à la mode Mikado*, 'many a vase and jar, many a screen and fan', and it was only in London that his *japonisme* took on real, if still limited, depth and understanding.

Tissot was ostensibly to abandon the painting of modern life at the end of the sixties. After 1868, his major effort was directed towards a group of pictures in Directoire costume. In many ways, however, these pictures have a modern senti-ment about them as great as that found in his pictures of contemporary life, for he seems to have used historic costume essentially to give a gloss of distance to their suggestive narratives. Period costume allowed him a latitude in treating overtly sexual themes which was inadmissible in modern subjects, as Courbet and Manet had already discovered. At the same time, it allowed him to slip un-obtrusively back into his 'magasin de curiosités' unburdened for the nonce with

---

[75] Champfleury, 'La Mode des Japoniaiseries', repro. in G. Lacambre, *Le Réalisme*, p. 145.

Leysian meaning, and to demonstrate a technical skill still thought admirable in historic genre but considered suspiciously 'inartistic' when applied to subjects from everyday life. If many of his admirers were put off by his regression, others —the Salon public not least among them—were delighted by the reappearance of his fascinating historical curiosities, especially since they had taken so delightfully wicked a turn. *Un déjeuner* (Pl. 60)[76] was the first to be exhibited and is typical of the new sentiment found in the group. Like the *Promenade sur les remparts* of 1864 (Pl. 18), it is, in its way, a comedy. Taking his tone from the amorous and disorderly society of the Directoire, a period not without parallels in the Second Empire, Tissot looked to the insincerity and mock innocence of the *éstampe gallante* for inspiration. Thoré described *Un déjeuner*, an assignation between a nacreous *incroyable* and a professional-looking *merveilleuse* as 'qui fait soupçonner un drame à ses premiers actes',[77] a description which sets the tone of these cold little comedies to perfection.

In the same review, Thoré voiced his disappointment at Tissot's slipping-away from the painting of modern life, a genre he had always encouraged him to pursue if he had not always praised the result—but his disappointment was not universal. In the *Gazette des beaux-arts*, Grangedor defended Tissot's right to paint the life of the past, seeing no reason why an artist's horizon need be limited by optical reality, especially since 'le fond des passions et des sentiments reste le même à travers les âges':

Où la représentation grossière finit, où l'image est muette, l'art commence. Ce qui est essentiel à faire sentir dans ses créations, c'est la puissance de la vie organique et de la lumière, qui sont immuables. Peu important le costume et les habitudes transitoires, exceptionnelles. Ce qui nous touche dans une œuvre d'art, c'est précisément ce qui échappe au changement et à la destruction.[78]

Other outdoor luncheons and a picnic mark Tissot's fondness for the theme. *Un souper sous le Directoire* (*c.*1869; Museum and Picture Gallery, Baroda, India) has a similar setting and shows the children of the Revolution toasting the new Republic. Tissot exhibited the picture at the Third International Exposition at Vienna in 1871, when its title was pointedly changed to *Vive la République!* The change may well reflect Tissot's political feelings, but it may simply demonstrate his ability to use circumstance to his own advantage. In a now unlocated picture, a couple flirt contentedly on a bench, Tissot's ubiquitous pug glowering in the lady's lap, waiting for a servant girl to lay the table for their luncheon beneath the rustic arbour of a riverside inn. (A closely related picture of 1869

---

[76] Salon of 1868, no. 2389. A second version or replica of the picture, with minor variations (principally in the substitution of a triple onion dome for the medieval church tower in the background), is known (repro., *Connoisseur*, 207 no. 831 (May 1981), p. 15).

[77] Thoré, 'Salon de 1868', *Salons*, ii, 488.

[78] Grangedor, 'Salon de 1868', p. 16.

shows them sitting before a trellis on another bench, the pug at their feet: in both, the man wears the scarlet postillion's coat and huge tricorn seen in *Un déjeuner* and at the left of *Partie carrée* (Pls. 60 and 61); the girl, the white dress and ribboned hat of *A la rivière* and *Jeune femme en bateau* (Pls. 66 and 67), for which she also served as a model.)

Partie carrée (Pl. 61),[79] the most important as well as the most attractive of the group, was exhibited at the last Salon before the war. Popular enough, its success was soon overshadowed by political events, and if it dimly recalled Manet's *Déjeuner sur l'herbe* (1863; Louvre), which may well have inspired it, the public generously allowed any resemblance to that unfortunate masterpiece to pass unnoticed at the Salon. Like Moreau le Jeune's *Le Souper fin* (Pl. 62), which it emulates in feeling, *Partie carrée* is openly sensual in intent, if lacking the warmth and good humour of its predecessor. In these *déjeuners*, Tissot consciously employs devices favoured by the *peintres gallantes* of the eighteenth century, and often a woman establishes contact with the viewer in a quizzically inviting way, making him an accomplice in sensuality. Human passions, as Grangedor suggests, traverse the ages, but if the manners of the Second Empire rivalled those of the Directoire, Tissot's picnics suffer none the less from a curiously constrained quality. There is a self-conscious and slightly shocked voyeurism about them which gives their coy eroticism the unmistakable aura of their own time. Tissot was essentially a *bon bourgeois* and he appears uncomfortable with such open eroticism. Although the relationship between the sexes became his favoured theme, and was clearly central to his concept of *modernité*, his treatment of it was always essentially psychological rather than sexual. His Directoire pictures are an anomaly in his work, and the direction they might have taken was to be cut off by the war. In London, he would paint costume pieces of superficial similarity, but their content has by then been completely transformed.

All things considered, Tissot's choice of the Directoire is surprising. The social life of the period, composed of *déclassés*, *nouveaux riches*, and adventurers, hardly paralleled his fastidious middle-class upbringing, and its zestful amorality seems even further removed from the narrow respectability to which he always adhered. Nevertheless, it appears to have been a personally motivated choice, and is without particular precedent in the visual arts. A taste for the art of the eighteenth century had never died out in France, and by the late 1860s interest had moved from the Louis XV of Louis Philippe to the Louis XVI–Impératrice of Napoleon III. By the end of the Second Empire, the cult of Marie Antoinette fostered by the Empress had brought fashionable taste close to 1789, but Imperial patronage stopped short at the Revolution.[80]

---

[79] Salon of 1870, no. 2748. There is an oil sketch for the picture in a private collection in Hawaii.

[80] For the revival of interest in the art of the eighteenth century, see principally S.O. Simches, *Le Romantisme et le goût esthétique de XVIIIᵉ*

II. *Jeunes Femmes regardant des objets japonais*, 1869.

Tissot's fascination with the Directoire may have grown out of a reading of Edmond and Jules de Goncourt's *Histoire de la société française pendant la Directoire*, published in 1855 as part of their studies of the art and life of eighteenth-century France. The Goncourts' attitude towards their subject and their literary tone are very similar to the narrative aspects Tissot chose for his pictures, and they surely influenced his conception of the period. 'C'est l'été. —Où aller? —dit la bonne compagnie . . . où donc sera, l'été, la statue du Plaisir, ce veau d'or du Directoire?—En mille bosquets, en mille réduits verts, sur les gazons', setting the stage for Tissot's out-door luncheons and picnics, while a later remark that under the Directoire 'La France n'est plus qu'un vaste lieu de prostitution'[81] sets the moral tone with equal precision. If Tissot's original interest derived from a literary source, he clearly turned to contemporary visual sources for his inspiration. There appears to have been little interest in the Directoire among his contemporaries—no models as he had found in Leys and Stevens —and this study of primary sources was to add to his increasingly complex conception of narrative, focusing a feeling of underlying sexuality, at once powerful and ambiguous, that marks many of his best pictures. Is it not possible to discover the ultimate refinement of those means—openly provocative and uncomplicatedly humorous in *Partie carrée*—in the glacial sensuality and ironic narrative of a work like *London Visitors* (Pl. 106)? Tissot's choice of the Directoire again demonstrates a purposeful estrangement in his choice of sources. With few visual counterparts in the 1860s, these Directoire comedies must have seemed far more novel to his contemporaries than they do today. Tissot was, in fact, a pioneer in a genre not to become popular for several decades, and looks forward to a fashionable taste in France and England which made the Directoire popular at the turn of the century.

If his subject was unusual, his artistic approach was familiar. Although popular taste leaned heavily towards the overblown pastiches of artists like Besson and Chaplin after Boucher or Natoire (a taste Tissot obviously admired in the decorative arts, filling his house with the chic pastiches of Grohé, Tahan, or Monbro *aîne* which appear in his paintings), he studiously avoided such neo-rococo fantasy in his own work. His approach is in fact closer to that of his friend Meissonier, whose 'conception bourgeoise du genre XVIIIe'[82] had deliberately applied realist banality to minuscule pictures of readers and smokers tied to the eighteenth century by costume alone. Tissot himself exhibited two of a series of six comedians at the Cercle de l'Union Artistique in 1869 which are close to Meissonier in

siècle, pp. 23–47, and Reitlinger, *The Economics of Taste*, ii, 130–2.

[81] Edmond and Jules de Goncourt, *Histoire de la société française pendant le Directoire*, pp. 210–11, 181. The Goncourts' role as pioneers in their interest in the Directoire was recently noted by Denys Sutton in 'L'Europe sous les aigles', *Apollo*, ciii (June 1976), 463–85.

[82] Simches, p. 44.

their approach: little full-length figures set against essentially neutral backgrounds. Judging from the photographs of the series in Tissot's albums, it seems likely that he intended to describe the spectrum of comic life, from the polished *sociétaire* of the Comédie-Français found in *Premier comédien*, to the sad clown of the *Sixième comédien* (Pl. 63), the only canvas from the group now located, avoiding the chill wind in a travelling circus as best he can with his makeshift costume.[83]

Both Tissot and Meissonier sought situations and types 'characteristic' of the period, documented their work with careful research, and kept actual costumes and props which reappear from canvas to canvas. In his Directoire pictures, Tissot shows all the archaeological care he had lavished on his medieval works, and if the delicate intangibles which give the art of the late eighteenth century much of its good-natured humanity fade under his relentless scrutiny, at least the greater force of their human element maintains itself against the onslaught of documentation which had extinguished human feeling in his earlier works.

As a painter of *la vie mondaine*, Tissot must have felt a kinship with the artists of the eighteenth century, and may even have considered himself as the heir to their traditions. But strangely enough, few of the neo-rococo artists appear to have been drawn to the art of the eighteenth century purely for its intrinsic beauty or to have completely understood its aesthetic approach. As often as not, they appear to have used it for what would now be described as its period charm or as the justification of their own genre. In his *Impressions sur la peinture*, Stevens clearly identifies his own work with that of the eighteenth century rather than with painters of modern life like Courbet or Manet: 'Les maîtres du XVIIIe siècle sont surtout intéressants parce qu'ils se sont sérieusement inspirés des mœurs le leur époque et les ont interprétées avec ésprit.'[84] Like so many of his academic contemporaries, Stevens failed to recognize the true heirs of the *modernité* of the eighteenth century in peers who were dismissed and scorned. It is hardly surprising that Meissonier's tiny figures look like the members of a London club, or that Tissot's *merveilleuses* are suspiciously like Cora Pearl or Marguerite Bellanger in fancy dress. As with the art of Japan, it was left to others to bring true understanding of the spirit of the eighteenth century to their work. Leaving the rococo costumes in the wardrobe of the Comédie-Française and faded sentiment to the cult of Marie Antoinette, Courbet, Manet, Degas, and

[83] *Premier comédien* is repro. Laver, *Vulgar Society*, pl. XII; the unlocated fourth and fifth comedians—both wearing the familiar Directoire postillion's coat and tricorn—are perhaps more remarkable. Viewed from above against the sharply receding planes of painted stage flats, as they might be from a box in the theatre, their compositions, no less than their play on the contrast of reality and theatrical illusion, offer striking parallels with devices and attitudes which later become commonplace in the ballet pictures of Degas.

[84] Stevens, *Impressions sur la peinture*, no. CLXIV, repr., Lemonnier, p. 48. Stevens himself never departed from his modern genre for historical costume pieces, finding that 'Le public s'intéresse aux sujets à costumes comme il s'éprend des travestissements mondains d'un bal masquée' (Ibid., CCXVII, repr., Lemonnier, p. 51).

Renoir found a meaning truer than superficial manner and a grace more vivid in the world around them.

A number of Tissot's Directoire pictures focus suggestively on the figure of an errant young woman. If a work like *La Cheminée* (Pl. 64) remains essentially a charming and accomplished exercise in the manner of Stevens, thinly disguised by its historical costume, others strike a more immediately personal note. *Jeune Femme à l'éventail* (Pl. 65), in which the young woman gazes with languid impertinence from behind a fan, is quite another thing, as is *A la rivière* (Pl. 66), where she now sits casually with a daisy in her mouth and stares at the viewer. The Salon picture *Jeune Femme en bateau* (Pl. 67)[85] is another scene from the same play, and if there is any doubt as to its meaning, the title under which it appeared as a Salon photograph, *A la dérive*, or *Adrift*, leaves little room for nautical or moral speculation.

One of the last of Tissot's canvases to be exhibited before the war, *Jeune Femme en bateau* can serve in retrospect as a summary of his development in the sixties. It looks back to the sensuality and heightened realism as well as the subject of Courbet's *Les Demoiselles des bords de la Seine*, although Courbet's overflowing sensuality is carefully contained in a veneer of the fashion-plate chic learned from Alfred Stevens which gives it an archness foreign to its meaning. As a narrative, it heightens intensity of 'mood' at the expense of 'subject', creating context without plot in the manner of Millais and the Pre-Raphaelites and giving Stevens's bland genre new sharpness and bite. Its focus is comic as much as sentimental, and turns, as will be the case with many of his most effective works in the seventies, on manners and *double entendre*. A clear attempt to suggest character and narrative by a careful choice of 'typical' pose can doubtless be traced to interaction with Degas. Like the majority of Tissot's works of the sixties, *Jeune Femme en bateau* is carefully and competently designed. A growing understanding of the principles of Japanese design can be sensed in the sharp cutting of the boat, its diagonal placement, and parallel arrangement of elements in relation to the picture plane. Over everything, technical meticulousness and careful documentation of detail give an almost archaeological quality to his visual research.

The 1860s were a period of continual experimentation for Tissot, and *appassionnement* followed upon *appassionnement* in his search for technical and narrative means of expression. Technically, he remained an imperfect and essentially unimaginative painter, although by the end of the decade he had become extremely personal in his manner. Insistence on high finish and minute rendering had the effect of reducing a wide range of influences to a single stylistic denominator, and as a result one speaks more of iconographical than technical

---

[85] Salon of 1870, no. 2747, as in the collection of W. H. Stewart.

development. Tissot's technique at the end of the decade was accurately summarized by Thoré, who characterized it as 'Pre-Raphaelite' and found it pretentious but undeniably accomplished: 'M. James Tissot est toujours très-personnel et très-distingué dans sa manière un peu prétentieuse et—pour essayer une expression vulgaire—tirée à quatre épingles. Il vaut mieux que l'art rougeaud et vulgaire. Il est petit maître, mais il est maître puisqu'il fait ce qu'il veut et comme il veut.'[86]

Tissot was more willing to experiment with narrative, and within the narrow limits he set himself his imagination functioned with inventive finesse as he developed in the sixties. Even at his most derivative, his canvases bear the irreducible imprint of his personality. By 1870, the broad outlines of his style had been set, and development became a matter of variation and refinement rather than change.

In the early months of 1870, Tissot must have faced the future with complacency. Official recognition had come with gratifying ease, and fashionable success had matched fame with fortune. Life in the avenue de l'Impératrice must have seemed ideal. But the pattern of halcyon days was then suddenly broken by the violence of the Franco-Prussian War and the Commune which followed the siege of Paris.

The sense of foreboding which had begun to grow in France after the Prussian defeat of Austria in 1869 deepened as Bismarck slowly goaded France into a war for which she was unprepared. On 15 July 1870, the excuse of the Spanish succession and the insult of the Ems dispatch pushed the Empire into a declaration of war. In Paris, crowds surged through the boulevards singing the *Marseillaise* and shouting 'à Berlin', but what began as *La Grande-Duchesse de Gérolstein* proved to have a Prussian *Götterdämmerung* for its last act.

On 2 September 1870, Napoleon III surrendered with 80,000 men at Sedan after the most humiliating defeat in French history. The war had lasted less than two months. Two days later, a Republic was proclaimed in Paris and for a few days Parisians forgot the advancing German armies in their joy at the fall of the Empire. Their euphoria was short-lived, for on 19 September the investment of Paris was complete, and a few days later the capital had been cut off from the outside world. As Europe waited for the modern Babylon to crumble, amazement turned to admiration as the dark, starving city held out through the coldest winter of the century.[87]

During the siege, there was a concerted attempt on the part of the Government and many citizens, artists chief among them, to preserve historical landmarks and

[86] Thoré, 'Salon de 1868', *Salons*, ii, 487.

[87] Historical material on the siege of Paris is based mainly on Robert Baldick, *The Siege of Paris* (New York: Macmillan, 1964); that on the Commune on Alistair Horne, *The Terrible Year: The Paris Commune* (London: Macmillan, 1971).

works of art from destruction.[88] Tissot remained in Paris and took an active part in its defence, serving in two companies of the Garde Nationale, first with the Éclaireurs de la Seine, and when that unit was dissolved, with the Trailleurs de la Seine. In 1869, Tissot had met Thomas Gibson Bowles, the editor of *Vanity Fair*, who had hired him to draw caricatures for the new magazine; they met again by chance during the siege, and it is thanks to Bowles, in Paris as special correspondent for the *Morning Post*, that we have much of our information about Tissot's personal conduct at this time.[89] The two men met at the end of October after a sortie at Malmaison–La Jonchère. According to Bowles, Tissot was in the front line of the fighting, under the walls of Malmaison itself, and seventeen of the company of sixty were killed or wounded.[90] Manet, writing to Eva Gonzalès of the engagement on 19 November 1870, confirms Bowles's account: 'Tissot s'est couvert de gloire à l'affaire de la Jonchère. Jacquemart en était. Leroux, blessé très grièvement, est prisonnier à Versailles. Le pauvre Cuvelier a été tué.'[91]

Bowles met Tissot again at the end of January 1871, at Boulogne, and they spent an uncomfortable night with three other *corps de garde* in an abandoned house. After the capitulation of the city, they met once again and with a certain bravado strolled into the occupied fort at Vanves, saluting the Bavarian sentries as they passed, gaining the interior of the fort before they were noticed and summarily ejected.[92]

Tissot recorded his military experiences in a number of drawings and water-colours, some of which were later used as the basis for prints and illustrations. Seven drawings were engraved on wood in London in 1871 to illustrate Bowles's *Defence of Paris*; between 1875 and 1878 other drawings served for the six etchings which bear the subtitle *souvenir du siège de Paris*.[93] Some, like *Le Foyer de la Comédie-Française pendant le siège de Paris*, are important both as works of art and as historical documents; but as effective as any in its quiet comment about the futility of war is the single painting known from this time, a sketch of a house bombarded during the siege (Pl. 68).

---

[88] For an account, see A. Darcel, 'Les Musées, les arts, les artistes pendant le siège de Paris', *Gazette des beaux-arts*. Darcel suggests Tissot's service was with the eclaireurs and later with Trailleurs, although another reading might suggest that the company was not dissolved but rather merged with the latter company during the siege (see J. d'Arsac, *Memorial du Siège de Paris* (Paris: Saint-Sulpice, 1871), p. 414, where he speaks of a Compagnie des Trailleurs–Éclaireurs as part of the Garde Nationale de la Seine).

[89] For Bowles, see L. Naylor, *The Irrepressible Victorian*, which also reproduces a drawing of Bowles by Tissot as the frontispiece.

[90] T. G. Bowles, *The Defence of Paris*, pp. 151–2. For a tactical account of the sortie, see A. Duquet, *Guerre de 1871: Paris, La Malmaison, Le Bourget et le Trente et un Octobre*, pp. 8–40.

[91] Moreau-Nélaton, *Manet raconté par lui-même*, ii, 127.

[92] Bowles, pp. 335–8, 387–8.

[93] For Tissot's etchings and illustrations, see Wentworth, *Catalogue Raisonné of Prints*, nos. 15, 16, 19, 27, 41, and 42, and illustrations by Tissot, no. 2. The majority of Tissot's known drawings and water-colours related to the siege are reproduced under those numbers.

One of Tissot's drawings made during the siege led to the angry exchange between him and Degas which is recorded by Lemoisne: the evening of the Sortie de la Malmaison, Tissot met Degas and Manet as he returned from the battle and told them that he had seen Cuvelier, a mutual friend, among the dead and had made a drawing of him. When he took out the sketch to show them, Degas pushed it angrily away, telling Tissot it would have been more fitting to bring back the corpse.[94] What insights the story gives into the characters of the two men perhaps better remains a matter of personal opinion.

After the siege and the capitulation of the city on 28 January 1871, the German occupation was of short duration. French agreement to the conditions of peace was so swift that the German army had no sooner staged its triumphal entry into Paris on the first of March than it was again withdrawn. The upper classes fled the city if they possibly could as soon as the siege was lifted, Degas, Manet, and Berthe Morisot among them, and it remained for the lower classes and the unlucky to witness the ceremonial triumph of the enemy. German presence was considered a humiliation inflicted on the city by the provinces, and when the Government slighted the capital by moving from Bordeaux to Versailles, suppressed six newspapers, and ordered the army to seize six cannon which the Garde Nationale had refused to surrender to the Germans, revolution broke out.

The Commune was proclaimed on the eighteenth of March, and Paris experienced a nightmare worse than the winter's siege. Tissot's participation, or his non-participation, in the Commune has always been a matter of conflicting rumour. There does not, in fact, appear to be any evidence to substantiate a definite conclusion. Whatever his actual involvement, however, he almost certainly must have felt himself to be in danger of reprisal when the Versailles Government retook Paris at the end of May, for no other reason seems sufficient to have motivated his precipitous flight and the abandonment of a decade of successful work.

The only contemporary source we have which makes an attempt to clarify Tissot's behaviour during the Commune is Bastard's biographical article. He absolves Tissot of any connection with the Commune, but his explanation of his flight as the action of offended patriotism does not ring quite true. Had Tissot left France of his own choice, it would hardly have been necessary to have gone with such haste. Indeed, it would hardly have been necessary to have gone at all. He must have been one of very few to do so if he went for patriotic reasons. According to Bastard, Tissot returned to his house in the *ci-devant* avenue de l'Impératrice at the beginning of the Commune to assure himself that his paintings, representing the sum of his artistic career as well as a large potential capital, were

---

[94] Lemoisne, i, 67. A slightly different version of the story is given in D. Halévy, *My Friend Degas*, p. 118. It is likely that the etching *Le Premier* *Homme tué* (W. 19) is related to the now unlocated drawing.

not in danger. Finding that they were, situated between the forces of the Communards and the Versailles troops, he selflessly abandoned the house to the hands of fate and went to work as a stretcher-bearer among the wounded. It was in this capacity that he came to the attention of the Commune. Pressed by a group of *dames infirmières* to take them to the Comité Centrale des Fédères to ask for help and supplies, Tissot spontaneously opposed the minting of some museum silver he heard being debated by the Communards. Returning home, appalled by the double cataclysm of foreign invasion and civil war, finding nothing to look forward to from an artistic point of view, and now frightened by his unpremeditated opposition to the Comité Centrale, he fled Paris.[95]

In a more widely circulated version of the story, Tissot is said to have been alarmed by the persistent rumour that the Commune intended to confiscate the possessions of the rich and burn their houses. In order to protect his belongings, he joined—or pretended to join—the Commune, and even dressed in the uniform of its officers.[96] Jacques-Émile Blanche, whose memoirs are apparently the original source of information about Tissot's selfishness and cowardice during the Commune clearly believed this to be true. Blanche also postulated a nervous collapse as the result of Tissot's behaviour: visiting London in the seventies, his father, a doctor with a fashionable sanatorium outside Paris, suggested calling on Tissot: ' "May God forgive him his cowardice!" said my father, the kindest of men. "Let's go and see Tissot; he's a nervous wreck, just like my patients at Passy!" '[97] Blanche had no doubt that Tissot had joined the Commune in order to save his possessions. Considering conflicting evidence, it seems possible that the strain of the Commune had proved beyond Tissot's nervous strength after the long hardship of the siege, and caused some hasty or poorly-considered decision. Although there is slight evidence that Tissot was as 'nervous' as Dr Blanche's patients, his behaviour in other moments of stress does not appear entirely rational. Looking forward to the death of Mrs Newton, we find his answer was once again flight, and his subsequent dependence on the occult and the biblical visions of the nineties are not particularly reassuring as signs of stability.

If Tissot thought himself insured by his Communard activity for the interim, and able to justify the necessity of his actions later, the uncontrolled fury of the Versailles Government as it retook the city must quickly have dispelled the idea. It was necessary to flee for his life before the reprisals of the notorious 'Bloody Week' in which the defeated Communards burned buildings as imposing as the Tuileries and shot hostages as venerable as the Archbishop of Paris, while government troops massacred 20,000 suspected Communards in the streets.

[95] Bastard, pp. 261–2.
[96] Laver, *Vulgar Society*, p. 24. For life during the Commune and tales of Communard retaliation against the rich, see Lillie de Hegermann-Lindencrone, *In the Courts of Memory* (New York: Harper, 1912), pp. 277–334. The condition of the avenue de l'Impératrice during the Commune is described, pp. 292–3.
[97] J.-E. Blanche, *Portraits of a Lifetime*, p. 25.

The image of Tissot as a Communard is a hard one to accept, but it is not impossible. He was always fiercely patriotic, and in England refused to give up his French citizenship, declining, as he said, to be 'one of those who change their country as they change their shirt'.[98] There are also hints of a fitful social conscience in his work. The origins of the Commune are to be found in the conditions of the siege itself rather than political or ideological theories. It was a patriotic movement, but it was not Socialist or Marxist. The Commune was a day-dream shared by many classes of society, and there is no reason why Tissot should not have been caught up in its ideology. Henri Zerner suggests that reports like Blanche's, presenting Tissot's Communard activities as an expedient for saving his house, were the ironic and disparaging excuses of friends to whom a Communard was no better than a bloodthirsty animal, in justification of something which was beyond their comprehension,[99] and this seems correct. Tissot may well have joined the Commune in the outraged patriotism of one who had fought through the siege only to be betrayed by an ineffectual government. He would not have been alone in his rage that venality had been replaced by incompetence. After his conversion in 1885, Tissot painted a strange visionary picture called *Inner Voices*, unlocated but known through an engraving (Pl. 196), which appears to be his only direct statement about the Commune. Set in the ruins of the Tuileries, or the Cour des Comptes, it depicted 'Jesus, crowned with the Crown of Thorns, seated and resting against two working people, also wounded and suffering, amidst the ruins of a smoking edifice'.[100]

Bastard concludes his examination of Tissot's activities during the siege and the Commune by saying that the charges levelled against Tissot were the result of a simple case of mistaken identity. About 1874, Tissot's English career was being adversely affected by the rumours of an unsavoury political past. Hearing of them, he went to the French Embassy in London and then to the Préfet de Police in Paris where he was quickly cleared of any charges, his name having been confused with that of 'un nommé Tissot (Antoine)'.[101]

Considerable credence is given to the chronology if not the content of Bastard's account by a letter from Degas to Tissot of about 1874, which has not previously been considered in reference to this question. The letter obviously refers to Tissot's successful efforts to have his name removed from the list of the proscribed, and the possibility of his return to Paris: 'I should like to spend a few days with you. But I am afraid of missing you, for de Sermet told me that after the official news he had given you, you were returning. Returning sounds nice. It is my expression, not his. It would take too long to talk the whole matter over in a letter.'[102]

[98] Lostalot, 'Tissot', p. 384.
[99] Zerner, Introduction, in Brooke, Wentworth, Zerner, *Tissot*, no page number.
[100] R. Sherard, 'James Tissot and his Life of Christ', *Magazine of Art*, p. 3.
[101] Bastard, p. 263.
[102] Degas, *Letters*, p. 34.

Although he was not to return permanently to France until 1882, it is clear that after 1874 Tissot crossed freely back and forth to Paris, took part in the Salon of 1876, and had no need of the protection of the general amnesty of 1880. For the rest, it is clear that until definitive evidence concerning his activities during the Commune can be located, it is safer not to discount any possibility. More to the point, perhaps, is the strange fact that the violence of the siege and the Commune left little trace in his subsequent work. His career continued in England virtually without a break. Bastard justifies Tissot's exile by saying that he had nothing to expect from an artistic point of view in Paris, his market having been ruined by the chaotic fall of the Empire and the economic disaster of the war. Nevertheless, the carnival of 1872 was of particular brilliance, the Salon reopened in 1873, and by 1878 the prosperity and splendour of the *Exposition Universelle* had triumphantly affirmed the latent power and resilience of France.

On a January afternoon less than six months after Tissot had fled to London, Edmond de Goncourt saw traffic blocked by fashionable carriages in the rue de la Paix: 'je me demandais quel était le grand personnage qui avait sa porte assiégée par tant de grand monde, quand levant les yeux au-dessus d'une porte cochère, je lus: Worth. Paris n'a pas changé.'[103]

[103] Goncourt, *Journal*, ii, 869.

IV. The Siege of London

But, as the Elizabethans knew, an addiction to foreign ways is a powerful dissolvent of English propriety, and the impact of French Naturalism, in particular, was certain, sooner or later, to call for the intervention of the police. To bards and painters a certain limited eccentricity had always been permitted, but the notion of art as an enclosed world, obedient to its own laws only, did not come easily to a race which took its pictures much as it took its tunes, less for the excellence of the work than the pleasure of the response; and thought of a painter as an upper-class decorator, a recorder of domestic incident, winning landscapes, and right sentiments.

G. M. Young, *Victorian England* (1936).

TISSOT probably arrived in London soon after the fall of the Commune. At a stroke, he gave up the settled life of a fashionable painter to take his chances on a new career in a city he can have visited only briefly.[1] Although he was to remain

---

[1] Tissot may have come to London for the International Exhibition of 1862 (see chap. III above, n. 31); he may have been there in 1864 for the opening of the Royal Academy, the catalogue giving an address in Kensington, 7 St. Philip's Terrace, as well as his Paris address; and he must have come late in 1869 or early 1870 for sittings with Burnaby and his *Vanity Fair* subjects. In early August 1868, Degas visited London and wrote to Tissot in Paris telling him of his arrival and his attempt to find him at Victoria Grove, Bayswater: Lillian Browse, *Degas Dancers* (London: Faber and Faber, 1947), p. 21, n. 3, cites an unpublished letter from Tissot in reply and summarizes its contents. Tissot advises Degas to call on Legros, Prevost, and Whistler; to visit Richmond and Windsor, and Greenwich by boat; and above all not to miss seeing the London docks. For this, he said, Degas would need at least a month. Browse's assumption that Tissot was already resident in London is incorrect. Degas clearly thought Tissot was there and expected to see him, but Tissot had returned to Paris without telling him and they did not meet. Tissot was then serving as drawing instructor to Prince Akitake in Paris, and two entries in the diary of Eiichi Shibusawa, a member of the prince's suite, suggest the dates of Tissot's English trip: 3 June, 'From today the drawing instructor leaves for a journey', and 5 August, 'In the afternoon the painter appeared' (quoted in Ikegami, 'James Tissot, "Drawing Instructor" of Tokugawa Akitake', p. 151).

Although not resident, Tissot's letter demonstrates that by the end of the decade he was familiar with the city and had already developed an interest in the subject-matter of his English works. His presence in London can probably be related to more than his interest in English art and the presence of his pictures in the exhibitions of the Royal Academy and the Royal Society of British Artists: it was doubtless also financial, and may well relate to his dealings with Ernest Gambart, who was selling his works by 1866 (see chap. III, n. 30), and would publish engravings after his pictures in the early 1870s (see Wentworth, *Catalogue Raisonné of Prints*, 'Prints After Tissot', nos. 1 and 2). Tissot's relations with Gambart (and other London dealers) have yet to be fully explored; it seems certain that knowledge of them will do much to explain Tissot's association with England in the sixties no less than the seventies.

in London for eleven years, he may at first have thought to stay only long enough for the violence directed against participants in the Commune to come to an end. The fury of government reprisals soon made him realize that even this period would be of some duration, and from the beginning he must have thought in terms of extended residence. In Paris he had borrowed money to arrange for the long-term maintenance of his house, and is said to have arrived in London with only a hundred francs in his pocket.[2]

London was the obvious place of refuge. It was the home of friends like Bowles and Whistler, to whom he could turn for advice and support, and its sights and exhibitions were already familiar. Second only to Paris in its active cultural life, there was no other city in Europe which could have offered him as many aesthetic, social, and financial possibilities. The notion cherished by Degas that the riches of Manchester were ripe for exploitation was correct and to the point, for the seventies and eighties in England were the golden age of the living artist. Even painters of minor skill and limited appeal lived on a scale which would have astonished most old masters, and for a really popular painter like Millais or Landseer, there was no limit to what might be achieved. Both were to be paid an astronomical 4,000 guineas for a picture in the seventies, and in 1874, William Holman Hunt was to set a record for the century when the dealer Agnew paid him 11,000 pounds for *The Shadow of the Cross.* The illusion that modern British painting was the culmination of all art had been foisted by artists and dealers on a *nouveau riche* buying public hungry for status and already familiar with the rewards of speculation. Millionaire patronage, coupled with a lucrative copyright market for steel engravings, had made it possible for an artist to become socially acceptable and immensely rich.[3]

Tissot was not unknown as a painter when he arrived in England, having sent a picture to the London International Exhibition in 1862, another to the Royal Academy in 1864, and two to the Society of British Artists Exhibition the same year.[4] More immediately, he must have been known to society readers as a caricaturist for *Vanity Fair*, having provided sixteen drawings for the magazine between 1869 and 1871.

It was to the editor, Thomas Gibson Bowles, that Tissot turned when he arrived in London, going directly to his house, Cleve Lodge, in Queen's Gate, and

---

[2] Bastard, p. 262.

[3] See Reitlinger, *The Economics of Taste*, i, 143–74, for a discussion of the position of the artist in England in the second half of the century. Material on prices and the buying public is based on his research. Maas, *Gambert*, chap. I, pp. 15–21 also gives an excellent summary of English patronage at mid-century and later.

[4] For the International Exhibition of 1862, the *Handbook of the Picture Galleries* (London: Grant, 1862), no. 192, gives the title of Tissot's picture as *Sleighing*, but Graves, *A Century of Loan Exhibitions*, iii, 1315, gives it as *A Walk in the Snow*, lent by Émile Pereire, presumably the picture exhibited at the Salon of 1859 (see chap. II above, no. 48); for the Royal Academy of 1864, see chap. II above, n. 125; for the Society of British Artists, see chap. II above, nn. 111 and 125.

remaining there for several months.[5] Besides the emotional comfort that Bowles's open-handed welcome must have given, he also provided an immediate source of income, commissioning the drawings for *The Defense of Paris* and making Tissot a staff caricaturist for *Vanity Fair*, a position he shared with 'Ape', Carlo Pellegrini, the protégé of the Prince of Wales and friend of Degas and de Nittis, and 'Spy', Leslie Ward, a young man 'groomed for society' discovered by Millais in 1873, who was to remain with the magazine for forty years and draw over a thousand caricatures for it.

Tissot's work for *Vanity Fair* falls into two distinct groups.[6] The first consists of sixteen drawings made before the Franco-Prussian War which are signed with the sobriquet 'Cöidé', the significance of which is not known, and is made up of *portraits chargés* of Continental royalty and political figures, although the series ends with two English ecclesiastics and an earl. Like the French models on which they are directly based,[7] these drawings are as much political cartoons as caricatures, their purpose being symbolical ridicule and moral comment rather than "true" caricature: what Max Beerbohm later defined as 'the delicious art of exaggerating, without fear or favour, the peculiarities of this or that human body, for the mere sake of exaggeration.'[8]

Typical of them is a drawing of Napoleon III (Pl. 69), titled 'le regime parlementaire', a regimen clearly not to the taste or indeed the benefit of the Imperial patient. Prematurely aged and in constant agony from the stone ('You're right, I don't look too frisky,' he is said to have answered the princess Mathilde when she commented on his unhealthy appearance at the beginning of the war), he walks supported by the figure of France *en garde malade*, of necessity putting an uneasy trust in the hands of the people. In others, Victor Emanuel of Italy, 'il rè galantuòmo', whose libidinous vulgarity had scandalized even the Tuileries, stands stolidly in corduroy with a hunting rifle, looking like the gamekeeper he longed to be, and Henri de Rochefort, 'la voyoucratie', hovers over Paris like a great bird of prey.

These drawings have a real sting, although they hardly approach their models in ferocity and bile. With their political charge, bright colour, and elaborately studied satire, 'Cöidé's' caricatures can be easily separated from Tissot's later work in London. After coming to live in London, his caricatures are without exception of British subjects, and they quickly fall under the spell of Pellegrini's

[5] Naylor, *The Irrepressible Victorian*, p. 37.

[6] For a list of Tissot's caricatures for *Vanity Fair*, see Wentworth, *Catalogue Raisonné of Prints*, pp. 348–9: for a stylistic study of the various caricaturists for *Vanity Fair*, which includes valuable material on Tissot's caricatures and his practice of drawing his own lithographic key stones, see the introduction by E. Harris in *Vanity Fair*.

[7] For numerous examples, see Susan Lambert, *The Franco-Prussian War in Caricature* (London: Victoria and Albert Museum, 1971).

[8] M. Beerbohm, 'The Spirit of Caricature', repr., *The Incomparable Max*, p. 94.

style of strictly personal satire and limited range of colour, the familiar '*Vanity Fair* style', which had brought Pellegrini success in England. Since Bowles was obviously willing to indulge Tissot in such matters, his change of manner was clearly dictated as much by *appassionnement* as editorial policy.

Tissot's English caricatures depend almost entirely on the delineation of personal foible in the mildest possible terms for their effect. More often than not, he seems to eschew caricature altogether, content with 'a playful touch adventured here and there if his sitters be not very eminent, nor very ugly, nor of noble birth',[9] and his drawings are really better characterized as witty portraits. Gentlemanly and flattering, it is difficult to believe that these caricatures ever offended their subjects, and Tissot was probably far too clever to have it otherwise, as he sought new sources of patronage among his distinguished sitters.

Typical of these caricatures, and obviously taken from life, is a caricature of George Whyte-Melville, 'the novelist of society', sitting fashionable and world-weary on a sofa (Pl. 70). In others, Charles Darwin looks suspiciously simian perched atop a pile of cushions in a caricature called 'natural selection', and Frederick Leighton languishes in a doorway at a soirée, graciously presenting his classical profile to a throng of shadowy admirers in 'a sacrifice to the graces'.

Vanity Fair artists were not generally involved with the reproduction of their drawings for the magazine. Editorial policy as well as standard commercial procedure required only that the artist submit a finished, coloured drawing, sometimes with a careful tracing to assure a correct outline, to the printer. Tissot, however, chose to draw the outline or black 'key' stone himself, and later made corrections and added final details and colour to a trial proof taken for the purpose. Doubtless this concern reflects something of the French tradition of original artist's lithographs, and it gives his work for *Vanity Fair* added interest as well as a limited status as quasi-original prints.

It is not clear why Tissot took up caricature in the late sixties. If not commissioned by Bowles, as seems likely, his interest could have developed out of his serious work, as the pictures of six comedians suggest, or even out of political feeling. Tissot drew a total of sixty-two caricatures for *Vanity Fair*: sixteen appeared before he left France, and thirty-nine more had appeared by the end of 1873. The remaining eleven, appearing in 1876 and 1877, doubtless represent little more than a debt of gratitude to Bowles. What had been a sideline in Paris became a financial necessity when he arrived in London, and it was abandoned as soon as he had established an English market for his pictures.

Despite their charm and skill, Tissot's caricatures are of no particular originality and contribute little to the genre. Strangely, their most salient feature is probably a fundamental lack of humour. Undeniably clever, and with a closeness

[9] Ibid.

of observation that comes near to wit, they lack entirely that indefinable quality of laughter which has made the caricatures of Pellegrini retain their charm even though their subjects have been forgotten. In his narrative genre, Tissot grew increasingly accomplished, and many of his best English pictures are comic in intent, but his humour was not really of a kind to lend itself to the demands of pure caricature. If his work in the genre had any effect on his art, it lay only in a comic exaggeration of type and social situation in his serious work which led the English to fear, and not perhaps without reason, that they were being teased. There was always to be a lurking suspicion that Tissot was making fun of English types and English tastes with straight-faced but wickedly satirical parodies of English pictures. Critics were not slow to discover malicious intent: 'the supercilious air of the sandy-haired officer seems to smack of French satire', the *Illustrated London News* would say of *The Thames* (Pl. 115), although they acknowledged that the two young women were 'rather more acceptable types of *belles anglaises* than the disdainful misses the artist usually selects'; the *Graphic* discovered 'a tinge of caricature to flavour quaintness with satire' in the 'faces and figures of a kind inseparable from drawing-rooms' of *Hush!* (pl. 103); and the *Athenaeum* was not alone in remarking that the 'smart vulgarity' of *Rivals* (Pl. 159) justified their assertion that Tissot wished to 'satirize the British plutocracy'.[10]

Whatever the immediate financial support *Vanity Fair* offered, it was of even greater indirect benefit in bringing Tissot to the attention of the fashionable public he sought on a scale impossible in any other medium. It was doubtless his caricatures as much as his canvases at the Royal Academy or the International that first established his name in England. As he must have intended, his caricatures demonstrated a remarkable talent for flattering likeness, and he was soon launched on a successful secondary career as a portrait painter.

Tissot had already demonstrated a dazzling gift for *soigné* genre portraits and conversation pieces, and the English were not slow to take advantage of his skill. The general style of such portraits had been established in works like *Le Cercle de la rue Royale* (Pl. 39), and it is unfortunate that the opportunity to duplicate the triumphant accomplishment of that picture was denied in England through want of a commission of equal importance. On a smaller scale, however, his approach remained as flexible and subtle, and in his attempt to find familiar and typical attitudes he is sometimes as audacious as Degas himself in his solutions, if not always as skilful in their resolution.

---

[10] 'Royal Academy Exhibition', *Illustrated London News* (13 May 1876), 475; 'The Royal Academy', *Graphic* (8 May 1875), 447; 'The Grosvenor Gallery Exhibition', *Athenaeum* (10 May 1879), 607. See also the material cited below in notes 35 and 100. Such suspicion, however, was not universal: in the text which accompanied the engraving of *The Thames* (pl. 75) in the *Graphic*, they merely found it exceptional that Tissot had been able to enter the spirit of English character with such success, remarking that 'nothing could be more typically John Bullish than these young ladies and the officer at their side' (8 February 1873), 119.

Tissot made his début as a resident artist at the Royal Academy and the International Exhibition in the spring of 1872, having arrived too late the previous year to send in any work. Two of the four pictures he sent to the International were English narrative portraits, and they demonstrated his talent in the genre with irresistible charm.

Colonel Frederick Augustus Burnaby (Pl. 71)[11] might be called the last of Tissot's French pictures or the first of his English ones, but it is surely the master-piece among these little portraits. Strength and silken elegance are combined in a seamless binding of detail which holds the claims of portraiture and genre in perfect suspension. Like the best of Tissot's works, it distils the essence of its age with flawless instinct. Taking its bold harmony from Burnaby's uniform of vermilion, black, and white and softening it with pinks, yellows, and pale blue, there is a more atmospheric rendering of tone than usual, and it gives added effectiveness to piquant colour. The composition, built along the long vermilion stripe of the uniform, skilfully suggests Burnaby's great height and has much of the relaxed yet tensile strength of the sitter himself. Painted with technical delicacy and brio, it is one of Tissot's most felicitous performances.

Previously unidentified, the second portrait Tissot sent to the International can now be said to be the picture called *Gentleman in a Railway Carriage* (Pl. 72).[12] In an essay on Tissot's work at the exhibition, Jules Claretie described both portraits in some detail:

Il exposait en 1872, dans la galerie française de l'exhibition de Londres, deux *portraits*: l'un fort comique, représentant un colonel d'artillerie anglaise, lustré et propre comme une figure de cire: l'autre, un gentleman assis dans un wagon, costumé comme un touriste et lisant un livre, le Guide Bradshaw ou le Guide Joanne.[13]

Claretie was not surprised by the audacity of Tissot's approach to a portrait: 'il y a là d'ailleurs une idée, une recherche, et il n'est point mauvais, certes, de peindre les contemporains dans ces situations communes de la vie de tous jours.' But if he liked the idea well enough, a railway carriage being a familiar part of modern life and as such a suitable background for a portrait, he was less sym-pathetic to what he called 'cette éternelle tendance au pastiche qui lui fait imiter M. Millais ou Mulready après avoir lui avoir fait imiter Leys'. Lacking any artistic

---

[11] International Exhibition, London, 1872, no. 1282, as *M. le Colonel* * * *. Tissot also made a drawing of Burnaby at this time in preparation for a *Vanity Fair* caricature which was not published (repro., Naylor, p. 49). A remarkable, but surely coincidental, similarity between Tissot's *Burnaby* and the hero of Ouida's *Under Two Flags* (1871) has been noted by both of her recent biographers: see

Yvonne ffrench, *Ouida: A Study in Ostentation* (London: Cobden-Sanderson, 1938), pp. 47–8, and Eileen Bigland, *Ouida: The Passionate Victorian* (London: Jarrolds, 1950), p. 49.

[12] International Exhibition, London, 1872, no. 1219b, as *Portrait of Capt.* * * *.

[13] J. Claretie, 'M. James Tissot', *Peintres et sculpteurs contemporains*, p. 374.

personality of his own, 'il avait déserté Leys pour courir aux japonais, et le voici qui laisse là le Japon pour demeurer à Londres'.[14]

Tissot had done just that. Immersed in new surroundings, he had immediately turned to new sources of inspiration, and his early London work is a series of variations on the themes of English narrative painting. Although the impact of English art is more clearly seen in his narrative pictures, it is evident enough in the *Gentleman in a Railway Carriage* to make the portrait read virtually as a genre picture, and if British artists had been quick to realize the narrative possibilities of the railway for their work, Tissot's use of its 'energized punctuality' to give flavour to a portrait appears to be unique in the genre. Taking his clue from a picture like Abraham Solomon's *First Class* (1854; National Gallery of Canada, Ottawa), exhibited at the Royal Academy of 1854 and immensely popular through steel engravings, Tissot transforms its anecdotal narrative into a portrait philosophically worthy of Degas.[15] It was at this time that Tissot also painted the less audacious but no less remarkable *Waiting for the Train (Willesden Junction)* (Pl. 98),[16] which seems suspended between the literary narrative of Frith's *The Railroad Station* (1863; Cooper-Bridgeman Library, London) and the dispassionate objectivity of Pisarro's *Lordship Lane Station, Lower Norwood* (1871; Courtauld Collection, London).

In speaking of the portraits Tissot sent to the International, Claretie also made an extremely valuable observation about their physical presentation, calling them: '*portrait-cartes* agrandis par M. Tissot et mis sous verre, à la mode anglaise, comme les tableaux de la *National Gallery*'.[17] Tissot is also known to have exhibited the series *La Femme à Paris* under glass in the eighties, and it may well have become his practice after he came to England. Claretie obviously found it pretentious, as did later critics, but its quality of foreignness if not its preciousness must have appealed to Tissot.

Similar to the portraits at the International in all but scale is a large work of 1871, *Chichester Fortesque, later Lord Carlingford* (Pl. 73), a commission

---

[14] Ibid., p. 375.

[15] The Scottish moralist Samuel Smiles wrote that the railway 'energized punctuality, discipline, and attention; and proved a moral teacher by the influence of its example' (quoted in John W. Osborne, *The Silent Revolution: The Industrial Revolution as a Source of Cultural Change* (New York: Charles Scribner's Sons, 1970), p. 31; a statement of values as well as an opinion, it captures an essential Victorian attitude, and it is possible that Tissot's portrait, called *La Première Classe* after the original title was lost, was intended to offer proof by example of a similar lesson. Degas also painted two portraits at this time which hint at travel, *Marie Dihau* (L. 172, 1867–8; Metropolitan Museum of Art, New

York), in which he alludes to her frequent trips by portraying her in street dress and placing her valise conspicuously in the foreground, and an unfinished portrait of a young woman (L. 174, *c.*1867–8; private collection) which uses a railway carriage as its setting.

[16] The setting is identified in C. Hamilton Ellis, *Railway Art* (Boston: New York Graphic Society, 1977), p. 70.

[17] Claretie, 'Tissot', p. 374. The *Gentleman in a Railway Carriage* is known to have retained its original glazing and gilt frame with pilasters and arched top until recently; it has unfortunately been reframed.

doubtless prompted by the success of the portrait of Burnaby and his growing fame at *Vanity Fair*. At the time of the sittings, Fortesque was the president of the Board of Trade, and the portrait was commissioned as a present for his wife by a galaxy of seven peers, forty-nine members of Parliament, and five Roman Catholic bishops to commemorate his popular and successful term as Chief Secretary for Ireland between 1868 and 1870.[18] It demonstrates the rapid artistic and social ascent Tissot had made in London and the good use to which he had put the introductions provided by Bowles and *Vanity Fair*. The portrait itself might be said to share something of Tissot's approach to his drawings for the magazine; personality is stated with bold directness and a vivid sense of presence which links it to them, while the painter's more complex approach to documentation of feature and environment gives refinement and dimension to the image. Like many of his portraits, *Chichester Fortesque* is essentially a reworking of the aesthetic and philosophical elements first used in *Mlle L. L . . .* (Pl. 26), devices Tissot continued to find attractive and which form the basis of many of his English portraits.

Nevertheless, Tissot had not come to England as a caricaturist or a portrait painter. His most serious attention must have been directed to his narrative pictures, and it is to them that one must turn to sense the full degree of his response to new surroundings and new subjects. Captivated by the unfamiliar aspects of English life—a response reflected in a new range and flexibility of subject-matter—his pictures demonstrate new aesthetic *appassionnement* as he sought to adjust his work to its new audience. Tissot's painting is always more responsive to art than life, despite its meticulous documentation of reality, and it is hardly surprising that he cast the novelty of English life in what were, for him, the equally novel conventions of English painting.

He had, in fact, long demonstrated a marked affinity for English painting. In the middle sixties, a taste for the Pre-Raphaelites had superseded his interest in Leysian genre, and French critics had remarked pointedly about his reliance on Millais for both the subject and mood of a work like *Le Printemps* at the Salon of 1865. When he arrived in London, his anecdotal realism was already but a step away from the brand practised at the Royal Academy in the wake of the Pre-Raphaelites, although it is of a philosophical difference greater than its similarity suggests.

Willingness to reorient his work must have been in large part financial. Tissot was always keenly aware of his market, and his penchant for money-making can only have been reinforced by the pressing need to establish himself as an artist in London. He had already considered England as a market for his work and had tested the water with an occasional picture sent to English exhibitions in the

---

[18] For biographical information and circumstances of the commission, see I. Thomson, 'Tissot and Oxford', *Oxford Art Journal*, no. 2, pp. 53–4.

sixties. In London, he appears to have grown enthusiastic about the ready market for French pictures and almost euphoric about the ease with which a clever French painter could part the English from their money. Although Tissot's letters to Degas at this time have not been preserved, Degas's replies suggest their content well enough: 'entertain me with some juicy ideas and some veritable sums of money', or 'and you, what news is there since the 700 pounds?' or 'you are getting on like a house on fire! 900 pounds, but that's a fortune?'[19] Tissot may well have been the deciding factor in Degas's decision to send two pictures to London for exhibition in 1872, and he wrote to Tissot from New Orleans, where he had gone to visit his family, about their reception in England and their possible sale.[20] Having developed what he called 'a taste for money' in the New World, Degas later thought of placing the most important of his American pictures, *Portraits in an Office: The Cotton Market, New Orleans* (L. 320, 1873; Musée Municipale, Pau), with Agnew in London. He may well have conceived it in what he considered the English manner, with the English market in mind, and he wrote to Tissot that Agnew should place the picture in Manchester, 'for if a spinner ever wished to find his painter, he really ought to hit on me'.[21] The next year he tried still another English market, submitting a drawing of a ballet rehearsal to the *Illustrated London News*, which was rejected because its subject was not thought suitable for a magazine with a rectory circulation.[22]

Tissot proved more skilful at the business: it is perhaps the only area in which his talent actually surpassed that of Degas, who remained an amateur at the manipulating of his work in order to exploit a foreign market: 'give me some idea how I too could gain some profit from England' he asks wistfully in a letter from New Orleans in obvious response to one of Tissot's tales of financial acumen.[23] Tissot's skill soon became well known. In 1874, Edmond de Goncourt noted reports of his great success in England, calling him with justice if not charity, 'cet ingénieux explorateur de la bêtise anglaise', and John Singer Sargent is said to have referred to him disparagingly as 'a dealer of genius'. Their sentiments are supported by hard fact: according to Bastard, Tissot earned 1,200,000 francs while he lived in England.[24]

As the aesthetic interest in English painting Tissot had shown in the sixties

---

[19] Degas, *Letters*, pp. 33, 18, and 30.

[20] Ibid., p. 21. The two pictures Degas sent to London were *Aux courses en province* (L. 281; Museum of Fine Arts, Boston) and *Le Foyer de la danse à l'opéra de la rue Peletier* (L. 298; Louvre, Paris).

[21] Degas, *Letters*, p. 21.

[22] The work sent to the *Illustrated London News* was the *Repetition de ballet sur la scene* (L. 400; Metropolitan Museum of Art, New York); the identification, correct date, and Degas's inten-

tion to publish the drawing, now hidden beneath oil washes, as a wood engraving, were discovered and published, as was the identification of the two works referred to in n. 20 above, in Ronald Pickvance, 'Degas's Dancers, 1872–1876', *Burlington Magazine*, 105 (June 1963), pp. 259–66.

[23] Degas, *Letters*, p. 12.

[24] Goncourt, *Journal*, ii, 1001; Sargent quoted in Laver, *Vulgar Society*, p. 33; and Bastard, p. 265, n. 1.

was transformed into the desire to turn an English profit in the seventies, he must have attempted to define English taste in order to suit his product to the market. On the basis of his pictures and the adjustments he made in them after arriving in England, it is obvious that he assumed there was a wide interest in the depiction of contemporary life. His idea was based on a study of painters like Millais, Solomon, and Frith, but probably even more on the evidence of English illustrated magazines like the *Graphic* and the *Illustrated London News*. The wood engravings Tissot saw in such magazines had a kind of contemporary subject-matter and a tone of level reportage which already paralleled the objective approach and lack of narrative emphasis of his painting of modern life. It seems certain that the style of the illustrated magazines had a significant effect on his work, suggesting both subject and a clue to its treatment, which developed in his work throughout the seventies. Tissot began to paint subjects from contemporary life as soon as he arrived in England, but soon discovered English taste for *la peinture de la vie moderne* to be less widespread than he had assumed, and although he sent a modern subject to the International, he also sent a safely anecdotal costume picture which easily proved the more popular; and for his more important début at the Royal Academy, he sent only costume pictures of an even more conservative cast. It was not until the following year that he was willing to hazard modern life at the Academy, and even then it was given a heavy gloss of Victorian respectability with clear narrative, sentimental decorum, and moral import, seemingly presented without a trace of satire or criticism. Only as his modern subjects grew increasingly uncompromising, after 1874, did he fail to placate Victorian respectability with some hint of narrative meaning or moral content: turning then to the impassive delineation of what Ruskin distastefully called 'vulgar society',[25] he began to alienate his public. As the creator of *base* art, 'art directed to the representation of base and unworthy things',[26] he condemned himself in his own time to an aesthetic respectability lower than that of Millais or Watts and the creators of certifiably *high* art. 'To have the power of painting almost perfectly anything in the world, and to choose to paint a five-o'clock tea-table,' the *Spectator* mused in 1879—'Could any condemnation be really more severe than the one the artist passes upon his own work by the choice of such subjects?'[27]

Even more than moral import, Tissot felt that narrative content was essential

---

[25] Ruskin, *Fors Clavigera*, in *Works*. For Ruskin, such vulgarity lay in a lack of sensibility and an undue regard for appearances. Although insensitivity, pretence, and affectation of manner in the vulgar were of themselves unimportant, they were symptomatic of a basic failure to understand, rightly and instinctively, relations of importance between oneself and others. By the end of the decade, charges similar to Ruskin's were being made by virtually every informed English critic about Tissot's work. For Ruskin's definition of vulgarity, see Henry Ladd, *The Victorian Morality of Art: An Analysis of Ruskin's Esthetic* (New York: Octagon Books, 1968), pp. 270–91.

[26] 'French Art: A Comparative Sketch', *Spectator* (18 August 1877), 1038.

[27] 'The Grosvenor Gallery', *Spectator* (31 May 1879), 691.

for success in England. Once in London, he brought his views into sharp focus, discovering that a narrative with comic overtones generally served better than one without, and that sentimental subjects could be outsold only by keepsake pictures of pretty girls engaged in attractive occupations, truths equally obvious at the Academy or in the pages of the illustrated magazines. On his arrival, he not only chose conservative costume subjects for his début, he gave them a heightened narrative obviously calculated to appeal to English taste. This story-telling approach was also used in his first pictures of modern life at the Academy, but after 1873 it disappeared almost completely as he began the series of 'social conversation pieces', which occupied him in the middle of the decade, and it took with it no small part of his popularity as it went. Narrative content is essentially absent, despite an occasional picture whose title suggests anecdotal meaning, until the end of the decade when it reappeared with new insistence in the pictures of the series *The Prodigal Son in Modern Life*, hand in hand once again with sentiment and morality, surely in an attempt to regain a following now bored and annoyed by opaque narratives and a seemingly endless supply of pictures of Kathleen Newton taking her leisure in St. John's Wood. This return to narrative was paralleled by a short-lived attempt to create *high* art, and suggests that Tissot felt his lack of aesthetic respectability more sharply than might be imagined. Like his 'unworthy' subjects, Tissot's narrative, wanting clarity, could not aspire to the heights: 'The picture is without distinct and intelligible meaning,' the *Art Journal* said of *London Visitors* (Pl. 106), 'and, lacking this, it also lacks the higher distinction of pictorial grace.'[28]

Tissot was not entirely alone in his predicament. As more and more rumours of the superiority of French painting reached London in the seventies, the delicate balance of a long-standing aesthetic provincialism began to suffer a series of increasingly violent shocks. In 1876, the *Spectator* found it necessary to mount a general attack on 'some of the glaringly bad pictures' perpetrated by the new adherents of the irredeemable genre which they found in the second room of the Royal Academy exhibition—Tissot's *A Convalescent* and *The Thames* (Pls. 113 and 115) conspicuous among them. Even after six years in England, Tissot must have found their reaction exceedingly strange. Schooled in the admiration of Alfred Stevens, to display 'a tendency to apply all the labour to the accessories of the picture, and give but little time or thought to the working-out of any great idea or noble conception' cannot have struck him as being quite as misdirected or 'wilfully' offensive as it did the *Spectator*:

It cannot be too much insisted upon that no amount of harmonised furniture and dress will make a picture, but that, on the contrary, the more labour that is bestowed upon the purely

---

[28] 'The Royal Academy', *Art Journal* (June 1874), 164.

artificial surroundings, the less likely is the composition to be of any greater value than a magnified fashion-plate or a photographic interior. These remarks apply especially to many of the pictures in the second room, in which there is a superabundance of what may be called the 'Clapham School of Art,'—art, that is to say, which is calculated to raise no unpleasant feelings or undue excitement, but whose aim is to depict trivial incidents of manners and society in as 'elegant' a style as possible.[29]

In his discussion of Tissot's work at the International, Claretie had found that in giving up his artistic nationality, the most Tissot could hope to become was 'un peintre anglais sans naïveté et sans conviction',[30] two qualities which Tissot must have thought to be essential elements of English popularity. The heritage of the Pre-Raphaelites and the genre tradition, naïveté and sincerity were thought by the French to give English painting its unmistakable character and vivid emotional power, but they were not without danger for foreign practitioners:

Mais s'il est bon de reconnaître dans le peuple anglais une façon toute particulière de voir, de sentir et de rendre la nature, il est, à mon avis, dangereux d'imiter ses procédés et sa manière de traduire la vérité! C'est pourtant ce qui arrive à l'heure qu'il est à M. Tissot, qui se *britannise*, si je puis dire, tout à fait, et va perdre certainement bientôt sa nationalité artistique.[31]

Tissot's painting was hardly naïve, but it did not lack conviction. It is likely, however, that he sought to give both qualities to the subject and narrative, if not the composition, of his pictures after he arrived in England. A narrative like *The Captain's Daughter* (Pl. 81) is certainly naïve in comparison with pictures like *Une Veuve* and *L'Escalier* (Pls. 51 and 52); if all three can be said to be treated with equal artistic conviction, such diligence might indeed be judged better-suited to the more sophisticated drama of the two earlier pictures. *The Captain's Daughter*, lacking the *naïveté* which is demanded by its subject, and which might have saved it in the hands of a native painter, might easily be thought to dissipate conviction with patent insincerity. Throughout the decade, Tissot would be found to have soured *naïveté* into satire and conviction into cynicism: 'It is art brought to the doors and laid at the feet of the monde, if not the demi-monde, with an almost cynical sincerity. Thus far it is French rather than English, alike in the ideas it suggests and the skill it shows.'[32]

Much contemporary criticism of Tissot's pictures uses them as the basis for a consideration of 'Frenchness' and 'Englishness' in the art of the time,[33] and

---

[29] 'The Royal Academy', *Spectator*, 27 May 1876, p. 681.

[30] Claretie, 'Tissot', p. 376.

[31] Ibid., p. 374.

[32] 'The Grosvenor Gallery', *The Times*, 2 May 1878, p. 7.

[33] For a more than usually thoughtful example, see 'French Art: A Comparative Sketch', *Spectator* (18 August 1877), 1036-8. In his memoirs, the dealer Gambart recalled the tremendous prejudice again French painting in London at mid-century: '. . . not only was the English taste, insular like the English character, attracted only by English painting; what is more, English taste responded almost with disdain. Leaving the Gallery . . . one of the English painters, whom a collector was consulting about the

although the comparisons are seldom on a level higher than the suspicion of 'French satire' in his depiction of English manners and the notion that his pictures had an air of Parisian wickedness about them which was dangerous, if glitteringly attractive, to the native born, they make his position as an outsider very clear.

National character, as Maurice Grosser has pointed out in relation to van Dyck's English career, is profoundly exotic. To a native, the land of his birth may be irritating or idyllic, but it is never exotic or strange. People exhibit individual characteristics and separate lives, but they have no visible nationality. This national character might then be said to be made up of what a national considers normal, that is, unremarkable behaviour. To a foreigner, however, it is precisely this unremarkable behaviour, so different from the unremarkable behaviour of his own country, which is exotic and strange. To him, individual characteristics have less impact than a composite of what is, to him, striking behaviour.[34]

Seen in this light, the reason for much contemporary criticism and suspicion becomes clear. The danger of an outsider's view is a strong tendency to caricature, and Tissot was found to have fallen into the trap:

But, though a very keen observer, M. Tissot, like most other of our foreign critics, fails in sympathy and falls into vulgar exaggeration. The particular types prevalent in his works—the lanky faces, crane necks and falling shoulders—are not always recognizable by us as English; they are besides, always curiously cold and antipathetic.[35]

At the same time, Tissot's position as an outsider also gave his pictures much of their unique quality, accounting for the striking difference in approach between his work and that of native painters of similar subjects like William Quiller Orchardson. For Tissot, the Mayfair of *Too Early* and the Cowes of *The Ball on Shipboard* had an exotic flavour they could never have for a native artist. Indeed, Tissot was among the first to use subjects like society dances for pictures at all, and their novelty was welcomed by the public: 'Strange to say, a foreign artist—M. Tissot—sets our painters an example in choosing English subjects so characteristic that they seem to be neglected only because they are so near at hand'.[36]

As a foreigner, Tissot had another distinct advantage in his approach to his subject-matter. He was never caught up in the English class system as native painters were by birth, and as a result never felt compelled to turn class worry into moral worry as they did, transforming their canvases into philosophical tracts. Class is the central theme of British art in the nineteenth century, but

purchase of a picture, left him with the words, "Yes, but it's only a French picture." ' (Quoted in Maas, *Gambart*, p. 55.)

[34] Maurice Grosser, *The Painter's Eye* (New York: Rinehart, 1951), pp. 37–41.

[35] 'The Royal Academy Exhibition', *Illustrated London News* (25 May 1872), 502.

[36] Ibid.

being classless, as foreigners often are in highly structured societies, Tissot was free to record rather than judge, and this sets his work apart from that of native painters. Tissot was willing to take society at its own valuation, and if he did not treat it with the detachment and integrity Degas would have brought to the study, he was equally careful to avoid making it serve as a moral lesson.

Tissot took full advantage of his position as a foreigner. Given his taste for estrangement, it is likely that he found a degree of alienation as personally attractive as it was professionally useful. He may have been, one fears, something of a professional Frenchman, a tendency doubtless heightened by his anomalous position as a political exile. For Tissot and his public, foreignness stimulated a kind of romantic fiction. Distance lent enchantment to the view, giving his work a novelty and chic native painters could not hope to reproduce.

Tissot's stylish and expensive canvases, carefully promoted by fashionable dealers, soon found their natural clientele among a *nouveau riche* plutocracy which found that he made their chic look both more chic and more gratifyingly French than it really was, although in their insecurity of ascent and imperfection of achievement they never lost the suspicion that he might also be making fun of their pretentions.[37]

If Parisian gloss was admired by the happy few, a more conservative element of society still found addiction to foreign ways only too powerful 'a dissolvent of English propriety'. By the end of the decade, the *Spectator* had lost patience with Tissot's 'swells': ' "Swells" is a very appropriate word, we may mention, for there is always a suspicion of the "snob" about Tissot's personages; their purple has too much of the Tyrian dye upon it, and their linen forces itself upon one's attention in somewhat offensive quantity and brilliance'.[38]

The 1870s were to see the destruction of the unostentatious and self-contained society of mid-Victorian England. As a rising tide of industrial wealth displaced older social and economic structures, it quickly realized the extent of its power and began to demand wider outlets for its new social and political aspirations. For many in the seventies, the immediate past already seemed a lost paradise of simplicity, structure, and duty understood. The emergent cosmopolitan society immediately became the subject of bitter criticism for its licence, vitiated standards, and questionable connections. The decorous England recorded by writers like Trollope was bought out or thrust aside by a plutocracy ostentatious with

[37] For a study of Victorian taste which gives clear definition to its complex evolution, see W. Ames, *Prince Albert and Victorian Taste*. In this remarkable study, Ames identifies Tissot's patrons with what he calls 'parvenu taste', a kind of late nineteenth-century version of the Frenchified taste of the Regency which had inherited some of its fluid sense of style but more of its worldly pretence.

It had a love of well-buttoned upholstery, sharp colour, hard surfaces, and a taste for artists 'whose high prices reflected good value for thorough work'. As Ames suggests, 'it had swallowed Ruskin without bothering to try to understand, still less believe, him' (p. 185).

[38] 'The Grosvenor Gallery', *Spectator* (31 May 1879), 690–1.

new-found power, but its destruction was not allowed to pass unnoticed, and was accompanied by dismayed and angry lamentations.

Tissot was perhaps unwittingly caught between the two factions. The chic which was his stock-in-trade had been an unquestioned essential in the parvenu style of the Second Empire, and he was probably taken by surprise when it was met with the indignation of the just in the London of Queen Victoria. His position in England and the impact of his work on English sensibilities becomes clear in this context, and the social threat as well as the artistic novelty of his work is immediately comprehensible only in reference to it:

In its best days, Victorian society had never been 'smart'. During the forties, under the influence of Louis Philippe, Courts affected to be simple; and they succeeded. The taste of Louis Philippe was *bourgeois* beyond any taste except that of Queen Victoria. Style lingered in the background with the powdered footman behind the yellow chariot, but speaking socially the Queen had no style save what she inherited. Balmoral was a startling revelation of royal taste. Nothing could be worse than the toilettes at Court unless it were the way they were worn. One's eyes might be dazzled by jewels, but they were heirlooms, and if any lady appeared well-dressed, she was either a foreigner or 'fast'. Fashion was not fashionable in London until the Americans and the Jews were let loose.[39]

It was on moral rather than aesthetic grounds that Tissot came to grief in England. In his glorification of 'vulgar society', he identified himself with a breakdown of moral values which was deeply disturbing in the seventies:

The only things that are real are the dresses, and the abominably artificial atmosphere of a certain style of society, which might be called the Neo-French-English, the essential parts of which are to dress like a French actress, and to care for nothing under or above the sun; energy, truth, brains, heart and life, all disappearing rapidly, and a talented artist revelling in the spectacle and painting the result.[40]

Tissot failed to realize—or perhaps simply chose not to notice—the degree to which a constant ideal of order pervaded English life. The objective portrayal of the material world was absolutely inseparable from a clearly defined moral attitude towards that world, and Tissot's 'swells' offered a moral lesson he can hardly have intended. Yet if he came to grief on social or moral grounds, his aesthetic welcome was open and warm. His choice of English subjects was held up as a model for native artists, and his technical skill was judged in much the way it would be today. Even when his pictures were found to be *base* art, unworthy in subject, or vulgar, lacking in proper sensibility, they were never found to be

---

[39] Henry Adams, *The Education of Henry Adams*, ed. Ernest Samuels (Boston: Houghton-Mifflin, 1974), p. 195. First published in 1905, but written much earlier, the material here quoted is dated 1864. An example of everything objectionable in the world of 'swells' is to be found in Trollope's darkly pessimistic *The Way We Live Now*, which was first published in serial form between February 1874, and September 1875.

[40] 'The Grosvenor Gallery', *Spectator* (31 May 1879), 691.

false art, 'art without meaning, mere art-upholstery, representative of nothing save a great deal of mis-directed labour' as much contemporary British painting was adjudged to be.[41] Tissot's real merit as a painter and his seriousness as an artist were never questioned even when his critics had given up on his subject-matter. After the *Spectator* had attacked the false moral tone of his pictures, it was unbiased enough to give the most generous praise to his gifts as an artist: 'It must be said that his pictures, however vulgar in conception and common-place in subject matter, are always artistic. It is quite unquestionable that for purely technical mastery of colour and of arrangement in shadow and sunlight, Tissot has but one rival in England, and that is Alma Tadema'.[42]

After Tissot arrived in London, he immediately began to seek unmistakably English subjects and narratives for his new pictures. As Thomas Gibson Bowles had been the financial mainstay of Tissot's early months in England, it seems likely that it was Whistler who helped him to find his way in the English art world and offered him the clue he sought for the redirection of his work. Renewed familiarity with Whistler's pictures had the now predictable effect of inspiring a new *appassionnement*. Taking the pictures Whistler was doing of the Thames as his model, Tissot went to the river and the Pool of London to begin a series of pictures which were to extend through his English period and form the central focus of much of his English work.

For twelve years, Whistler had been exploring the visual possibilities of river life and the shipping in a series of etchings which took final form as *The Thames Set* in 1871. Beginning to paint the river at the same time, he visualized it in the way he saw his etchings. Writing to Fantin-Latour in 1861, Whistler likened the background of *Wapping* (Pl. 74) to an etching: 'maintenant par la fenêtre, on voit toute la Tamise, qui est comme une eau-forte'.[43] *Wapping*, which Tissot may well have remembered from the *Exposition Universelle* of 1867,[44] is the obvious prototype for one of his first pictures in the genre, *The Thames* (Pl. 75), and its composition and mood can still be found in paintings and prints like *A Passing Storm* and *Ramsgate* (Pls. 116 and 117) at the middle of the decade.

The press was not slow to notice the similarities of subject in the two artists' work, and in less abusive moments delighted their readers with historical

[41] 'French Art: A Comparative Sketch', *Spectator* (18 August 1877), 1038.

[42] 'The Grosvenor Gallery', *Spectator* (31 May 1879), 691.

[43] Quoted in Staley, *From Realism to Symbolism*, p. 37.

[44] It is not perhaps coincidental that Tissot first employed the shipping as a background for a picture in *Un déjeuner* (pl. 60), which must have been executed shortly after the *Exposition Universelle* of 1867. An unlocated picture dated 1864 would seem to be the single exception: a man in eighteenth-century dress stands on a *quai* which cuts at a sharp diagonal across the left half of the picture. Behind him, a sailing ship lies at berth surrounded by other vessels. The delineation of its hull and rigging has all the precision Tissot would bring to his Thames pictures a few years later. It is unlike them in composition, feeling, and intent, but none the less demonstrates that Tissot had the interest and the means to bring such a subject to a successful conclusion before Whistler suggested the approach he would come to favour for his nautical pictures.

comparisons like those of the *Daily Telegraph*, which said that if Whistler's robust 'Dutch' subjects qualified him as 'the Cuyp of Rotherhithe' or 'the Claude of Old Chelsea', Tissot's more social approach clearly made him 'the Watteau of Wapping'.[45] The distinction has accuracy as well as charm, for Tissot brought his own sensibility to the genre, and his shipboard galas and romances are often as deliciously rococo as anything in nineteenth-century painting. His ravishing young women display their *toilettes* against the brass and mahogany of yachts and pleasure-boats or on the rustic terraces of riverside taverns in Victorian *fêtes champêtres* that capture the aura of eighteenth-century painting far better than his costume pieces had done at the end of the sixties in France.

For Tissot, the wonders of the river and the pool were always as much social as nautical, and the evidence of his pictures is confirmed by the reminiscences of his friend Louise Jopling, who had been invited with her sister and the expatriot German painter Ferdinand Heilbuth[46] to join Tissot for sketching trips after she met him at the Academy in 1873.[47] Although Tissot was immediately attracted to the quiet upper reaches of the Thames and recorded its autumnal beauty in what must be among the first of his English canvases (Pls. 90 and 93), he betrays his affinity with Impressionism as well as with Whistler in his clear preference for the industrial suburbs below London.

Tissot must have begun to paint his Thames subjects immediately after his arrival in London, for he sent a picture called *The Thames* to the International Exhibition in 1872,[48] with the *Colonel Burnaby*, the *Gentleman in a Railway Carriage*, and a narrative costume picture called *Bad News* which can be identified with the work now often called *The Parting* (Pl. 78).[49]

The Thames itself is unlocated; it is described in the *Athenaeum*, however, as 'a skipper and two young girls at a table near a window in a tavern',[50] and a wood-engraving published in the *Graphic* (Pl. 75) early the next year doubtless records its composition.[51] It is also the subject of an extended discussion in

---

[45] 'The Royal Academy', *Daily Telegraph*, 21 May 1874, quoted in H. Taylor, *Whistler*, p. 182, n. 30.

[46] Ferdinand Heilbuth (1826–89). He was born at Hamburg and trained in Paris, *biederkeit* surviving a long course of Parisian experience to give flavour to pictures of cardinals, orphans, and fashionable women. Heilbuth settled in London after the Franco-Prussian War, where he became a popular rival of Tissot, whose portrait he painted, as well as a friend. He was the subject, with other Parisian artists of German origin, of a scornful attack in Claretie's *Peintres et Sculpteurs*, pp. 340–1, for his lack of gratitude in receiving French education and honours, only to abandon his adopted country. In that respect he appears a strange friend for the patriotic Tissot.

[47] L. Jopling, *Twenty Years of My Life*, p. 73.

[48] International Exhibition, London, 1872, no. 1176.

[49] International Exhibition, London, 1872, no. 1181. See also David S. Brooke, 'Tissot's "The Parting"', *Amgueddfa*, pp. 22–6.

[50] 'The London International Exhibition: Foreign Pictures', *Athenaeum* (6 July 1872), 22.

[51] There is an unidentified newspaper reproduction of the painting in the Witt Library, London, which identifies the painting as 'ex-collection Mrs. Bannister'; drawings for both female figures are in the collection of the Telfair Academy of Arts and Sciences, Savannah, Georgia.

Claretie's essay on Tissot's pictures at the International Exhibition, although Claretie mistakes its tavern setting as the deck of a steamer in mid-stream:

Tel de ses tableaux qu'il appelle *Thames* (*la Tamise*) est une étude fort curieuse et, si l'on veut, fort jolie! Deux jeunes misses, accoudées au bastingage d'un steamer, regardent devant elles cette forêt de mâts, de cordages, de tuyaux énormes qui se fond dans le brouillard du fleuve. Le capitaine du paquebot, assis, contemple à son tour les deux jeunes filles. Cela est très-vrai, à coup sûr, et les étoffes à carreaux blanc et noir, les lainages qui portent les deux misses ont été peints à la loupe et sortaient évidemment des fabriques de Leeds ou d'Huddersfield. Mais ce tableau d'une tonalité grise et d'un *fini* horriblement travaillé, tout à fait bon à être lithographié et pendu aux murs d'un salon bourgeoise, ce tableau laisse voir une déviation absolue dans le talent de M. Tissot.[52]

For his more important début in 1872 at the Royal Academy, Tissot did not risk even such winsome aspects of modern life, and returned to the late eighteenth-century costume pieces which had been successful at the last Salons of the Empire and the Vienna *Weltaustellung* of 1871, sending *Les Adieux* (Pl. 76), a sentimental leave-taking at a garden gate, and *An Interesting Story* (Pl. 77),[53] a comedy of manners with a background of the shipping.

Les Adieux, which was popular enough to be issued as a steel engraving,[54] is a remarkable summary of Tissot's narrative as it altered to conform to the exigencies of British taste. The mute and passionless lovers, separated by a fence which makes their parting tangible, are compelling enough in their discreet narrative suggestiveness and have a phlegmatic appeal Tissot doubtless considered 'British'. It is a world removed from the vivid emotions of the Directoire pictures. The painting was, in fact, very much to English taste, admired for its narrative simplicity and 'sentiment without sentimentality' in an exhibition where 'the *ad captandum* specimens of *genre*, the sentimental rustic and the namby-pamby domestic' had been characterized as 'especially bad' that year.[55] Casting about for typically English subjects, Tissot has taken a page out of Millais's book, and *Les Adieux* is one of the legion of descendants of *A Huguenot* (1853; Makins Collection), the prototype for endless variations on troubled lovers huddled beside garden walls. But if Millais suggested the subject, Tissot has given it an entirely personal treatment. If it is no less explicit in narrative than Millais's picture, its troubled mood is no longer tied to wider meaning. Holman Hunt had objected to Millais's original idea for the *Huguenot*—two lovers whispering at an orchard wall—as having no interest beyond a prurient intrusion of privacy and

[52] Claretie, 'Tissot', pp. 375–6.

[53] Royal Academy, 1872, nos. 644 and 389. See also David S. Brooke, ' "An Interesting Story" by James Tissot', *Art Bulletin of Victoria*, pp. 22–9.

[54] For the engraving by John Ballin, see Wentworth, *Catalogue Raisonné of Prints*, prints after Tissot, no. 1. A full-sized maquette by Tissot for the engraver is repro., Brooke, Wentworth, Zerner, *Tissot*, no. 49.

[55] 'The Royal Academy', *Spectator* (4 May 1872), 561.

suggested that their action be actuated by some generous thought of the larger world. Millais agreed and was delighted when he hit upon the subject, which he thought contained a high moral lesson.[56] Tissot had earlier adopted Millais's moral material in *Le Départ du fiancé* (Pl. 13), although the meaning of that confused picture is hard to determine with any degree of accuracy, but for *Les Adieux* he took only the composition and emotional formula of *A Huguenot* and eschewed moral significance. For Tissot, however, historicism did not carry the emotional charge it did for Millais, and once again costume limits the effectiveness of the image. For the public, costume without specific reference was unfamiliar and confusing, and it is not surprising that an audience familiar with the educated reference of *A Huguenot* sought unsuccessfully to turn *Les Adieux* into a picture of Becky Sharp at the gate of Minerva Hall.[57] (It was not until the subject was repeated in modern dress in *The Last Evening* (Pl. 84) that the full narrative and psychological possibilities of the subject could be realized. Tissot appears to have come to the conclusion himself, for with the completion of the costume pictures at this time he turned with resolution to modern life. Freed of historical costume, all the successful aspects of *Les Adieux*, its stylish attitudes, equation of setting and emotion, sophisticated narrative, and glossy pathos—even the wistful, unhealthy beauty of the young woman herself—find their place in Tissot's modern pictures with a compelling effectiveness.)

An Interesting Story (Pl. 77) was an even greater popular success, 'a capital piece of humourous characterization',[58] and demonstrates even more clearly than *Les Adieux* the skill with which Tissot transformed the material of his Directoire pictures to suit British taste. With unerring instinct, he hit upon the comic tradition of the English eighteenth century, transforming the erotic suggestiveness of works like *Partie carrée* (Pl. 61) into the robust humour and comic narrative of Goldsmith, Sheridan, and Sterne.

Its artistic means were nearly as widely admired as its narrative. Skilfully composed with its figures seen against the light in the manner Tissot favoured and continued to employ with great success (see, for example, Pls. 116 and 132), it confidently sacrifices a certain amount of modelling in deference to optical truth. Its technique, juxtaposing thin films of pigment in the flesh with dexterous impasto passages in the costume, and its fresh colour harmonies, based on the clear red of the officer's coat, also struck notes as bold and unfamiliar as its clever narrative. The *Art Journal* admired Tissot's originality and the risks he had taken in bringing the enterprise to so successful a conclusion: 'We have never seen anything more daring conducted to an issue so felicitous. All the small expedients of

---

[56] The genesis and content of Millais's *Huguenot* is summarized by Allen Staley in F. Cummings *et al.*, *Romantic Art in Britain*, pp. 317–19.

[57] 'Exhibition of the Royal Academy', *The Times*, 21 May 1872, p. 7.

[58] 'The Royal Academy', *Athenaeum* (25 May 1872), 659.

relief are whistled down the wind, and the simple oppositions are left to stand on their own merits. It is a picture which would tell in any gallery.'[59]

All Tissot's neo-Georgian costume pieces share something of this new comic irony and felicitous technique: *Bad News* (Pl. 78),[60] a farewell breakfast with a departing officer and two young ladies, and certainly the equal of *An Interesting Story* on both counts; *Le Thé* (Pl. 79), an exceptionally beautiful variation on the left-hand figure of the girl in *Bad News*; the unlocated *How We Read the News of Our Marriage*,[61] a couple sitting in the bow-window of a tavern overlooking the Thames reading of their wedding over the anvil; and *Histoire ennuyeuse* (Pl. 80), a variation on the left-hand figure of *An Interesting Story* which also served as the model for an etching of the same name.[62]

These little comedies of manners have a bright theatrical quality about them, and humour briskly undercuts sentimentality with all the polished archness of an epigram. Avoiding the *scène à faire*, Tissot seizes the moment when the comedy is at its most witty rather than its most active, setting his narrative obliquely to the action. The stock cast of eighteenth-century comedies settles into old familiar attitudes: the heroine and her confidante roll their eyes at the tedious reminiscences of some Uncle Toby with a military map, a red-coated officer goes off to find battle and see The World, and the story ends happily with that most exhilarating eighteenth-century pastime, a merry chase to Gretna Green.

The emphasis on narrative and unmistakably English subjects Tissot had brought to these costume pictures is even more evident in the first scenes of modern life he exhibited at the Academy in 1873: *The Captain's Daughter* (Pl. 81) and *The Last Evening* (Pl. 84), melancholy romances set against a background of the shipping, and *Too Early* (Pl. 101), the first of his three important 'social conversation pieces'.[63] *The Captain's Daughter*, a pretty narrative in which the father and the suitor of the young lady discuss her future as she stares listlessly at the water traffic on the Thames, might be considered simply an unpretentious and rather successful picture very much in the English taste and was, in fact, greatly admired for its character and feeling.[64] With its sentimental, if somewhat glossy, pathos, its decorous narrative of distempered hearts, and its idealized

[59] 'The Royal Academy', *Art Journal* (July 1872), 181. *The Times* also found that 'nothing could be more careful and complete' than the execution of the picture ('The Royal Academy', *The Times*, 21 May 1872, 7), although the *Athenaeum* thought it 'a pity that the spirit of this design is not worthily supported by care and thoroughness of execution. It possesses every good quality but finish' ('The Royal Academy', *Athenaeum* (25 May 1872), 659).

[60] A drawing for the figure, dedicated to Degas, is repro., Brooke, Wentworth, Zerner, *Tissot*, no. 50, recto.

[61] A related oil sketch or unfinished painting is also known: *The Tryst, Greenwich*, exhibited, Sheffield, *Tissot*, 1955, no. 14. A drawing for the composition is repro., Brooke, Wentworth, Zerner, *Tissot*, no. 50, verso.

[62] Wentworth, *Catalogue Raisonné of Prints*, no. 32.

[63] Royal Academy, 1873, nos. 108, 121, and 914.

[64] See, for example, the reviews in the *Art Journal* (June 1873), 167; the *Graphic* (3 May 1873) 411; and the *Spectator* (17 May 1873), 638.

representation of the lower classes, it seems as naïve and simple as the refrain from a ballad opera, and as such it was intended, cleverly fashioned to delight a native audience:

> Who could resist these two young hearts' laments?
> Sir, she is yours! I give you my consent,
> And a commission in my man-o'-war,
> Lieutenant, now, salute your commodore![65]

The concern for the smallest elements of pictorial imagery that had marked works like *L'Escalier* (Pl. 52) a few years earlier has been brought to bear on this simple tale, giving its ingenuous charm the most sophisticated innocence, and if today Tissot's acquiescence to the demands of sentiment appears a little too easy, suggesting all the 'French satire' and the 'cynical sincerity' the English feared in his bland propitiation of British taste, this Victorian *True Blue* appears to have been taken at face value by the public for the obvious pleasure of the response.

The Captain's Daughter is representative of a few pictures set apart from the complacent pleasures Tissot generally favoured for his nautical canvases in their less exalted subject-matter and in their faint odour of social significance. An oil sketch, *The Three Crows Inn, Gravesend* (Pl. 82), presumably a study for an un-located painting or a closely related print,[66] uses the same setting and hints at a similar, if now obscure, narrative. Some of the same actors appear once again in what may have been the most important picture of the group, a now unlocated *Emigrants*, which is known to have been damaged and reduced in height although its composition is fortunately preserved in the particularly beautiful small replica by Tissot exhibited at the Grosvenor Gallery in 1879 (Pl. 83), and in one of his most felicitous etchings.[67] Although these pictures suggest the fitful social conscience which flickers now and then in Tissot's narratives until it flames brightly in the proselytism of the illustrations to the Bible, it undoubtedly re-presents the more immediate desire to find 'English' subjects and to give a faintly moralistic quality to his narratives. Emigration was one of the greatest of the Victorian social problems, and it had supplied innumerable native artists with a subject for their work: Ford Maddox Brown's *The Last of England* (1855; City Art Gallery, Manchester) is perhaps the most moving and suggests itself as an immediate prototype for Tissot's experiments in the genre. But however picturesque or calculatingly British in their appeal, such subjects must also have spoken

---

[65] The denouement to *Nancy: or, The Parting Lovers*, often called *True Blue*, an interlude with libretto and music by Henry Carey (c.1687–1743), first given at Drury Lane in 1739 and the subject of numerous revivals.

[66] Wentworth, *Catalogue Raisonné of Prints*, no. 45.

[67] Grosvenor Gallery, 1879, no. 93; Wentworth, *Catalogue Raisonné of Prints*, no. 45. Although

what must have been the replica of the picture was not exhibited until the Grosvenor Gallery of 1879, where it was described by *The Times*, 2 May 1879, p. 3, as one of Tissot's smaller pictures, and the etching is dated 1880, it is clearly related to the Thames pictures of the early 1870s in style, composition, and subject, as well as costume, setting, and protagonists; it seems certain that at least the original version dates from this time.

directly to Tissot, representing aspects and emotions immediately attractive to his taste for estrangement and imbalance. Throughout the decade, travel and parting are the subjects of many of his most inventive pictures, culminating in the compositional and philosophical originalities of *Goodbye, On the Mersey* and *Les Deux Amis* (Pls. 147 and 148).

The Last Evening (Pl. 84), Tissot's second Academy picture in 1873, is at once more opaque in its meaning and more compelling in its atmosphere than *The Captain's Daughter*. The amazing precision and finish so often remarked in Tissot's delineation of a ship's appointments is seen at its most dazzlingly complex,[68] and it gives an hallucinatory quality to this narrative where time itself seems arrested by the mute anguish of the couple sitting together in passionless lassitude, powerless against their approaching fate. The two old men with troubled expressions discuss the lovers like the chorus in a Greek tragedy, and the little girl eavesdropping behind them like a child in a picture by Balthus, adds to the uneasy atmosphere without bringing it into focus. For the first time, Tissot aligns the 'repressed' narrative of his Parisian genre pictures with the anecdotal emphasis of his 'English' manner in the most subtle and distinctive way. From *The Last Evening* a genre evolves in which the investigation of psychological tension, innuendo, and unexplained relationships suggests context and meaning without labouring narrative. *The Last Evening* at once honours English narrative conventions and transcends them. Applying his own dramatic construction to the traditions of British painting, Tissot creates a hybrid form which serves as the flexible and transparent medium through which his own troubled spirit is given its most complete and integrated expression. In it, he establishes the formula for many of the finest of his English narrative pictures.

A number of preparatory studies in gouache over pencil or black chalk for paintings from this period suggest that Tissot used the medium extensively in the early seventies. Single figures drawn from life, these gouache studies establish expression and pose with an accuracy that required little more than their careful transfer to canvas. Among the most beautiful are studies for the young woman in *The Last Evening* and *The Captain and the Mate* (Pls. 85 and 86); they have a grace of spirit and a painterly distinction which places them directly in the tradition of the eighteenth-century French water-colour painters.[69]

If the narrative suggestiveness of *The Captain and the Mate* (Pl. III) is even more tentative than that of *The Last Evening*, the result is no less remarkable or poetic in its effectiveness. Tissot regroups now familiar protagonists in new aspects of troubled romance against skies as overcast and clouded as the future

[68] For a sailor's opinion of Tissot's skill, see Laver, *Vulgar Society*, p. 6.

[69] Among others of particular interest are studies for the young woman in *The Captain's Daughter* (unlocated); a study for the seated woman in *The Captain and the Mate* (Ashmolean Museum, Oxford); a study of a woman with a lap rug, not related to a known painting (Art Gallery of New South Wales); studies for two of the women in *Too Early* (unlocated, and private collection, New York); and *La Dormeuse* (Ashmolean Museum, Oxford).

of those silent and abstracted couples. Even such tenuous narrative dissolves in those studies of ships' rigging and feminine costume like *A Visit to the Yacht* (*c.*1873; Viscount Leverhulme), where a relaxed and desultory charm as well as an essential absence of anecdotal reference looks forward to the visual splendours of *The Ball on Shipboard* (Pl. 102).

Although the pale, overcast atmosphere of these pictures might be said to have communicated itself to Tissot's palette, he had in fact immediately begun to raise the tone of his pictures to the higher pitch of English painting, the Royal Academy having a distinctly higher 'exhibition pitch' than the Salon:

Every annual exhibition, as its day comes round, is thought to be rather worse than usual. I am not in a position to compare the Academy with itself, having seen hitherto but a single specimen of it. The most I can do is compare it with the Paris Salon. This, indeed, I found myself doing spontaneously, as I walked through the brilliant chambers of Burlington House. I call them brilliant advisedly, for the first impression one receives is that of extraordinary brightness of colour. The walls of the Salon, by contrast, seem neutral and dusky.[70]

He at first achieved the higher pitch of the Academy, the legacy of Constable, Turner, and the Pre-Raphaelites, with the addition of large amounts of white to his palette. The attempt to integrate local colour and aerial perspective in the 1860s, which had resulted in the grey-green of *Les Deux Sœurs* (Pl. 29), was also applied to these English works. Writing of *Les Adieux* (Pl. 76), the *Illustrated London News* found it as grey in tone as Claretie had found *The Thames* at the International: 'M. Tissot is evidently no colourist; his proclivity for rendering anything in black and white almost argues a form of colour-blindness; even the foliage in the last-named picture is *en deuil*, like the fair girl who mournfully turns from her lover'.[71] Both *The Captain's Daughter* and *The Last Evening* are white enough to appear a little chalky, and their pale colour was found to be exaggerated, if Whistlerian, at the time. The *Athenaeum* found the former to be 'a study in white, as many of M. Tissot's pictures are', and the *Graphic* that both 'might be called after Mr. Whistler's fashion, "Symphonies in White," only that, unlike certain of Mr. Whistler's works, they have the merit of distinct and accurate drawing.'[72] This conscious effort to heighten the tone of his pictures doubtless accounts for the extremely 'blond' effect of a picture like *London Visitors* (pl. 106), and if it also accounts for the unifying atmospheric effects of a work like *The Ball on Shipboard* (Pl. 102), its 'superadded tinting' not only restates problems of the past, it looks forward to the colourist effects Tissot developed in the late seventies in which Whistlerian harmonies give way to hot, saturated colour which suggests the polychrome excesses of *La Femme à Paris*.

[70] H. James, 'The Picture Season in London' (1877), repr., *The Painter's Eye*, p. 147.

[71] 'The Royal Academy Exhibition', *Illustrated London News* (25 May 1872), 502.

[72] 'The Royal Academy', *Athenaeum* (10 May 1873), 605; 'The Royal Academy', *Graphic* (7 June 1873), 539.

III. *The Captain and the Mate*, 1873.

From the beginning, Tissot varied the melancholy sentiment of his romances with episodes of comic briskness and wit. All are variations on a single theme, the comic possibilities of rivalry and choice in the affairs of the heart; for Tissot never tired of the dilemma of a young man's choice between two equally attractive young women as a subject for his works at this time.

Once again, chief among them is one of the first, *Boarding the Yacht* (Pl. 88), a comic masterpiece in which a stout mate squires two haughty ladies aboard with a subservient concentration that gives full credulity to their pretentions. The picture is composed with all the inventive brilliance and heightened sensibility Tissot was able to bring to his early London work, and its narrative quality is equally remarkable, not only for its precise phrasing of character and situation, but for a human sympathy which keeps its laughter from growing brittle or cold.

A nearly contemporary engraving like Arthur Hopkins's *The Last Croquet Game of the Season* (Pl. 87) makes clear what Tissot would have found had he studied the illustrated magazines with an eye to his own work. If the horizontal thrust of its rudimentary composition suggests something of the structural complexities of *The Captain and the Mate* (Pl. III), isolating figures along a triangle for psychological as much as compositional purposes, its inarticulate narrative is like a rough draft for Tissot's comedies of sentiment, charged with the hidden conflicts of civilized behaviour, where allusions to weather and season give lyric amplitude, and hints of finality a suitably bitter-sweet taste. The eloquent 'modern' beauty of Hopkins's lady in her fashionable 'Dolly Varden' costume at the centre also hints that Tissot would have discovered poetry as well as drama in the pages of the illustrated magazines.

The narrative effectiveness of *Boarding the Yacht* has been ascribed to a subtle *double entendre* between the apparent innocence of the situation and the salacious possibilities which lie close beneath the placid surface, creating a sharp tension between good-natured humour and what has been wonderfully called 'subliminal lickerishness'.[73] This dichotomy became an almost essential feature of Tissot's narrative construction, and although it now adds hugely to the enjoyment of his pictures, it caused considerable uneasiness at the time and accounts for the feeling in the seventies that his work was somehow not quite nice. Such a feeling accounts for the horrified reception of the Wakefield *Thames* (Pl. 115) in 1876; it also allowed *Punch*, unquestionably making direct reference to Tissot's

[73] G. MacBeth, 'Subliminal Dreams', *Art News Annual* (1970), 29. Often as Tissot could have encountered the theme in nineteenth-century English painting, he could also have found it among the sources for his eighteenth-century English costume pieces: an overtly bawdy model for such a trio, unknown in his work before the English period, can be found in typical form in a work like the anonymous mezzotint *Sir Timothy Thicketts First Reel to London: or, The Beauties of King's Place Drawing Lots*, in which a gentleman takes the line of least resistance in deciding between the charms of two well-dressed tarts. The subject in reverse was to be met in the illustrated magazines of the seventies; the *Graphic*, for example, offered *The Rival Blues*, in which two ladies contest a ribbon (April 8, 1871, p. 309).

private life, to spin the seemingly innocuous pictures exhibited at the Grosvenor Gallery in 1879 into a tale of lurid immorality in which Mrs Newton appears as the mistress of an errant clergyman and a City man simultaneously in *Scènes de la vie dans le Bois de S. Jean*, and a picture like *A Quiet Afternoon* (Pl. 144) is retitled *The Naughty Old Man: or, I'll Tell your Wife how you spend your Afternoons in Fair Rosamund's Bower-Villa, N. W.*[74]

The theme of rivalry and choice was a popular one in Victorian painting, and a work like John Calcott Horsley's *Showing a Preference* (Pl. 89), exhibited at the Royal Academy of 1860, is set apart from numerous other examples by its remarkable quality rather than its originality of subject. But when Tissot's *The Thames* (Pl. 115) was exhibited at the Academy violent exception was taken to its narrative. It was singled out for its blatant impropriety and proved to be the most unpopular of his works. The scandal it created marks the beginning of the long decline of his English popularity. Tissot must have been amazed and horrified at its reception. The *Spectator* called it 'a chalky abomination' and found that the 'undeniably Parisian ladies' no longer exhibited the least character or feeling. The *Athenaeum* thought it 'thoroughly and willfully vulgar', found the women 'ugly and low-bred', and called the background a 'libel' on the Pool. 'Questionable material', said *The Times*; 'a pleasanter thing in reality than on canvas'; while the *Graphic*, always among Tissot's strongest supporters, found it clever, 'but hardly nice in its suggestions. More French, shall we say, than English?'[75]

Another picture with a similar narrative and composition may date from this time, although it was not exhibited until the second half of the decade: *Portsmouth Dockyard* (Pl. 125), which was later etched with the descriptive title *Entre les deux mon cœur balance*,[76] and a third, *The Gallery of H.M.S. Calcutta* (Pl. 124) of 1877 is Tissot's last known treatment of the theme. Perhaps the central problem posed by these pictures for the viewers of the seventies was their feeling of cynical freedom from the unpleasant consequences of morality. As Tissot had isolated the sentimental subject of *Les Adieux* from the historical reference and wider human significance of Millais's *Huguenot*, divorcing it to his cost from the realm of *high* art, he also removed the moral dilemma of Horsley's *Showing a Preference* from its obvious social and emotional consequences. *Punch* had found that 'Mr. Horsley's naval lieutenant (H.M.S. Trifler) is showing a preference in a

[74] 'The Gay Grosvenor Gallery Guide (A Personally Conducted Tour Through the Collection of Curiosities)', *Punch* (21 June 1879), 286.

[75] 'The Royal Academy', *Spectator* (27 May 1876), 682; 'The Royal Academy', *Athenaeum* (13 May 1876), 670: 'The Royal Academy', *The Times*, 29 May 1875, p. 6; 'Exhibition of The Royal Academy', *Graphic* (13 May 1876), 471.

[76] It would not be surprising if *Portsmouth Dockyard*, which uses the costumes, props, and compositional devices of the nautical pictures of the early seventies, proved to be contemporary with them. For the etching, see Wentworth, *Catalogue Raisonné of Prints*, no. 30.

very indiscreet and decided manner. The very poppies hang their heads in shame', but one doubts that Tissot intended what the *Illustrated London News* called 'the mud-stained, tormented water reflecting a sky almost as sullied' of *The Thames* to make a similar iconographic comment.[77] It has been said that if the curtain were to rise after the last act of a comedy, we should see a tragedy, and a picture like Philip Hermogenes Calderon's *Broken Vows* (1857; Tate Gallery, London), in which a disappointed young woman overhears her future husband flirting with another, must have suggested itself as the pendant to *Showing a Preference* as it could not to *The Thames*:

> Love that hath us in the net,
> Can he pass, and we forget?
> Many suns arise and set;
> Many a chance the years beget;
> Love the gift is Love the debt,
> Even so.[78]

Seen in this light, the light by which the English viewed their pictures, *The Thames* must have appeared as a shocking caricature of morality and affection as much as an indecorous spectacle. If today the lobster and champagne of *The Thames* appear a good deal less objectionable, and the battle of the sexes has taken on a witty naval metaphor by its setting, it clearly struck a nerve in its own time. Young ladies of good family did not coast unchaperoned about the Pool with complacent officers, but they did frequent Burlington House and were able to characterize the 'undeniably Parisian ladies' Tissot depicted with shocked precision.

Even when Tissot depicted settings in which well-bred people might conceivably find themselves, the English had great difficulty in recognizing his caricatures in flashy clothes as accurate representations of their physical appearance, their manners, or their spirit. Discussing *The Ball on Shipboard* (Pl. 102), the *Athenaeum* could find 'no pretty women, but a set of showy than elegant costumes, some few graceful, but more ungraceful attitudes, and not a lady in a score of female figures'.[79] There is now a tendency to think of Tissot as the perfect recorder of Victorian social life. His perfection is retrospective: to his contemporaries, he was more a foreign exoticism than a flawless glass, was thought satirical and vulgar, and altogether too chic. Where the *Athenaeum* could find 'not a lady in a score of female figures', a later generation would decide that *The Ball on Shipboard* represented a dance on board the Royal Yacht at Cowes during the state visit of the Czar in 1873.[80]

---

[77] Quoted in J. Maas, *Victorian Painters*, p. 232.
[78] Alfred, Lord Tennyson, 'The Miller's Daughter' (1833, revised 1842), ll. 203–8.
[79] 'The Royal Academy', *Athenaeum* (30 May 1874, 738.

[80] S. Sitwell, *Narrative Pictures*, pp. 92–3. Sitwell offers a valuable summary of early twentieth-century attitudes towards the picture.

If Whistler's work had been the immediate inspiration for Tissot's Thames pictures, he soon moved away from his model and began to cast the subject in more personal terms, expanding its narrative possibilities and giving it the *odore di femmina* which was always the essential basis of his aesthetic. Tissot had begun to paint the Pool and the industrial suburbs below London immediately after he arrived in England, and if his canvases with a background of the shipping form the most important group of pictures from this time, he also experimented with other subjects which are no less indicative of his search for English subjects and his response to English life. Just as he painted at Greenwich and the Pool, he also turned to the quiet upper reaches of the Thames for inspiration, and a few pictures recording the autumnal stillness of the river around Oxford and Henley must have been painted in September or October of his first year in England.

On the Thames, a Heron (Pl. 90)[81] looks to the particularly English genre of the illustrated magazines for its subject and perhaps even its treatment and title. Numerous pages of the *Graphic* and the *Illustrated London News* are devoted to such English pastoral subjects in which sentiment is balanced by level factualism and great compositional originality. Young girls, often in contrasting pairs of keepsake beauty, gather violets and ferns, picnic, or linger in the autumn woods with melancholy pleasure, in engravings with titles of descriptive or topographical rather than sentimental reference.

The hushed and almost mystical rapture which Millais had brought to the evocation of nature and the changing season in a work like *Autumn Leaves* (Pl. 91) might be described as quintessentially English, what Claretie found to be the entirely individual English way of seeing, feeling, and rendering nature, and much of its quality is to be found in the often remarkably poetic evocations of the illustrated magazines (Pl. 92). Like the best of them, *On the Thames, a Heron* has something of this magical distillation of still mood and reverence for nature.

It was at this time that Tissot began to make consistent use of weather and season to give depth to his narratives. As the conventions of English narrative painting gave flexibility and range to his approach, they also gave direction and refinement to his dramatic technique. His use of such devices in France had been inconsistent, but after his arrival in England they became essential and remarkably effective elements of his narrative. Setting, weather, and season are made harmonious with psychological states and heighten dramatic intent, giving energy to the central image as they continually redirect attention to it. Everything now describes aspects and emotions, heightens and activates feeling.

---

[81] See also M. Wentworth, 'Tissot's "On the Thames, a Heron"', *Minneapolis Institute of Arts Bulletin*, pp. 35–49. The picture may be related to the unlocated *Waiting*, exhibited at the Royal Academy, 1874, no. 387, described as 'autumn leaves overhanging a figure of a young lady waiting in a boat' ('The Royal Academy', *Art Journal* (July 1874), 200) and as a young lady 'looking out for her "oars," yoke-lines in hand' (*The Times*, 26 May 1874, p. 6).

On the Thames, a Heron is as remarkable for its composition as it is for its hushed narrative, and suggests a clear debt to Japanese art in its daring juxtaposition of pictorial elements, shallow field, and high vantage point. Tissot's superficial *japonisme* of the sixties begins to take on depth through a growing understanding of the principles of Japanese design. The comprehension demonstrated by the *Jeune Femme en bateau* (Pl. 67) a year or two earlier is made clear in the sophisticated design of early London pictures like *The Thames* (Pl. 75) or *On the Thames, a Heron*.

Autumn on the Thames (Nuneham Courtney) (Pl. 93)[82] is similar in its narrative and also suggests a debt to Japanese art, calling to mind the bold design of Harunobo's *A Windy Day by the River* (Pl. 94). Or is it perhaps a debt to some English illustrator? Sidney Hall's *The Autumn Campaign* (Pl. 95) offers an equally attractive prototype. With its 'bird's eye' point of view and superb windblown young woman, surely one of Tissot's most beautiful figures, it reads with equal conviction as an image of the *ukiyo-e* or the illustrator's factual modern poetry.

In a related genre, Tissot also looked to what might be called the English Amazon for a subject. She appears in all her glory in *At the Rifle Range* (Pl. 96),[83] the ancestress of the self-possessed and larger-than-life heroines Tissot favoured for the drama of pictures like *The Letter* (Pl. 114) and sister to scores of sporting ladies in the illustrated magazines.[84]

Other subjects and themes introduced at this time were to be of a more pervasive importance. Travel appeared with a deceptive blandness in *Waiting for the Train (Willesden Junction)* (Pl. 98), the first of a long series of increasingly personal statements Tissot was to make of one of his favourite themes in the seventies. 'The course of true love' found its place in Tissot's iconography at this time, and it never did run smooth as he turned to the aspects of romance which offered opportunities for psychological complication. As *Les Adieux* had made physical separation tangible in the fence separating the two lovers, *Quarrelling* (Pl. 97) makes psychological disjunction tangible in the column which separates the petulant couple. If it duplicates something of the approach of the early

---

[82] The location is identified in Thomson, 'Tissot and Oxford', pp. 55–6.

[83] This picture, which has been assumed to date from after Tissot had taken up residence in London, was actually painted before the war, for the date *69* appears clearly beneath his signature in the photograph preserved in his albums. Since the setting was also used for *Les Adieux* (pl. 76) of 1871, it has been thought to represent the garden of his now-demolished house in Springfield Road, but given the date it seems almost certain that it is actually the garden of Bowles's house in Queen's Gate, where Tissot stayed while in London to paint Frederick Burnaby (pl. 71) and draw his *Vanity Fair* subjects

in 1869–70. The seated man partially hidden by the woman with a gun may be a portrait of Bowles, and the pastime—perhaps the first of Tissot's 'English' subjects—is one which he is known to have enjoyed. A drawing for the figure of the woman with a gun is known (private collection, London).

[84] See, for example, illustrations like *Ladies Golf* (7 June 1872, p. 540) and *An American Ten-Pin Alley: A Ladies' Game* (19 October 1872, p. 356) in the *Graphic*; or *Archery* (24 August 1872, pp. 176–7) and *The Last Croquet Game of the Season* (28 September 1872, p. 300; pl. 87) in the *Illustrated London News*.

Promenade dans la neige (Pl. 1), it does so without resorting to literary allusion, and it looks forward to the even more theatrical rendering of later quarrels in which disagreements are equated with passing storms and summer showers (Pl. 115).

Tissot also turned to illness as a subject. Like the Pre-Raphaelites, and surely influenced by them, he now began to associate sickness and passion in his narratives, and the spent victims of a disease which burns inwardly become the protagonists of some of his most compelling 'English' pictures. In these works, illness binds the seemingly contradictory attributes of a dematerialized spirituality which rejects appetite and a heightened sensual presence which celebrates it: the unfocused yearning and brooding eroticism of *A Girl in an Armchair* (Pl. 99) may well be but a variation on the theme of *The White Girl,* or the ripe, unnaturally vivid beauty of Elizabeth Siddall, but it strikes its ambiguous emotional chord with a sureness of touch worthy of Whistler or Rossetti. The baleful sentiment of *A Girl in an Armchair* makes it clear from the start that in Tissot's 'English' narratives, illnesses not physical may well prove fatal. Like Millais' *Mariana* (1851; Makins Collection), illustrating the poem by Tennyson, she is beyond the doctor's physic:

> She only said, 'My life is dreary,
>   He cometh not,' she said;
> She said, 'I am aweary, aweary,
>   I would that I were dead.'

So too the pathetically frail young woman in *A Morning Ride* (Pl. 100) as she reaches out for what is surely the last time to touch a rhododendron flower at some English spa, although the anxious gentleman in attendance suggests the fatally dilatory Armand Duval of *La Dame aux camélias* or the hero of William Lindsay Windus's *Too Late* (1859; Tate Gallery, London), illustrating Tennyson's 'Come Not, When I Am Dead', rather than simple unrequited love or an ordinary jilt:

> '. . . if it were thy error or thy crime
>   I care no longer being all unblest;
> Wed whom thou wilt, for I am sick of time:
>   And I desire to rest.'[85]

Sickness also supplied a plot for the important *A Convalescent* (Pl. 113) at the Royal Academy in 1876, but Tissot no longer attempts to storm the heights of Pre-Raphaelite feeling, and the piercing emotion of *A Morning Ride* gives way to a sentimental comedy of manners which matches the polished tone of his social conversation pieces to perfection. If the subject is now treated with mild irony and considerable wit, Tissot continues to rely on the unfailing charm of a heroine

---

[85] Alfred, Lord Tennyson, 'Mariana' (1830), ll. 9–12; 'Come Not, When I Am Dead' (1835) ll. 7–10.

for whom disease is only love transformed. Later, illness slips over into actual bereavement in *The Widower* and *Orphan* (Pls. 122 and 138), but the most touching of all these works are those sad documents which record the harsh reality of Kathleen Newton's suffering with a human directness and compassion which makes the literary conventions of earlier pictures appear theatrical and shallow (Pls. 171 and 172).

Although it may not have been immediately obvious at the time, Tissot's third picture at the Academy of 1873 signalled a clear change in the subject and narrative approach of his work. *Too Early* (Pl. 101) is the first of his canvases devoted to the unvarnished depiction of the pleasures of the rich. Offered seemingly at face value, without narrative implication or moral comment to mar the perfect reflection of its glittering trivialities, *Too Early* appears to have attracted less critical attention than either *The Captain's Daughter* or *The Last Evening* (Pls. 81 and 84), perhaps because its narrative approach was less clear-cut or appealing than that of its companion pictures, but it made a great popular impression and irrevocably identified Tissot as a painter of 'vulgar society', a genre which began to attract a number of painters at this time. Many years later, Louise Jopling still remembered the 'great sensation' *Too Early* had made at the Academy, describing its 'witty representation of modern life' as 'a new departure in modern art'.[86]

The *Art Journal* thought it realized with an 'extraordinary skill and power', which it attributed to Tissot's French training, and the *Graphic* found 'no more humorous yet strictly truthful picture' in the exhibition. But for the first time, the words *caricature* and *vulgarity* were used in considering Tissot's work. The *Spectator* found that *Too Early* failed at what it admitted was the perhaps impossible task of depicting 'the spirit of modern society' with 'genuine humour in the good old English sense of the word' without falling into caricature or vulgarity, although the picture was undeniably 'amusing and well-painted'.[87]

As might be expected, Tissot's 'new departure in modern art' was not without precedents. The 'witty representation' of English social life had a long and vigorous tradition among native caricaturists and painters, taking on real aesthetic importance in the hands of a master like Hogarth, and it is not without interest that Tissot cast these social conversation pieces in a traditional comic mould which gives them an immediately recognizable context to serve as a foil for their novelty and chic.

The subjects and narrative approach of his social conversation pieces were already familiar to the readers of the illustrated magazines. It may be coincidental that the *Illustrated London News* had offered its readers the subject of *Too Early*

[86] Jopling, *Twenty Years*, pp. 60–1.
[87] 'Exhibition of the Royal Academy', *Art Journal* (August 1873), 238; 'The Royal Academy', *Graphic* (7 June 1873), 539; 'The Royal Academy', *Spectator* (17 May 1873), 638.

the previous year in Frederick Barnard's *The First to Come*,[88] a satirical drawing in which an embarrassed young man is set adrift in a drawing-room by a daunting butler, but the illustrated magazines were full of engravings reporting functions at court and in society which make it clear that Tissot was quite familiar with their compositional devices and narrative approach.

Warming description with a faint anecdotal colour and pointedly avoiding the *scène à faire*, illustrations like *Preparing to Enter Her Majesty's Presence*, reporting a Drawing Room but showing the débutantes adjusting their trains in an ante-room rather than the actual presentation, or *Ascot Races: Luncheon Time Behind the Grand Stand*,[89] set well away from the event it ostensibly describes, offer obvious parallels to Tissot's narrative approach, and must have strongly re-inforced his inherent love of oblique narrative. In the same way, an illustration like *Her Majesty's State Concert at Buckingham Palace* (Pl. 104)[90] can be taken as representative of the compositional devices which lie in the immediate back-ground of a picture like *Hush!* (Pl. 103).

If the subjects of Tissot's social conversation pieces were widely known, his ready acceptance of the genre—amusing enough in the illustrated magazines but hardly thought suitable to the dignity of canvas[91]—can only be traced to his familiarity with advanced trends in French painting. Although they are tran-scriptions of the illustrator's subjects and approach, their transference to canvas and their appearance on the walls of the Academy is the result of Tissot's position between French and English painting. His social conversation pieces are as much the spiritual descendents of a picture like Manet's *La Musique dans le jardin des Tuileries* (Pl. 105) as they are reflections of English illustration, and it is only in reference to such French works that his essential purpose is made clear.

The French aesthetic of these pictures was noticed by the *Art Journal*, which with unusual perception related *The Ball on Shipboard* to French painting:

If we look for the source of this movement we shall find it, not as some suppose in the prin-ciples of what was once called Pre-Raphaelitism, but in the general and well accepted ideal of a certain section of contemporary French painters. In the galleries of the *Salon* we meet with a

---

[88]   21 December 1872, p. 534. The depictions of society published in *Punch* and the *Illustrated London News* by the now too little-known artist and illustrator Frederick Barnard (1846–96), a pupil of Bonnat in Paris, offer numerous clear prototypes for Tissot's social conversation pieces. An engraving like *Supper Time* (*Illustrated London News*, 27 April 1872, double-page supplement), for example, could easily have served as the inspiration for Tissot's *Hush!*, which is remarkably close in both its composition and approach. Barnard's *Crowd Before the Guards' Band, St. James's Park* was compared to

Tissot's *Ball on Shipboard* at the Royal Academy of 1874 by the *Art Journal* (August 1874), 228.
[89]   *Graphic* (30 May 1874), 524–5; *Illustrated London News* (15 June 1872), 572–3.
[90]   *Graphic* (1 July 1871), 12–13.
[91]   *The Times*, 1 May 1877, p. 10, for example, found the subject of Tissot's unlocated *Summer* 'more appropriate to the wood block than the canvas' in its depiction of contemporary manners, in a review of his work at the Grosvenor Gallery Exhibition.

number of these transcripts of modern life, wherein the chief endeavour is to mark exactly the changing facts of costume and the slight and subtle manifestations of various social distinctions.[92]

As such, Tissot's social conversation pieces seem balanced between his essentially French aesthetic outlook and his desire to satisfy English taste for narrative, and it is this hybrid quality which gives them their unique distinction. Of the three, *Too Early* achieved near-perfect balance and great popularity; *The Ball on Shipboard* proved too opaque in its meaning, too French in its purely visual approach, and did not achieve the same success; while *Hush!* went in the opposite direction and took on too obvious a hint of caricature and satire in its attempt to reproduce the charm which had distinguished *Too Early*. These 'mere coloured photographs of vulgar society' are the first clear statement of the conflict between Tissot's aesthetic and an English insistence on intelligible meaning which would effectively destroy his English career.

The success of *Too Early* was probably responsible for Tissot's repetition of the formula in *The Ball on Shipboard* (Pl. 102)[93] at the Academy the next year, but with its impenetrable narrative and steely hardness it failed to please. The *Athenaeum* regretted that he had not made the most of the splendid opportunity offered by his subject, although the picture had 'considerable merit' and 'a certain charm in its piquancy', and it was generally felt that his approach to colour and pictorial values had become disagreeably excessive. The *Illustrated London News* found that the picture was conceived in black and white, and said that however gay the 'superadded tinting', it could 'hardly be regarded as "colour" in the higher artistic sense'. They also felt that Tissot had no perception of relative pictorial values, painting 'a ship's rigging with as much mechanical precision and zest as a young lady's countenance', and found that although the picture was clever in its perspective and elaboration of detail, it was 'garish and almost repellent' in its effect.[94]

In terms of colour, *The Ball on Shipboard* represents Tissot's most extreme attempt to raise the tone of his painting to English standards and to gain control of a problem which had troubled him since the beginning of his career. The *Illustrated London News* found it 'strange to find a foreigner painting in a still brighter key than the highest "exhibition pitch" of our native artists, to the entire neglect of tone and "keeping" which usually distinguishes Continental from British pictures'.[95] Ten years earlier, Thoré had pointed out that the true qualities of the colourist lay in the relationship of one tone to another and not in the hard rendering of local colour, but it was a lesson Tissot had still failed to learn. His interest in aerial perspective is intermittent at best, and in combination with a

[92] 'The Royal Academy', *Art Journal* (August 1874), 228.

[93] Royal Academy of 1874, no. 690.

[94] 'Fine Arts Exhibition of the Royal Academy', *Illustrated London News* (16 May 1874), 470.

[95] Ibid.

growing relish for brilliant colour it gives a picture like *The Ball on Shipboard* an arbitrary tone far removed from the realistic—what was then called the 'truthful'—colour of *Too Early*. What little attempt there is to bring tone into harmony comes through the use of a coloured atmosphere, the green tint of the sea, as in the early *Les Deux Sœurs* (Pl. 29), and, as with that picture, it gives *The Ball on Shipboard* a cold and watery light.

In all three social conversation pictures, composition focuses on a brilliant use of empty space to set off complex figure groups and to balance asymmetrical design. Whether one is to discover the lesson of the Japanese print, the illustrated magazine, or knowledge of pictures by Degas and Manet, remains an open question, but Tissot's approach is remarkably sophisticated in comparison with that of his English peers at the Academy. If *Too Early* has a tentative quality about it and the figure groups are not quite sufficient to activate the empty space around them—Tissot in this instance using empty space with far less effect than Orchardson later achieved in similar compositions like *The First Cloud* (1887; Tate Gallery, London)—*The Ball on Shipboard* and *Hush!*, essentially the same picture in terms of composition, are remarkably effective in their spatial disposition. *The Ball on Shipboard* does so with crisper effect and avoids a fussiness which makes the design of *Hush!* somewhat confusing, but in both pictures the figures pull to the edges of the composition, leaving a neutral void and displaying once again Tissot's marked taste for cutting form at its edges. They suggest the extremes of much of his later work, looking forward to the compositional devices of pictures from the end of the decade like *Good-bye, On the Mersey* (Pl. 147).

The Ball on Shipboard is the most formally ambitious and artistically important of Tissot's English pictures. It shows him at his most sophisticated as a creator of evocative imagery and at his most successful in the resolution of widely disparate sources. It is probably the most beautiful of his English works and shows him at the height of his artistic power in its complexity of design and brilliance of execution. It is also the most entirely personal of his English works in its neurotic intensity, and the sharp flavour of its individuality is unmistakable. Like all of his best work, it is a series of clever paradoxes which are resolved in great part by the very force of their contradiction. Neither sentimental narrative nor facetious anecdote finds a place in its stunning compilation of dresses, but the very accuracy of its descriptiveness demands the narrative its hard neutrality rebuffs. Painted with unblinking concentration and absolute conviction, it has all the impenetrability of a polished glass. Cold and acid in its vivid colour, it creates an effect at once garish and yet magically colourless. Its composition is boldly informal, but for once informality is the result of a formal structure only too rare in his work. Wilfully cold and antipathetic in its approach, and eccentric in every detail, *The Ball on Shipboard* surely stands alone among the minor masterpieces of the nineteenth century.

Much the same can be said of *London Visitors* (Pl. 106)[96] which was seen with it at the Academy in 1874, where its lack of meaning and frigid atmosphere made it as unpopular as its companion. The *Art Journal* was not alone when it regretted a want of 'distinct and intelligible meaning' which deprived it of 'the higher distinction of pictorial grace'; and without narrative to extract, criticism fell back on character assassination: the *Illustrated London News* thought the couple 'good-looking but singularly uninteresting', the *Art Journal* was sure they were Scotch, the *Athenaeum* thought the lady sneering and the blue-coat boy foolish. The *Athenaeum* also found the architecture preposterous, the colour vile, and the atmosphere dirty, sentiments echoed by the *Illustrated London News*, which found the 'arctic frigidity' of the picture even more disagreeable than the garishness of *The Ball on Shipboard*. *The Times* alone seems to have fathomed something of Tissot's intention, finding the execution 'very clean and clear', and discovering some beauty in the Whistlerian harmonies of grey and brown, although it thought the atmosphere to be hard and dry.[97] *London Visitors* is in fact one of Tissot's most successful pictures. Daring in composition, refined in colour, and subtle in psychological implication, it must rank among the handful of his master-pieces. It is a considerably larger picture than he usually attempted, but its size contributes to its effectiveness. Its firm execution activates the entire surface with a glassy perfection, and its scale, resulting in the protagonists appearing above eye level, gives it great dramatic effectiveness.

At the Academy the next year, *Hush!* (Pl. 103)[98] made an obvious attempt to conciliate the public with intelligible meaning and a technical approach less determinedly eccentric, and it was rewarded with a popularity equal to that of *Too Early* in 1873. Everyone attempted to identify the personages depicted ('Shall we call her Neruda?' asked *The Times* of the lady violinist[99]), and for once with real justification, for Tissot quite probably included a number of portraits in order to avoid the glacial impersonality of *The Ball on Shipboard*:

[96] Royal Academy of 1874, no. 116. There is a replica of the painting, reduced in size and with minor variations, in the Layton Art Gallery, Milwaukee, Wisconsin. The setting was used for the etching of 1878, *London Visitors*, which omits the two figures on the left and includes Kathleen Newton in the left foreground; see Wentworth, *Catalogue Raisonné of Prints*, no. 40, which also reproduces the Layton Art Gallery version.

[97] 'The Royal Academy', *Art Journal* (June 1874), 163; 'Exhibition of the Royal Academy', *Illustrated London News* (16 May 1874), 470; 'The Royal Academy', *Athenaeum* (30 May 1874), 738; and 'The Royal Academy', *The Times*, 2 May 1874, p. 12.

[98] Royal Academy of 1875, no. 1233.

[99] 'The Royal Academy', *The Times*, 29 May 1875, p. 6. Perhaps the earliest attempt to identify various sitters is to be found in C. Yriarte, 'Exhibition of the Royal Academy of Arts II', *L'Art*, p. 255, but Laver's assertion in *Vulgar Society* (pp. 33–4), on the basis of information supplied by Mrs Frank Pownell, that Tissot was secured an invitation by her mother for a party at the Coopes at which Neruda played, but that not having permission to take portraits, 'most of the people are just types', is surely correct. The exception would seem to be the portraits of friends like de Nittis and Heilbuth (standing in the doorway) which Tissot included for his own amusement. *Hush!* was bought by Agnew directly from the walls of the Academy for 1,200 guineas (Laver, *Vulgar Society*, p. 33).

Many of the portraits will be recognized by persons 'in society,' and possibly with pleasure by the ill-natured; for if there is not a tendency to caricature, something smacking, as it were, of a Gallic sneer runs throughout. But polite people will, of course, be thankful to see themselves as a polished Frenchman sees them.[100]

'What fun!', the Marlborough House set must have said, finding delightfully wicked caricatures of friends on the walls of the Academy, for evidently even ridicule was a small price to pay for the comfort of intelligible meaning. The success of *Hush!* at the Academy was clearly dependent on what Charles Yriarte described for his French readers as 'le vif de la société anglaise',[101] and English society was quite willing to take the picture as a Gallic compliment to its own taste and importance without pondering any possible double meaning. Although Yriarte considered the picture at length in terms of its *modernité*, such philosophical and aesthetic overtones escaped English viewers, who read it exclusively in terms of narrative, likeness, and suspected satire. Since *Hush!* is the most seemingly documentary of Tissot's social conversation pictures, it raises the question of caricature and satire in them with the most insistence, but it is a question which still cannot be answered. Balanced between non-commital description, the 'exotic' view of national character common to foreigners, and unconscious exaggeration, if not purposeful caricature, *Hush!* remains as maddeningly inscrutable in its purpose as it was a hundred years ago.

The picture was less remarkable technically than those which preceded it. The accomplished sheen of *The Ball on Shipboard* gives way to a laboured accuracy which only occasionally equals the brilliant execution of its immediate predecessors, and its colour is at once less integrated and strikingly personal. The *Graphic* voiced the general regret that a subject 'so deserving of applause' had not been honoured with workmanship of a less sketchy sort, and remarked the unpleasantness of effect which resulted from an excessive use of white.[102]

Hush! is the first of Tissot's major exhibition pictures to move away from the meticulous rendering of detail in a smooth, waxen pigment which had characterized his early pictures—culminating in the finish of a work like *The Ball on Shipboard*—towards the drier pigment, relief textures, and somewhat more painterly approach of his later work. Although the short, square brush-strokes laid in parallel patterns which follow and define form had been a feature of his work almost from the beginning, they now begin to take on an independent existence and often create textural patterns which underlie entire surfaces without reference to composition. In *Hush!*, Tissot stands half-way between the smoothly

[100] 'Royal Academy Exhibition', *Illustrated London News* (22 May 1875), 486.
[101] Yriarte, 'Exhibition of the Royal Academy of Arts III', *L'Art*, 255.
[102] 'The Royal Academy', *Graphic* (8 May 1875), 447.

controlled *facture* of the school of Ingres and the dry, broken surfaces which carry his late pictures into the world of the Post-Impressionists.

With *Hush!*, Tissot also exhibited *The Bunch of Lilacs* (Pl. 107),[103] a keepsake which offered the chic of the social conversation pictures on a domestic scale. A *tour de force* of polished reflections, subtle textures, and tender finish, it is a last ravishing exercise in the untroubled manner of Alfred Stevens. Painted in the winter garden of Tissot's house in Grove End Road, it suggests that the collector as well as the artist was still enamoured of Japanese art, and if it looks backward in its mood and its combination of elements (see Pls. 47 and 56), it is also a clear predecessor of important works like *Rivals* (Pl. 159) whose tropical settings were to be praised for their technical brilliance at the end of the decade.

As might be expected, most of the canvases Tissot painted at this time can be related to his Academy pictures, and each group suggests another of those *appassionnements* by which his career progressed. *Reading the News* (Pl. 108) retains something of the narrative suggestiveness of the pictures which preceded it, but its insistent modishness as well as the young woman's costume relate it to the abstract social splendours of *The Ball on Shipboard*. As a Royal Hospital pensioner reads the newspaper, the black and white dress which appears twice at the centre of the *Ball* is studied at leisure. The subject is one which Tissot found attractive enough to repeat in *A Quiet Afternoon* (Pl. 144).

The costumes of a picture like *Still on Top* (Pl. 109)[104] are familiar from a number of Thames pictures (see Pl. 88), and it is not unlikely that their heraldic brilliance suggested the ingenious setting of *The Ball on Shipboard* itself. Flags and a holiday spirit also pervade a picture of a somewhat later date which is now called *A Fête Day at Brighton* (Pl. 110). The setting of *Waiting for the Ferry* (Pl. 111) likewise relates it to earlier pictures (see Pls. 81 and 82), but again its fashion-plate emphasis as well as its costume suggest that it is contemporary with *The Ball on Shipboard*. The young woman who posed with such superb grace for the central figure was clearly herself something of an *appassionnement* at this time, and her haughty elegance also adds to the chill perfection of pictures like *The Ball on Shipboard* and *London Visitors*.

Tissot's standing as a portrait painter in England, or possibly the memory of his standing in France, was confirmed at this time by what is probably the most historically significant of his pictures, *The Empress Eugénie and the Prince Impérial in the Uniform of a Woolwich Cadet in the Grounds of Camden Place, Chisleburst* (Pl. 112). Commissioned either to mark the majority of the Prince Impérial in March, 1874, or his passing out of Woolwich at the end of the year,[105]

---

[103] Royal Academy of 1875, no. 48.

[104] The three figures and the setting are repeated in *Preparing for the Gala* (exhibited, Sheffield, *Tissot*, no. 35).

[105] 'M. Tissot is painting portraits of the Empress Eugénie and of Prince Louis Napoleon in his Woolwich uniform' ('Fine Arts', *Illustrated London News* (19 December 1874), 590).

this diminutive state portrait is of engrossing iconographical and social interest in its tactful search for the proper approach to the portrayal of a family of importance in reduced circumstances, and its real human warmth and sympathy are perhaps the best denial of anti-Bonapartist feelings on Tissot's part one could ask. In the tender, passive figure of the Empress he captures better than most the elusive beauty and the incomparable grace so often remarked in the memoirs of her contemporaries but so seldom caught in her portraits, and her appropriate gesture, at once maternal and deferential, focuses attention on the figure of the Prince, whose physical shortcomings are minimized and even given a touch of style, if not quite command, by his optimistic stance.

For sitters of the highest station in the nineteenth century, the conversation piece often took on the function of the state portrait of earlier centuries. The most attractive of Winterhalter's state portraits combine baroque *grandezza* with nineteenth-century domestic virtue, and Tissot's portrait of the exiled Bonapartes has more than a little of the manner Winterhalter had perfected in his portraits of Queen Victoria and her family, in which a life of exemplary dullness takes place amid the trappings of power. The lawn at Camden Place, furnished like a drawing-room with a Turkish carpet, a coaching table, and unpretentious wicker furniture, is indicative of more than the taste for fresh air and bourgeoise comfort endemic among nineteenth-century princes: reminiscent of life at Windsor, it has an indisputable air of legitimacy. In the background, the shadowy figures of the Imperial Household linger like the last leaves on the trees, the pathetic yet comforting regalia of exile, ghosts of what had recently been the most brilliant court in Europe. The choice of season itself suggests symbolic if not political significance, and like the bouquet of violets, doubtless gave bitter-sweet pleasure to the Empress, who was both realistic and histrionic by temperament.

The Royal Academy of 1876 saw the disaster of *The Thames* (Pl. 115), and did lasting damage to his reputation. *A Convalescent* (Pl. 113)[106] fared better, although a now predictable appreciation of its listlessly sentimental narrative was more or less lost in the storm of abuse which greeted *The Thames*. While its narrative relates it to earlier pictures, a new integration of narrative and visual means looks forward to the boldly stated themes of pictures like *A Passing Storm* and *Holyday* (Pls. 116 and 123). Setting now becomes the clear visual metaphor for narrative, and a work like *A Convalescent* gains considerably in authority from the simplicity of its statement. Set in the garden of Tissot's house in Grove End Road, it is not impossible that its new integration of means owes something to the portrait of the Empress Eugénie and the Prince Impérial, to which it bears an unlikely resemblance, transforming that picture's evocative reality into a scene

---

[106] Royal Academy of 1876, no. 530. An incomplete etching of the figure of the convalescent dated 1875 is known (see Wentworth, *Catalogue Raisonné of Prints*, no. 6).

from a romantic comedy where a hat on a chair and the anxiety of an old lady are hardly less suggestive in their conviction than the documentation of historical reality itself.

Tissot also sent two etchings to the Academy in 1876, reproductions of *Quarrelling* and *The Thames* (Pls. 97 and 115).[107] After a few tentative experiments with the medium as a student in the early sixties (see Pl. 23), Tissot lost interest in etching for ten years before taking it up again in 1875, probably inspired by Whistler and guided by Seymour Haden. Mastering the technique with astonishing ease, it became a major preoccupation and resulted in a graphic *œuvre* of eighty-eight plates, the majority of which reproduce his paintings and date from his English years. Tissot always exhibited his etchings as widely as possible, and he clearly considered them an important part of his work if not an essential supplement to his income.[108]

With his popularity at *Vanity Fair*, his standing as a portrait painter, and the fame of his carefully tailored narrative pictures, Tissot's success in London had been immediate. By the time of the International Exhibition and the Academy of 1872, he had been able to leave Bowles in Queen's Gate for a semi-detached villa at 73, Springfield Road, St. John's Wood—then a popular residential area for successful artists and kept women—and by the spring of the next year he had bought a Regency house in the Dutch style nearby at 17, Grove End Road. Tissot kept the house until he left England, and made many improvements to it, adding a ship's window for use in his paintings to the studio, and a winter garden and a pool with a colonnade reminiscent of one in the Parc Monceau to the grounds.[109]

As word of Tissot's quick financial recovery and easily won artistic reputation filtered back to Paris, there was a flurry of surprise not unmixed with resentment, which suggests that the luxuries dispensed in the house in the avenue de l'Impératrice may have been a trifle ostentatious. Degas, who had visited Tissot briefly in London in the autumn of 1871 and evidently remembered him as a refugee living with Bowles or only recently in Springfield Road, was perhaps not entirely pleased to hear that Tissot had acquired another large house: 'I hear you've bought a house. My mouth is still open.'[110]

By 1874, Tissot was once again a considerable success, and when Degas wrote

[107] Royal Academy of 1876, nos. 1098 and 1156; see Wentworth, *Catalogue Raisonné of Prints*, nos. 20 and 18.

[108] For a stylistic and historical study of Tissot's prints, see Wentworth, *Catalogue Raisonné of Prints*, Introduction, pp. 11–32.

[109] The chronology of Tissot's moves is reflected in the addresses given in the catalogues of the Royal Academy Exhibitions; for his additions and improvements to the house, see Laver, *Vulgar Society*, p. 32. Tissot sold the house to Alma-Tadema after he left England, when it was enlarged and transformed into an Anglo-Roman villa. In the twentieth century, much of the garden was sold off as the site for a block of flats, and the colonnade was pulled down to make room for a garage.

[110] Degas, *Letters*, p. 33.

to invite him to take part in the first Impressionist exhibition, he found it necessary not only to dredge up the Commune and appeal to aesthetic nationalism, but
also to tell him bluntly that there were times when money really should not
come first:

Look here, my dear Tissot, no hesitations, no escape. You positively must exhibit at the Boulevard. It will do you good, you (for it is a means of showing yourself in Paris from which people
said you were running away) and us too. . . . The realist movement no longer needs to fight
with the others, it already is, it *exists*, it must show itself as *something distinct*, there must be a
salon of realists. . . . So forget the money side for a moment. Exhibit. Be of your country and
with your friends.[111]

In this case, Tissot found his friends altogether too compromising and preferred to remain within the sanctified purlieu of the Royal Academy rather than
savour independence with what even the mild Corot called 'the gang in the boulevard des Capucines'.[112]   From Tissot's point of view, his decision surely was the
correct one, for such company would have done little to allay British fears about
his work. Giuseppe de Nittis was more adventuresome and found that the pictures
he sent to the exhibition were indeed tarred with the Impressionist brush, ruefully
noting that while his pictures at the Salon were praised, those in the boulevard were
dismissed for a lack of finish, although they were in fact technically identical.[113]
The road to fame and fortune clearly did not lead through the boulevard des
Capucines.

Tissot had never been considered a painter of the first rank by Parisian critics
in the sixties, and his English success counted for little in France in the seventies.
The fact that it was based on a total modification of his manner to suit English
taste was a matter of suspicion, regret, or amusement, depending on one's point
of view, but it was hardly a matter of surprise. However dubious its quality in
French eyes, however, it was granted grudging recognition by the indisputable
reality of what Yriarte bluntly called 'des preuves *sonnantes*'.[114]

Edmond de Goncourt, familiar with both Tissot and the splendours of the
house in the avenue de l'Impératrice, was not surprised by the news of his success
or his surroundings, and on 3 November 1874 noted in his *Journal*:

Hier, Duplessis me racontait que Tissot, ce peintre plagiare, avait le plus grand succès en
Angleterre. N'a-t-il inventé, cet ingénieux exploiteur de la bêtise anglise, d'avoir un atelier
précédé d'une antichambre, où il se trouve, en tout temps, du champagne frappé à la disposition des visiteurs, et autour de son atelier, un jardin où l'on voit, toute la journée, un
domestique en bas de soie occupé à brosser et à faire reluire les feuilles des arbustes?[115]

[111] Degas, *Letters*, p. 39.
[112] Quoted in J. Rewald, *The History of Impressionism*, p. 314.
[113] Ibid., p. 339, n. 24.

[114] Yriarte, 'Exhibition of the Royal Academy
of Arts II', *L'Art*, 256.
[115] Goncourt, *Journal*, ii, 1001–2.

At the centre of all this was Tissot himself, bandbox fresh and delighting everyone with his finished manner and open hospitality. Louise Jopling found him quite as polished as Goncourt imagined his shrubberies: 'James Tissot was a charming man, very handsome, extraordinarily like the Duke of Teck, or rather the Prince, as was then his title. He was always well groomed, and had nothing of artistic carelessness either in his dress or demeanour'.[116]

In London with her husband in 1875, Berthe Morisot was invited to come and see the wonders in St. John's Wood for herself. She speaks of her visit in a letter to her mother written at the height of an August heatwave:

Il fait atrocement chaud; les nuages sont bas, l'air étouffe; on est comme dans une pièce sans air. Ce matin, j'ai laissé Eugène courir tout seul et je suis restée tranquillement à mon lit où je serais encore si je n'en avais été tirée à l'instant par une lettre de Tissot; une invitation à dîner pour demain soir; il m'a fallu de me lever, bousculer tout pour trouver une feuille de papier intacte et répondre comme je sais répondre; je ne suis pas fâchée de voir quelqu'un; puis cela nous changera de l'ordinaire du boarding. Nous avons déjà été chez lui hier, il est très bien installé et fait de très jolis tableaux. Il vend pour trois cent mille francs à la fois. Comment trouvez-vous le succès de Londres? Il a été très aimable; il m'a fait des compliments, sans avoir jamais rien vu de moi probablement.[117]

Perhaps the dinner was a little trying in the heat, for a well-bred chill belies the compliment in a letter to her sister written soon after:

. . . nous avons été chez Tissot qui fait de très jolies choses qu'il vend fort bien et qui est installé comme un prince; nous y avons dîné; il est très gentil, très bon garçon quoiqu'un peu commun; nous sommes au mieux ensemble, je lui ai fait beaucoup de compliments et vraiment il les mérite.[118]

The diary of Alan S. Cole also suggests the comfortable life of the successful artist, as well as some of Tissot's friendships in the seventies. Although there must have been occasions of more ostentatious social sheen, the small dinners given by Whistler which Cole records must have been among the most stimulating:

November 16 (1875):
Dined with Jimmy; Tissot, A. Moore, and Captain Crabb. Lovely blue and white china and capital small dinner. General conversation and ideas on art, unfettered by principles. Lovely Japanese lacquer.
December 7 (1875):
Dined with Jimmy; Cyril Flower; Tissot; Storey. Talked Balzac.[119]

[116] Jopling, *Twenty Years*, p. 60.
[117] B. Morisot, *Correspondance*, p. 89.
[118] Ibid., p. 88.
[119] The diary of Alan S. Cole, quoted in Pennell, *Whistler*, i, 189. Cole was the son of the Keeper of the South Kensington Museum; Albert Moore was to have an influence on Tissot's pictures at the time of the Grosvenor Gallery exhibitions; Cyril Flower, later Lord Battersea, was a passionate amateur of the arts whose Rothschild wife preferred political to artistic influence and directed him to Parliament (a portrait of him by Sandys of 1872 is repr., Maas, *Victorian Painters*, p. 219); Storey [sic], probably Julian or Waldo Story, sons of the American sculptor William W. Story, who divided their time between London and Rome; Capt. Crabb has not been identified.

Then, once again, things were to change. The Royal Academy Exhibition of 1876 can be seen in retrospect as the end of a clear period in the development of Tissot's career. By the following spring he had switched his allegiance from the Academy to the controversial but socially lustrous Grosvenor Gallery, among the happy few invited to challenge the supremacy of Burlington House from its lavish galleries in Bond Street. At the same time, he flouted social convention and effectively disappeared from society when a divorced lady appeared in Grove End Road to share an illicit but obviously happy domesticity. If anything had been lacking in his success, it was a heroine to share it, and in 1876 she was waiting in the wings.

V. The Earthly Paradise

The earthly paradise is a static vision of humanity. In it life holds its breath, its busy events are stilled. Nothing happens: man is simply there, surrounded by an everlasting present indistinguishable from any past or future. He does not recognize the passing of time and knows neither age, nor decay, nor any seasons. He neither remembers nor looks forward. His is eternal youth, an everlasting existence that has no history.

Werner Hofman, *The Earthly Paradise* (1961).

THE pretty woman who wears her simple clothes with such style in many of Tissot's canvases after 1876 was long the subject of romantic speculation. Tissot recorded her sweet domesticity with an almost neurotic adoration, and even the most casual acquaintance with his work soon makes her modest charm familiar. Entertaining children in the garden in Grove End Road, dreaming on a flight of steps, or reading in a Brazilian hammock, she is the fulfilment of an ideal, the bourgeoise Eve of a nineteenth-century paradise. Long familiar, she was to remain nameless for fifty years after her death, known only as *la mystérieuse*.

Kathleen Newton's absence from the biographical literature published during Tissot's lifetime is understandable, and she makes her first appearance in Thiébault-Sisson's necrology in 1902, where she is called Kitty King, and again in Bastard's biography, now simply as Kitty, where she is tactfully, if erroneously, described as a widow with three children, and is gracefully compared to La Fornarina in her influence on Tissot's art.[1] Both articles make it clear that Mrs Newton's existence was well known at the time, and they have a real degree of accuracy, although it seems likely that Tissot himself had purposefully confused certain facts in order to protect the memory of his dead mistress and put the liaison in a better light.

In the memoirs of the seventies which began to appear in this century, an unidentified and until then forgotten Mrs Newton began to garner romantic legend. Jacques-Émile Blanche told Laver that Tissot had kept his mistress a virtual prisoner in Grove End Road, the nameless sister to scores of kept women hidden in discreet but luxurious obscurity by Victorian men of fashion behind the walls of little villas in St. John's Wood. Only Helleu among Tissot's friends was said to

---

[1] F. Thiébault-Sisson, 'J. James Tissot', *Les Arts*, p. 6; Bastard, p. 263.

have even seen her, and then only by accident when he opened the wrong door in the unfamiliar house. Arnold Bennett recorded the apocryphal story of her suicide after a confusion of letters revealed that Tissot had grown tired of the liaison and planned to leave her. Although it was later established that she had died of consumption rather than by her own hand, rumours of Tissot's guilt (Bennett thought that he regarded himself as her murderer) and remorse (he thought Tissot had become *dévot* as a result) had already displaced fact.[2]

La mystérieuse was identified only in 1946 when a plea for information published by Marita Ross, a London journalist, was answered by Lilian Hervey, Mrs Newton's niece. Miss Hervey's memories should be approached with caution since she was seven when her aunt died and was presumably given a version of her life suitable for a child, but they are of the greatest interest as the only first-hand account of life in Grove End Road apart from Tissot's own paintings. It was from Miss Hervey that Marita Ross obtained the few photographs known today which served Tissot as the basis for paintings and prints in the late seventies (Pls. 120, 161, 164, 165, and 173).[3] More recently, research by David Brooke at the time of the 1968 *Tissot Retrospective Exhibition* has led to an accurate biography of Mrs Newton.

Kathleen Irene Ashburnham Kelly (1854–82), the motherless daughter of Charles Frederick Augustus Ashburnham Kelly, a major in the Indian Army and later Governor of Alderney, was educated in a convent and given in marriage when she was seventeen years old to Isaac Newton, a surgeon in the Indian Civil Service, at Hoshiarput, on 3 January 1871. The marriage had been arranged by her brother, Frederick Kelly, and the bride had been sent out to India for the purpose, but the couple separated almost immediately after the wedding when Mrs Newton confessed an association with, and a continuing preference for, a certain Captain Palliser whom she had met on the ship from England. Divorce proceedings were instituted on the grounds of her adultery in May 1871, and the case was not defended. A decree nisi was granted on 20 December 1871, and made final on 20 July 1872. Mrs Newton returned to England during the latter half of 1871, where a daughter by Captain Palliser, Muriel Mary Violet, was born at her grandfather's house in Coinsborough, Yorkshire, on 20 December 1871. Nothing is known of Mrs Newton's life between 1871 and March 1876, when she registered the birth of another child, Cecil George, imaginatively giving Isaac Newton as the father. The child was born at the house of her elder sister, Mary Hervey, the wife of Augustus Frederick Hervey, a colonel in the Indian Army, at 6, Hill Road, St. John's Wood, not far from Tissot's house, where the two women

---

[2] Laver, *Vulgar Society*, pp. 39–40, records Blanche's remarks, and, pp. 48–9, quotes Bennett's *Journal* concerning the liaison; E. Knoblock, 'The Whimsical Seventies', p. 679, first established the true cause of her death.

[3] M. Ross, 'The Truth About Tissot', *Everybody's Weekly*, pp. 6–7.

had recently moved. It is not certain how or when Tissot and Mrs Newton met or whether he was the father of her son. In any case, Mrs Newton moved into Tissot's house sometime in 1876 and remained there until her death in 1882.[4]

Despite increased factual information, little is known of Kathleen Newton's character. Her few remaining letters, written at the time of the divorce, are romantic, confused, and touching in their *naïveté*: 'I am going to speak to you as if I were standing before God,' she wrote to Isaac Newton of Captain Palliser. 'It is true that I have sinned once, and God knows how I love that one too deeply to sin with any other.'[5] She clearly had second thoughts. Her failure to marry Tissot may have been based on mutual religious conviction, but doubtless they felt 'married in the eyes of God', as Lilian Hervey appears to have been told by her mother. Had Tissot been discreet or callous enough to keep Mrs Newton hidden away in the approved Victorian manner, there would have been little more than knowing looks, but in publicly installing her in his house he challenged convention in a way which could not be ignored. It was all very well to be called Mme Tissot by the servants, but it was without benefit of clergy, and nobody was taken in by it.[6]

As much has been written of Tissot's withdrawal from society as of Mrs Newton's seclusion. Certainly, a great deal of time was spent at home bringing up the children, as a long series of pictures proves, and it is hardly surprising that either took to a settled domesticity with relief after the upheavals of the preceeding years. Nor is it surprising that, its conventions flouted, society withdrew with a shudder from the open irregularity of the curious ménage of a fashionable painter with a mistress and a ready-made nursery of illegitimate children. Tissot ceased to be that desirable social quantity, the 'extra' man, and Mrs Newton

[4] David S. Brooke, 'James Tissot and the "Ravissante Irlandaise"', *Connoisseur*, pp. 55–9. Biographical material on Mrs Newton is based on that article and on his 'Author's Note' in Brooke, Wentworth, Zerner, *Tissot*. Brooke, in 'A Postscript to "La Mystérieuse": A Speculation on Motives and Movements' (unpublished typescript circulated by the author, 1971), has traced the movements of Mrs Newton's children after 1882: Violet (Palliser?), aged 11, and Cecil (Tissot?), aged 6, were brought up with their aunt, Mary Hervey. By 1884, they had left the house at 6, Hill Road, St. John's Wood: Violet was educated in a convent in Belgium, later became a governess in Golders Green, and is thought to have died in the 1940s; Cecil became a captain in the army, and, after making a brief but striking appearance in 1933 at the first Tissot exhibition at the Leicester Gallery, to announce 'that was my mother', disappeared (Laver, *Vulgar Society*, p. 46), and is thought to have died at Worthing about 1941. Both children harboured (or at least professed) mistaken ideas about their parentage which were probably fostered by their mother and aunt. Violet never tried to contact Isaac Newton, but Cecil visited him in 1895. Despite a polite rebuff, he later laid claim to a portion of Dr Newton's estate, although it was quickly disqualified by his birth certificate. Violet, however, motivated by her mistaken belief or pure greed, also laid claim to the estate. She won her case on a legal technicality and was granted a settlement of ten thousand pounds. Both children are said to have occasionally visited Tissot in Paris, and he left them each a thousand francs in his will (Misfeldt, p. 326). Considering the size of the bequest, Tissot may have made some other provision for the children during his lifetime, especially if he was actually Cecil's father.

[5] Quoted in J. Abdy, *Tissot*, no page number, from letters in the possession of Dr and Mrs John Newton.

[6] Lilian Hervey, quoted by Ross, p. 6.

would hardly have been made welcome in the drawing-rooms of Mayfair, or even their less exalted counterparts in St. John's Wood. The couple did what people in their position generally do, and ignoring the rebuffs of society took their pleasure in restaurants and places of public amusement, in travel, at seaside resorts, and in 'their own little literary and artistic circles, in which the absence of a conventional wedding ring made no difference'.[7]

If a veil of romance was drawn over the liaison by later generations, Mrs Newton's position in Tissot's household was clearly common knowledge in the seventies, and it was labelled with the lack of sentiment with which society always judges its errant members. Remarks in *Punch* about the Grove End Road pictures exhibited at the Grosvenor Gallery, referring to their settings as 'Fair Rosamund's Bower-villa, N.W.,' are surely too accurately pointed to be general references, and they echo the more generalized moral indignation of periodicals like the *Spectator*. Far from keeping her a hidden beauty, Tissot flaunted Mrs Newton and the liaison in his pictures, and his continued reference to his domestic arrangements is undoubtedly the source of the moral indignation directed against his pictures at the end of the decade. That a pretty woman of equivocal position and with children of mysterious antecedents was able to enjoy herself in such obvious tranquillity was bad enough, but that the Grosvenor Gallery exhibitions were made the stage for the public display of her happiness was an affront too great to be borne with equanimity.

The central position Mrs Newton occupied in Tissot's life has led to her being given an equal importance in his artistic development. There is certainly a tangible proof-by-number for the assumption, and her appearance marks a clear shift from the chic of the social conversation pieces to subjects of a more intimate but hardly less smart domesticity. Yet to make her into some kind of bluestocking muse is romantic and superficial. That she became the central ornament of Tissot's canvases after 1876 is obvious to even a casual observer: whether she was their inspiration must remain a matter of conjecture. Tissot had begun to shift away from the large-scale depiction of society before they met, and Grove End Road had already provided the setting for essentially domestic pictures like *A Convalescent* (Pl. 113). Elaborate social conversation pieces had been the exception rather than the rule among Tissot's English pictures, and the canvases which now made Mrs Newton the chief ornament of his art hardly represent a break in his subject-matter although she soon gives them a particular flavour of their own.

[7] Ibid. Lilian Hervey told Marita Ross that this circle included Whistler, Oscar and Willie Wilde, Sir Charles Wyndham, and Sir Henry Irving. In 1886, Tissot made his own list in the form of a small plaque in *cloisonné* enamel decorated with the names of friends from his English career: the painters Whistler, Millais, Alma-Tadema, Seymour Haden, George du Maurier, P. R. Morris, R. W. Macbeth, Louise Jopling, and Clara Montalba, the composer-conductor Sir Julius Benedict, the medium William Eglinton, and also the names F. Pils, Robert, and N. Hemy. For the plaque itself, see below, n. 35.

For Tissot, happiness did not prove to be without aesthetic danger. His repetition of Mrs Newton's uneventful beauty strengthened a strong natural tendency towards typification which might not otherwise have become as powerful as it did in his later work. Even at the time, love seems to have made him singularly blind to what character her face possessed. In his pictures she often becomes a stylish cypher as generalized as the heroine of any penny romance, and it is telling that the one known portrait of her from another hand, an oil sketch by de Nittis, shows a less 'absolute' beauty but a good deal more individual character.[8]

The St. John's Wood pictures are the most clearly autobiographical of Tissot's works: a happy existence is recorded without irony, narrative, and often even anecdote. They are also perhaps the most uncomplicated of his images, clothing reality with an order and meaning that compensates for their static vision. Nowhere does Tissot come as close to the philosophy of Impressionism as in these pictures, and a number of them seem to experiment timidly with Impressionist techniques. If Tissot seems to imitate Manet in a sketch like *Mrs. Newton with a Child by a Pool* (Pl. 135), which is not unlike Manet's *The Monet Family in Their Garden at Argenteuil* (1874; whereabouts unknown), the similarity probably springs as much from like impulse as conscious emulation, but the approach was clearly conditioned by Impressionism and differences are more of quality than kind.

Henley Regatta (Pl. 136) suggests what Tissot might have been as an Impressionist. It is unique among his large works both for its freedom of touch and its direct visual approach to its subject. It is also virtually his only landscape. Unlike the Impressionists, Tissot was interested in landscape exclusively as a background for human activity and narrative content. A study of a lake (private collection, London), sketches for a few backgrounds among the Bible illustrations, and one or two studies of the River Loue as it passes through the grounds at Buillon (whereabouts unknown) would seem to complete the short list. *Henley Regatta* is anomalous among Tissot's pictures, but its success demonstrates what he might have done had he found the technique and philosophy of Impressionism more than intermittently attractive.

But Tissot was not an Impressionist, and his aesthetic did not really lend itself to such uncomplicated visions of reality rescued from time, or to a technique which summarized the detail essential to his dramatic construction. For that reason, the St. John's Wood pictures are in many ways his most uninteresting. Lacking a sense of estrangement, neurotic imbalance, and the carefully phrased

---

[8] For a discussion of de Nittis's portrait, which was painted about 1880 during sittings for a portrait by Tissot called *Promenade dans la neige*, see Wentworth, *Catalogue Raisonné of Prints*, no. 48, where both works are reproduced.

vocabulary of his narrative, their attractiveness does not always compensate for the absence of Tissot's greater gifts. It is only when some kind of tension can be felt beneath the untroubled surface that these works are compelling, as in the remarkably effective *Quiet* (Pl. 169), where superficial charm makes no attempt to conceal the far more interesting impatience of Mrs Newton or the bad temper of her bored and overheated daughter, giving the picture an impact far greater than the face of its narrative suggests. At the end of the decade, a sense of estrangement and imbalance returns with a pent-up violence that hints it had been forced underground rather than dissipated. It colours many of the late London pictures and the series *La Femme à Paris* with a force which projects something almost insane.

After the liaison began, Mrs Newton was fitted with facile ease into pictures which employed the subjects Tissot had long favoured, and she appears at the centre of familiar narrative pictures, genre subjects, and 'specimen' portraits which are given fashionably allegorical overtones. If these works are familiar iconographically, there is a marked stylistic development and a new attitude towards subject-matter which transforms them completely by the end of the decade. Nowhere is this continuity and change more clearly seen than in the pictures with nautical backgrounds which occupied him continuously during his English years.

A room overlooking the harbour in Goldsmid Place (now Harbour Parade) at Ramsgate[9] provided the setting for what proved to be among Tissot's most accomplished English pictures. It must have been one of the first to include the figure of Mrs Newton, since the group can be dated to the summer of 1876 or very soon after. *A Passing Storm* (Pl. 115), is contemporary with broadly conceived pictures like *A Convalescent, The Letter*, and *Holyday* (Pls. 113, 114, and 123), and casts Mrs Newton as the actress in a drama which is among Tissot's most compelling in its equation of setting and emotion and its realization of psychological tension in terms of physical separation, vacant looks, and atmospheric conditions. It is a picture which looks back to the very beginning of his career for its definition of wintry emotion in terms of season (Pl. 1); to the most mysterious and evocative of his Parisian genre pictures for its atmosphere (Pl. 52);[10] and to the best of his English works for its narrative approach and wit (Pl. 88), but its elements are blended with a concinnity which makes it tremendously effective.

The same setting served for what is surely Tissot's most beautiful print, *Ramsgate* (Pl. 117)—as dazzling as an image from the *ukiyo-e*, which probably inspired its composition, technique, and fluid grouping of figures—and for the

---

[9]   The location is identified in Brooke, Wentworth, Zerner, *Tissot*, no. 27.
[10]   The similarity of *A Passing Storm* to Tissot's Pre-Raphaelite works of the sixties is pointed out by Reff in 'Degas's "Tableau de Genre"', pp. 333–4.

domestic incident of *A Room Overlooking the Harbour* (whereabouts unknown), for which an oil sketch of the kind Tissot favoured at this time is known (Musée Magnin, Dijon).[11] Ramsgate also served as the background for pictures like the water-colour *Woman at a Piano* (*c*.1881; Rhode Island School of Design, Providence), which was painted several years later in Grove End Road with a nostalgic forest of masts added outside the studio window to give atmosphere, and for portraits like *July* (Pl. 132), which includes a view of Ramsgate Light in the background and colours its atmosphere with the sunny indolence of summer afternoons by the water.

Settings already familiar around Mrs Newton reappeared. The dock beside the Falcon Tavern, Gravesend, which had long since served as a background for works as various as *The Captain's Daughter* and *Waiting for the Ferry* (Pls. 81 and 111) now becomes the location, perhaps by way of photographs, water-colours, or drawings, for pictures in which an abstracted Tissot gazes at Mrs Newton, hidden like an idol behind a heavy travelling veil (Pl. 118), or waiting with the children for yet another boat (Pl. 119), a canvas for which a compositional photograph has been preserved (Pl. 120).[12] In the latter picture, the cool greys of the earlier marine pictures are replaced by the sooty lavender and vermilion of polluted skies lurid in the dying light and reflected in oily water, giving the bland subject a strangely menacing overtone. In other pictures, Tissot returned to Greenwich to savour its pleasures in Mrs Newton's company in works like *The Terrace of the Trafalgar Tavern* (Pl. 121), and this setting empty of figures also served for one of his most brilliant etchings.[13] The river itself appeared again in works like *The Ferry* (Pl. 145), which is a little reminiscent of *The Thames* (Pl. 115), although comic narrative gives way to autobiography and composition looks forward to the last works of the decade, characteristics even more clearly evident in the little panel *Crossing the Channel* (Pl. 146),[14] which was exhibited at the Grosvenor Gallery in 1879.

The most important aspect of the marine pictures of the late seventies, however, is the remarkable change of emotional key which takes place. Earlier, the sea and ships had existed entirely as excuses for genre and narrative for pictures like *Boarding the Yacht* (Pl. 88), but at the end of the decade the same subjects are invested with a new urgency and a tangible feeling of flux and change as the scene shifts from the decks of yachts and warships *en fête* to the hectic departure-piers of channel boats and transatlantic steamers. Travel itself becomes the subject of

[11] See Wentworth, *Catalogue Raisonné of Prints*, no. 22, for the relation of the print to Whistler's etchings and to the prints of the *ukiyo-e*; *Room Overlooking the Harbour* is repro. under that number, fig. 22b.

[12] Tissot also used the figure of the girl at the left for another picture, *The Artist, Mrs. Newton,*

and her Niece, Lilian Hervey by the Thames at Richmond, for which, see below, n. 21; the figure of the boy at the right was also used for the dry-point *Sa Première Culotte* (W. 51).

[13] *Trafalgar Tavern, Greenwich* (1878; W, 36).

[14] Grosvenor Gallery, 1879, no. 100.

these pictures, and departure and parting become facts which alter the tenor and meaning of life itself.

Good-bye, On the Mersey (Pl. 147),[15] which was one of Tissot's last Academy pictures, is eloquent of parting. On a tug in Liverpool harbour, a group of figures wave a ritual 'goodbye' to a transatlantic steamer as it puts out to sea beneath a louring sky. Tissot had always tended to paint overcast skies, but in many of these late travel pictures the weather becomes absolutely foul. In an equation of feeling and atmosphere, even the sky weeps in this grey picture, its greyness relieved only by the white wings of circling gulls, and fluttering handkerchiefs. Much the same can be said of *Les Deux Amis* (Pl. 148), an oil sketch related to an etching of 1882 and possibly to a now unlocated painting,[16] and of similar works like the water-colour *Waiting at Dockside* (Pl. 149). As travel itself replaced narrative as the subject of these pictures, Tissot added settings like the platforms and cab stands of Victoria Station to his repertoire, but his approach remains otherwise the same in a picture like *The Cabstand* (*Victoria Station*) (Pl. 150).[17]

In all these pictures, new feeling required new compositional approaches. Figures now pull to the edges of the canvas, leaving the centre for a symbolic statement of the theme: the waving handkerchiefs in *Good-bye, On the Mersey*, the clasped hands in *Les Deux Amis*, or the mountains of luggage in *Waiting at Dockside*, and reduce figures to part of an overall statement which focuses on theme rather than narrative interest or psychological content. These random views, composed with a studied indifference to formal composition which reflects the technical advancements of instantaneous photography and the lesson of the Japanese print, can be seen as the culmination of Tissot's English aesthetic, transforming narrative and subject into abstractions of emotion and theme and carrying the noncommital approach of his best modern genre pictures to its logical conclusion.

At the end of the decade, certain other pictures which can be grouped with these travel subjects indicate that Tissot had begun to turn from the intimacy of his Grove End Road subjects to the movement and agitation of the city for his themes. *Going to Business* (Pl. 151)[18] takes London life as its subject, and its sulphurous sky and old City man reading his *Times* in a hansom recalls a remark the artist made to Edmond de Goncourt: 'il me dit aimer l'Angleterre, Londres, l'odeur du charbon de terre, parce que ça sent la bataille de la vie.'[19] Like many of the travel pictures, the increasingly vertical orientation, crude·realism, and

[15] Royal Academy, 1881, no. 981.

[16] For the etching, see Wentworth, *Catalogue Raisonné of Prints*, no. 55; the elaboration of the sketch and its emphasis on colour suggests that it was meant to serve for a painting; Tissot's known maquettes in oil for prints are more often *en grisaille*.

[17] For a related picture in gouache, see Laver, *Vulgar Society*, pl. 21.

[18] Grosvenor Gallery, 1879, no. 98. It is possible that the present work is a replica rather than the picture actually exhibited at the Grosvenor Gallery.

[19] Goncourt, *Journal*, iii: 174.

sense of suppressed tension look forward to the excesses of *La Femme à Paris*. A number of pictures suggest that the life of the city was of continuous interest to Tissot throughout the decade. A preoccupation with monumental architecture, clearly in evidence in works like *London Visitors* (Pl. 106) as early as 1874, is manifest in the little panel *A Convalescent* (Pl. 152), for which an oil study of the setting is known (Pl. 153),[20] and in which Mrs Newton is juxtaposed with the splendid neo-classic architecture of Regent's Park as she walks beside an old man in a bath chair.

In other pictures from this time, she visits Richmond and is seen against familiar local attractions. Seated on an embankment beside the Thames in *Richmond Bridge* (c.1878; Stair-Sainty Fine Arts Ltd., New York), whose pointed centre arch frames her head, she wears the smart autumn toilette of the Manchester *Convalescent*, confronting the spectator with a haughty, or perhaps simply indifferent, stare from lustreless eyes, while Tissot himself, his face hidden by the brim of a soft hat, lounges beside her toying with his stick. As an image it is already familiar (see Pls. 118-19), but it takes on added meaning from a new feeling of anxiety or tension, and an unusually honest contrast of Mrs Newton's fastidious chic and her obviously precarious health.

Lifted on to the podium of Sir William Chambers's Temple of the Sun in *Kew Gardens* (c.1878; whereabouts unknown), she sits passively, her hands in a muff and her feet dangling off the ground, dreaming, or perhaps simply dozing, in the thin autumn sunlight, while the old man from the Manchester *Convalescent* reads at her side. If *Kew Gardens* is also composed of familiar elements (see Pls. 108 and 144), the key to its meaning is perhaps only to be found in a photograph taken soon after, and in the illustrations to *Renée Mauperin* for which it served. As abstractions of travel and parting became the subjects of related pictures (see Pls. 145-50), the melancholy contemplation of Mrs Newton's failing health replaces genre and narrative in these little pictures. As the autobiographical records of what must often have been intolerably poignant attempts to amuse and divert a young woman already under sentence of death, they can take on a retrospective pathos quite removed from their ostensible subject-matter and their inconsistent, and sometimes indifferent, artistic quality.[21]

[20] A full-sized replica of the Manchester picture, sold Christie's, London, 25 May 1979, lot 242, is known.
[21] *Richmond Bridge*, sold Phillips, New York, 16 February 1982, lot 164, is repro. in both colour and black and white in the catalogue; there is a study for the figure of Tissot in the Musée Magnin, Dijon. A picture with the same setting, *The Artist, Mrs. Newton, and her Niece, Lilian Hervey, by the Thames at Richmond*, was sold Sotheby Parke Bernet, New York, 28 May 1981, lot 95, and is repro. in colour in the catalogue; for the latter picture, see also above, n. 12. *Kew Gardens* is thought to exist in damaged condition in an American collection; a line drawing after the painting is repro. in Lostalot, 'Tissot', p. 383; a water-colour replica of the picture was exhibited at the Société d'Aquarellistes Française in 1883, no. 2; and an oil study for the figure of Mrs Newton was at one time in the possession of the Leicester Galleries, London.
Contemporary prints also show Tissot's concern with similar juxtapositions: *Le Joueur d'orgue* (W.

In most of the pictures in which Mrs Newton is seen in a public setting, Tissot portrays her as she would appear to an outsider. Even when he depicts himself with her, admiring or protective, but always clearly proprietary (Pls. 118 and 119), the impression she makes is the one he might proudly have imagined—that of a beautiful stranger glimpsed and admired, but soon lost, in the flow of urban life, whose chance regard, sometimes almost hostile (Pl. 152), establishes a fleeting contact which at once paradoxically enhances and destroys the anonymous quality of city life. This concept engaged both Manet and Degas in the 1860s and 70s, and Tissot's continued use of it can doubtless be traced to his French training. The Parisian *peintre-flâneur* stands behind many of Tissot's English pictures: the early *Waiting for the Train (Willesden Junction)* (Pl. 98) can be clearly related to pictures like Manet's *Le Chemin de fer* (1873; National Gallery of Art, Washington DC); the Mrs Newton of *A Convalescent* (Pl. 152) equally clearly descends from it, as do pictures from the series *La Femme à Paris* such as *La Mystérieuse* (Pl. 181).

Tissot's flouting of Victorian social convention in the middle seventies was paralleled by a bold dismissal of its artistic hierarchy. The hue and cry which had greeted *The Thames* at the Academy of 1876 had confirmed his standing as a 'fast' painter, as well as a clever painter-delineator of high life, and when he was invited to take part in the opening exhibition of Sir Coutts Lindsay's Grosvenor Gallery in 1877, he left the Academy and was not to exhibit there again until 1882.

Although it was intimated by the ill-natured that Sir Coutts, an amateur painter, had really spent his hundred thousand pounds in order to have a place to exhibit his own pictures, the Grosvenor Gallery was purportedly founded to challenge the monopoly of the Academy and to protest its overcrowded exhibitions. The Grosvenor provided a sumptuous setting of green and crimson brocade, architectural elements from diverse sources, and lavish antique furniture, a combination which succeeded in overpowering most of the pictures displayed in the palatial rooms. Commercialism was muted and discreet, and a number of what Henry James called 'peculiar' artists were invited to hang their works beside those of the gods of the Royal Academy and the amateur efforts of Sir Coutts's artistic friends.[22]

38), an organ grinder with Cumberland Terrace, Regent's Park, in the background, and *Le Portique de la National Galerie à Londres* (W. 40), Mrs Newton descending the steps of the National Gallery in a composition similar to *London Visitors* (Pl. 106); while others suggest an interest in the evocative power of settings empty of figures: *Trafalgar Tavern, Greenwich* (W. 36) and *Mon jardin à S.-John's Wood* (W. 39).

Tissot's response to Mrs Newton's illness was obviously both deeply-felt and complex. In certain pictures, he seems to have tied personal feeling to widely-held nineteenth-century concepts of disease: often, her uneventful beauty seems charged with the fatal attractiveness of the consumptive for the Romantic imagination. She has become 'interesting'. For a study of nineteenth-century attitudes towards tuberculosis, see Susan Sontag, *Illness as Metaphor* (New York: Farrar, Straus and Giroux, 1978).

[22] For the Grosvenor Gallery, see F. Spalding, *Magnificent Dreams*; Henry James describes the Grosvenor artists as 'peculiar' in his review of the exhibition for the *Galaxy*, repr., *The Painter's Eye*, p. 139.

Among the 'peculiar' artists represented in the inaugural exhibition, Alma-Tadema, Burne-Jones, Millais, Leighton, Whistler, Watts, Poynter, and Albert Moore remain familiar. The exhibition made the reputation of Burne-Jones, who had not exhibited publicly in several years, and put the finishing touches on the ruin of Whistler's when Ruskin's remarks about 'Cockney impudence' brought them into the courts.[23] But most of Sir Coutts's painters seem to have paid less attention to the carping of the press than to strict punctuality at Lady Lindsay's Sunday afternoons 'at home' in the galleries, when the worlds of society and high finance mingled with the artistic élite in the admirable, if risky, attempt to open new avenues of patronage. Inviting Whistler and the Prince of Wales into the same room was not without its obvious dangers, but the result was clearly worth the effort, and the Grosvenor was the social success of the season.

Tissot was represented by ten works in the first exhibition, six of which can be identified with some certainty (? Pl. 6 (see n. 28 below) and Pls. 122-6). It was the largest assembly of his work yet seen in London, and critics were impressed by its scope. *The Times* was struck not only by the variety of his subject-matter, but by the corresponding change in his manner of painting from picture to picture which they found demonstrated 'his great command of all the executive resources of his art'.[24] Most of the works were in the genre of 'coloured photographs', but there were a few surprises.

According to J. Comyns Carr, Tissot had been deeply struck by Burne-Jones's 'ideal' art at mid-decade, and decided to try his hand, much to the amusement of friends, who could never decide whether it was the moral elevation or the financial possibilities of Burne-Jones's pictures which attracted him most.[25] In either case, Tissot was faced with increasingly critical disapproval of his mundane subject-matter at this time, and the idealized nature of his fellow exhibitor's work at the Grosvenor can only have brought his lack of 'aesthetic respectability' into painfully sharp focus. In the face of Watts's pontifical statement that he painted 'ideas not things', his artistic aim being 'to urge on to higher things and nobler thoughts', Tissot must have felt distinctly odd man out among the high priests of meaning.[26]

The stock-in-trade of the Grosvenor was immediately identifiable as 'high' art, and only Whistler, Heilbuth, and Tissot fell consistently below the general level of seriousness. Whistler was beyond the pale, and Heilbuth clever enough to blunt the edge of his modernity with sufficient cardinals and orphans to give it a sentimental *biederkeit* which could be mistaken by the careless for content (although his fashion-plate reading of Watteau was also found sadly wanting in 'purpose'),

[23] Ruskin, *Works*, vii, 161. Whistler asked Tissot to testify on his behalf at the trial, but Tissot refused, and the friendship ended. Whistler commented that he did not want 'un ami malgré lui' (MS in the Whistler Collection, University of Glasgow, quoted in Staley, *From Realism to Symbolism*, p. 132).

[24] 'The Grosvenor Gallery', *The Times*, 1 May 1877, p. 10.

[25] J. C. Carr, *Coasting Bohemia*, p. 31.

[26] Quoted in Spalding, p. 34.

which left Tissot and his 'swells' alone in unredeemed modernity. His response was a conciliatory gesture towards the 'ideal' doubtless intended to demonstrate a becoming contrition, a new sense of purpose—and temper the cold wind of critical disapproval.

After the death of Burne-Jones in 1898, Lady Burne-Jones wrote to Tissot in Paris to tell him of the pleasure her husband had taken in the 1896 exhibition of the Bible illustrations and took the opportunity to ask if the two men had known one another in London or had ever corresponded. Tissot's answer refers openly to the sense of artistic inferiority he felt in the seventies, and despite a pious dismissal of worldliness, which marks all his statements at the end of the century, it expresses the new self-confidence the Bible had conferred:

J'ai très peu connu votre mari. Je me rappelle seulement que vers 1875 j'allais le voir; il me reçut avec beaucoup de simplicité et je jugeais l'homme d'après ce que je vis dans son atelier—c'est à dire de grandes choses sur le chevalet rendues avec une simplicité touchante de primitif. Je sentais les hauteurs où il planait et la matérialité où je luttais alors de plus en plus; tout cela m'intimida tellement que je n'allais plus le voir. Il grandit alors beaucoup et je quittais l'Angleterre. Depuis j'ai fait cette Vie de Christ, il a été la voir je le sais. J'ai su qu'elle lui plaisait, et je me faisais une vraie fête d'aller le voir à un de mes voyages à Londres quand j'appris sa mort. Il ne m'a jamais écrit, sans cela je mettrais à votre disposition ce qui me resterait de ce grand artiste, une des glories les plus pures de votre pays.[27]

Perhaps because he had little suitably 'ideal' art on hand at such short notice, a long-unsold Marguerite was pressed into service, a gothic interior 'which the painter calls "Meditation" but which if we mistake not, has been elsewhere described as Marguerite in agonized self-question in church from the paintings of the *Faust* series'.[28] With this backward glance at a troubled past, Tissot exhibited the first, and what was to be the only, completed work in a series of five pictures in an 'ideal' series, *The Triumph of Will* (called with high Grosvenor aesthetic seriousness, 'A Poem in Five Parts'). *The Challenge*,[29] to have been followed by *Temptation, Rescue, Victory*, and *The Reward*, was a block-buster of an allegory which impressed even Ruskin, who found it proved Tissot capable, 'if he would obey his graver thoughts, of doing much that would, with real benefit, occupy the

---

[27] Quoted in G. B.-J. (Lady Burne-Jones), *Memorials of Edward Burne-Jones*, ii, 282.

[28] Grosvenor Gallery, 1877, no. 21; described, 'The Grosvenor Gallery', *The Times*, 1 May 1877, p. 10. It seems probable that the Grosvenor picture can be identified with the work illustrated in Pl. 6, which appears to have remained with the dealer Goupil who acquired it in 1860 (see chap. I, n.60) and sold it in 1876 at Christie's where it was acquired by Algernon Moses Marsden. Tissot had either

bought the work back from Marsden or had borrowed it for the Grosvenor exhibition. There was method in his approach: according to Yriarte, 'Exhibition of the Royal Academy of Arts II', 256, Tissot had been extremely successful in creating an English market for his early canvases. It is also possible that the work exhibited at the Grosvenor is the unlocated Salon painting or the Dublin version of the same subject (Pls. 7 and 8).

[29] Grosvenor Gallery, 1877, no. 22.

attention of that part of the British public whose fancy is at present caught only by Gustave Doré.'[30]

In an attempt to elucidate what it called the 'severe symbolism' of *The Challenge, The Times* struggled with the iconography of the now unlocated picture:

. . . behind a knotted brood of coiled pythons and vipers—types of human vices and passions, Will, typified by a fair woman with pale cheeks, delicate features and calmly resolute blue eyes, strides triumphant, armed with sword in hand over the vanquished monster, half fair woman, half tiger, which symbolizes the temptation of carnal lusts; while before the thick wood, of which one of the tree trunks carries a scutcheon with the words 'Audere, volle, tacere' stand Will's two squires, Daring and Reserve, also typified in female forms—the one all in red, with a tiger skin knotted over her head, the other in black and white, with a pale sad face, and her mouth bandaged, bearing the helm of Will, with its flowing lambrequin.[31]

Even without the picture, faced with its description one can only sympathize with the critic for the *Spectator*, who found the picture completely unintelligible despite the gloss in the catalogue, and confessed, 'it appears to us more like a scene from an inferior burlesque than anything else'.[32]

The complicated symbolism of this bevy of superwomen and serpents is Tissot's aesthetic—or financial—homage to 'high' art. The heavy-handed allegory of *The Challenge* was fortunately without lasting influence in his painting but it was continued, even elaborated, in the little-known sculpture in bronze and *cloisonné* enamel which absorbed his attention at this time. *Fortune* (Pl. 158), the most ambitious of his sculptures, was not exhibited until 1882, but its elaborate iconography is not unlike that of *The Triumph of Will*:

THE GODDESS, no longer balancing herself upon her revolving wheel, is seated at ease upon our globe, and raises the bandage from her eyes in order to discern her favorites. Beneath her feet, Time, typified by the months of the Zodiac, is flying. Patience, the principle of all success, and the true basis of all fortune, is represented by the tortoise; whilst the two leading impulses of man, Selfishness and Sympathy, are represented by the types of Ambition and Love. The motto, 'WAIT AND WIN' in various languages—French, German, Russian, Hebrew, Arabic and Latin—runs round the base. The intention of the artist is to adapt this work to a life size monument or fountain.[33]

Tissot's work of a more decorative function in *cloisonné* sometimes also leaned towards the allegorical symbols favoured by Lord Leighton. A vase in the Dudley exhibition of 1882 was described, for example, as having supports in the

[30] Ruskin, *Works*, vii, 161.
[31] 'The Grosvenor Gallery', *The Times*, 1 May 1877, p. 10.
[32] 'The Grosvenor Gallery', *Spectator* (26 May 1877), 665.

[33] *J.J. Tissot: An Exhibition of Modern Art*, Dudley Gallery, London, 1882, no. 71.

form of entwined human figures, and surfaces enamelled with black serpents on a yellow ground. Most, however, appear to have been less elevated in their symbolism, and at least one vase employed elements from paintings of Mrs Newton and her children in the garden at Grove End Road (Pl. 141). Others incorporated similar domestic subjects or the familiar red monogram which he had designed for use on his prints.[34] From the examples known at present, Tissot's work in *cloisonné* and bronze owes its greatest formal debt to those contemporary Japanese enamels and bronzes to which it bears such distinct resemblance, and it even seems possible that the actual metal supports he used in his work were sometimes of Japanese origin. Unfortunately, too few pieces are known to yet permit the study of his *œuvre* in depth:[35] it doubtless offers a fascinating footnote to his career as a painter and printmaker, but little more.

The other pictures at the Grosvenor exhibition in 1877 were less importunate in their meaning than *Meditation* or *The Challenge*, although *The Widower* (Pl. 122)[36] hints that Tissot was aware of Heilbuth's sentimental excursions into the damper varieties of sentimental narrative. It is saved, however, by its tart rendering and by an eccentric composition which once again can be read as either a painterly assimilation of Japanese influences or a simple rehash of Millais's *Autumn Leaves* (Pl. 91). In any case, it was a composition which Tissot employed with regularity in the seventies, as the very similar design of works like *Spring* (Pl. 131) and *Orphan* (Pl. 138) clearly demonstrate.[37]

Reviewing the Grosvenor exhibition, Oscar Wilde thought all Tissot's pictures

[34] Dudley Gallery, 1882, no. 72; no. 73 was similar; nos. 74 and 75 employed supports described as 'female figures kneeling on monsters' heads'; the two vases with Grove End Road subjects, nos. 78 and 80, were entitled *Children in a Garden* and *The Old Brick Wall*; the monogram, no. 90, was described as a trial piece in sealing-wax red and turquoise blue; and no. 91 was made up of a number of trial pieces.

[35] It seems likely that nos. 71–91 in the Dudley catalogue, some of which cover more than one work, represent the total of Tissot's finished work in the medium at the time. The material was again exhibited in the same order at the Palais de l'Industrie in 1883, nos. 1–20, and at the Galerie Sedelmeyer in 1885, nos. 1–20, although the latter exhibition was enriched with the addition of eight knife-rests (no. 21). Tissot continued to work in *cloisonné* after 1885: a small plaque bearing the names of English friends in stylized cartouches (for which see n. 7 above), dated 1886, and a panel representing three Egyptian goddesses depicted in the style of ancient wall painting, dated 1888, were sold at Sotheby's, Monte Carlo, 15 June 1982, and are repro. in the catalogue. In the same sale were two teapots of Japanese form decorated with *cloisonné* patterns of Japanese inspiration (lots 835 and 836), which can be identified with nos. 85 and 81 in the Dudley, and nos. 14 and 10 in the Palais de l'Industrie and the Sedelmeyer exhibitions; also an oval jardinière entitled *Lake and Sea* (*Un lac et la mer*) in *cloisonné* mounted in ormolu (lot 833), repro. in colour in the catalogue, which can be identified with no. 74 in the Dudley and no. 3 in the Palais de l'Industrie and Sedelmeyer exhibitions. This jardinière (Bury Street Gallery, London) is decorated with *cloisonné* landscapes *à la japonais* and mounted on feet in the form of claws and tenticles clasping glass balls. It has elaborate gilt handles in the form of mermaids 'kneeling' on monsters' heads that are reminiscent of Japanese lion or dog masks, and is clearly among the most ambitious and artistically important of Tissot's *cloisonné* enamels.

[36] Grosvenor Gallery, 1877, no. 20. A replica, sold at Sotheby's Belgravia, 1 October 1979, is known. For the etching after the painting, see Wentworth *Catalogue Raisonné of Prints*, no. 28.

[37] The etching *Matinée de printemps* (W. 13), which is dated 1875, is the first of Tissot's pictures to employ the composition: its clear reference to the *Manga* and to Japanese actor prints in which figures are silhouetted against a dark ground suggest that it has its origin in a study of Japanese prints.

IV. *En plein soleil, c.*1881.

except *The Widower*, which he found 'full of depth and suggestiveness', were 'deficient in feeling and depth', his young ladies 'too fashionably over-dressed to interest the artistic eye', and found 'a hard unscrupulousness in painting uninteresting objects in an uninteresting way', which suggested nothing more to him than the horrors of 'the photographic' style of Frith.[38] These failures were particularly marked in *Holyday* (Pl. 123),[39] which he described disdainfully as representing 'over-dressed, common-looking people, and [the] ugly, painfully accurate representation of modern soda-water bottles', and compared unfavourably with seventeenth-century Dutch pictures of civic banquets with their 'beautiful grouping of noble-looking men and still lives aglow with light and wine'.[40] If modern opinion demurs at Wilde's conclusions, it must none the less be admitted that there is a calculated avoidance of depth and feeling in *Holyday*, pointed up by its relentless technique and impassive narrative. Its *modernité* must have been far more shocking to Tissot's contemporaries than it is today, with the heavy patina of period charm it has taken on. Compositionally, *Holyday* restates the broad horizontal format of *A Convalescent* (Pl. 113) and establishes the ample pattern common to many of Tissot's most impressive pictures from the middle of the decade, such as *The Letter* and *A Passing Storm* (Pls. 114 and 115).

The Gallery of H.M.S. Calcutta (Portsmouth) (Pl. 124),[41] the last of Tissot's major nautical pictures, is another of his 'souvenirs' of shipboard galas, and like *The Ball on Shipboard* (Pl. 102), it is set well away from the dancing, and now even the crowd, with great dramatic effectiveness. Like so many of the most striking scenes in nineteenth-century literature, its oblique narrative gains immensely from the unseen crowd and the music of the band. Seeking the fringes of pleasure, Tissot as usual discovers private drama, and the emotional relationship of these three sitters-out at a ball offers what is perhaps his most finely wrought triangular puzzle.

The dilemma of reading this language of looks and gestures, for us no less than the protagonists themselves, is now made splendidly complex, like the picture itself, by the artful gesture of the woman closest the viewer who hides her face with a fan from the young officer who studies her with such open admiration. Although we might be said to know more than he in viewing the drama from the opposite side, added knowledge is of little use in unravelling a drama which is now clearly, in the manner of Thoré, in its second act. Its psychological opacity, like that of *Les Adieux* (Pl. 76), and its comic stance, like that of *Boarding the Yacht* (Pl. 88), are familiar, but they have never before appeared in a combination quite as subtle and discreet—nor will they again.

[38] O. Wilde, 'The Grosvenor Gallery', in *Dublin University Magazine*, repr., *Works*, xv, 20–1.

[39] Grosvenor Gallery, 1877, no. 23.

[40] Wilde, 'The Grosvenor Gallery', repr., *Works*, xv, 21.

[41] Grosvenor Gallery, 1877, no. 19. For the etching after the painting, see Wentworth, *Catalogue Raisonné of Prints*, no. 25.

The design of the picture is as skilful as its narrative, reiterating the psychological states of the protagonists as it subtly heightens them. The thrust and imbalance of the composition, suggested by the form of the ship and cast in terms of the Japanese print; the watery reflections in the slanted glass; the unmodulated chalky light; and the hypnotic repetition of the 'Trafalgar' chairs: each seems to comment on the impenetrable conflicts and lack of emotional equilibrium among the three figures, with their listless sensuality as heavy as the overcast sky.

The 1877 Grosvenor exhibition also had the distinction of a review by Henry James, who singled out the *Calcutta* for special notice. Like Wilde, James found Tissot's fashionable affectations and exacting attention to the fall of a dress to be lacking in depth and suggestiveness, however clever the subject and brilliant the execution. Remarking that he would not be able to live a week with the *Calcutta* without finding it 'intolerably wearisome and unrefreshing', he sharply characterized Tissot's painting as 'hard, vulgar, and banal', his humour as 'trivial', and his sentiment as 'stale'.[42] He too uses the Dutch masters as a touchstone for Tissot's painting of modern life, and again the comparison is invidious. James found that long acquaintance had done nothing to diminish the delight and pleasure he took in the Dutch little masters of the seventeenth century and their scenes from contemporary life, although he did not speculate on whether the passage of time might not actually have increased it.

Even so, his objections retain much of their force and point, for if the *Calcutta*, now divorced from its own time by a gulf James could hardly have imagined, has acquired the enduring if not inexhaustible charm of a period piece, time has done little to dull what he found trivial, stale, and vulgar. There is a nearly imperceptible distaste on Tissot's part and a core of emotional hardness which is perhaps impossible to articulate, but when the *Calcutta* hung beside *The Challenge* at the Grosvenor, it must have been as deeply offensive to its audience as Tissot's subject-matter, if part and parcel with it, and the source of much contemporary critical rage.

In England, Tissot was made to feel his lack of aesthetic seriousness, and critical resentment was at its height at the end of the decade. He was at once considered one of the most brilliant among the foreign painters established in London, as James described him, and yet somehow dismissed because of his foreign mannerisms. His reaction was complex. On one hand, he sought to appease British taste with custom-made pictures like *The Challenge*, and on the other to flaunt it with increasingly uncompromising examples of his modernism—ladies dangling slippers from Brazilian hammocks and old gentlemen reading newspapers in hansom cabs. Left to his own devices, Tissot might well have become an 'ideal' artist. His early and late pictures bracket his subjects from modern life with

---

[42] James, 'The Grosvenor Gallery', repr., *The Painter's Eye*, pp. 140–1.

unrelieved moral seriousness, and he always seems most comfortable when he is able to preach. The unvarnished modern sentiment of the *Calcutta* is a triumph of taste and perception, but, as with other pictures from this time, it is out to prove something and is perhaps a little forced. The 'wearisome and unrefreshing' quality James discovered may well begin there. 'Is there to be no more *delightful* realism?' James wondered, perhaps unwittingly identifying the quality the *Calcutta* lacks. 'I sometimes fear it.'[43]

If the *Calcutta* refrains from any obvious moralizing, its absence is strangely felt in the void. For modern taste, it is only when a moralizing tone is transmuted into genre that Tissot is entirely successful. Surely *The Letter* (Pl. 114) translates the didactic iconography of *The Challenge* into the *mœurs* of the society novel without any loss of power. The lady in black who tears her letter with such splendid theatrical forcefulness is like the heroines of Ouida's romances—one-dimensional and hyperbolic, but larger-than-life and more than a match for the superwomen of *The Challenge*. What lesson more chillingly effective could there be than those bits of torn paper fluttering down to lie with the dead leaves on the grass?

Portsmouth Dockyard (Pl. 125),[44] which was quickly given the title of the eighteenth-century song, *How Happy I could be with Either*, and etched as *Entre les deux mon cœur balance*, restates the composition and narrative of *The Thames* (Pl. 115), but it failed to offend the public at the Grosvenor as its predecessor at the Academy had done, perhaps because its picturesque Highlander made the subject more palatable. Its comic triangle actually amused, and even its laboured technique found admirers.

The subject appeared yet again in a picture whose original title has not been preserved but which is now called *In the Conservatory* or *Rivals* (Pl. 137) and has been understandably confused with a picture of the latter title exhibited at the Grosvenor in 1879 (Pl. 159). It looks to the opulent world of the social conversation pieces, but combines their neutral display of millinery with a triangular comedy of manners—surely Tissot's favourite English narrative subject—as twins in juvenile blue preen before a gentleman who takes refuge in conversation, or at least embarrassed silence, with a lady presumably their doting mother. Treated in broad areas of pale, light-struck colour, with its tonal range established by the unshadowed greenish light of the conservatory, the picture is not unlike *The Ball on Shipboard* (Pl. 102) in its approach, if less technically perfect and glacially incisive in the result, and doubtless is close in date as well as spirit to a work like

---

[43] Ibid., p. 141.

[44] Grosvenor Gallery, 1877, no. 25. For the etching after the painting, see Wentworth, *Catalogue Raisonné of Prints*, no. 30. For reviews of the picture, see, for example, 'The Grosvenor Gallery', *The Times*, 1 May 1877, p. 10, which says of the picture: 'How perfectly he has painted the cold gray light on English water, and the multiplicity of crowded craft and crossing ropes.'

The Bunch of Lilacs (Pl. 107), from mid-decade. If its narrative pushes satire dangerously close to caricature, a drift clear in comparison with the deliciously subtle comedy of early works like *Boarding the Yacht* (Pl. 88), its loquacious vulgarity at least has a life which marks it out from the often less than incisive narratives set in St. John's Wood.

A Portrait (Pl. 126)[45] is one of the 'specimens' Tissot regularly sent to exhibitions to attract commissions, although it is probably somewhat freer in its approach to the genre than a paid example would have been at this time. The sitter was a professional model, Miss Lloyd, whose function was soon taken over by Kathleen Newton (as was the dress she wears), and the next year two portraits of Mrs Newton, *Spring* and *July* (Pls. 131 and 132), were given the subtitle 'Specimen of a Portrait' at the Grosvenor. *A Portrait* recalls the vivid immediacy of the portraits of the early seventies (Pls. 71 and 72), and like them it has a suggestiveness which is riveting. Here, it gives the picture an interrogatory atmosphere fraught with possibilities.

About this time, Tissot received the commission for an important conversation piece, *The Chapple-Gill Family of Lower Lea, Woolton* (Pl. 127), a portrait of Katherine Chapple-Gill with her two-year-old son, Robert Carey, and six-year-old daughter, Helen, which was painted in the drawing-room of their house near Liverpool. The portrait is among Tissot's largest works, and it is perhaps a little too large for its technique, which fails to activate large areas, its casually unstructured composition, and its conventionally pretty colour, which goes chalky on this scale and lacks the agreeable bite of Tissot's usual combinations, although it can be related to the pale tonalities he favoured at this time in works like the *Calcutta*. Tissot lived at Lower Lea for eight weeks while working on the canvas, and a mutual affinity is said to have developed between the artist and Katherine Chapple-Gill—who was well known for her lavish taste in dress: the perfect patron for the painter of *The Ball on Shipboard*—which caused her husband considerable distress.[46] If this is true, the affinity must have overlapped the appearance of Mrs Newton, who was living in Grove End Road by this time; for the portrait is dated 1877. But despite Tissot's admiration for the sitter—or perhaps because of it—the picture is strangely lacking in the brio and inventiveness which gives works like *Colonel Burnaby* their vivid life, and it relies on generalized charm and the obvious appeal of its subject rather than on any particular refinement of artistic means for its effect.

A similar drift towards generalization can be felt in a contemporary portrait

[45] Grosvenor Gallery, 1877, no. 18. For the etching after the picture, see Wentworth, *Catalogue Raisonné of Prints*, no. 23, under which (n. 1) the identification of the present work with the Grosvenor exhibition is established.

[46] Biographical data on the Chapple-Gill family are based on information supplied by the son of Robert Chapple-Gill when the picture was sold, and were included in typescript material assembled by Messrs Neuman, London.

of the art dealer *Algernon Moses Marsden* (Pl. 128), although it is sharply contradicted by the obvious knowledge and affection with which the sitter is characterized. Once identified as a portrait of Marsden in his study, the picture was actually painted in Grove End Road, and many of the objects appear in other works. Even if borrowed for the occasion, the luxurious objects doubtless reflect Marsden's taste, and contribute an added dimension to Tissot's delineation of his character. Interestingly enough, the composition of the picture seems to derive from Pre-Raphaelite conventions; the tiger-skin on the chair takes on the function of a Renaissance tablet, Marsden's pose is reminiscent of Rossetti, and even the horizontal format of the picture seems to reflect the unusual shape of many Pre-Raphaelite portraits. Imbued with a discreet and vague lavishness rather than a precise and meticulous iconography, *Algernon Moses Marsden* most resembles a society version of Holman Hunt's *Henry Wentworth Monk* (1858; National Gallery of Canada, Ottawa).

The second Grosvenor exhibition in 1878 was to be the apotheosis of Mrs Newton, for at least five of the nine works Tissot exhibited were portrait sudies of her in various guises (Pls. 129, 130, 131 and 132), a percentage which is probably an accurate reflection of their proportion in his work at this time.[47] The etching *Mavourneen* (Pl. 129)[48] quickly proved to be the most popular of Tissot's prints, and it reflects a kind of image Tissot favoured when he etched her, in which high chic and girlish charm are present in more or less equal measure. It is related to *October*, a large etching of Mrs Newton wearing the same costume which was also exhibited at the Grosvenor: like *Mavourneen*, it records a large painted portrait of 1877, a small replica of which is also known (Pl. 130).[49] Both portraits are presented in the allegorical personification which Tissot found extremely congenial in the possibilities it offered for an extension of the pure portrait.[50] *October* is of particular interest because it suggests a new *appassionnement* at this time. Albert Moore was a friend of Whistler and at least an acquaintance of Tissot's, and his influence on Whistler has long been the subject of scholarly study. Tissot also seems to have been interested in his work, and *October*, with its graceful figure set against a background of leaves, suggests that the lesson of the Japanese print had been augmented by a careful study of Moore's

[47] In addition to the five works known to portray Mrs Newton, it is possible that two others were also of her: *Evening* (no. 33), presumably the picture now in the Musée d'Orsay, Paris (see below, chap. V, n. 23), and *A Study* (no. 35), 'of which only a pretty simple head is finished' ('The Grosvenor Gallery', *The Times*, 2 May 1878, p. 7). It is possible that *A Study* can be identified with the picture repro. *Connoisseur*, 129 no. 526 (June 1952), xxxii.

[48] Grosvenor Gallery, 1878, no. 156; W. 33. The etching records what is said to have been Tissot's first portrait of Mrs Newton, which is repro. in Wentworth, *Catalogue Raisonné of Prints*, fig. 31c.

[49] Grosvenor Gallery, 1878, no. 155. The large portrait is in the Montreal Museum of Fine Arts.

[50] For a discussion of Tissot's use of allegorical personifications in his portraits of Mrs Newton, see Wentworth, *Catalogue Raisonné of Prints*, no. 48. All but one of Tissot's etched portraits of Mrs Newton bear allegorical titles.

poetic, decorative painting. Like its design, the technique and extremely large scale of *October* also points to Moore. Its use of an unusually chalky pigment, its high-keyed colour, and its insistence on decorative patterning are not unlike that of Moore's *Sea-Shells* (1870–1; Walker Art Gallery, Liverpool) which was commissioned by Frederick Leland and exhibited at the Academy in 1874; and both its technique and decorative intention suggest that Tissot may have taken an active interest in the architectural schemes which occupied Moore and Whistler at this time.

Spring (*Specimen of a Portrait*), another portrait of Mrs Newton exhibited at the Grosvenor in 1878 in both a painted and etched version (Pl. 131),[51] is perhaps even more clearly indebted to Moore. If the marked interest in reflected light is peculiar to Tissot, its format and flower-tinted subjectlessness bring it close to Moore, whose single figures in light-struck muslin, framed in narrow vertical canvases, half classical, half Japanese 'pillar print', hung near Tissot's at the Academy and the Grosvenor. But Tissot was unwilling to give up the Parisian chic of his canvases for Greece or Japan, and pictures like *October* and *Spring* hover half-way between the archaic poetry of Moore and the brittle elegance of the fashion plate. Tissot's *appassionnement* is to be seen at its most intense as well as its most attractive in oil sketches like *Listening to Music* (Pl. 134) whose subject, now a world removed from the cultural pretense of *Hush!* (Pl. 103), suggests those musical analogies between painting and music which gave musical titles to so many pictures in the seventies, and its ravishing palette of pink, wine red, and pale green offers a clear parallel to the colourist approach employed by Whistler for sketches whose colour notes he described as harmonies or likened to symphonies.[52]

The same conditions and approach are to be found in another of the 1878 Grosvenor studies of Mrs Newton, *July* (*Specimen of a Portrait*) (Pl. 132).[53] It is the most accomplished of Tissot's readings of Moore (Pl. 133) and the most

[51] Grosvenor Gallery, 1878, nos. 31 (oil) and 158 (etching); for the etching after the painting, see Wentworth, *Catalogue Raisonné of Prints*, no. 34. It is possible that the present work is a replica rather than the picture actually exhibited at the Grosvenor Gallery; its support and scale are atypical.

[52] For the analogies between music and painting cultivated by Whistler and Moore, see A. Staley, 'The Condition of Music', *Art News Annual*, and *From Realism to Symbolism*, no. 104. Although Tissot is not discussed, a work like *July* fits easily into a tradition which included Moore's *The End of the Story* (1876; Mr and Mrs J. M. Tanenbaum, Toronto) and Whistler's *Mrs. Leland* (1872–73; Frick Collection, New York) and ends with Lord Leighton's *Flaming June* (1895; Museo de Arte, Ponce, Puerto Rico).

[53] Grosvenor Gallery, 1878, no. 34. There is a replica of the painting (repro., Wentworth, *Catalogue Raisonné of Prints*, fig. 35b) which appears to have been repainted at some point to make the severe hair-style of the time more attractively *fin-de-siècle* to a later generation, a process which the now-cleaned *Quiet* (Pl. 169) is also known to have undergone. For the incomplete etching after the painting, see Wentworth, *Catalogue Raisonné of Prints*, no. 35. An exhibition label on the stretcher of the Grosvenor version of the painting, in Tissot's hand, gives the title as *Sea-side*, under which it was exhibited at the Palais de l'Industrie, 1883, no. 13; it is inscribed to E. Simon, the director of the Théâtre L'Ambigu, to whom Tissot must have given it in the mid-eighties.

individual of his approaches to 'the condition of music'. If it owes no small part of its drowsy, summer luxuriousness to Moore's sleepy classical beauties, which it also resembles in its colour and technique, it casts its borrowed ideas in the vocabulary of his own aesthetic with unfaltering style and precision.

Whatever the debt of *July* to Moore and the Aesthetic Movement, its particular sophistication also suggests that Tissot had kept abreast of the work of friends and contemporaries in France. Tissot's ties with Paris were clearly closer during the seventies than has been thought, and he probably went to France with some frequency after he was free to do so again in 1874. He remained on especially close terms with Manet, and in 1875 probably travelled to Venice with him for a brief visit in September or October, afterwards buying his *Blue Venice* (1875; Shelburne Museum, Shelburne, Vermont) *en souvenir*—and probably also to help his less financially secure friend pay for the trip.[54] It seems likely that a picture like Manet's *Marguerite de Conflans* (1873; Smith College Museum of Art, Northampton) lies in the immediate background of *July*, offering a model of relaxed sophistication which tempers the classical sobriety of Moore's canvases. In other works, such as the sketch *Mrs Newton with a Child by a Pool* (Pl. 135) the bravura technique suggests that Manet's technical approach was also of more than passing interest at this time.[55] Although there is no documentary evidence to support the conjecture that Tissot may have visited the second Impressionist Exhibition in 1876, such a visit would have provided him with models for the aesthetic of his St. John's Wood pictures, and there is no reason he should not have made it.

The third Grosvenor exhibition in 1879 returned to a more judicious mixture of subjects, although Mrs Newton remained very much in view. *Rivals* (Pl. 159),[56]

[54] Hanson, *Manet*, p. 145. It has been questioned whether Tissot actually accompanied Manet and his wife on the trip, since Manet's departure from Paris was delayed when he was forced to wait for a rich buyer (whom he mentioned in a letter to Mallarmé on September 19); there is, however, no evidence for assuming that he did not.

[55] Manet's portrait of Nina de Callias, *La Dame aux éventails* (1874; Louvre, Paris) might also be suggested as a prototype for *July*; the relationship of Tissot's sketch of Mrs Newton in a garden to Manet's *The Monet Family in the Garden at Argenteuil* has been pointed out by Zerner in the introduction to Brooke, Wentworth, Zerner, *Tissot*, no page number.

[56] Grosvenor Gallery, 1879, no. 95. Although Pl. 137 has recently been identified with the Grosvenor *Rivals* (as in Misfeldt, p. 162, and at Christie's, 16 October, 1981, lot 84), the position of a photograph of Pl. 159 in Tissot's albums between *A Quiet Afternoon* and *Orphan* suggests that this is the Grosvenor picture, and that assumption is surely confirmed by

a description in *The Times*: '[Tissot] finds his subjects, as usual, in the boudoir life of luxuriously appointed villas, where graceful ladies, in irreproachable costume, keep a brace of rivals in play at five o'clock tea, playing their crochet pins the while as demurely as if men's affections were women's natural playthings. Such a scene is the subject of one of Tissot's cleverest pictures here, the scene of which is laid in a conservatory with a background of tropical plants wonderfully painted' ('The Grosvenor Gallery', 2 May 1879, p. 3). *The Times* also says that two other Grosvenor paintings show 'the same lady swinging in the shade in a Brazilian hammock, in one case, alone, under a Japanese sun-shade of black and yellow; in the other with a grey haired elderly gentleman to keep her company (ibid.): clearly the unlocated *The Hammock*, a photograph of which is preserved in Tissot's album, and *In the Shade* (Pl. 144). The Grosvenor *Rivals* was almost certainly sold by Christie's in 1911 with its proper title: the dimensions given (35 1/2 × 26 1/2 in.) are of approximately the same proportion as Pl. 156.

in which she has clearly charmed two distinguished old gentlemen, offers a familiar situation in reverse. Even so, the picture elicited a habitual response, being at once castigated for the vulgarity of its subject and praised for the marvellous technical skill of the work itself. The *Athenaeum* found it 'a clever but rather coarse painting of unpleasant persons seated at afternoon tea', and discovered in its complacent enumeration of social affectations proof enough of Tissot's desire to satirize the plutocracy he delineated with such consummate skill—ideas repeated by the *Spectator*, although it found the painting itself 'better even than usual', and remarked the artistic perfection in the handling of tropical plants which make up the background.[57]

Although there was no new attempt to scale the heights of 'high' art, social meaning reappeared with the early narrative *Emigrants*, a replica of which appears to have been exhibited (Pl. 83),[58] and there was an obvious attempt to duplicate the success of *The Widower* (Pl. 122) with a pendant *Orphan* (Pl. 138).[59] But the depth and feeling which had been widely admired in the earlier picture was found to have been dissipated by the strangeness of the setting, the suspicious chic of the protagonists, and the lurid overtones of the narrative. *The Times* thought the waist-deep bulrushes and reeds suggested 'nothing short of suicide and by the muddiest of deaths', and, despite the sentimental directive offered by the title, found it impossible to discover any meaning in the picture beyond 'an arrangement in black and green'.[60] The *Athenaeum* also took note of its Whistlerian approach and was inspired to compare the two painters, finding that they were 'at one in not rejecting a subject merely because it is unrefined, not to say vulgar', but while Tissot was not 'capable of anything so bizarre as *Miss Connie Gilchrist*', his work descended to a 'lower order of taste'. Tissot's colour was found inferior to Whistler's, or, more precisely, he was found to have no colour at all: 'M. Tissot has nowadays no colour, . . . he is at present regardless of tone, and affects bright, isolated, and unbroken tints. Black to him is black; not so to Mr. Whistler.'[61] If such criticism restates familiar objections to works like *Les Deux Sœurs* and *Les Adieux* (Pls. 29 and 76), focusing once again Tissot's peculiar problems, it also seems likely that the deliberately close-keyed colour of *Orphan* reflects a continuing interest in Whistler's work, and it is perhaps not coincidental that the picture is strangely reminiscent of Whistler's full-length portraits.

Orphan is anomalous among the works of the St. John's Wood period in its curiously morbid subject, probably chosen to capture the public imagination.

---

[57] 'The Grosvenor Gallery Exhibition', *Athenaeum* (10 May 1879), p. 608; 'The Grosvenor Gallery', *Spectator* (31 May 1879), p. 691.

[58] Grosvenor Gallery, 1879, no. 94; for the etching after the painting, see Wentworth, *Catalogue Raisonné of Prints*, no. 45.

[59] Grosvenor Gallery, 1879, no. 96; for the un-finished etching after the painting, see Wentworth, *Catalogue Raisonné of Prints*, no. 44.

[60] 'The Grosvenor Gallery', *The Times*, 2 May 1879, p. 3.

[61] 'The Grosvenor Gallery Exhibition', *Athenaeum* (10 May 1879), p. 607.

More often, Mrs Newton and her children find themselves unbereft in their paradise, as is suggested by paintings like *The Gardener* (Pl. 139), a work which is related to both a sketch of Mrs Newton (Pl. 140), an etching,[62] and one of Tissot's vases in *cloisonné* enamel (Pl. 141). Life in Grove End Road was represented at the 1879 Grosvenor by *A Quiet Afternoon* (Pl. 144)[63] and by *The Hammock* which is unlocated although its composition is probably preserved in an etching of 1880.[64] Like *Croquet* (Pl. 142) the previous year, they represent the *dolce far niente* which reigned in Tissot's earthly paradise at its most ravishing: summer afternoons of lazy tranquillity and warm sunshine.

Whatever feelings they distil for modern taste, both *A Quiet Afternoon* and *The Hammock* were found particularly offensive when they were exhibited at the Grosvenor. Neither the arch vulgarity of *Rivals* nor the studied 'arrangement' of *Orphan* were found quite as arrogant as these innocuous and remarkably accomplished tributes to domestic happiness. This was due in some part, as has been suggested, to the transparency of their reference to the liaison, but also to their determined adherence to 'base' subjects and a lack of narrative at the cost of 'feeling' and 'intelligible meaning'. The *Spectator* pointedly compared them to the earlier Academy pictures *The Captain's Daughter* and *The Last Evening* (Pls. 81 and 84), which it found had 'a considerable amount of character' and 'a hint of real feeling', and remarked the 'abominably artificial atmosphere of a certain style of society' which characterized Tissot's current work: 'This year he tries our patience somewhat hardly, for these ladies in hammocks, showing a very unnecessary amount of petticoat and stocking, and remarkable for little save a sort of luxurious indolence and insolence, are hardly fit subjects for such elaborate painting.'[65] In the same manner, the *Athenaeum* discovered 'a "smart" vulgarity' about them which they found justified 'the saying that M. Tissot wishes to satirize the British plutocracy'.[66] *Punch* was decidedly witty at the expense of *The Hammock* and its 'very unnecessary amount of petticoat and stocking', suggesting it might better have been called *The Web:*

> Will you walk into my Garden?
>   Said the Spider to the Fly.
> 'Tis the prettiest little garden
>   That ever you did spy.
> The grass a sly dog plays on;
>   A hammock I have got;
> Neat ancles you shall gaze on,
>   Talk—*à propos de bottes.*
> *Elle est bien botté alors.* Is it so? *'Tis so.*

---

[62] *L'Été*, W. 43.

[63] Grosvenor Gallery, 1879, no. 97.

[64] W. 46 is either a replica or a variation of the Grosvenor picture.

[65] 'The Grosvenor Gallery', *Spectator* (31 May 1879), p. 691.

[66] 'The Grosvenor Gallery Exhibition', *Athenaeum* (10 May 1879), p. 607.

To complete the story, *A Quiet Afternoon* was retitled *The Naughty Old Man; or, I'll tell your Wife how you spend your Afternoons in Fair Rosamund's Bower-Villa, N.W.*, and *Going to Business* (Pl. 151), off to the City leaving Fair Rosamund in the bower, was tagged with the question:

'Drive on, Cabby!
Ah! is she good,
She of the Abbey
Road, St. John's Wood?'[67]

Tissot ceased to exhibit at the Grosvenor Gallery after the 1879 season. He did not appear in any major London exhibit in 1880 and returned to the Royal Academy in 1881, exhibiting *Good-bye, on the Mersey* and *Quiet* (Pls. 147 and 169).[68] His reasons for leaving the Grosvenor are not known, and although it has been suggested that he ceased to be invited to exhibit, no documentary evidence remains to attest such a decision by Sir Coutts, and it seems equally probable that Tissot came to regret his defection from the Academy or that he decided to try still another approach after critical abuse had demoted him to a position of secondary importance in the ranks of the Grosvenor painters. After 1881, most of his efforts must have been directed towards the important one-man exhibition he held at the Dudley Gallery in May 1882 in which the series *The Prodigal Son in Modern Life* (Pls. 154-7)[69] was the *pièce de résistance* among the paintings. Only eight other pictures, mostly small-scale Grove End Road pictures and one or two travel subjects, appeared with the new series.[70] The entire etched production of his London years was also exhibited, but it was already familiar, and only the twenty-one pieces in *cloisonné* enamel offered novelties to compete with the *Prodigal*.

After a steady exhibition diet of Mrs Newton at home and abroad, *The Prodigal Son in Modern Life* must have come as a considerable relief. With clear narrative progression and immediately intelligible meaning, its laboriously witty blend of biblical import and piquant modernism remains a paradigm among Victorian conceits, and it was rewarded with immense popularity when it appeared. The series became Tissot's chief exhibition piece in the years before the Bible

---

[67] 'The Gay Grosvenor Gallery Guide', *Punch* (21 June 1879), p. 286.

[68] Royal Academy, 1881, nos. 561 and 981.

[69] *J. J. Tissot: An Exhibition of Modern Art*, Dudley Gallery, London, 1882, nos. 1-4. Watercolour replicas of the pictures were also available for inspection upon application to the secretary. Because of the difficulty of photographing the oil versions, which are in damaged condition, the etchings after them have been reproduced. It was at the Dudley exhibition that Tissot made available photographs of

his entire *œuvre* in three albums (1859-70); 1870-6; and 1876-82: the albums, together with photographic material which postdates the Dudley exhibition, were sold Sotheby's, Monte Carlo, 15 June 1982, lot. 838, and are now in a private collection in the United States.

[70] None of the pictures, despite familiar titles, can be identified with known works, except no. 5 and Pl. 170; see also n. 84 below for the relationship of Pl. 163 with Dudley no. 6.

illustrations swept everything before their exemplary dullness, and the *Prodigal* made regular appearances at the principal World's Fairs at the end of the century.[71] Even the master of the *Vie de Jésus* did not repudiate their instructive fun, leaving them to the Luxembourg in his will as his most important works,[72] and when he came to illustrate the parable for his Bible, he could do no better than repeat the central group from *The Return* in Bedouin dress.

For its late Victorian audience, the *Prodigal* offered not only the comfort of intelligible meaning and the usual wealth of patently symbolic detail; the old story with a new twist[73] came in an immediately recognizable format, for such moralizing series had been popular in England since Hogarth had brought the genre to prominence in the eighteenth century. *The Prodigal Son in Modern Life* restates Hogarth's *The Rake's Progress* (as do the lucrative engravings which were issued after it), despite the fact that Tissot offers a less horrific glimpse into the void than his predecessor, equipping his prodigal with a suitably bourgeois fate after he has 'wasted his substance in riotous living' with all the abandon of a curate on a Cook's tour—a social contrast which reflects to a nicety the evolution between Hogarth's free-wheeling 'modern occurrences in high life' and Tissot's plutocratic Victorian caution. If the *Prodigal* offered reassuring kinship with the engravings which lined the corridors of clubs and country houses, it also had modern peers of great popularity in series like Frith's *The Road to Ruin* (1877; whereabouts unknown), issued in photogravure in 1882, or the fay equivalents Burne-Jones was offering the public with great success at the Grosvenor Gallery.[74]

The parable of the prodigal son must have held great appeal for Tissot, for having treated it twice in the sixties as an operatic and arbitrary costume drama (Pls. 14 and 16), he played it again in modern dress as a mildly cautionary tale. Between the sixties and the eighties, he covers the spiritual ground between Gounod's *Faust* and Puccini's *Madama Butterfly*, although the essential approach remains fixed in its concentration on the externals of the narrative. A letter of credit carries Tissot's middle-class Tom Rakewell from domestic ennui (Mrs Newton is seen suitably employed with the mending), to a tea-house which is the ultimate reverie of the ageing *japoniste* and surely based on a photograph,[75]

---

71 See appendix V.

72 Bastard, p. 278; Misfeldt, p. 326.

73 Putting the prodigal in contemporary dress was an old conceit; see, for example, a series of six in Directoire costume, by Auguste Legrand, engraved by Duthé around 1800.

74 For the development of the genre in the eighteenth century, see William Gaunt, *The World of William Hogarth* (London: Jonathan Cape, 1978), chap. 12, 'Modern Moral Subjects'; Burne-Jones's series, *The Days of Creation* (1875–6; Fogg Art Museum, Harvard University), were exhibited at the Grosvenor Gallery in 1877.

75 Photographs of Japan had been available as early as 1870 when work by Felice Beato was reproduced in Aimé Humbert, *Le Japon illustré* (Paris: Librairie Hachette, 1870), a work which was doubtless familiar to Tissot (see Weisberg, 'Photographic Documentation: Japan as Known to Early Japonists', in *Japonisme*, pp. 313–14.

to a verismo scene on the London docks which lights the emotional path he was to travel in the Bible illustrations (Mrs Newton astonished in her furs), and finally to respectability regained in a summer-house beside the Thames, with an impressive roast about to make its appearance from beneath its silver dome (Mrs Newton demurely festive). While the settings and the cast are familiar, it is difficult to guess what significance the story held for Tissot himself. Despite exile in London and illicit domesticity in St. John's Wood, it is hard to think of the cautious Tissot in terms of his thriftless Victorian, and parables of passionate error and Christian forgiveness seem less relevant than the symbolism of his *cloisonné Fortune* where Patience, 'the principal of all success and the basis of all fortune', seems about to be cheated of her just rewards by a minx of a goddess, Fortune, 'who raises the bandage from her eyes the better to discern her favorites'.[76]

At the time of the Dudley exhibition, one senses a solidification of opposition to Tissot's position as a successful outsider in the London art world. Insular resentment of his success, and his failure to heed the advice of critics like Ruskin to pursue 'high' art, at last tried the English beyond all patience, and they closed ranks against the outsider. Although the *Illustrated London News* found the Dudley exhibition 'displayed with a taste in the arrangements that is rarely seen in this country',[77] it was not a critical success, and even this faint praise hints that Tissot's attempts to raise the standards which prevailed in British exhibitions were not particularly appreciated by his peers. Writing with Tissot's knowledge and surely recording his own views in the matter, Lostalot openly attributed the failure of the Dudley exhibition to its over-abundance of success:

James Tissot has done the injustice—in the eyes of British painters and dealers—of importing a taste, for almost the first time, for 'Continental pictures' on English soil. This sort of thing is not readily forgiven; especially since the taste in question has now developed considerably, so as to lead to a real neglect of the works of insular artists. Add to this that the market of the continent and that of America are almost closed to their works, it is easy to understand that the painters of the soil have closed their ranks strictly against all art that is not English. Tissot felt the effects of this at the last exhibition of the Dudley Gallery. Artists as well as critics showed him something more than coolness.[78]

As Lostalot suggests, British objections to Tissot, however grounded in personal resentments and jealousies, were also symptomatic of a much greater crisis in English art in the seventies. Appearing in 1871 with the tremendous psychological advantage of a fully formed style, Tissot's accomplished pictures were

---

[76] From the description of the sculpture given in the Dudley catalogue, no. 71.

[77] 'Dudley Gallery Exhibition', *Illustrated London News* (27 May 1882), p. 552.

[78] Lostalot, 'Tissot', p. 383.

lauded at the expense of the native product, and only deepened a lack of confidence in English painting as growing awareness of the 'international' standards demonstrated by his work made the supremacy of French painting a patent fact. As G. M. Young suggests, the idea of 'art as an enclosed world, obedient to its own laws' did not come easily to the English, but once acquired, it was applied with a ruthlessness that struck at the very heart of the English school and left it with a lack of confidence which persisted well into the twentieth century.[79]

If the dozen odd paintings with intimate domestic subjects which were exhibited in London in the late seventies and early eighties were found remarkable for 'little save a sort of luxurious indolence and insolence' in their own time, a hundred years later they have come to represent the *sine qua non* of Tissot's popular reputation. He introduced the subject and the mood at the first Grosvenor exhibition with *Croquet* (Pl. 142),[80] which is also known in a highly finished gouache replica (Pl. 143). David Brooke has perfectly captured the vague uneasiness which underlies its placid surface, giving the picture its arresting psychological fascination:

It is a lazy, intimate and rather delectable secret garden in which we are invited, and at the same time prevented from entering. There is a suggestion of a threshold to be crossed, and we are further hindered by various objects at our feet—a croquet ball, a small dog, flowerpots and a watering can. A girl with a croquet mallet bars our way and seems almost to challenge us as intruders into a private and ideal world.[81]

The luxurious domesticity which marked the autobiographical *A Quiet Afternoon* (Pl. 144) and *Rivals* (Pl. 159) at the 1879 Grosvenor is also clearly present in works of equally remarkable quality like *Hide and Seek* (Pl. 160) and *En plein soleil* (Pl. IV) for which no definite record of contemporary exhibition has been preserved.

A number of little pictures can be grouped around these major works which offer variations on the themes they establish. Perhaps the most interesting aspect of the pictures, usually small in scale and painted on wooden panels, is their almost total reliance on photographic sources as the basis of composition. A handful of photographs, preserved for reasons of family sentiment by Lilian Hervey and later given to Marita Ross, doubtless represent only a fraction of those which existed. Fortunately, all of them can be related to known paintings or prints, and they shed invaluable light on Tissot's working method in the late seventies. According to Lilian Hervey, Tissot would develop his idea for a painting, pose his models, and have his studio assistant make a photograph. It was then used, with a

[79] G. M. Young, *Victorian England*, p. 161.
[80] Grosvenor Gallery, 1878, no. 32; for the etching after the painting, see Wentworth, *Catalogue*

Raisonné of Prints, no. 37.
[81] Brooke, 'James Tissot and the "Ravissante Irlandaise"', p. 57.

suitable adjustment of background, as the basis for one or more pictures, a process clearly demonstrated in the nautical background given to a photograph taken in the garden in Grove End Road (Pls. 119 and 120).

In other cases, a photograph of Mrs Newton with an unidentified man (Pl. 161) was said by Miss Hervey to have served for a now unlocated picture called *The First Cloud*;[82] it also served for the figure of Mrs Newton and a child in an oil sketch now called *Rêverie* (Pl. 162), which may in fact be the maquette for an etching of the same title.[83] Another photograph of Mrs Newton with a child and a woman—presumed to be her daughter, Violet, and her sister, Mary Hervey—(Pl. 164), served as the basis for an etching called *La Sœur aînée*,[84] and the same or a closely related but now unknown photograph served as the basis of a painting now given the same title (Pl. 163). Another photograph of Mrs Newton (Pl. 165) served in part as the basis for a painting, *En plein soleil* (Pl. IV)—certainly among the most beautiful of these works in its composition, fresh colour, and sentiment —and for the etching after it.[85]

Many paintings for which compositional photographs are not preserved also betray their source, and works like *The Picnic* (Pl. 166), a theme Tissot often treated at this time, or *The Park* (Pl. 167) clearly suggest photographic models. Such pictures continued to be painted even after the death of Mrs Newton and the dissolution of the household in Grove End Road, and two mezzotints which were scraped after Tissot's return to Paris, if not the sketches or photographs for them, clearly postdate their concept by a year or more. Drawn with no reference to the actual sitter, the highly animated yet strangely inexpressive features of Mrs Newton in the mezzotint *Le Banc de jardin* (Pl. 168) take on a waxen typification and hysterical liveliness which marks *La Femme à Paris*.

Tissot's reliance on the photograph during his last years in London can doubtless be traced in no small part to Mrs Newton's failing health and her growing inability to sustain difficult poses for long periods of time. It may also account for the tendency to repeat certain backgrounds—the Falcon Tavern or Richmond Bridge—from what were clearly photographs or careful studies made for the purpose, as the sites themselves became more and more inaccessible in terms of her physical strength. A now unlocated oil sketch for her figure in *Kew Gardens*, obviously taken from life—she sits on a model's stand—and quickly brushed in monochrome, may well have been supplemented by a photograph of the pose. The sketch itself may well represent her only physical participation after a visit to the gardens—and perhaps a compositional photograph or an oil sketch like that of Regent's Park (Pl. 153) of the Temple of the Sun itself—established the design of the picture.

---

[82] Ross, p. 7.
[83] W. 52.
[84] W. 53; a painting of the same title but of a different size was exhibited at the Dudley Gallery, 1882, no. 6.
[85] W. 54.

The chief aesthetic effect of Tissot's new reliance on the photograph was a dilution of the careful design of the pictures of the middle seventies which had been based on his Ingriste training and the study of Degas, Whistler, and the Japanese print. The increasing capacity of the camera to capture instantaneous effects translates itself into a random quality in the paintings which, no matter how carefully contrived in actuality, gives an effect of discursiveness which was clearly intended to keep his work 'modern'. Japanese art and the photograph had tended to validate one another in the seventies when the actual 'truthfulness' of many seemingly abstract effects in Jananese prints was corroborated by the evidence of the photograph, and this double influence had often struck a balance in works like *En plein soleil* (Pl. IV). When photographic sources are fully assimilated in his work, they tend to give it new direction and dimension; the clear reference to source in the least interesting of these little pictures, however, makes them appear little more than the 'mere coloured photographs' Ruskin called them. Unassimilated photographic sources, in combination with a sometimes gummy pigment and a growing insensitivity of touch, can make them singularly unattractive objects. They represent a transition from the technique of his Parisian training and the palette he had adopted in England to the open brushwork and often garish colour of *La Femme à Paris*. Only at their best can they honestly be said to maintain the standards of earlier pictures, but when they do they are often of the greatest beauty.

The earthly paradise Tissot had sought to preserve was already lost. Mrs Newton appears unnaturally thin and drawn in *Quiet* (Pl. 169),[86] and if the contemporary *Soirée d'été* (Pl. 170) disguises a harsh truth in its lavish approach, the rapid advance of illness is shocking in the less idealized *Jeune femme souffrante* (Pl. 171). Sometime after the Dudley exhibition, Tissot had asked Edmond de Goncourt for permission to illustrate his novel *Renée Mauperin*.[87] Mrs Newton posed as the heroine for the ten etchings which were based on photographs, and the most touching of them shows her sitting in the sun with Tissot shortly before her death, and was transcribed directly for one of the illustrations (Pls. 172 and 173).

Kathleen Newton died of consumption in Tissot's house on 9 November 1882, at the age of twenty-eight. Draping the coffin in purple velvet he prayed beside it for hours, prostrate with grief.[88] After the burial in Kensal Green Cemetery, Tissot abandoned the house and went to Paris. According to a visitor, his paints, brushes, and several incomplete canvases remained in the studio. In the garden, the old gardener was burning the mattress of the mysterious lady.[89]

[86] Royal Academy of 1881, no. 561. There is a water-colour replica of the picture in the collection of the Hon. James Tennant, London. The figure of Mrs Newton was repeated in another now unlocated picture which is vertical rather than horizontal in format.

[87] For the illustrations to *Renée Mauperin*, see Wentworth, *Catalogue Raisonné of Prints*, nos. 62–71.

[88] Ross, p. 7.

[89] Knoblock, 'The Whimsical Seventies', p. 679.

VI. La Femme à Paris

O Muses modernes! vous dont les chapeaux tout petits sont des merveilles de caprice et dont les robes éffrénées semblent vouloir engloutir l'univers sous des flots d'étoffes de soie aux mille couleurs, inspirez-moi! soyez mes soleils, grappes, agrafes et nœuds de diamants! Parfums de la poudre de fleur de riz à l'iris et du savon vert tendre au suc de laitue, donnez à cette œuvre une actualité agaçante!

Théodore de Banville, *Esquisses parisiennes* (1876).

ON Wednesday the fifteenth of November, 1882, Edmond de Goncourt noted in his journal that Tissot had arrived in Paris the previous evening, having made the momentous decision to resume his career in France after an absence of eleven years. He was forty-six years old.

Kathleen Newton's death need not have brought his career in London to its abrupt end. Nothing on the face of it seems to have required that he give up his acknowledged, if somewhat anomalous, position in the city that had been his home for a decade. It is understandable that he might not have wanted to continue to live and work in the setting so intimately associated with his dead mistress, but such feelings need not have necessitated total upheaval. Although his precipitate flight has all the appearance of deep-felt impulse, such new beginnings are seldom undertaken lightly, and he had plenty of time for thought during the last months of Kathleen Newton's inexorable decline. Tissot's behaviour rarely gives the impression of spontaneity. Indeed, a careful manipulation of circumstance never seems far from the spring of action, and his flight is surely the result of complicated and perhaps conflicting emotions rather than a simple response to the loss of Mrs Newton.

Perhaps Tissot's life was no longer as idyllic as his pictures suggest. James Laver proposes that the social exile imposed by the liaison had begun to grow tedious, that Tissot and Mrs Newton may have begun to regret the sacrifices they had made for love, and that he found himself tied down when he attempted to take up his former London acquaintances at the end of the decade.[1] In truth, life in Grove End Road must have been circumscribed to a great degree by

---
[1] Laver, *Vulgar Society*, pp. 47–8.

Kathleen Newton's dependants and relatives, and by the eighties they may well have lost much of their interest to Tissot both as companions and as pictorial subjects. His paintings seem to bear this out, for they reflect an increasing concern with a more public social life.

On the basis of what little contemporary evidence we have, however, it seems that Tissot's feelings for Kathleen Newton were of greater depth. Edmond de Goncourt, who never found Tissot particularly convincing emotionally, was obviously moved by the reality of his grief when they met in Paris a week after her death: 'Visite, ce matin, de Tissot arrivé dans la nuite d'Angleterre et qui me dit, dans la conversation, être très affecté de la mort de la Mauperin anglaise, qui, déja bien souffrante, lui avait servi de modèle pour l'illustration de mon livre'.[2] Lilian Hervey's memories of this time, admittedly those of a child, were also coloured by the excess of Tissot's grief, and his later dependence on spiritualism in the hope of making contact with his mistress in the next world is heart-rending, if faintly comic, in its misplaced faith.

If Tissot's position in the English art world had been acknowledged, it remained peculiar and by no means unassailable. His pictures sold well, but he never scaled the heights occupied by Millais and Alma-Tadema where criticism dissolved in paeans of admiration, and as the decade progressed, insular resentment intensified and critical tolerance wore thin as his narrative remained insensible to the requirements of native genre. With a wide artistic acquaintance in London, but cut off by his liaison, by his position as an outsider, and perhaps by temperament as well, Tissot seems to have made few close friends and is surprisingly seldom mentioned in the memoirs of the time. Whatever Tissot's feelings about his English career and his private life, the death of Kathleen Newton made a clean break in the pattern of his existence. With his personal links to England severed, perhaps he felt his position with added sharpness, and like his own prodigal son was ready to return home.

In Paris, he went about rebuilding his life and career with the laconic practicality that had marked his first years in London. Opening the house in the avenue du Bois, he renewed old friendships and set about planning a large retrospective exhibition to bring the Parisian public up to date on the evolution of his work during the previous decade. The majority of the hundred and two works exhibited at the Palais de l'Industrie in March, 1883, under the auspices of l'Union Centrale des Arts Décoratifs[3] were English works, and *The Prodigal Son in Modern Life* was again the *pièce de résistance* as it had been at the Dudley Gallery the previous year. With that series, *London Visitors* (Pl. 106) was exhibited as *Au musée de Londres; Good-bye, On the Mersey* (Pl. 147) as *Le départ d'un Cunard* (Liverpool);

---

[2] Goncourt, *Journal*, ii, 204–5.
[3] Palais de l'Industrie, *Exposition des œuvres de* M. J.-J. Tissot *organisée par l'Union Centrale des Arts Décoratifs* (Paris: Quantin, 1883).

and *July* (Pl. 132) as *Sea-side*. Virtually all Tissot's London etchings and his work in *cloisonné* enamel were also shown. Works which had not been seen in London included an unlocated series of decorations called *Le Jardin des Hespérides* and described as 'panneaux décoratifs pour la salle à manger de M. H. Oppenheim, de Londres'. There were also eight new pastels—all, from the evidence of titles and the examples known, bust portraits, usually of women or children, and decorative heads. *Le Journal* (Pl. 174) is the only one of the group which can now be identified with certainty from the allegorical titles and ellipsis-points of sitter's names in the catalogue, although an unlocated *Dimanche Matin* is recorded in an etching of the same title made the next year.[4]

Tissot's pastels had an immediate critical and popular success. Alfred de Lostalot found them to be the best of the works exhibited at the Palais de l'Industrie, far superior to the English works which had generally failed to please the Parisian public:

Les meilleurs des tableaux exposés par M. James Tissot sont des pastels, portraits de femmes et d'enfants traités librement et qui ceperndant doivent ressembler à leurs modèles, car le dessin est très cherché et souligné avec vigueur; les colorations sont justes et leur franchise de la touche leur a lassé tout leur fraicheur originelle.[5]

They were also a great success with *le tout Paris*. In 'Le Journal d'une parisienne', Jules Claretie records a visit to the Palais de l'Industrie in March between 'une demi-heure à l'exposition des aquarellistes', more calls than the coachman thinks good for the horses, and 'un tour au bois pour me reposer': 'Et ne pas oublier, aux Arts Décoratifs, la visite aux paysages de Lépic et aux pastels de Tissot, un Parisien de Londres devenu Londonien de Paris'.[6]

Pastel had been neglected in France since the Revolution, dismissed no doubt because of its associations with the rococo fripperies of the *ancien régime*, but with the general revival of interest in the art of the eighteenth century which began in the 1840s and reached flood tide in the eighties, artists had rediscovered the sympathetic qualities of the medium. Tissot had used pastel little if at all in the past, but after his return to Paris he employed it extensively. He was an early member of the Société de Pastellistes Français, a somewhat self-consciously *dix-huitième* organization founded in 1885 which exhibited at the Galerie Georges Petit, although his participation in its activities appears to have been minimal. With the possible exception of Helleu, the names now associated with the great revival of pastel in the eighties are not to be found in its membership lists, and

---

[4] Tissot made etchings after both *Dimanche Matin* and *Le Journal*: see Wentworth, *Catalogue Raisonné of Prints*, nos. 72 and 73.

[5] A. de Lostalot, 'Exposition de M. le Comte Lepic et James Tissot', *Gazette des beaux-arts*, p. 452.

[6] J. Claretie, *La Vie à Paris: 1883*, p. 114.

the presence of Jean Béraud, Madeleine Lemaire, and Léon Lhermitte—or even Puvis de Chavannes and Jean Raffaëlli—today hardly appear sufficient compensation for the absence of Degas and Redon (Manet had died in 1883 before its foundation).

Tissot, however, was also clearly familiar with the pastels of Degas and Manet. Certain aspects of his portraits appear to have been influenced by Degas, who was the most experimental of his generation in the use of the medium, but both his philosophical and technical approaches are far closer to Manet, whose aesthetic, like his own, was always more *faire joli* than probing or experimental. After 1880, Manet had used pastel almost exclusively to capture the spirit and charm of the fashionable *parisiennes* who sought souvenirs of their graces, and Tissot did the same.[7]

Virtually all of Tissot's portraits in the eighties and nineties appear to have been executed in pastel. He continued to be extremely popular as a portraitist, and was—as Philippe Jullian succinctly puts it—'the favoured portraitist of actresses and cocottes'.[8] These works exist in numbers larger than has been suspected, since they are for the most part still unlocated. As a group, they appear an overwhelming assemblage of feather fans, fur boas, and satin dresses—an impression only strengthened by the presence of an occasional *jeune personne* dressed for a *bal blanc* or *le tennis* and several babies done up to the nines for the painter's delectation: couturier's visions launched on seas of tufted upholstery and set in forests of potted palms or among the gilt mazes of folding screens. (Now and again, Tissot varies this rich diet with a more sharply characterized male portrait which comes as something of a pleasant shock among the photographic sequences of his albums.) The considerable variation in the quality of these portraits is doubtless largely the result of Tissot's response to his sitters. None the less, in almost every case bright smiles and melting glances defeat all but the most superficial and flattering characterization. If nothing else, these portraits capture the Louis XVI-Empire modishness of Parisian society in the eighties and nineties. Unfailingly clever in composition, pale and bright in colour, and remarkably skilful in technique, Tissot's brittle social images offered worthy competition (and also, no doubt, useful models) for the bravura flights of his friends Helleu, Boldini, and Forain.

Created concurrently with his illustrations to the Bible, and between trips to the Holy Land, these provocative and worldly images contrast strangely with his religious works. It is a contrast which gives us pause, but it is indicative of an attitude not uncommon in France as the Catholic revival drew more and more

---

[7] For the revival of pastel in France and critical studies of the pastels of Manet and Degas, see John Rewald, *Edouard Manet Pastels* (Oxford: Cassirer, 1947) and Douglas Cooper, *Pastels by Degas* (Basel: Holbein, 1952).

[8] Jullian, *Dreamers of Decadence*, p. 137.

converts from the ranks of fashionable artists. It never seems to have struck Tissot as odd or incongruous that drawings of Jesus—the result, as he blandly told the press, of divine revelation—were interspersed with sittings for portraits like that of the actress Réjane (whereabouts unknown), or the one of the princesse de Broglie perched on an Empire table against a background of palms (Pl. V).

Not unexpectedly, Tissot brought both his insistent technique and a sharp sense of psychological tension to his pastels. *Berthe* (Pl. 175),[9] which can be dated to 1882–3 on the evidence of the etching after it, is a clever, if unsettling, mixture of rococo affectations and nervous personal mannerisms. As fashionable taste for the eighteenth century became widespread, such portraits were often consciously conceived as extensions of an older tradition. The pastel portraits of Manet, Forain, Helleu, and Blanche can be considered in these terms, but the parallels between those of Tissot and Degas and the eighteenth century are particularly instructive. Jean Boggs has compared the portraits of Degas with those of Perroneau or Quentin de la Tour, noting that in each a delight in elegance and unaffected prettiness never distorts a basic honesty in the depiction of physical and psychological characteristics, but that honesty itself is always tempered by a deep human sympathy on the part of the artist for the dignity and spirit of his sitters.[10] By comparison, Tissot's insistence on topical descriptiveness, affected gesture, and spiritual *malaise* gives his portraits an eccentricity which has little of the timeless about it.

The portrait *Woman with a Gun* (Pl. 176) is even more extreme in its psychological insistence, and can be dated to the middle 1890s when the illustrations to the Bible already had occupied his attention for a decade. Unusual only in its particularly high quality, this late work serves as a perfect example of Edmond de Goncourt's criticism of Tissot's 'Hard' pastels which, with the 'bland' portraits of Helleu and the 'nervous' ones of Blanche, he thought had lost the spirit of their eighteenth-century predecessors in their insistence on psychological oddity: '. . . leurs roses d'engelures et leurs violets plombés on dirait qu'ils ne veulent exprimer que l'éreintement, l'ahurissement, le barbouillage de cœur, enfin tous les malaises physiques et moraux d'une physionomie de femme.'[11] If this psychological reportage distressed Goncourt, it now seems an essential part of *fin-de-siècle* artistic expression, a virtue in Tissot rather than a defect.

In 1883, Tissot's election as a *membre titulaire* of the Société d'Aquarellistes Français gave him an additional place to exhibit, and his retrospective at the

---

[9] Although not exhibited until 1885 at the Galerie Sedelmeyer with *La Femme à Paris* (no. 36), the etching after it is dated 1883: see Wentworth, *Catalogue Raisonné of Prints*, no. 74.

[10] J.S. Boggs, *Drawings by Degas*, p. 196. In one instance, Tissot attempted to emulate the pastellists of the eighteenth century: for the un- located portrait of a young woman, presumably an actress in a costume rôle, he deploys the flashier repertoire of rococo graces. The result, if one is not too closely critical, is an attractive facsimile of a minor eighteenth-century portrait.

[11] Goncourt, *Journal*, iii, 1157.

Palais de l'Industrie was supplemented by the works he sent to the Society's annual exhibition at the Galerie Georges Petit. Although he remained a member until the early nineties, Tissot exhibited only three times, in 1883, 1884, and 1886.[12] In the biographical article which marked Tissot's election to the Société d'Aquarellistes Français, which is one of the most valuable sources of information about Tissot, Alfred de Lostalot avoided the whole question of Tissot as a water-colourist, confining his remarks to saying that he had 'a high opinion of his talent'.[13]

Like his prints, Tissot's water-colours are usually repetitions of his paintings, but unlike his prints, they bring little technical originality to the medium and are undeniably cramped in execution. Only the best have any particular interest: among these water-colour replicas, *Le Confessional* (Pl. 33) and *Waiting at Dockside* (Pl. 149) have both intelligence and sensibility in their approach, but they are otherwise typical of the replicas Tissot appears to have made in some number in the eighties after both English and French works. More generally rewarding are the studies he made in gouache for numerous pictures in the early seventies. He clearly enjoyed the opaque, powdery quality of gouache, which approximated to the surface of his paintings, and used it with an attractive freshness. A study for *The Last Evening* (Pl. 85) is among the finest of them and represents a number of particularly accomplished works. In at least one instance, gouache was used for an ambitious replica of a picture (Pl. 143). In general, however, Tissot's work in water-colour is without particular interest.

In his private life, Tissot tried to take up where he had left off at the outbreak of the Franco-Prussian War, frequenting *boîtes de nuit* and fashionable salons, but always getting up in the morning to go to mass. His companions in his revels, and perhaps church in the case of Forain, are said to have been Boldini, Helleu, and Forain.[14] An early dry-point by Helleu (Pl. 177), inscribed by the artist 'le peintre Tissot chez la princesse de Polignac', suggests a taste for smart society untouched by religious fervour, and conjures up the world Proust was already preserving in its mandarin complexity.

In 1885, Edmond de Goncourt recorded two pathetic if humorous attempts on Tissot's part to find new romantic interest. In the first, both Tissot and Aurélien Scholl are said to have competed for the favours of the tightrope dancer who appears in pink tights and artificial flowers in *L'Acrobate* (Pl. 183), walking a rope over the heads of the crowd at a *café-concert* in *La Femme à Paris*. It is a vignette worthy of the series itself:

un moment, il nous parle joliment d'une danseuse de corde, à laquelle il faisait concurrement la cour avec le peintre Tissot, qu'il nous peint,—le vieux romantique,—accompagnant sa belle à la

---

[12] See the catalogues of the Société d'Aquarellistes Française (Paris: Jouast) for the years 1883–90.

[13] Lostalot, 'Tissot', p. 382.
[14] Laver, *Vulgar Society*, pp. 52–3.

gare, tenant d'une main le cerceau dans lequel elle saute, de l'autre la *couseuse* mécanique avec laquelle elle a l'habitude de *répetasser* ses costumes.[15]

Later the same year, Tissot transferred his affections and even became engaged to a certain Mlle Riesener, described by Edmond de Goncourt as 'une fille déja d'un certain âge', adding a floor to his house in anticipation of the marriage. But the match, which had been arranged by Mme Daudet, was abruptly terminated: 'un jour, sur la vision de la silhouette vieillotte du dos de Tissot décrochant son paletot dans une antichambre, elle lui faisait dire par sa mère que son envie de se marier était passée'.[16]

It was also in 1885 that Tissot, unlucky in love with the living, first tried to establish contact with the dead Kathleen Newton through a course of seances which were, in his opinion at least, entirely successful. Spiritualism went hand in hand with the 'attractive irrationality' of the Catholic revival which was also to claim him at this time, and these two unlikely *appassionnements* were to give his career its surprising final twist.

From the time of his return to Paris in 1882, Tissot's major occupation must have been the creation of a series of fifteen large canvases which showed *parisiennes* of various classes at their occupations and amusements. Completed some three years later, *La Femme à Paris* was exhibited at the Galerie Sedelmeyer in the spring of 1885 and at the Arthur Tooth Gallery in London the following year.[17] Without narrative progression, the series was unified only by the standard size of the canvases and their single theme: the fabled chic, and sometimes *chien*, that set the *parisienne* apart from all other women in her unerring sense of style.

By the eighties, the *parisienne* had psychologists, poets, artists, historians, philosophers, humorists, musicians, and inquisitors, not to mention flatterers, devoted to her study, all spiritual descendants of Baudelaire's discovery that fashion was an integral part of modern beauty. Study had set certain guidelines. To be a true *parisienne* was only slightly less difficult than to enter the kingdom of heaven: no provincial and no foreigner, by effort, emulation, or length of residence, could hope to become one: 'Vous connaissez sans doute la proverbe qui dit: Grattez le Russe, vous trouverez le Cosaque. Eh bien! soulevez le voile tisse d'artifice dont ce couvre depuis quinze ans la femme qui est à Paris et qui n'en est point, vous reconnaîtrez la provinçale'.[18]

But if the true *parisienne* was born only in Paris, geographical accident in no

---

[15] Goncourt, *Journal*, iii, 413.
[16] Goncourt, *Journal*, iii, 498. She was Louise, daughter of the painter Léon Riesener (1808–78). According to an inscription on the back of an oil sketch for the picture (Mr and Mrs Joseph M. Tanenbaum, Toronto), Tissot portrayed Mlle Riesener in *Le Sphinx* for *La Femme à Paris* (Jane Abdy, oral communication): for a portrait of Louise Riesener by her father, dated 1876, see Geneviève Viallefond, *Le Peintre Léon Riesener* (Villeneuve-Saint-Georges: Morancé, 1955), pl. XI.

[17] For both exhibitions, see appendix IV.
[18] P. Perret, *Physionomies parisiennes: 'la parisienne'*, p. 12.

way conferred birthright: 'On n'est Parisienne par droit de naissance, comme on est reine ou duchesse. Il y a même de duchesses qui ne seront jamais Parisiennes; —il y a,—il y avait plutôt—des grisettes qui l'étaient'. This exclusive creature was a gorgeous creation in which art and artifice had triumphed over nature: 'Si ce n'est pas le chef d'œuvre suprême de la forme, c'est le suprême de l'élégance'.[19]

Alas, this modern sphinx was without a riddle. Artifice and cynicism had vitiated true feeling, and the *parisienne* had become merely a superb doll in the contemporary puppet-show:

> Les petites marionettes font, font, font:
> Trois petits tours et puis s'en vont.[20]

The doll was undeniably lovely, but her beauty had become disturbing and dangerous. The 'fruit suprême de la civilization' had become 'toujours un fruit vert'.[21]

It was the citizens of this quicksilver democracy of chic that Tissot took as his subject. With discretion as well as wisdom, he attempted definition only by example. The fifteen actresses in the little comedies of *La Femme à Paris* are placed at the centre of tableaux vivants which suggest the bounds of their charm without attempting to define it too closely.

The pictures of *La Femme à Paris* are the logical extension of the approach and subject of much of Tissot's London work, to which serial format now gives a superficial continuity. But if a serial format is a logical development in his work, it also demonstrates yet again his impressive ability to bend the most advanced currents of the art of his time to his own conservative uses. *The Prodigal Son in Modern Life* had retained the strict narrative progression and moral implication of Victorian painting, although it may have turned his thoughts to the series form as a means of giving narrative unity to his pictures. *La Femme à Paris* is quite different and rather more complex in its aesthetic implications.

After a decade of aesthetic provincialism, renewed contact with French painting acted almost like a drug on Tissot, and *La Femme à Paris* shows an interest in complex formal problems and a sense of excitement long absent in his English work. His new concern with scale corresponds to the search for monumentality which had prompted Renoir to abandon Impressionism and Seurat to begin his first great projects; his interest in the series parallels that of Monet, as does his palette, dense brushwork, and decorative patterning; and his subject, treated as a programmatic series, reflects those which occupied Manet and Degas: shop-girls, society ladies, the *demi-monde*, and circus performers, caught up in the ceaseless life and agitation of the city, whose friction gives them a hysterical brilliancy which is surely the 'real' subject of the series.

---

[19] Perret, pp. 13–14, 21.   [20] Uzanne, *Fashion in Paris*, p. 166.   [21] Perret, p. 11.

Advanced painting gave Tissot both the courage and the means to attempt the resolution of his genre within a grand design that at once imposed formal, philosophical, and iconographic order. In the past, his narrative had alternated between the anecdote of *Le Gôuter* or *A Convalescent* (Pls. 48 and 113) and the subject-lessness of *L'Escalier* or *London Visitors* (Pls. 52 and 106): *La Femme à Paris* attempts to combine both within a single pattern, and at its best it succeeds admirably. Modern beauty and modern temperament had always been at the heart of Tissot's narrative; they now become the stuff of mythology, modern life the stuff of history. *La Femme à Paris* is not the series of clever snapshots of Parisian life it is often assumed to be, it is an ambitious and often successful attempt at history painting. Like the barmaid in Manet's *Le Bar aux Folies-Bergère* (1881–2; National Gallery, London), which is perhaps the one truly viable proto-type for the series, Tissot's *parisiennes* are the goddesses of modern life—'dull and subtle', as Degas found Manet's barmaid, and perhaps dangerous—and like the abstractions which people Seurat's *La Grande Jatte* (1884–5; Art Institute of Chicago), they exist in a world where irony gives the most subtle flavour to the formal order of *la grande peinture*.

At the Galerie Sedelmeyer, the exhibition was made up of the fifteen pictures of the series, two others of the same size intended for an incomplete second series devoted to foreign women, to be called *L'Étrangère, The Prodigal Son in Modern Life*, and a number of paintings, pastels, prints, and *cloisonné* enamels which had been exhibited before. *La Femme à Paris* was divided into three groups of five canvases:[22] *L'Ambitieuse* (Pl. 178), of which an earlier version is known,[23] *Ces dames des chars* (Pl. 179),[24] of which a water-colour replica on silk of the left half is known (Musée de Dijon), *Sans dot* (Pl. 180),[25] *La Mystérieuse* (Pl. 181), for which an oil sketch is known (Roy Miles Gallery, London), and *La Plus Jolie Femme de Paris* (Pl. 182). The second series was made up of *L'Acrobate* (Pl. 183), *La Menteuse* (Pl. 184), *La Mondaine* (Pl. 185),[26] *La Demoiselle d'honneur* (Pl. 186), and *Les Femmes d'artiste* (Pl. 187). The third series was

---

[22] This subdivision of the series relates to the proposed publication of etchings after the paintings: the first five etchings, which were completed before the project was abandoned, are repro., Wentworth, *Catalogue Raisonné of Prints*, nos. 77–81.

[23] This picture, in the Musée d'Orsay, Paris (oil on canvas, 90.17 × 50.17 cm.; RF 2253), is thought by Misfeldt, (pp. 185–6) to be *Evening*, exhibited at the Grosvenor Gallery, 1878, no. 33, on the basis of descriptions in contemporary reviews like that of *The Times*, 2 May 1878, p. 7: 'The crush at the entrance to a west-end *soirée*, with a young lady in a daring "arrangement," in which yellow predominates in head-gear, fan, and dress, all of the most pronounced fashion of modern millinery, a figure

worthy of Worth.' If so, the lapse of seven years between the d'Orsay *Evening* and the Buffalo *L'Ambitieuse* does much to explain Parisian quips that the lady's ambition was clearly not to be thought *à la mode*: her 'daring arrangement' was hopelessly outmoded in 1885 (see Wentworth, *Catalogue Raisonné of Prints*, p. 304).

[24] See H. Gourley, 'Tissots in the Museum's Collection', *Bulletin of the Museum of Art, Rhode Island School of Design*, pp. 1–11.

[25] For *Sans dot*, see also the entry by Willard Misfeldt in d'Argencourt and Druick, *The Other Nineteenth Century*, s.v. 'Tissot', no. 67.

[26] For *La Mondaine*, see also ibid., no. 68.

made up of *Les Femmes de sport* (Pl. 188),[27] *Les Demoiselles de province* (Pl. 189), which is a variation of the central group of *Too Early* (Pl. 101),[28] *Le Sphinx* (Pl. 190),[29] *La Demoiselle de magasin* (Pl. 191), for which an oil sketch is known (Art Museum of the Socialist Republic of Romania, Bucharest), and the still unlocated *Musique sacrée*, the photograph of which has been removed from Tissot's album.

The two works from the incomplete series *L'Étrangère* were *La Voyageuse* (Pl. 192), for which an unlocated oil sketch is known, and *L'Esthétique* (Museo de Arte de Ponce, Puerto Rico), for which a study of the gallery empty of figures is known (Rhode Island School of Design, Providence) as well as a particularly attractive replica in oil (Pl. 193). *L'Esthétique* is of independent interest as the most ambitious of a group of pictures of tourists in the classical galleries of the Louvre which occupied Tissot in the middle of the decade. Although its composition and narrative are in the manner of the most successful *Femme à Paris* pictures, others seem more closely related to the travel works of the late London period (Pl. 146). Since they usually include a figure readily identifiable as Mrs Newton, their origin is doubtless connected with the works from that time although they were almost certainly painted in Paris after her death. None of them seems to have been exhibited before 1883, when a water-colour version of *Visiteurs étrangers au Louvre* (Pl. 194) was shown at the Société d'Aquarellistes Français,[30] the figures from which were used in various combinations for a number of other works (see Pl. 195). If it is possible to trace the germ of these images to pictures like *Jeunes Femmes regardant des objets japonais* (Pls. II and 59), they now take on a sense of paradox which suggests intentional play upon the role of the artist, who is seen at work in a number of them, the viewer, never particularly attentive, and the work of art itself. Degas was interested in the exploration of similar relationships at this time, as works like *Mary Cassatt au Louvre* (L. 581, *c*.1880; private collection, New York) make clear, but his approach is quite fundamentally different, making Tissot's careful record of sculptural fact and his simplistic humour appear pedantic and rather pale in comparison with the formal and iconographic analogies which give Degas's treatment of the theme its depth, wit, and meaning. Tissot's pictures remain narrative in

---

[27] For *Les Femmes de sport*, see also D. Brooke, 'James Tissot's Amateur Circus', *Boston Museum Bulletin*, pp. 4–17.

[28] Misfeldt, p. 231.

[29] For *Le Sphinx*, see also the entry by Misfeldt in d'Argencourt and Druick, s.v. 'Tissot', no. 69.

[30] It has not been determined whether the present work is the one exhibited under that title at the Société d'Aquarellistes Français in 1883, no. 3, although a reproduction in Lostalot (p. 376) proves

it to have been of the same composition. There was a now unlocated oil version of the picture in the Seney collection (American Art Association Galleries, New York: *Modern Paintings from the Collection of George I. Seney*, 11 February 1891, lot 90), and there is an oil study of the setting empty of figures in the Louvre (repro., Charles Sterling and Hélène Adhemar, *Musée Nationale du Louvre: peintures, école française XIXe siècle*, 4 vols. (Paris: Musée Nationale du Louvre, 1958–61), iv, 706).

intent, and their charm is reminiscent of the *veduta* paintings of the late nine-teenth century which were aimed directly at the tourist trade they portray.[31]

La Femme à Paris was Tissot's last major attempt at society painting. Its large scale and intriguing subject were intended to bring him to the attention of the public and re-establish his artistic reputation in Paris, but the ambitious under-taking was a failure. The pictures were found to be unco-ordinated as a series, cumbersome in design, and unattractive in technique. Caught between the con-ventions of Victorian narrative painting and the avant-garde, they pleased hardly anyone. For a public not concerned with technical and aesthetic matters, Tissot's reportage was found superficial, 'easy reading like a clever, not too profound modern novel', and, even worse, not particularly Parisian: 'De la Parisienne, il n'en est pas question, le peintre nous met simplement sous les yeux une série de quatorze de genre plus ou moins réussis de la vie anglaise où le Bar's maid a été son seul modèle. On dirait des caricatures agrandies et coloriées de Punch'.[32]

In discussing individual pictures, *La Vie parisienne* again remarked on their English bias, finding *La Plus Jolie Femme de Paris* 'au contraire la plus simple des Anglaises', and *La Menteuse* 'toujours la même Anglaise'; the narratives comi-cally inept, pairing *La Demoiselle d'honneur* and *La Mondaine*, for example, as 'Le prince de Galles à 20 ans faisant monter une jeune fille dans un locati, rue Saint-Denis' and 'le prince de Galles 20 ans après, en extase devant une casque turque de velours rouge brodée d'or'; and the preponderance of circus pictures ridiculous in its lop-sided presentation of Parisian types, remarking sarcastically of *L'Acrobate*: 'quelques acrobates sur la corde raide complètent cette série de manifestations de la vie élégante d'une Parisienne'.[33]

The series is peopled with strange, elongated dolls, and individual character-ization gives way to complete and radical typification. There had always been a bias towards typification in Tissot's work, which was doubtless reinforced by his repetition of Mrs Newton's features in the late seventies, but in *La Femme à Paris* it reaches a new extreme. Typification gives a troubling unity to the series: each canvas, repeating the same animated but inexpressive face, projects some-thing hallucinatory, if not insane.

This unity of feature points up what appears to be the only apparent under-lying concept of the series: the equation of character and situation. For Tissot, the occupations and amusements of these women *are* their character. Suspended at the centre of these elaborate stagings, they are truly playing a doll's part: 'Ce sont de gracieux pantins mis en mouvement sur le théâtre où ils ont l'habitude

[31] For a study of Degas's use of such images, see Reff, 'The Pictures Within Degas's Pictures', pp. 125–9, 156–8.

[32] 'Art Chronicle', *Portfolio* (January 1886),

p. 144 and 'La Femme à Paris: Exposition Tissot', *La Vie parisienne* (2 May 1885), p. 255.

[33] 'La Femme à Paris', *La Vie parisienne*, p. 255.

d'évouler, qui n'appellent ni commentaires ni gloses, n'inspirent ni admiration ni répugnance ni désirs, et se contentent d'être interessants et agréables à voir'.[34]

These *parisiennes* are denizens of the Musée Grevin, spiritual precursors of the wax mannequins of the Palais de la Mode at the *Exposition Universelle* of 1900 where scenes of Parisian life were created with dummies dressed by Worth and Doucet for the delectation of provincials and foreigners who studied *The Departure for the Opera* or *The Fitting of the Wedding Dress* with rapt attention.[35]

Tissot had always used psychological and compositional devices to involve the viewer in his narratives, but in *La Femme à Paris* they are pushed to new extremes. Action is no longer confined within the frame, it spills out into 'real' space and the actors now speak directly to the viewer in a way that demands reaction. Direct visual contact with the painted figures and physical proximity to the scene itself are used in almost every picture. Both are familiar, and only the extremity of the attempt to blur the line between the painted and the real strikes a new note, but in the most successful pictures they have a shock which approaches originality.

In the past, Tissot had built the compositional and psychological effectiveness of many pictures on similar devices. *London Visitors* (Pl. 106) is based on the direct and penetrating glance of its protagonist, but at the same time its aesthetic and psychological distance is guaranteed by its 'arctic coldness' and the discouraging barrier of the flight of steps which raises the actors above the viewer's head. The same ambiguity is present in *Croquet* (Pl. 142), where openness and sensuality are contradicted by a feeling of challenge.

In contrast, the glances of the protagonists in *La Femme à Paris* are uncomplicated, given a hint of character more by their uniform look of smiling hysteria than by a psychological subtlety. Their fixed looks seem forward and impertinent, if not sometimes brazen. The glance of the woman in *Les Femmes d'artiste* (Pl. 187) is as central to its effect as that in *London Visitors*, but it partakes of none of the paradoxical quality which gives the latter picture its subtle fascination. It is merely sociable, commonplace, and more than a little vulgar, saved only by the omnipresent hint of hysteria which rivets the attention.

As psychological involvement is achieved by a repetition of the unequivocal stare, physical involvement comes through the elimination of middle distance. *Ces dames des chars* (Pl. 179), precipitates the viewer into the ring, practically under the wheels of the chariots, in a composition which guarantees a response. The principle is the same, if far less forced, in a picture like *L'Ambitieuse* (Pl. 178) where the lady's train sweeps across one's feet, or in *La Demoiselle d'honneur*

---

[34] *Courrier de l'Art* (1885), p. 200, quoted in D. Brooke, 'James Tissot's Amateur Circus', *Boston Museum Bulletin*, p. 9.

[35] For the Palais de la Mode at the *Exposition Universelle of 1900*, see P. Jullian, The Triumph of Art Nouveau, pp. 151–2.

(Pl. 186), where one is beside the lady as she steps into her cab. Both devices are merged in successful pictures like *La Demoiselle de magasin* (Pl. 191), where psychological and physical involvement are combined in a clever manner. In the pictures where composition and narrative are thus close-knit, *La Femme à Paris* succeeds best on its own terms.

In others, composition is less successful in heightening narrative. The conservative design of *Sans dot* (Pl. 180), which does not involve the viewer in the action, or *La Mondaine* (Pl. 185), where the superb glance of the woman is not quite able to activate the composition, results in pictures of less concentrated impact.

Within the fifteen pictures, there is similar variety of success in terms of subject and narrative. The three pictures which deal with popular theatrical performances are particularly successful: *L'Acrobate* (Pl. 183), the tightrope-walker Tissot had courted balancing over a sea of upturned faces, *Ces dames des chars* (Pl. 179), a performance at the Hippodrome de l'Alma where the glittering Amazons appear almost beautiful 'under the glamour of the electric light and amid the applause of the amphitheatre', and *Les Femmes de sport* (Pl. 188) a scene at a *cirque de High-Life* where *le tout Paris* took turns playing at being clowns and tightrope artists.[36] The success of these pictures lies in great part in the presence of a crowd which adds still another dimension to their effectiveness. The viewer is confronted by hundreds of staring faces which focus their attention on him, watching through glasses if necessary. In other pictures, *La Plus Jolie Femme de Paris* (Pl. 182) and *L'Ambitieuse* (Pl. 178) chief among them, the oppressive crowd not only stares, but whispers behind upraised hands. In all these canvases, the effect is overpowering as one has the uncomfortable feeling of being whispered about and watched. These simple devices prove remarkably effective in making the painted world intrude itself upon the viewer.

Others are less successful in terms of narrative, when their subjects are unsuited to presentation in simple visual terms or are treated with a dramatic ineptitude heretofore uncommon in Tissot's work. There is little mystery to be discovered in *La Mystérieuse* (Pl. 181), discounting her peculiar expression—a lady walking her dogs in the Bois followed by a socially reassuring footman; little allure about *La Plus Jolie Femme de Paris* (Pl. 182), a head-on confrontation which leaves nothing to the imagination; little to justify *La Menteuse* (Pl. 184) in a lady who seems about to tell a bold domestic fib about the price of coffee, sugar wafers, and cut flowers; and little riddle about *Le Sphinx* (Pl. 190), who seems only to puzzle about what has become of the man whose hat and stick she finds in her salon.

For modern taste, however, psychological strangeness and eccentric composition often take the place of narrative with great effectiveness. *La Mystérieuse*

---

[36] From the descriptions of the pictures given in Tooth, *Pictures of Parisian Life*, nos. 7 and 11 (Bibliography, s.v. 'Tissot'): see appendix IV.

pushes a tendency towards typification to new extremes; the last traces of aerial perspective disappear from *La Plus Jolie Femme de Paris*, so that the throng pressing into the room towards the viewer looms like the dilated figures of a dream; *Les Femmes d'artiste* (Pl. 187) has all the menace—and the sharp teeth—*La Menteuse* lacks; and if *Le Sphinx* is indeed without a riddle, its narrative—a Parisian staging of *A Convalescent* (Pl. 113)—is clever if hardly profound. At their best, these pictures look to the Symbolist painters for visual parallels, if not beyond them to the Surrealists.

La Femme à Paris was conceived on a scale larger than Tissot generally attempted, and he was forced to find a way to keep his small-scale technique from becoming monotonous. To do so, he animated the entire surface of the canvas with a relief texture of brush-strokes in the ground itself, and this independent texture underlies the actual painting, remaining visible although unrelated to what lies above it. Like the theme and composition of the series, this technique appears to have been fully developed before Tissot left England, for the same curious relief textures underlie the surface of works from the late seventies and early eighties.

The high key and decorative function of colour in *La Femme à Paris* suggests that Tissot attempted, with some timidity, to approximate the effects of late Impressionism. The greenish or greyish tonality of his earlier pictures, coloured essentially by carefully placed spots of bright local colour, gives way to a new brilliance of hue and a decorative use of colour he might have observed in the rich pattern, decorative contrasts, and complex textures of Degas's pastels of the eighties. Like many painters, Renoir notable among them, Tissot's palette grew warmer as he matured, and in *La Femme à Paris* a ruddy tone predominates. Even in pictures of a familiar cool grey cast, like *La Demoiselle d'honneur* (Pl. 186), red accents raise the temperature, and in those of a warm pinkish cast like *Les Femmes de sport* (Pl. 188), they bring it to the boiling point. Yet despite their new brilliance, it is not difficult to find Tissot's essentially black-and-white picture immediately beneath the surface of many pictures in the series.

La Vie parisienne did not trouble itself with technical terms, but it put an old complaint nicely none the less: 'J.-J. Tissot a une passion malheureuse et rétrospective pour les coquelicots; il aime cette couleur rouge, il en fourre partout: aux corsages, dans les cheveux, dans les traines. C'est pour lui le comble de l'élégance.' Their appreciation of colour was perhaps somewhat inhibited by another of Tissot's foreign mannerisms, for the physical presentation of the series at the Galerie Sedelmeyer was as alien to Parisian taste as its narrative genre. As he had done before, Tissot exhibited the pictures under glass in the English manner: 'Pour donner un air encore plus anglais à cette suite de tableaux, le peintre les a fait mettre sous verre. On ne sait pas plus si c'est de l'huile que de l'aquarelle, du pastel que de l'oléographie'.[37]

---

[37] 'La Femme à Paris', *La Vie parisienne*, p. 255.

Today, it is those pictures in the series which are most extreme that are the most rewarding. Their sense of pressurization or imminent explosion, the result of crowded surfaces, violent perspective, physical involvement, airlessness, and hard, decorative patterning, gives them a tautness and neurotic intensity which disturbs and excites. It is pointless to make any exaggerated claims for the paintings of *La Femme à Paris* as works of art, but it is equally difficult to deny their strange and compelling fascination.

A search for the visual predecessors and the peers of the series is not particularly rewarding. Such subjects lie close to popular illustration and the fashion plate, and it is only Tissot's narrative gift which lifts them into a higher category. But for a novelistic twist, paintings like *La Mondaine* (Pl. 185) have little to distinguish them from the trade cards of fashionable shops or the illustrations of society novels. It is also easy enough to make comparisons between *La Femme à Paris* and works like Renoir's *Moulin de la Galette* (1876; Louvre) or *Bal au Bougival* (1883; Museum of Fine Arts, Boston), Degas's *Miss La La au cirque Fernando* (1879; Tate Gallery, London) or *Chez la modiste* (1882; Museum of Modern Art), and Manet's *Nana* (1877; Kunsthalle, Hamburg), but it is difficult to press such comparisons further than iconographic similarities, for beyond a common impulse the differences are as fundamental as the similarities are superficial.

If we look in vain to find precise equivalents for *La Femme à Paris* among its visual peers, when we turn to contemporary literature the search is more rewarding, and the meaning of the series comes quickly into focus. Its impulse is almost entirely literary, and if it is considered as a group of short stories like the *mœurs parisiennes* which Daudet was writing at this time, psychological studies with surprise endings à la Maupassant, they take their proper perspective.[38]

As if to point up to the literary nature of the series, Tissot planned to issue etchings after the pictures in the series, and each was to be accompanied by an illustrative text written by a suitable contemporary author. According to an extended review of the exhibition which appeared in the *New York Times*,[39] Jules Claretie was to write on *L'Ambitieuse*, Théodore de Banville on *Ces dames des chars*, Georges Ohnet on *Sans dot*, Henri Meilhac on *La Mystérieuse*, Ludovic Halévy on *La Plus Jolie Femme de Paris*, Aurélian Scholl on *L'Acrobate*, Alphonse

[38] Studies of the *parisienne* were common at this time. Works like *Les Français peints par eux-mêmes*, published in 1841 and reissued in 1876-8, contain sketches of Parisian women, a number of which have titles similar to those used by Tissot for his series. Such subjects were also popular with magazines like *La Vie moderne*, which published numerous sketches of Parisian women in the eighties, some of which were collected by their author, baron de Vaux,

under the title *Les Femmes de sport* in 1885 (see Brooke, 'James Tissot's Amateur Circus', n. 15, p. 17). Somewhat later, Octave Uzanne's *La Femme à Paris*, a series of articles published between 1879 and 1894, was also collected in book form.

[39] 'Tissot's Novel Art Work', *New York Times* (10 May 1885), p. 10. I am indebted to Willard Misfeldt for this bibliographical source.

Daudet on *La Menteuse*, Sully-Prudhomme on *La Mondaine*, François Coppée on *La Demoiselle d'honneur*, Albert Wolf on *Les Femmes d'artiste*, Charles Yriarte on *Les Femmes de sport*, Guy de Maupassant on *Les Demoiselles de province*, Paul Bourget on *Le Sphinx*, Émile Zola on *La Demoiselle de magasin*, and Charles Gounod on *Musique sacrée*.

The ambitious project was never completed, abandoned when Tissot experienced his rebirth of faith while working on *Musique sacrée* and swallowed up in the huge task of illustrating the Bible. Only the first five etchings were completed, although they were never published, and the question of the accompanying texts is complicated and perhaps now insoluble. Although it seems quite certain that the project was well under way and that the authors had been invited to expand on Tissot's visual themes, few appear to have complied with his request by the time the project was abandoned.

From the evidence which remains, it is possible to speculate that Alphonse Daudet played a major role in the form and content of *La Femme à Paris*. If the series is a logical development of Tissot's aesthetic, it also represents a change of direction, but for Daudet such loosely related narratives under a covering title, his *mœurs parisiennes*, had long been a familiar feature. Friends from their earliest youth, the two men had grown close once again after Tissot's return from England, and it is very likely that Tissot drew his inspiration and the formal organization of his series from Daudet.

That Daudet took an active part in the organization of the literary aspects of the series is proved by an unpublished letter of introduction for Tissot to François Coppée in which Daudet describes the series and invites Coppée's contribution, accepting his terms or those of his publisher for Sedelmeyer in advance.[40] Daudet was given the text of *La Menteuse* for the series, and a short story of the same title was published in a collection of his works which appeared under the familiar title *Les Femmes d'artiste* in 1885. The degree of correspondence between text and picture was doubtless left to the individual authors, and the texts which have been located all tend to correspond more in spirit than fact. Daudet's *Menteuse*, for example, the mistress of an artist who lives in the avenue de l'Impératrice, dresses in mourning for a husband conveniently lost in the colonial service, and often returns home with flowers or jewels which she explains to her lover as the gifts of people to whom she gives piano lessons. She dies in the closing pages of the story, and all her stories are proved to be lies when her lover tries to locate her friends and relatives. She never reveals her secret, but it is obvious that the lady has been playing her naïve lover false with a vengeance.

[40] Manuscript collection, Boston Public Library (Department of Rare Books and Manuscripts, *MS. E.9.4 (65.12). Coppée's response to the invitation is not known: there is nothing in his work which suggests a correspondence with *La Demoiselle d'honneur*, the painting with which he is associated by the *New York Times*.

The *New York Times* describes Tissot's *Menteuse* as entering a room filled with what they call the 'mysteries' of 'false luxury', and with its sunflowers and flowering cherry, its Japanese 'nothings', and its furniture straight out of a Turkish bazaar, it sounds distressingly like the du Maurier *Punch* cartoon of a 'serious', aesthetic interior: 'In the background, coming between the opening portière, is the figure robed in a pretentious furbelow of black lace; her features have an unpleasant smile, inviting yet repulsive. In her arms she carries huge bunches of jonquils, forget-me-nots, and wall flowers'.[41]

Daudet's participation in *Ces dames des chars* is more complicated. The *New York Times* gives the text for the etching to Théodore de Banville, but there are correspondences so direct in Daudet's novel *Sapho*, which was published in 1884, that it clearly served Tissot for the painting. The novel is based on a youthful affair Daudet had with a woman named Marie Rieu, who is called Fanny Legrand in the novel, and the intriguing possibility exists that Tissot, having known Daudet since the 1860s, knew the story first-hand. In any case, Fanny Legrand numbers among her possessions 'un beau portrait par James Tissot, une épave des anciennes splendeurs de la fille', and has as a confidante a woman named Rosa, 'une ancienne "dame des chars" à l'Hippodrome'. A reminiscence by Rosa's elderly lover of his first sight of her twenty years earlier could be a description of Tissot's picture:

Moi, voilà vingt ans que je vis avec Rosa, vingt ans que revenant d'Italie après mes trois années de prix de Rome, je suis entré à l'Hippodrome, un soir, et que je l'ai vue debout dans son petit char au tournant de la piste, m'arrivant dessus, le fouet en l'air, avec son casque à huit fers de lance, et sa cotte d'écailles d'or, lui serrant la taille jusqu'a mi-cuisse. Ah! si l'on m'avait dit . . .[42]

The mention of Tissot's portrait of Fanny is surely a joking compliment to Tissot's fame as a fashionable portraitist during the Second Empire, but the reminiscence by Rosa's lover is precisely the kind of visual situation Tissot sought for the series. It demonstrates the essentially literary inspiration of the series even before it was given the pointed literary reference of textual illustration.

In at least one other instance, Tissot seems to have based his painting on an existing literary source. A passage in Ouida's novel of 1880, *Moths*, once again appears too close to be coincidental. Although the text of *La Mystérieuse* is given to Henri Meilhac, Ouida's hero sees the mysterious Anglo-Russian Princess Zouroff during a ride in the Bois: 'As he returned two hours later, he saw her walking in one of the *allées des piétons*; she was in black, with some old white laces about her throat; before her were her dogs and behind her was a Russian servant'.[43] The

[41] 'Tissot's Novel Art Work', *New York Times*, p. 4.

[42] Alphonse Daudet, *Sapho (mœurs parisiennes)*, *œuvres complètes* (Paris: Librairie de France, 1931), x, 45, 74, 83.

[43] Ouida (Louise de la Ramé), *Moths*, 3 vols. (Leipzig: Tauchnitz, 1880), ii, 141.

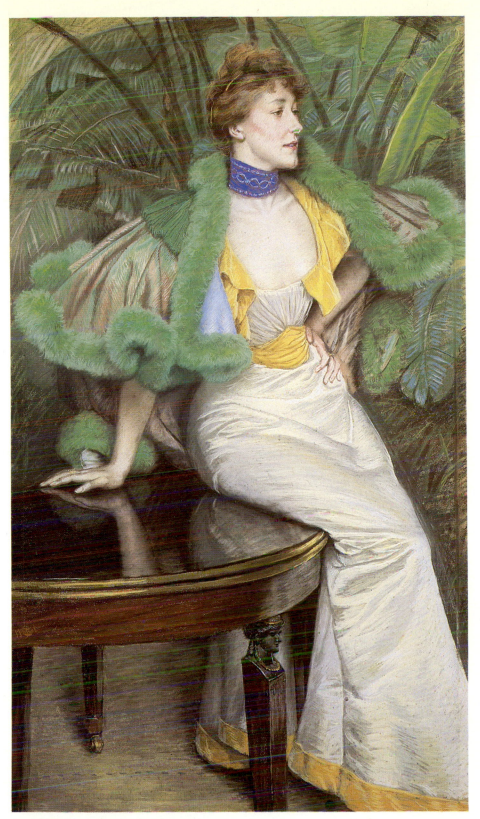

V. *The Princesse de Broglie, c.*1895.

presence in the picture of other passers-by, the visual representations of Ouida's *allée des piétons*, and a servant who wears what might well be the costume of a Russian coachman seems to confirm the source. It seems impossible that Tissot did not read Ouida while he was in England. Most people did, and her depiction of society has a theatrical perfection about it which is not unlike his own.

The correspondence between other pictures in *La Femme à Paris* and their texts is more direct. Ludovic Halévy was to write about *La Plus Jolie Femme de Paris*, and a story of that title was later published in English translation in *Parisian Points of View*.[44] At a performance of Ernest Reyer's *Sigurd* at the Opéra (presumably with Rose Caron singing and an enraptured Degas in the audience) Mme Derline, the wife of a Parisian lawyer, is singled out by the *abonnés* as 'the prettiest woman in Paris'. But fame is fickle, and the next day her title is reassigned to a musical comedy actress. Tissot captures her triumph at the Opéra, which lasts only as long as an entr'acte.[45]

Georges Ohnet was to write about *Sans dot*, and a story of that title later appeared in *Les Lettres et les arts*.[46] The dowerless orphan of a colonel, the young lady spends the melancholy autumn of her father's death with her mother listening to the music at Versailles, but love triumphs over material concerns, and the story ends with her engagement.

Perhaps other correlations can be made between the remaining pictures and their authors, although those that have been established have all been early in the series, and it is possible that the later texts were never actually solicited. None the less, it is tempting to identify *La Demoiselle de magasin* with Zola's *Au Bonheur des dames*, and it would be a pleasure to have the stories by Maupassant and Bourget. At present, however, there are more than enough examples to determine the working pattern of *La Femme à Paris* and to clarify its essential literary orientation.

There is absolutely nothing in *La Femme à Paris* which suggests the radical change Tissot now made in his art. Suddenly, the gorgeous *pantins* were swept away by religious devotion, the occult, and the decision to illustrate the Bible instead of society novels.

According to Tissot's own account, it was while he was completing the last painting for *La Femme à Paris* that he experienced the mystic vision that changed him completely. *Musique sacrée* represented a *femme à la mode* singing a duet

[44] L. Halévy, 'The Most Beautiful Woman in Paris', *Parisian Points of View*, pp. 83–110. It has been impossible to discover if, where, and when the story was published in France. There is no bibliography of Halévy's works: incredibly prolific as a writer, he contributed to numerous periodicals, and it is virtually impossible to trace many of his works.

[45] Rose Caron, Reyer, and Degas were all friends of Halévy: the choice of *Sigurd* for the opera in *La Plus Jolie Femme de Paris* was obviously in the nature of a private joke (see Lemoisne, i, 148–9, 212, and 254).

[46] Georges Ohnet, 'Sans dot', *Les Lettres et les arts* (New York: Scribner's Sons, 1888), pp. 121–7. I am indebted to Harold Peterson for this bibliographical source.

with a nun in the organ-loft of a church,[47] repeating the subject, and perhaps the composition, of a picture he had painted in the middle sixties, *Jeune Femme Chantant à l'orgue* (Pl. 35). While making studies for it, Tissot returned to the churches from which he had long been absent:

It came about in a mysterious way—one that I do not pretend to understand. I was then painting a series of pictures, to be called 'La Femme à Paris,' representing the pursuits of the society woman of the gay capital. At that time it was the fashion to sing in the choir of some great church, and I wished to make a study for my picture 'The Choir Singer.' For this purpose I went to the church of St. Sulpice during mass, more to catch the atmosphere for my picture than to worship. But I found myself joining in the devotions, and as the Host was elevated and I bowed my head and closed my eyes, I saw a strange and thrilling picture. It seemed to me that I was looking at the ruins of a modern castle. The windows were broken, the cornices and drains lay shattered on the ground; cannonballs and broken bowls added to the debris. And then a peasant and his wife picked their way over the littered ground; wearily he threw the bundle that contained their all, and the woman seated herself on a fallen pillar, burying her face in her hands. Her husband, too, sat down, but in pity for her sorrow, strove to sit upright, to play the man even in misfortune. And then there came a strange figure gliding towards these human ruins over the broken remnants of the castle. Its feet and hands were pierced and bleeding, its head was wreathed with thorns, while from its shoulders fell an Oriental cloak inscribed with the scenes, the Fall of Man, the Kiss of Judas. And this figure, needing no name, seated itself by the man, and leaned its head upon his shoulder, seeming to say, more by the outstretched hands than in words: 'See, I have been more miserable than you; I am the solution of all your problems; without me civilization is a ruin.' The vision pursued me even after I had left the church. It stood between me and my canvas. I tried to brush it away, but it returned insistently. Finally I was attacked by fever, and when I was well again I painted my vision.[48]

The Ruins, sometimes called *Inner Voices*, unlocated and known only through an engraving in Levy's article (Pl. 196), is the first tangible product of Tissot's conversion, and must have been painted at the end of the *Femme à Paris* series. In the exhibition of the illustrations to the Bible which took place in 1894, after nearly ten years of dedicated labour, it was assigned the first number in the

---

[47] It is indicative of the religious feeling of the time that this paradoxical subject was also treated the same year by Henri Lerolle whose *A l'orgue* was exhibited at the Salon of 1885 and is now in the Metropolitan Museum (repro., Charles Sterling and Margaretta M. Salinger, *French Paintings: A Catalogue of the Collection of the Metropolitan Museum of Art*, 3 vols. (New York: Metropolitan Museum, 1966), ii, 211).

[48] C.H. Levy, 'James Tissot and his Work', *New Outlook*, pp. 954 and 956. The painting was sold with the contents of the artist's studio in 1903 where it is called *L'Apparition* and described as 'le Christ revêtu d'habits sacerdotaux, au milieu des

ruines de la Cour des Comptes, vient au secours d'un malheureux abusé de la Commune' (Hôtel Drouot, Paris, *L'Atelier de M. James Tissot*, lot 1). The subject of *The Ruins* suggests that Tissot was already familiar with certain dogmas of the Catholic revival. If there was an *éminence grise* in his return to the church, it may well have been the missionary priest père Bichet, the brother of Tissot's sister-in-law, Claire, who had been a widow since the death of Tissot's brother Marcel-Affricani in 1877, and to whom he was particularly attached. For Tissot's portrait of père Bichet, inscribed *à Claire*, and now in the Musée de Nantes, see appendix VI, 1889, no. 1309.

catalogue, the acknowledged progenitor of the series. It appears to be a curious picture, as far as can be judged from the engraving, but it is also less visionary than Tissot would have one believe, for it is curiously doctrinaire. It is, in fact, practically a textbook illustration of the most popular doctrines of the Catholic revival, the suffering of the poor and the moral superiority of the peasant.

It was not unusual, it seems, for 'the figure needing no name' to make such personal appearances for the benefit of late nineteenth-century Christianity. In what is surely the most winsome of them, Jean Béraud's *Saint Mary Magdalen Prostrate before Christ in the House of the Pharisee* (1891; Walker Collection, Paris), Jesus abandons the Third Estate in order to attend a gentleman's dinner where the famous *horizontale* Liane de Pougny, as Mary Magdalen—in a *toilette* made especially for the picture by Redfern[49]—prostrates herself at his feet. The group includes all the Catholic revival's particular *bêtes noires*: Ernest Renan, the hated author of a sceptical *Vie de Jésus*; the chemist Chevreul, representing the enemy science; Alexandre Dumas's *fils*, representing immorality; and Clemenceau representing the anti-clerical Third Republic. Jesus is personified by the pious duc de Quercy, giving a lecture, apparently about Mlle de Pougny, but the gentlemen register only well-bred surprise at the intrusion of the Tolstoyan figure wearing a bed-sheet. Doubtless one is meant to know that Christianity retains its force even in such Godless company, although it is a little hard to tell, but it would be impossible to find another image which so precisely characterizes the religious emotions and confusions of the *fin de siècle*.

Tissot's illustrations to the Bible were to be his last major undertaking and were left unfinished at the time of his death. In their scope, they might be said to be among the most significant visual monuments of the Catholic revival, although it can also be said that their often indifferent artistic quality places them essentially outside the realm of art. As reflections of the theological implications of the Catholic revival in the visual arts, and as a curiously logical development of Tissot's aesthetic, they are of the greatest interest. In a real sense, the 'Tissot Bible' is as accurate a representation of 'vulgar society' in the nineties as his genre pictures of the previous decades had been, for society had got religion and liked to think of itself *portée à la devotion*. As Béraud's *Mary Magdalen* points out with such directness and charm, the man who came to dinner in the nineties was Jesus Christ.

---

[49] Jullian, *The Triumph of Art Nouveau*, pp. 127–8.

VII. God and the Blessed Spirits

> *. . . the veil*
> *Is rending, and the voices of the day*
> *Are heard across the voices of the dark.*
>
> Alfred, Lord Tennyson, *The Ring* (1889).

ALTHOUGH Tissot's career appears in retrospect to have been consistently successful, it is possible that it seemed the opposite to him. Certainly few artists ever made better use of a limited talent, but his ambition always exceeded his artistic gift, if not his entrepreneurial skill, and it is likely his laborious intelligence recognized its own limitations if not the genius of many of his friends. His career was the repeated victim of circumstance, much of it suspiciously of his own making, and at the mercy of those *appassionnements* which give his art new direction. External events divide his career into neat segments, each ending with upheaval and change. His successful career as a Salon painter in the sixties ended in the confusion of the Commune, a second career in London was terminated in the emotional cataclysm of Kathleen Newton's death, and the first half of the eighties saw the total failure of his attempt to recapture a significant Parisian following. But success was yet to crown his efforts, and Tissot was to have one triumph unalloyed: the 'Tissot Bible'. It is difficult to believe that these overworked little pictures ever aroused particular interest: that they were met with hushed reverence and immense popularity on two continents is nearly incomprehensible.

Considering the emotional climate of the eighties in France, it is not surprising that Tissot turned to the religion of the Catholic revival and to spiritualism for comfort, for both of those failed movements were at the height of their considerable popularity and drew countless numbers with their soothing doctrines. He was in need of spiritual comfort. The death of Mrs Newton had left an emotional void which his tragi-comic attempts at romance had not filled, and the several Parisian exhibitions of his work in the early eighties had made it clear that he could not recapture the position he had enjoyed in the sixties. A chance return to a church for the worldly research of *La Femme à Paris* may well have touched sentiments dormant since the religious training of his childhood and suggested a professional and emotional alternative.

The Goncourts found Tissot a complex blend of mysticism and phoniness, and it will never be known how much of his vision in St. Sulpice he actually believed to have taken place and how much was fabricated, the creation of opportunistic self-dramatization and a thirst for publicity at the time of the exhibition of the illustrations to the Bible. Tissot had been profoundly impressed by the idealized aesthetic of Burne-Jones in the late seventies and had made a temporary revision in his own work to conform to its standards, as his abandoned *The Triumph of Will* demonstrates, but the tremendous success of Burne-Jones at the Grosvenor Gallery of 1877 had also demonstrated the commercial possibilities of 'ideal' art with a clarity that must have struck Tissot with equal force. Whether the Tissot Bible represents piety and pure faith, commercial exploitation, or a blend of the two, as seems most likely, it becomes increasingly difficult to speak of Tissot in terms of rational behaviour after that afternoon in St. Sulpice in 1885.

The form of Tissot's conversion was the fashionable one of the day. The *fin de siècle* offers the repeated spectacle of the most unlikely converts returning to the church after experiencing visions worthy of Puvis de Chavannes or Gustave Moreau. Tissot was one among many. Visions were in the air, and each with its trappings of mystic innocence and magical revelation was usually recorded by its grateful recipient with the same hollow, if hysterical, sound. Tissot's mystic vision of Christ the Comforter was in the best theological company, however, for even Léon Bloy, the leader of the Catholic revival, also had the lamentable tendency to 'confondre le surnaturel avec le merveilleux'.[1] Small wonder that Tissot did the same, or that his mystical Catholicism went hand in hand with an apparently unshakeable belief in spiritualism and the materialization of the dead.

The Catholic revival and the spiritualist movement can be traced to the same nineteenth-century *malaise*. As Ronald Persall has pointed out in his comprehensive study of Victorian spiritualism, beneath the rational optimism of the century lay the fear that the dismissal of God from his universe had left only a yawning chasm.[2] Spiritualism and the Catholic revival are two sides of the same coin. The Catholic revival was a reaction against the claims of science, a suspension of knowledge and intellect in favour of absolute faith. The rejection of scientific knowledge and the attempt to recreate a world of faith which had been lost since the Middle Ages, if it ever existed at all, at once repelled the intellectuals who might otherwise have been drawn to the movement and attracted those hungry for sentimental

---

[1] Marie-Joseph Lory, *La Pensée réligieuse de Léon Bloy* (Paris: Desclée et de Brouwer, 1971), p. 41.

[2] R. Persall, *The Table Rappers*, p. 9. Persall offers what is probably the most balanced and palatable study of Victorian spiritualism to date.

historicism, romantic piety, and hysterical mysticism, as well as a plain old-fashioned lunatic fringe. In rejecting intellectualism, the Catholic revival lost those who could best have defended it and gained those who would ultimately bring it to disgrace.

Spiritualism doubtless began as an attempt to bring the technological equipment of science to bear on certain phenomena in the belief that science would ultimately unravel the mysteries, not only of this world, but of the next. But the number of true *savants* was small, the number of frauds and entrepreneurs large, and whatever claim it might have made to scientific credibility was quickly lost in the angry lamentations of the tricked who found it out and the paeans of those who did not. As Persall says, if even one of the hundreds of supposed materializations which took place in the nineteenth century had proved legitimate, the whole movement would have to be reassessed in a new light; none of them has. In the face of scientific evidence, to believe in spiritualism in the nineteenth century also required a total suspension of intellect and a powerful will to believe.[3]

Tissot was seriously attracted to both movements simultaneously, although he may already have dabbled in the occult in the late seventies, in London. According to Bastard, he had been plunged into 'une profonde tristesse' by the death of his brother Marcel-Affricani in 1877, and 'influencé par le ciel brumeux de la perfide Albion qui jeta dans le mysticisme quelques'uns de nos meilleurs artistes, tel que Gounod, se mit en relations avec les plus éminents médecins anglais, n'épargnant ni le temps ni les efforts pour étudier les choses occultes'.[4] Certainly Tissot had opportunity enough to observe spiritualism close up in those years. Whistler was caught up in the movement, probably at the enthusiastic insistence of Lady Archibald Campbell, but until the years after Kathleen Newton's death Tissot's interest appears to have remained more or less academic. As far as can be determined, it was not until 1885 that he attempted to make contact with the other world.

Tissot was introduced to spiritualism by William Eglinton.[5] Eglinton was one of the most famous mediums of the century and practised not only in England and Europe, but also in North and South America, India, and South Africa. He was the leading exponent of slate writing, a form of communication in which spirits were invited to leave tangible records of their presence in chalk on school slates, a process facilitated by a whole series of ploys and tricks. He was also a materialization medium, and when slate writing, which he urbanely termed

---

[3] Ibid, p. 9.

[4] Bastard, p. 264.

[5] For Eglinton, see John S. Farmer, *'Twixt Two Worlds: A Narrative of the Life and Work of William Eglinton* and Arthur Conan Doyle, *The History of Spiritualism*, ii, 42–54, both of which contain material related to Tissot's spiritualist activities; for a more sceptical view, see Persall, pp. 109–17; for the portrait of Eglinton by Tissot which served as the frontispiece of *'Twixt Two Worlds*, see Wentworth, *Catalogue Raisonné of Prints*, no. 84.

'psychography', was combined with materializations, 'there were endless opportunities for sharp practice'.[6] Tissot met Eglinton in Paris in February 1885, and after a successful seance followed him to London for a prolonged series of materializations. On 20 May 1885, Kathleen Newton appeared to Tissot's complete satisfaction:

At the last and culminating *séance* he had a touching and unique experience. The veil was lifted, and he saw one whose sweet companionship had been his joy and solace in years gone by. It is not possible or right that such sacred experiences should be revealed in their fullest expression to an unsympathetic world, but the few details of the *séance* I am enabled to give will no doubt be acceptable to those whose knowledge bids them lend a listening ear.

The *séance* (a private one) took place on the 20th of May, and there were present, besides M. Tissot and the medium, three ladies and one gentleman. After the usual preliminaries of a dark *séance*, Mr. Eglinton took his place in an easy-chair close to M. Tissot's right hand, and so remained the whole time. The doors were all locked, and the room otherwise secured. After conversing for a time two figures were seen standing side by side on M. Tissot's left hand. They were at first seen very indistinctly, but gradually became more and more plainly visible, until those nearest could distinguish every feature. The light carried by the male figure ('Ernest') was exceptionally bright, and was so used as to light up in a most effective manner the features of his companion. M. Tissot, looking into her face, immediately recognized the latter, and, much overcome, asked her to kiss him. This she did several times, the lips being observed to move. One of the sitters distinctly saw 'Ernest' place the light in such a position that while M. Tissot was gazing at the face of the female form her features were 'brilliantly illuminated'; it also lighted M. Tissot's face. After staying with him for some minutes, she again kissed him, shook hands, and vanished.[7]

Like the vision at St. Sulpice, the materialization of Mrs Newton was duly recorded. *L'Apparition médiunimique* [*sic*] (Pl. 197) is known only in mezzotint, but it doubtless records a lost painting.[8] According to Farmer, the mezzotint at least became 'the wonder and talk of the artistic world': 'As a work of art there is no question of its merit. Powerfully conceived and happily rendered, the picture tells its own tale, and is a lasting monument of the artist's appreciation of the blessing bestowed by spirit communication'.[9]

The memento always occupied a special place in Tissot's life. Edmond de Goncourt spent an afternoon with Alphonse Daudet and his wife at Tissot's

[6] Persall, p. 109.

[7] Farmer, p. 187. A less successful sitting is recorded in Blanche, *Portraits of a Lifetime*, pp. 65–6: at a seance held at the house of the painter Albert Besnard in London, the spirit form of Mrs Newton was revealed to be Besnard's model and the medium was jailed for fraud, a fate Eglinton always seems to have avoided.

[8] For the mezzotint, see Wentworth, *Catalogue Raisonné of Prints*, no. 76; Edmond de Goncourt

mentions the painted version in 1890 (*Journal*, iii, 1118, quoted below), but Bastard, p. 278, says that it was found to be missing after the artist's death; for a photograph of Eglinton with what was purported to be the fully materialized spirit-form of his guide Ernest, and clearly the figure recorded in Tissot's mezzotint, see Fred Gettings, *Ghosts in Photographs* (New York: Harmony Books, 1978), fig. 31.

[9] Farmer, p. 187.

house in 1890 to see the illustrations to the Bible which had been completed. The visit began with Tissot playing hymns on a harmonium as they arrived and closed with an unsettling visit to the little room where he had hung *L'Apparition médiunimique* and made his experiments in the occult:

Nous montons un moment, avec Mme. Daudet, voir l'arrangement de l'intérieur du haut qu'il a bâti, quand il a cru se marier avec Mlle. Riesener. C'est très joliment arrangé dans le goût anglais, dans des compartiments de bois aux murs, en fenêtres garnies de lierre. Et dans le crépuscule, se refusant à chercher des allumettes, avec une voix qui se fait tout à fait mystérieuse et des yeux vagues, il nous montre une boule de cristal de roche et un plateau d'émail, qui servent à des évocations, où l'on entend, assure-t-il, des voix qui se disputent. Il tire d'une commode des cahiers, où il nous montre des pages entières, contenantes l'historique de ces évocations, et nous montre enfin un tableau représentant une femme aux mains lumineuses, qu'il dit être venue l'embrasser et dont il a senti sur sa joue ses lèvres, des lèvres pareilles à des lèvres de feu.[10]

To understand something of Tissot's relationship to the art of the Catholic revival, it is necessary to consider some of the sources and characteristics of the movement as it relates to the arts.[11] Although it may not have appeared so at the time, a Catholic revival was only to be expected about 1880 as two centuries of disbelief culminated in the positivist philosophy of the Second Empire and the Third Republic. That the reaction began in the arts where sensibility and imagination play an essential part is hardly surprising; artists, especially writers, concerned themselves for the first time in two hundred years with the embodiment of religious values in their work. It was generally through a new sense of religious involvement, often heralded by visionary conversions like Tissot's, that these changes took place. Today, the Catholic revival is best known in the arts because of the 'Catholic' works of Gauguin and Bernard, and although those revolutionary works spring from the same now essentially forgotten philosophy, they are hardly typical of the artistic production of the movement. For the most part, theology dominated aesthetics, or aesthetic quality was simply lacking, and the monuments of the Catholic revival in the arts are better forgotten. The Tissot Bible is a quintessential example of the kind of works this infusion of faith created. In it he attempts to make his familiar genre approach create a kind of Christian, and, later, Old Testament, super-reality in which reportage combines with mystical and visionary elements, and the uncomfortable result is typical of the period.

The beginnings of the Catholic revival coincided with the first period of

[10] Goncourt, *Journal*, iii, 1118.

[11] For much of the general material on the Catholic revival which follows, I am indebted to Richard Griffiths's definitive study of the literature of the period, *The Reactionary Revolution: The Catholic Revival in French Literature 1870–1914*. While touching only marginally on the visual arts, its application to them is clear, and more useful than many of the works devoted entirely to painting. His scholarship, however, should not be judged by any distortions I may have made in applying it to a different art.

republican reaction against the church in France. Throughout the eighties, it was brought home that the church stood in danger in a secular republic, and the anti-clerical actions of the Third Republic created a spirit of violent opposition and a mistrust of compromise with a government now seen as the sworn enemy of the church. This deep enmity was to reach its height in the infamy and anguish of the Dreyfus affair at the end of the century.

Enmity was not confined to politics. A deep-seated mistrust of science and fear of the ideals which sprang from it led to the rejection, not merely of intellectualism, but to the use of the intellect itself in matters of religion. This anti-rationalism manifested itself as belief based entirely upon divine revelation and, even more dangerously, upon miraculous revelation. This mystical element quickly gained immense popularity and was ultimately to colour the entire movement by the effect it had upon its more unbalanced followers. It grew increasingly difficult, and ultimately impossible, for the rational to sympathize with its extreme claims. In their uncontrolled enthusiasm, miraculous revelation was hopelessly confused with spiritualism and the occult, and the confusion did little to give the movement a good name. Tissot, with his crystal ball and his visions of the Passion and the creation of the world, is too sadly typical.

Visionary revelation practised on a widespread scale had unfortunate consequences. Not least among them, it engendered an almost total dependence on the external aspects of faith rather than on its meaning. For this reason, the real, concrete descriptions of Anna Katherine Emmerick, who saw in detail scenes from the life of the Virgin and the Passion of Christ, had more impact than intangible philosophies of belief, and it is not surprising that Tissot expressed his thanks to her in the preface to his New Testament illustrations. This insistent physical approach to the intangible accounts for many of the dubious characteristics of the Tissot Bible, in which sacred legend is often sorely tried by descriptive detail.

If the adherents of the Catholic revival had the sense of being embattled martyrs in the society of the Second Empire and the Third Republic, they felt hardly more comfortable with the church itself. Attacked from the outside by democracy and science, they were betrayed from within by a weak and inadequate clergy and by the falsities and compromise of the Vatican itself. The vitality and social change which Leo XIII was bringing to the church met with no sympathy from the adherents of the Catholic revival. Modern Catholicism was irredeemably mediocre, and their response was retreat into an ever more intractable mystical traditionalism. Everyone longed to have lived like the early fathers of the church in the age of faith, asceticism, and heroic suffering.

One of the most telling examples of the spiritual failure of the modern church was found in the influx of sentimentality it had allowed. Contemporary faith was altogether despicable in its well-meaning insistence on the pleasant aspects of faith and the playing-down of suffering. Nowhere was this weakness seen more clearly than in contemporary church art. Its misguided falseness caused it to distort belief in an evolution of error which stretched back to the Renaissance. Léon Bloy was particularly violent in his condemnation, thundering like an early Christian in the middle of the Forum: 'Qu'ils eussent ou non le talent divin qu'on a si jobardement exalté sur les lyres de la rengaine, ils n'en furent pas moins les matelassiers du lit de prostitution où le paganisme fornicateur vint dépuceler la beauté chrétienne'.[12] In the same way, J. K. Huysmans looked to the art of the Middle Ages for salvation, the Renaissance having been the death of true Christian feeling in art: 'Il fallut l'époque interlope, l'art fourbe et badin du paganisme, pour éteindre cette pure flamme, pour anéantir la lumineuse candeur de ce moyen âge où Dieu vécut familièrement, chez lui, dans les âmes, pour substituer à un art tout divin un art purement terrestre'.[13] If the art of the Renaissance was bad, the art of the nineteenth century was infinitely worse, summed up for writers like Huysmans by the simpering Virgins of Lourdes and the *bondieuseries* of Place Saint-Sulpice.

It was to correct such errors and bring Christian art back to a purer truth that Tissot undertook his illustrations to the New Testament. In the introduction he wrote to accompany the works when they were published, he gives an account not unlike Huysmans's although he passes over even the Middle Ages in favour of topographical exactitude. On his return from Jerusalem in 1886, Tissot showed 'the sketches, drawings, and all the documents' he had brought with him from the Holy Land to aid him in his work, to his father, 'a Christian of the old-fashioned sort':

When he saw the various scenes in their exact proportions, the view of Golgotha especially, he exclaimed: 'It seems I have got to change all my preconceived ideas about things! What! Is not Calvary after all a lofty sugar-loaf mountain, covered with rocks and brushwood?' 'Well, no,' I replied, 'Calvary, though it did occupy the summit of the town, was not more than from 20 to 22 feet high at the most. In just the same way the Holy Sepulchre was near it, but under conditions totally different from what you imagine. Your error is very much that of the faithful. For a long time the imagination of the Christian world has been led astray by the fancies of artists; there is a whole army of delusions to be overturned, before any idea can be entertained approaching the truth in the slightest degree. All the schools of art have worked, more or less conscientiously, to lead astray public opinion in these matters. Some of these schools, preoccupied, as were those of the Renaissance, with the setting of the scenes represented, others, like those of the mystics, with the inner meaning of the events, were of one accord in ignoring the evidence of history, and dispensing with topographical accuracy. Is it not time in this exact century, when such words as nearly or almost have no longer any value, to restore to reality—I do not say to realism—the rights which have been filched from it?'[14]

---

[12] Léon Bloy, *Le Désespéré*, vol. 3, *Le Retour*, in *L'Œuvre complète* (Paris: Bernouard, 1948), vii, 230.

[13] Joris-Karl Huysmans, *La Cathédrale* (Paris: stock, 1898), p. 153.

[14] Tissot, *The Life of Our Saviour Jesus Christ*, i, p. ix.

The subtitle of *The Life of Our Saviour Jesus Christ* is *Three Hundred and Sixty-Five Compositions from the Four Gospels with Notes and Explanatory Drawings*. 'Notes and explanatory drawings' is the key to Tissot's approach, for the reader is told everything from the way the Virgin dressed her hair and the correct number of wings on the cherubim to the proper cartographical adjustments between the site of Calvary and the Church of the Holy Sepulchre. Historical fact and theological doctrine are stated for this world and the next with equal conviction. The Tissot Bible is a kind of sacred travel book, and his approach to the traditional sites of the Holy Land is not unlike that of many turn-of-the-century travel writers and lecturers who attempted similar combinations of topographical information, human interest, and sacred legend.

Topographical accuracy was reasonably easy to come by for an artist of Tissot's determination. 'I started on October 15th, 1886,' he tells us in the introduction, adding with cabalistic significance, 'I was just fifty years old'.[15] His departure was noted with ripples of amusement among his friends: the ageing *boulevardier* had got religion and was making the most of it. Aurélian Scholl, their rivalry for the *danseuse de corde* perhaps not quite forgotten, told Tissot that his pilgrimage to the Holy Land would do nothing but make him an agnostic. Tissot's arrival in Egypt on the first leg of his journey immediately proved him wrong, for Alexandria and Cairo made the past palpable in the present, and alone were enough to recompense him for the journey.[16]

The Middle East was the China of the *fin de siècle*. Its exoticism fulfilled the need for strangeness in the late nineteenth century that China had in the eighteenth, although its impact was greater in that it was not historic or imaginative, but accessible and real. As Delacroix had found the classical antiquity he sought in the Morocco of the 1830s, Tissot found the world of the Bible in the Middle East of the 1880s. But where Delacroix was looking for an attitude or a spirit, Tissot was looking for data and documentation. In him, scientific method had stifled direct response, and the 'facts' of costume and setting were no longer the stimulants

---

[15] Ibid.

[16] Bastard, p. 270. Bastard also says that it was persistently rumoured in Paris at this time that Tissot's faith had grown so intense upon exposure to the Holy Land that he planned to abandon France permanently and retire to a monastery on the Dead Sea. Such rumours must have been fairly widespread, and with the pious falsehood Tissot adopted in dating his correspondence from the 'abbaye de Buillon', confusion was soon complete. As the memoirs of the late nineteeth century began to appear, some truly remarkable variations on the theme *frère Tissot* were put in circulation. Easily the most gothic of them is the version told by Tissot's fellow caricaturist at *Vanity Fair*, Leslie Ward, who thought that Tissot had turned to religion in his remorse at the death of Mrs Newton, had gone hopelessly insane, and died after becoming a monk (*Forty Years of 'Spy'*, p. 102), although the notion entertained by his old friend Louise Jopling that he had joined a Trappist order at Rome is also typical (*Twenty Years of My Life*, p. 60). The understandable confusion of country house and monastery was made by most of Tissot's later biographers, and is to be found in both Laver, *Vulgar Society*, pp. 62–3, and Ross, 'The Truth About Tissot', p. 7. It was widely repeated in more general literature, and although its ghost has been generally laid to rest, it is still to be met in some recent literature.

of artistic creation they had been for Delacroix: they became ends in themselves in a process of documentation. Tissot had always used a similar documentary aesthetic in the composition of his pictures, but here historicism distorted what had always been a perfectly natural way to compose a genre picture, and under the guise of historical accuracy he gathered a mass of material with a nearly total lack of discrimination. Putting his trust in the faultiest of sources and in his own intuition, he made a collection of material without the slightest claim to historical or archaeological accuracy. In that respect, time has told; for today no one would mistake his historical verities for anything but what they are, the near relatives of the novels of Loti and the religious operas of Massenet.

Reaching Palestine, Tissot found that the Holy Land also lived up to his expectations as he set to work gathering data. An article by Cleveland Moffett which was published in *McClure's Magazine* as a sales pitch, the McClure Company having gone into partnership with Tissot in the publication of an American edition of the New Testament, gives a description, with wonderfully solemn adjectives, of Tissot's life in Jerusalem. Rising at six for mass at the Convent of Marie-Réparatrice, he set off on a sketching trip in search of visual documentation, returning for lunch and then going out to work again in the afternoon. Evenings were spent in research, in reflection on sacred events, and in making thumb-nail sketches for the pictures he planned to paint.[17]

In reconstructing the Palestine of Christ's time, Tissot observed local peculiarities of dress, physiognomy, architecture, and topography, drawing them meticulously or photographing them for even greater exactitude. Unfortunately, the bulk of this photographic material can no longer be located, although numerous sketches were reproduced among the Bible illustrations. Tissot must have relied heavily on photographs when he began actual work on the illustrations in Paris. The single photograph now known was published in *McClure's Magazine* and shows Tissot standing, as McClure puts it, in 'the place where the Sermon on the Mount was pronounced'. It is with a certain surprise that one compares the photograph with the illustration taken from it in which Jesus in white draperies replaces a dapper Tissot in riding clothes.[18]

To people his sacred landscapes, Tissot used a method already familiar at Oberammergau and soon to become the province of the casting director: he looked until he found faces he thought suitable. Having decided that St. Joseph, for example, was a younger man than is generally thought:

I took as a model one of the Yemenites, a race of Arabia Petrea, which, thanks to the autonomy it has been able to maintain in the midst of the manifold influences which have so

---

[17] C. Moffett, 'J. J. Tissot and his Paintings of the Life of Christ', *McClure's Magazine*, p. 393.

[18] For the photograph and the illustration, see Moffett, pp. 386 and 387. A now unlocated album of seventy sheets made up of such documentary material was sold with the Deglatigny collection in Paris in 1951 (see Brooke, Wentworth, Zerner, *Tissot*, nos. 56–9).

greatly modified other branches of the Jewish race, has remained to the present time one of the noblest and most characteristic groups of purely Jewish descent.[19]

In Paris after his return, Tissot used his sketches of Armenians and Jews to people the Holy Land of Christ's time, a single male model serving for reference in establishing poses. For the Roman oppressors of the Jews, 'a bust in the museum at Naples' provided a Pontius Pilate, and the waiters in Parisian cafes 'with their clean-shaven faces and classical profiles' the rest of the alien population.[20]

With this pseudo-scientific file of visual materials, Tissot set about his illustrations. If the 'facts' of his *fin de siècle* Jerusalem are superficial and personal, they still smack of the naturalists' approach in their insistence on realistic detail, and stand in the long shadow of his Leysian 'genre résurrectionniste'. Like several artists of the Catholic revival whose training had taken place earlier in the century, Tissot brought his approach into line with the Catholic revival through what he must have considered a new use of his material. For him, such 'facts' now had meaning only in an interpretative symbolic context. Their importance lay neither in themselves, nor in their usefulness as the key to a narrative—as it had in his genre pictures—but as the means of unravelling divine meaning. Archaeology, costume, and topography were now simply the pieces of a vast puzzle which if correctly pieced together would strip away error and clarify divine word. The only real difficulty lay in discovering a means of utilizing this mass of data. Tissot's method, which he set down in the second part of his illustrations to the New Testament, is not surprising: 'The general data put me on the right track for the studies I had to pursue. *All that was needed now was intuition*'.[21]

With that seemingly innocuous statement, Tissot lets the entire undertaking slip comfortably back into the realm of the subjective and irrational where he had become so much at home. In the past, intuition had served Tissot well in sharpening the narrative of his genre pictures, and despite its new and awesome context, it serves precisely the same purpose in the Bible illustrations. Formerly clever and suggestive, it now becomes a solemn pontifical force directed by divine will, and hardly a thing to be taken lightly. Tissot gives a glimpse of just how imposing a thing it had become:

Sometimes, indeed, as I trod the very path over which the feet of the Saviour had passed; when I realized that my eyes were reflecting the very landscape on which He had gazed, I felt that a certain receptivity was induced in my mind which so intensified my powers of intuition, that the scenes of the past rose up before my mental vision in a peculiar and striking manner. In the same way, penetrated as I became with the spirit of the race to which the actors in these scenes belonged, realizing as I did, the character of the districts in which they lived and moved; with

---

[19] Tissot, *Life of Christ*, i. p. 14.   [20] Sherard, p. 4.   [21] Tissot, *Life of Christ*, i, p. x.

the local colour of the familiar objects by which they were surrounded; when, thus prepared, I meditated on any special incident in its own particular sanctuary, and was thus brought into touch with the actual setting of every scene, the facts I was anxious to evoke were revealed to me in all their identity and under the most striking forms. Is not the artist, indeed, a kind of sensitive plant, the activity of which, when concentrated upon a certain point, is intensified, and through a kind of hyperaesthesia, is powerfully affected by contact with objects outside of itself; this contact producing vivid images on the brain?—I will not enter here into the details of the brilliant light, almost amounting to divination, which was thrown on various points by the sight of certain stones, and certain apparently insignificant topographical details; to do so would be to run the risk of being accused of mysticism.[22]

Despite his protestation, mysticism is surely the thing of which he wanted to be accused. The vision at St. Sulpice had received an excellent press, and as word spread of the scope of the Bible illustrations, Tissot's visions grew progressively more elaborate. No longer confined to Parisian churches, the Holy Land, or the privacy of his studio, they now took place in the street:

One day, for instance, while strolling in Paris, near the Bois de Boulogne, M. Tissot suddenly saw before him a massive stone arch out of which a great crowd was surging—a many colored crowd—with turbaned heads and Oriental garments. And the multitude, with violent gestures, lifted their hands and pointed to a balcony high up on the yellow stone wall where stood Roman soldiers dragging forward a prisoner clad in the red robe of shame. Hanging down from the balcony was a piece of tapestry worked in brilliant colors, and over this the prisoner was bent by rough hands and made to show his face to the crowd below, and it was the face of Jesus. What M. Tissot saw in this vision he reproduced faithfully on canvas in his painting 'Ecce Homo.'[23]

While there were full-cast productions in the street, the chief actors in the sacred drama were invited to the avenue du Bois to sit for portraits. It was all very well to leave Pontius Pilate to a Roman bust and the Romans to Parisian waiters, but the central figures of the drama demanded special treatment. The creative process, as recounted by Tissot to Moffett, was to rough the figure in with charcoal, forming the body with a few smudges and the head with an oval, and then attend divine revelation:

And this is it—and it happened over and over again, until it became an ordinary occurrence—M. Tissot, being now in a certain state of mind, and having some conception of what he wished to paint, would bend over the white paper with its smudged surface, and looking intently at the oval marked for the head of Jesus or some holy person, would see the whole picture there before him, the colors, the garments, the faces, everything that he needed and had already half conceived. Then, closing his eyes in delight, he would murmur to himself, 'How beautiful! Oh, that I may keep it! Oh, that I may not forget it!' Finally, putting forth his strongest effort

---

[23] Ibid., p. xi.   [23] Moffett, p. 395.

to retain the vision, he would take brush and color and set it all down from memory as well as he could.[24]

With truly unattractive coyness, Tissot also told Moffett that splendid as these visions were, there was still a higher category which was *hors commerce:*

But many of his best pictures were never painted at all, because the very gorgeousness of the scene made it slip from him as a dream vanishes, and it would not come back. 'Oh,' he sighed, 'the things I have seen in the life of Christ, but could not remember! They were too splendid to keep.'[25]

Whatever the tantalizing claims of mysticism, the real basis of Tissot's illustrations lay in the years of unremitting labour between 1886 and 1894, when two hundred and seventy of the illustrations were exhibited at the Salon du Champs de Mars, and 1895, when the now complete set of three hundred and sixty-five gouaches was completed and arrangements made for their publication.[26] As the work progressed, the ambition and dedication, if not the aesthetic value, of Tissot's undertaking became more and more apparent.

After his original trip to Palestine between October 1885 and March 1886, he returned again in 1889 to make further studies and to augment his impressions, making yet a third trip in 1896 after he had decided to illustrate the Old Testament. Time in the Holy Land was spent accumulating data and impressions, but the actual painting was done in France. He seems to have divided his time between the house in Paris and the château de Buillon which he had inherited from his father in 1888. The château was to become his principal residence towards the end of the century, and he paid a sanctimonious tribute to it in Moffett's article which is worth quoting if only because it perfectly captures the tone of humourless piety and self-importance Tissot now adopted in speaking of himself and his work:

To do my work best I must be able to think and feel quite alone; I must have solitude. So, for weeks at a time, I withdraw from Paris to a wonderful lonely valley, shaped like a vast amphitheatre, where the wind blows always and a little river runs. This is one of nature's worship spots, where reverence is in the air. Hundreds of years ago godly men chose this place for a monastery, and on the ruins of their buildings I have made my home for contemplation. Ah, the days that I have spent there listening to the wind sigh and watching the river flow![27]

Even the most informal occasions involving the Bible illustrations were given a heavy varnish of religious ceremony. During the visit of Edmund de Goncourt

[24] Ibid.
[25] Ibid., p. 394.
[26] Goncourt, *Journal*, iv, 595. Although officially a part of the Salon of 1894, the pictures were given a gallery and a special catalogue of their own at the Champ-de-Mars—the general catalogue, s.v. 'Tissot', directing the attention of the public to both. Tissot was a member of the Commission d'Examen for paintings that year.
[27] Moffett, p. 396.

and the Daudets to the avenue du Bois when they had seen *L'Apparition médiunimique*, the Bible illustrations had also been carefully displayed. Tissot commented on them in a hushed and reverent voice, now and again falling with unintentional charm into the Parisian slang of his former life:

A notre entrée, le bruit terrestrement céleste d'un orgue-mélodium· dont joue l'artiste; et pendant qu'il vient à notre rencontre, les regards soudainement attirés par un trou illuminé, devant lequel est une aquarelle commencée, un trou fait dans l'ouverture d'une étoffe, jouant la toile levée d'un théâtre d'enfant et dans lequel se voit, figurée par des petites maquettes, une scène de la Passion, éclairée par une lumière semblable aux lueurs rougeoyantes éclairantes un Saint-Sépulcre, le soir du Vendredi-Saint.

Puis aussitôt commence le défilé des cent vingt-cinq gouaches, dont Tissot fait le boniment à voix basse, comme on parle dans une église, avec parfois détonnant dans sa parole religieuse, des mots d'argot parisien, disant d'une étude de la Madeleine encore pécheresse: 'Vous voyez, elle est un peu *vannée*!'[28]

In addition to the drawings and photographs made in the Holy Land, the 'children's stage' which Edmond de Goncourt alone mentions, and various degrees of visionary contemplation, Tissot also turned to theological and archaeological literature for inspiration and factual material. In the introduction to the Bible illustrations, he says that in addition to the 'authorized authorities', he read Josephus, the Talmud, the Gospels, and the early Christian authors, among the ancients, and von Munk, Sepp, Stapfer, Didon, and Ollivier, among the moderns, turning to the German architect Herr Schieck for the 'conscientiously executed' relief plan of the Temple of Herod which he used in his pictures.[29]

Particular mention is made of Anna Katherine Emmerick, the Westphalian nun who had begun to have ecstatic visions after her convent was suppressed by Napoleon in 1811. Translated into numerous languages, her visions had an enormous and lasting popularity. Despite their supernatural origin, they are in fact extremely tedious records of biblical topography and events, the physical characteristics and genealogical background of sacred personages, and hour-by-hour chronologies of events, some of which, as the church now carefully phrases it, are correct, others mistaken.[30] According to Bastard, it was a reading of her works which led to Tissot's decision to illustrate the Bible.[31] He was tremendously impressed by the precision of her visions and was quite ready to employ her method himself, with equally paradoxical results.

La Vie de Notre Seigneur Jésus-Christ was given to the public in the spring of 1894 at the Salon du Champ-de-Mars. Edmond de Goncourt noted the exhibition and its audience in June:

[28] Goncourt, *Journal*, iii, 1117. *Vannée* is perhaps best translated as *faded*, or *past her prime*.

[29] Tissot, *Life of Christ*, i, p. xi.

[30] For Anna Katherine Emmerick, see the preface by the abbé de Cazales to her *Dolorous Passion* of *Our Lord Jesus Christ* (Hawthorne, Calif.: Christian Book Club, 1968), a translation of the edition which Tissot doubtless used.

[31] Bastard, p. 268; see also Tissot, *Life of Christ*, i, p. ix.

L'exposition de LA VIE DE NOTRE SEIGNEUR JESUS-CHRIST de Tissot au Champ-de-Mars, cette monographie réaliste de Jésus composée de 350 peintures et dessins, dont 270 sont exposés cette année et le restant sera exposé l'année suivante. Un public nombreux, très enthusiaste, où se trouvent mêlés au public élégant des expositions une foule d'étrangers et un certain nombre de prêtres.[32]

After the exhibition in the Champ-de-Mars, the pictures were exhibited in London in 1896 and again in Paris in 1897 before beginning a tour of North America in 1898 which is said to have brought Tissot the huge sum of $100,000 in entrance fees. The pictures were acquired by subscription for the Brooklyn Museum at the end of the tour for an equally impressive $60,000. Moved by such tangible evidence of American admiration, Tissot was reported to have offered to come to Brooklyn to supervise the decoration of a permanent gallery for the series and to paint a large head of Christ to serve as the focal point of the display.[33]

The Tissot Bible brought out the crowds wherever it was exhibited. Its subject and treatment, bringing faith and science into uneasy alliance, probably guaranteed its success in the emotionally charged religious climate of the times, but the response exceeded all expectations. Its reception had been prefigured in 1889 when Millet's *L'Angélus* had come up for auction in Paris and that murky peasant couple had briefly become a nation's glory as spectators wept, or swooned, or stood in reverent awe before it as before a shrine.[34] Even such behaviour pales before the reception accorded the Tissot Bible:

Some extraordinary scenes revealing the deep impression produced were frequently to be seen. Even the callous and the sceptical were observed to remove their hats, as slowly and with marked attention, they passed from one picture to another, and followed step by step the wondrous life of 'God who became man.' And women were seen to sink down on their knees as though impelled by a superior force, and literally crawl round the rooms in this position, as though in adoration.[35]

[32] Goncourt, *Journal*, iv, 595.
[33] 'To Buy Tissot's Paintings. Brooklyn Institute Secures Option on the Collection', *New York Times*, 7 January 1900, p. 7, and 'Tissot's Christ. Steps to Secure the Paintings for the Brooklyn Institute', *New York Times: Saturday Review*, 17 February 1900, p. 101. Tissot is now known to have visited the United States twice in 1898: his presence in New York to make arrangements for the tour of the Bible illustrations is noted in 'The Week in the Art World', *New York Times: Saturday Review*, 26 February 1898, p. 130, and his return later in the year for the opening of the exhibition in 'The Tissot Pictures and Drawings', *New York Times*, 15 November 1898, p. 6. Notice was taken of him once again four days later in an article with the self-explanatory headline 'French Artist Bruised and Shaken up in an Attempt to Board a Madison Avenue Bus', *New York Times*, 19 November 1898, p. 12. Misfeldt, p. 276, cites a letter from Tissot to Maurice de Brunoff dated from Buillon in July which shows that he had returned to France between February and November, and quotes from an article published in the *Chicago Post*, 22 October 1898, which indicates that he had travelled as far west as that city to make arrangements for the exhibition of the Bible illustrations before going to New York for the opening there in mid-November. I am indebted to Willard Misfeldt for bringing bibliographical sources relevant to Tissot's American trips to my attention.
[34] For the response to *L'Angélus* in 1889, see Wesley Towner, *The Elegant Auctioneers* (New York: Hill and Wang, 1970), p. 125.
[35] Sherard, pp. 1–2.

The runaway popularity of the three hundred and sixty-five little pictures in gouache and water-colour quickly suggested wider, commercial, possibilities to Tissot. The Bible could be made to pay, and pay it did. Before the American tour, Tissot arranged with the firm Mame et fils, of Tours, to publish the pictures in 1896-7, and received a million francs for the reproduction rights of their two editions, a sumptuous *édition de luxe*, which reproduced the gouaches in facsimile, and a regular edition.[36] Soon after, arrangements were made with other publishers for editions in England and America, and by the end of the century Tissot had even gone into partnership with the McClure Company in New York to take full financial advantage of the popularity of the illustrations as they toured the United States.[37] In quality, these editions range from the dazzling *tour de force* of the Mame *édition de luxe*, with its facsimilies—perhaps unrivalled in technical complexity by any other work of the century—printed on handmade paper and protected by silk bindings and wooden boxes, to the last of the sorry McClure-Tissot Company reprint editions of 1910, with plates printed badly off-register on poor paper and bound in cheap textbook cloth.

It is with disappointment that we turn to the objects which aroused such enthusiasm and remarkable behaviour. For modern taste, this 'monographie réaliste de Jésus' is acceptable only in small doses. To spend an afternoon turning the pages of the Tissot Bible is a disheartening task, although now and again a little work like the gouache illustrating the text 'Behold, he standeth behind our wall, he looketh forth at the window shewing himself through the lattice' attracts by its genre approach and ornamental treatment (Pl. 198).

Genre is the salient feature of a number of the Bible illustrations. At least three are known to have been translated into oil versions which are of an aesthetic significance greater than that of their gouache counterparts.[38] *The Sojourn in Egypt* (Pl. 199) suggests its kinship with earlier works like *Emigrants* (Pl. 83), and most of its interest derives from a similar delight in the depiction of a maze of masts and from its mildly narrative approach. *The Magi on Their Way to Bethlehem* (Pl. VI) also suggests a rendering of the visual world more immediate and compelling than its symbolic message. It is of particular interest in technical terms, pushing the method suggested by *La Femme à Paris* firmly into the dry,

---

[36] The actual printing, however, was done by Lemercier, the venerable firm of Parisian lithographers which had been founded in the early nineteenth century. According to Edmond de Goncourt, Tissot had considered doing the work himself and had thought of buying land at Jerusalem to build a studio 'où il aurait imprimé et gravé son livre, un atelier qui, disait-il, serait devenu un atelier d'art religieux en même temps qu'une colonie française, faisant revivre l'influence de notre pays dans les

Lieux Saints' (*Journal*, iii, 1112).

[37] For bibliographical information on the various French, English, and American editions, see Misfeldt, p. 272, n. 21.

[38] Of the oil versions, only the two reproduced have been located, although the existence of three others is proved by the catalogue of the Vente Tissot, lots 7, 8, and 9; Misfeldt, p. 327, citing Tissot's will, suggests that there are at least seven of these oil versions.

broken surfaces and pale pastel colours of Monet and late Impressionism or Symbolist painters like Le Sidaner.

But genre is more often than not overbalanced by an approach which admits of miracles, and tangible reality gives way to visionary revelation and a now total confusion of the 'surnaturel avec le merveilleux'. There is a whiff of the ultimate cosmic séance about *The Soul of the Penitent Thief in Paradise* (Pl. 200), which brings *L'Apparition médiunimique* immediately to mind, as a pair of celestial *dames des chars*, their liturgical splendours combining the bird's wings and bandages of Burne-Jones with the Byzantine bric-à-brac of Sarah Bernhardt, 'guide' the soul of a tiny felon upward from a receding terrestrial sphere whose visual truthfulness would not be confirmed until the generation of the astronauts. The crucified Christ of *It is Finished* (Pl. 201) takes on a hieratic significance which completely displaces human meaning in the abstract fulfilment of Old Testament prophecies, and visionary revelation is made tangible and explicit.

It was the scenes of the Passion which were most admired in the nineteenth century, and their effect was immediate and vivid.[39] Tissot's attempt to heighten the spiritual drama resulted in a crude verism that gives these works great violence if not additional meaning. *Christ Falls Beneath the Cross* (Pl. 202), with its reduced foreground and low eye-level, brings the viewer into the action with physical and psychological tricks already familiar. Here, as in most of his depictions of Christ, Tissot makes a concentrated attempt to give him an expression of great spiritual significance. But, with the eyes of a medium or a hypnotist, he is more like Eglinton in a trance, or Rasputin.[40] The setting, for the archaeologically curious, is a representation of the spot in the Via Dolorosa where the event is traditionally said to have taken place, a tradition substantiated for the faithful by one of the visions of Anna Emmerick.

But even the theatrical excess of such a picture hardly prepares one for what is doubtless among the strangest religious pictures in Western art, *What Our Saviour Saw from the Cross* (Pl. 203). In it, the viewer is made Christ and looks down at the sorrowing figures at his feet—which, in an excess of misplaced empathy, protrude into the bottom centre of the picture. It seems impossible to imagine a more immoderate or distasteful misuse of kinaesthetic composition or Christian iconography, but it was precisely this fanatical blend of mysticism, empathy, pseudo-science, and vulgarity that brought out the crowds in 1900.

The series ends with a *Portrait of the Pilgrim* (Pl. 204), a self-portrait surrounded by funeral paraphernalia which was reproduced as the last illustration in the series. Beneath it a text invites the reader to pray for the soul of the author.

---

[39] For the popularity of the scenes from the Passion, see, for example, Levy, p. 963.

[40] For what might be called the 'Rasputinization' of Christ in the art of the *fin-de-siècle*, see P. Jullian, *The Symbolists*, p. 49.

The Bible had been made to pay, but there were those who did not find Tissot's clever juxtaposition of God and Mammon convincing or attractive. Degas, whose friendship with Tissot came to a permanent end in the middle of the decade when the latter sold a picture Degas had once given him, was understandably annoyed by Tissot's conduct and deeply suspicious of his lucrative piety:

Now he's got religion. He says he experiences inconceivable joy in his faith. At the same time he not only sells his own products high but sells his friends' pictures as well . . . To think we lived together as friends and then . . . Well, I can take my vengeance. I shall do a caricature of Tissot with Christ behind him, whipping him, and call it: *Christ Driving His Merchant from the Temple*. My God![41]

Despite its seemingly irrational appeal to the general public, the Tissot Bible was judged more calmly by a part of its audience. Edmond de Goncourt transcribes a discussion of the series which took place in May 1894, at a dinner given by Alphonse Daudet, his wife, and his son Lucien, which was attended by the Zolas, Raffaëllis, Rodenbachs, and Charpentiers. After a somewhat heated discussion of the illustrations, the general consensus was that the real value of Tissot's work lay in its impassioned historical re-creation rather than its sacred impact:

Dans les paroles de ce soir, chez les hommes, chez les femmes, il y a de la bataille, et la bataille éclate à propos de la monographie peinte du Christ par Tissot, que Zola déclare l'avoir complètement empoigné et à laquelle il regrette de ne pouvoir faire un article, que Daudet assure être une œuvre qui l'aurait converti, s'il n'avait pas la tête en pomme, que Rafaeli éreinte avec une injustice révoltante et proclame l'ouvrage d'un cireur de bottes! Et quand il est établi que la qualité de ces peintures est d'être surtout une reconstitution, il y a le parti de ceux qui disent que l'histoire du Christ doit être traitée légendairement, sans s'aider aucunement de la vérité des localités et des races, et nous qui soutenons que l'histoire du Christ est une histoire comme celle de Jules César et que la reconstitution de Tissot est faite en correspondance avec le mouvement historique contemporain. Un moment, la discussion s'anime si bien que Daudet, parlant de Rafaeli, s'écrie: 'Quant à ce que dit *l'autre* . . .'.[42]

Goncourt, who was perhaps more impressed by the illustrations than he cared to admit, felt that the series was of significance if only because of 'l'effort, la conscience', and 'le travail haluciné' it exhibited. Not surprisingly, he was fascinated by the local colour and customs Tissot had recorded in the Holy Land, although he found his treatment of local colour excessive, 'trop turque, trop *bédouinante*', giving the series an aspect more exotic than sacred which recalled the *turquerie* of Horace Vernet's Bible paintings. He completely failed to detect the real source of the illustrations in the Japanese print: neither their dizzy perspectives nor their detached silhouettes were able to suggest the graces of

[41] D. Halévy, *My Friend Degas*, p. 95. For the picture Tissot sold, probably the *Chevaux dans la prairie*, see above, chap. III, n. 51.

[42] Goncourt, *Journal*, iv, 570.

the *ukiyo-e* to the old *japoniste* from beneath their Middle Eastern trappings. But what struck him most was the pedestrian quality of the visionary aspects of Tissot's illustrations:

Une chose qui me frappe, qui m'étonne, c'est chez ce fervent de l'occultisme, ce spirite, cet évocateur d'esprits, c'est qu'il ne réussit que ce que lui apporte l'observation des choses de la réalité, qu'il n'a pas l'invention des choses *visionées*, l'imagination des apparitions, et que le surnaturel de ses compositions est très médiocre; ainsi, ce sommeil de Jésus entouré d'anges bleus tendant vers lui leurs mains indigo et qui, avec leurs petites flammes au font, front l'effet d'une queue de paon.[43]

Despite Goncourt, the success of Tissot's 'monographie réaliste de Jésus' lay in great part with its flat documentation of local colour in this world and peacock's tails in the next, and in the response of 'an enormous public whose Christian feeling was incontestable, though fundamentally unresponsive to mystical thought'.[44] In its blend of discursive erudition, documentary reportage, and carefully delineated 'inspiration', the Tissot Bible is a mirror-image of the literal-minded faith prevalent at the end of the century. Fundamentally without pictorial imagination, a lack he had always disguised successfully with *appassionnements* and diligence, Tissot was also by now quite sincerely religious, and an artistic process which allowed the literal documentation of actuality in this world and the next was as welcome to the painter as the public he sought to instruct.

Ernest Renan's purely historical concept of Christianity which made Christ 'an incomparable man' had met with the implacable enmity of the Catholic party, but his approach had a profound effect none the less. For Tissot, the seemingly irresolvable contradition between absolute faith, the miraculous, and the irrational, was brought into moral and philosophical resolution with positivist trust in empirical proof by the uses he made of his material as the means of divine revelation.

In the conclusion to a long article devoted to the series in the *Gazette des beaux-arts*, Ary Renan hints at the means through which Tissot must have hoped to join reportage and sacred meaning and speak at once to reason and the heart:

Ce n'est pas par la couleur locale disséminée au gré d'un caprice d'artiste que le grand travail de M. Tissot se recommande le mieux; c'est par l'entente intime de la vie sociale de l'Orient à l'aurore du Christianisme, par l'expression de la *couleur morale*, pour ainsi dire, adéquate au texte évangélique et dont un grand nombre d'esprits ne redoutent ni l'exotisme, ni la prosaïque simplicité. Pour l'intelligence de la vie de Jésus c'est un grand pas de fait; personne, en tout cas, ne niéra que le plus grave événement qui ait changé la face du monde ne méritât

[43] Goncourt, *Journal*, iv, 491, 559, and 596. F. Bourgeat, *Salon de 1894*, p. 59, alone makes reference to the essential *japonisme* of the illustrations.

[44] Philippe van Tieghem, *Dictionnaire des littératures* (Paris: Presses Universitaires de France, 1968), iii, 3284, quoted in Čelebonović, *Some Call It Kitsch*, p. 50.

l'effort d'une reconstitution figurée, tentée de bonne foi devant les seuls vestiges qui parlent à la fois au cœur et à la raison.[45]

There was an attempt in the literature of the Catholic revival to stress the specific aspects of the Sacred Drama to point up the spiritual and eternal nature of Christ. The meaning of the Incarnation was found to glow more brightly against the specific data of Christ as a historical personage, the member of a working family at a certain place and time. As Griffiths points out, this contrast of burning divinity and genre specificity is made with singular effect in much of the literature of the movement, where it ultimately becomes something of a stock device.[46] It is far more effective in the writing of the period than it is in Tissot's visual monograph, for it is essentially a literary effect, and its application to the visual arts is difficult, if not impossible.

This is made clear by comparison with Péguy's *Le Mystère de la charité de Jeanne d'Arc*, where the contrast of realistic description, genre detail, and flashes of divine revelation are achieved with a literary aside impossible in the visual arts. At one point, for example, the Virgin, described unsentimentally as an ageing woman whose physical decay is emphasized, asks herself what she has done to bring such misery upon herself and her son. We are told, suddenly and starkly:

Je vais vous le dire:
Il avait sauvé le monde.[47]

It was an effect similar to this that Tissot must have sought in his New Testament illustrations. But if those hundreds of sad works demonstrate anything, it is the real impossibility of making a literary approach rise above illustration in the creation of vital and independent works of art. The young Maurice Denis was aware of the flaw in this documentary approach, and could have been describing the Tissot Bible when he said: 'The Christ of Byzantium is a symbol; the Christ of modern artists, even if clothed in the most authentic of *kiffeds*, is nothing more than mere literature. In the one it is the form itself which is expressive; in the other it is merely the imitation of Nature which would like to be so.'[48]

The task of completing the illustrations to the New Testament, having them exhibited and published, and making them pay, occupied most of Tissot's time in the nineties, and relatively few unrelated works were undertaken. The exception was the smart portraits which kept the pious artist in the mainstream of *le tout Paris*, but two independent, large-scale religious works were also executed at this

[45] A. Renan, 'Une nouvelle illustration des Évangiles par M. James Tissot', *Gazette des beaux-arts*, p. 68.

[46] See Griffiths, pp. 62–4.

[47] Charles Péguy, 'Le Mystère de la charité de Jeanne d'Arc,' *Œuvres poétiques complètes* (Paris: La Pléiade, 1962), p. 457, quoted in Griffiths, p. 64.

[48] Maurice Denis, quoted in Jullian, *The Symbolists*, p. 48.

time. Like the illustrations to the Bible, Tissot probably intended both as devotions, having already described his work on the Bible as 'not labour, but prayer'.[49] About 1895, he began a colossal *Christ Pantocrator* for the hemicycle above the high altar of the convent church of the Dominicans in the rue Faubourg Saint-Honoré, which was dedicated with great pomp in December 1897.[50] Local colour gives way to Byzantium in this huge, hieratic image of the Christ-Emperor with its theological vocabulary, mosaic stiffness, and lavish use of gold leaf.

According to Bastard, Tissot undertook a third trip to the Holy Land in 1896, partly to gather material for the second of these independent pictures, *La Réception à Jérusalem du légat apostolique du Saint-Siège, S. E. Mgr. le cardinal Langénieux par le patriarche S. B. Mge. Piavi.*[51] Painted for the baptistry at Reims Cathedral to commemorate the visit of Cardinal Langénieux, Archbishop of Reims, to the Holy Land in 1893, to negotiate a *rapprochement* between the Roman and Orthodox churches, it was exhibited at the Salon du Champ-de-Mars in 1897 and is now unlocated and perhaps destroyed. Tissot was the obvious choice for this modern history painting with its theological significance and Middle-Eastern local colour, but it had only a tepid *succès d'estime*, the reason for which is immediately apparent from even the poor reproductions of it which remain. Bastard says that Tissot also dreamed of painting 'un gigantesque panorama, destiné à l'exposition internationale de 1900', but the project came to nothing.[52]

The success of the *Life of Christ* turned Tissot's thoughts to another series of illustrations, and after toying with a *Life of Joan of Arc* and a *Bonaparte Intime*, he found, predictably, that although these stories would be 'interesting to construct, when one has passed ten years of his life on the most sacred subject that exists, all else appears puerile and commonplace',[53] and turned accordingly to

[49] 'Ce n'était pas un travail, c'était une prière', Moffett, p. 393.

[50] Henri Lehmann had been commissioned to paint the hemicycle above the high altar, but had died before the work could be begun, and soon afterwards the expulsions of 1880 made a new commission impracticable. Tissot was probably not invited to undertake the project, for which it is possible he volunteered, until after the success of the Bible illustrations had given him new respectability. The painting was dedicated with great pomp on 3 December 1897, at a service in which Fauré and Legain sang, Widor took the organ, and Père Sertillanges gave a eulogy 'très délicat de l'œuvre de M. Tissot' (souvenir pamphlet by père Jacques le Tilly, 'Évocations de cent ans: centenaire 1874–1974 du Couvent des Dominicaines. Deux causeries, les 12 & 19 Novembre 1974', première causerie, p. 7). The painting, often thought to be in fresco, is actually oil on canvas.

[51] Salon of 1897 (Champ-de-Mars), no. 1192. The painting is repro., *Exposition nationale des beaux-arts: catalogue illustré des ouvrages de peinture, sculpture et gravure exposés au Champ-de-Mars* (Paris: Bernard, 1897), pl. 7; for a lukewarm, but typical review of the painting which acknowledges the consideration due to the genius of the Bible illustrations, excuses it as an official commission, and then attacks its lack of aerial perspective and cohesion of parts in a manner disconcertingly reminiscent of the criticism of the sixties, see G. Schefer, *Le Salon de 1897*, pp. 81–2; for the history of the picture, see Bastard, p. 277, and Louis Demaison, *La Cathédrale de Reims*, Petites monographies des grands édifices de la France (Paris: Laurens, n.d.), p. 122.

[52] Bastard, pp. 277–8.

[53] Tissot, *Holy Bible: Old Testament*, i, p. ii.

the Old Testament. After a third trip to the Holy Land in 1896 to gather material, he set to work with a familiar dedication.

More than a decade of patient labour had already proved the former painter of bourgeoise idylls to have become a *pompier* of admirable seriousness. His art was now both respectable and lucrative, qualities often confused in 1900, and he joined the ranks of the artistic *demi-dieux*, a *cher maître* with moral standards and social obligations. His inborn sense of privacy and the enormous scope of his mystico-religious labour must have insured a degree of isolation, but with the Bible illustrations issuing from the fashionable hôtel a few minutes journey from the place de l'Opéra, Tissot was but another of those Parisian anchorites who have 'memorized the train schedules'. Portrait commissions, *mondaine* and *demi-mondaine*, kept him clearly in social view, although after the mid-nineties he seems to have willingly abdicated his position to Helleu, his highly visible faith assuring continuing moral credibility. Interviewing Tissot at this time, Clifton Levy described him with obvious relief as having 'none of the affectations of bohemia, a gentleman who might be anything respectable', and Bastard discovered 'une froideur quelque peu britannique' in his manner which was as reassuring as the English cut of his clothes.[54]

The house in the avenue du Bois also took on a more ponderous splendour. The pretty rooms in the English taste which had been added in anticipation of his marriage to Mlle Riesener were given over to spiritualist practices, and the daring Japanese studio of the 1860s became one of those *ateliers-musées*, the delight of *pompiers* and artistic ladies in 1900, where garden furniture, faded fabrics, Dutch marquetry, church candlesticks, Japanese sunshades, and choir stalls 'fraternized in significant promiscuity and announced the state of mind of the master of the house to new arrivals as soon as they set foot inside the door'.[55]

C'est là que l'artiste, après avoir tout regardé et bien examiné, s'asseyait en face des ses toiles, éclairées par les larges baies vitrées d'un atelier spacieux, orné de tentures et de drapeaux qui semblaient s'accrocher comme aux voûtes d'un palais. Salle vaste et lumineuse, envahie de plantes, décorée de potiches et de bronzes, où se jouait la gamme éblouissante des étoffes, qui mariaient entr'elles leurs couleurs vives, dans un fouillis de meubles de tous les styles et la confusion de carcasses de vaisseaux qui avaient servi de modeles au peintre.[56]

Towards the turn of the century, Tissot began to spend the majority of his time in quasi-religious retirement at Buillon, and most of the work on the Old Testament illustrations was probably done there. Religious devotion and artistic creation served as the focal points for the placidly correct *vie de château* which

---

[54] Levy, p. 954; Bastard, p. 276.

[55] Jean Lorrain, *Pelléastres* (1903), quoted in

Lethève, *Daily Life of French Artists*, p. 199.

[56] Bastard, pp. 275-6.

the New Testament illustrations had made possible on a truly ducal scale. Surrounded by faithful servants, visiting friends, and favoured relatives (among whom Jeanne Tissot, the daughter of Marcel-Affricani, appears to have served as honorary *dame du manoir* in the house where she would later spend the rest of her life as keeper-of-the-shrine), Tissot was at last able to enjoy the peaceful rewards of his fame. Leisure hours were spent in amateur archaeology, centring on the ruins of the abbey which gave its name to the estate; and in the improvement of the severely handsome late eighteenth-century house, not always entirely to its advantage. Tissot created a studio hung with the flags used in pictures of the London period in the former *abbatiale* of the monastery and happily embellished the grounds with rose arbours, sham ruins, ornamental lakes, and the other necessities of Victorian country life. It was while supervising the excavations for an ornamental pool that Tissot took an 'accès de fièvre pernicieuse' and died on 8 August 1902.[57]

Left unfinished, the Old Testament illustrations were completed by others and published by his friend Maurice de Brunoff.[58] The ninety-five pictures for Genesis which comprised the first of the four volumes were exhibited at the Salon of 1901,[59] and like their predecessors then toured the United States, finding a permanent home in the New York Public Library (which, however, transferred them to the Jewish Museum in New York in 1964). The religious climate that had guaranteed the immense popularity of the earlier series had already passed, and they attracted little attention. It can only be said of them that their combination of the mystico-religious and veristic local colour is already quite familiar.

After a number of memorial notices marking his passing, Tissot began his quiet descent into oblivion.[60] Under the terms of his will, the Louvre was offered *The Prodigal Son in Modern Life*, but should the gift be declined, the series was to be offered to the Musée de Nantes: it is now in the latter city. The Bibliothèque-Nationale and the museums at Nantes and Besançon were each to be given as complete a set as possible of his prints.[61]

---

[57] Bastard, p. 278. A photograph of the gardens is repro. by Moffett, p. 394.

[58] James Tissot, *La Sainte Bible: Ancien Testament*, 2 vols. (Paris: de Brunoff, 1904). Editions were also published in England and the United States. Excluding the illustrations to Genesis which Tissot himself exhibited, the actual degree of his authorship of the remaining illustrations has yet to be established. Misfeldt, p. 287, cites H.-J.-F. Bellery-Desfontaines, A.-F. Gorguet, Ch. Hoffbauer, A. de Parys, G. Scott, and M. Simonidy as having been employed by de Brunoff to complete the work, and the reproductions clearly show the participation of several hands. Tissot had obviously completed illus-

trations in addition to Genesis by the time of his death; others left incomplete must have been finished by de Brunoff's illustrators; while others, and perhaps a significant number, appear simply to approximate Tissot's style in the degree to which the six hands were able, often straying not only from Tissot's canon, but from one another, in the process.

[59] Salon of 1901 (Champ-de-Mars), no. 1405, une suite d'aquarelles sur *l'Ancien Testament 'Genèse'*. As previously, special rooms were reserved for the pictures.

[60] The most important is probably Thiébault-Sisson, 'J. James Tissot', pp. 1–8.

[61] Bastard, p. 278.

Setting aside only the portrait of his mother from the Salon of 1859, which was retained by the family, and the oil version of *L'Apparition médiunimique*, which had disappeared, the contents of his studio were sold at public auction.[62] The sale was not a success, and for a time after it was possible to buy impressions of his prints at the Magasins du Louvre.[63] Among the furnishings of the studio, relics described as 'meubles français et étrangers' or 'meubles de l'extreme orient' had doubtless figured in pictures painted in the sixties, and 'robes chinoises et japonaises en soie brodées' had clearly been the objects of Whistler's envy forty years before.

The darkness was complete, hardly broken by a now little-known version of the Passion filmed by Pathé in 1912, which was based on Tissot's Bible illustrations, giving those veristic little pictures the movement to which they always seem to have aspired and making them the unsung progenitors of generations of Hollywood biblical epics.[64]

Tissot's religious pictures proved detrimental in their effect on his posthumous standing as an artist. Their success in the nineties had the effect of forcing his earlier *mondaine* pictures into the background where they were soon forgotten. Tissot doubtless took a hand in this himself, for he also felt that his later work was not only 'high', but also 'great', art, and it was more rewarding to be compared to Mantegna, as Edmond de Goncourt compared him in a moment of unguarded enthusiasm,[65] than to Alfred Stevens or Giuseppe de Nittis, as was more generally the case. The *succès fou* of the Bible illustrations was of extremely short duration, however, and it is lucky they had found permanent homes away from the market-place without having to face the winds of change. With their mediocrity looming monolithically in the immediate historical background, they continued to exert a baleful influence, and earlier pictures which might have been appreciated for their own considerable merits were viewed with the same jaundiced eye. Their sanctimonious dullness antagonized the admirers of his earlier work beyond all patience, and their only lasting effect was to create a confusion about Tissot's aims and qualities as an artist which has persisted to this day, resulting in an aesthetic disrepute and diminished historical standing which is undeserved.

For thirty years after his death, Tissot's work was forgotten. Not one of his *appassionnements* had managed to put him in the mainstream, and he was written out of histories which saw nineteenth-century painting as a long scenario of revolt. Interest was kept alive only by those eccentric collectors of genre for whom his unfashionable pictures retained nostalgia and charm—and came at

[62] Hôtel Drouot, Paris, *L'Atelier de J. James Tissot*, July 9–10, 1903.

[63] Loys Delteil, *Manuel de l'amateur d'éstampes des dix-neuvième et vingtième siècles*, 2 vols. (Paris: Bornon-Aîné, 1925), ii, 332.

[64] A. Gowans, *The Unchanging Arts*, p. 291.

[65] Goncourt, *Journal*, iii, 1019.

bargain prices. By the 1920s, his pictures were worth little more than the price of their frames.[66]

The Depression and the Victorian revival of the thirties were to bring a new dawn. In London, the Leicester Galleries mounted an extremely popular Tissot exhibition in 1933, taking advantage of renewed interest in Victorian narrative paintings by virtually forgotten, and consequently cheap, artists which clients hard-hit by the rigours of the Depression could buy at reasonable prices.[67] James Laver's *Vulgar Society* was published in 1936 in response to this new interest. Often inaccurate, it remains a book of tremendous charm, and captures to perfection the social tone of the seventies in London and the gossip surrounding Tissot's liaison that had persisted up to Laver's time.[68] Twenty years separate it from the important retrospective exhibition held at the Sheffield Art Gallery in 1955 which concentrated on Tissot's English period but none the less gave a newly accurate picture of his particular qualities as an artist. Despite this interest, the market recovery for Tissot's work in the thirties failed, somewhat inexplicably, to get off the ground, and as late as the 1960s the prices given in the third volume of Reitlinger's *Economics of Taste* are not particularly elevated in comparison with those of many of Tissot's less attractive contemporaries. The next decade, however, was to see Tissot sky-rocket as an aesthetic commodity, and he has now taken his position, with other interesting minor painters of the Victorian period, among the fashionably overpriced.

American interest in Tissot led to the retrospective exhibition held at Providence and Toronto in 1968, the most complete review of his work since his death, and one which brought him to the attention of museums, scholars, and collectors. It was the first sustained attempt to treat Tissot from a scholarly point of view and to reassess his career, his position in relation to the art of his time, and his strange personality. It seems safe to say that Tissot has gone full circle: his works are sought, they fetch large prices, and are treated with respect by the scholarly community. One has the feeling it would not have surprised him at all.

---

[66] See Reitlinger, *Economics of Taste*, iii, 350.

[67] See M. Battersby, *The Decorative Thirties*, p. 169.

[68] For Laver's memories and some additional Tissot material, see *Museum Piece*, pp. 160–3.

VI. *The Journey of the Magi, c.*1886–95.

Appendix I. Pictures by Tissot exhibited at the Paris Salon

1859

2870. *Saint Jacques-le-Majeur et Saint Bernard; peinture à la cire* (unlocated)
2871. *Saint Marcel et Saint Olivier; peinture à la cire* (unlocated)
2872. *Promenade dans la neige* (Paul Touzet; Pl. 1)
2873. *Portrait de Mme T`. . .* (unlocated; presumably the portrait of the artist's mother mentioned by Bastard, p. 260)
2874. *Portrait de Mlle H. de S . . .* (unlocated)

1861

2969. *Pendant l'office* (presumably the picture now called *Martin Luther's Doubts*, Art Gallery of Hamilton, Ontario; Pl. 10)
2970. *Faust et Marguerite au jardin* (David E. Rust, Washington, DC; Pl. I)
2971. *Marguerite à l'office* (whereabouts unknown; Pl. 5)
2972. *Rencontre de Faust et de Marguerite* (Musée du Luxembourg, Paris; Pl. 2)
2973. *Voie des fleurs, voie des pleurs* (Museum of Art, Rhode Island School of Design, Providence; Pl. 12)
2974. *Portrait de Mlle M. P . . . .* (presumably the unlocated picture now called *A Girl in Black*; Pl. 24)

1863

1802. *Départ du fiancé* (unlocated; Pl. 13)
1803. *Retour de l'enfant prodigue* (Mr and Mrs Joseph Tanenbaum, Toronto; Pl. 14)
1804. *Départ* (also called *Le Départ de l'enfant prodigue à Venise*, unlocated; Pl. 16)

1864

1860. *Les deux sœurs; portrait* (Louvre, Paris; Pl. 29)
1861. *Portrait de Mlle L. L . . .* (Louvre, Paris, now called *Jeune Femme en veste rouge*; Pl. 26)

1865

2074. *Le Printemps* (unlocated; Pl. 30)
2075. *Tentative d'enlèvement* (Elliott Galleries, New York; Pl. 20)

1866

1843. *Jeune Femme dans une église* (unlocated; described, Thoré, 'Salon de 1866', *Salons*, p. 312, as: 'les stalles d'une église, où est assise une jeune femme absorbée dans ses contemplations.')

1844.   *Le Confessionnal* (Southampton Art Gallery; Pl. 32)

1867

1468.   *Jeune Femme chantant à l'orgue* (unlocated; Pl. 35)
1469.   *La Confidence* (unlocated; Pl. 31)

1868

2389.   *Un déjeuner* (Marquis of Bristol, London; Pl. 60)
2390.   *La Retraite dans le jardin des Tuileries* (unlocated; Pl. 45)
3337.   *Mélancolie; aquarelle* (unlocated; presumably a replica of the painting of the same title)
3338.   *Portrait; pastel* (unlocated)

1869

2269.   *Une veuve* (unlocated; Pl. 51)
2270.   *Jeunes Femmes regardant des objets japonais* (private collection, London; Pl. II)

1870

2747.   *Jeune Femme en bateau (appartient à M. W. H. Stewart)* (unlocated; Pl. 67)
2748.   *Partie carrée* (unlocated; Pl. 61)

1876

3985.   *Une eau-forte: La Tamise* (T. 14; B. 13; W. 20, repro.: a replica of Pl. 115)
2986.   *Une eau-forte: Quarrelling (une querelle)* (T. 11; B. 11; W. 18, repro.: a replica of Pl. 97)

1894

Société Nationale des Beaux-Arts, Champ-de-Mars. 270 illustrations for *La Vie de Notre Seigneur Jésus Christ* (exhibited in separate galleries with a special catalogue) (Brooklyn Museum, Brooklyn)

1897

Société Nationale des Beaux-Arts, Champ-de-Mars, no. 1192. *La Réception à Jérusalem du légat apostolique du Saint-Siège, S. E. Mgr. le cardinal Langénieux par le patriarche S. B. Mgr. Piavi* (formerly Reims Cathedral)

1901

Société Nationale des Beaux-Arts, Champ-de-Mars, no. 1405. 94 illustrations for *L'Ancien Testament 'Genèse'* (Jewish Museum, New York)

Appendix II.   Pictures by Tissot exhibited at the Royal Academy

1864

408.   *At the Break of Day* (unlocated; described, 'The Royal Academy', *The Times* 11 May 1864, and quoted in the present work, chap. II, n. 125; also described, 'The Royal Academy', *Athenaeum*, no. 1907, 14 May 1864, p. 684)

1872

389.   *An Interesting Story* (National Gallery of Victoria, Melbourne; Pl. 78)
644.   *Les Adieux* (City of Bristol Museum and Art Gallery; Pl. 76)

1873

108.   *The Captain's Daughter* (Southampton Art Gallery; Pl. 81)
121.   *The Last Evening* (Guildhall Art Gallery, London; Pl. 84)
914.   *Too Early* (Guildhall Art Gallery, London; Pl. 101)

1874

116.   *London Visitors* (Toledo Museum of Art; Pl. 106)
387.   *Waiting* (unlocated; described, 'The Royal Academy', *Art Journal*, no. 151 (July 1874), p. 200, as: 'autumn leaves overhanging the figure of a young lady waiting in a boat'.)
690.   *The Ball on Shipboard* (Tate Gallery, London; Pl. 102)

1875

48.   *The Bunch of Lilacs* (Richard Green Galleries, London; Pl. 107)
1233.   *Hush!* (City of Manchester Art Galleries; Pl. 103)

1876

113.   *The Thames* (Wakefield Art Gallery and Museums; Pl. 115)
530.   *A Convalescent* (Sheffield City Art Galleries; Pl. 113)
1098.   *The Thames* (etching) (T. 14; B. 13; W. 20, repro.: a replica of Pl. 115)
1156.   *Quarrelling* (T. 11; B. 11; W. 18, repro.: a replica of Pl. 97)

1881

561.   *Quiet* (Private Collection, London; Pl. 169)
981.   *Goodbye, On the Mersey* (Forbes Magazine Collection, New York; Pl. 147)

Appendix III. Pictures by Tissot exhibited at the Grosvenor Gallery

1877

17. *Summer* (*from a series of the Four Seasons; lent by E. F. White, Esq.*) (unlocated)
18. *A Portrait; lent by the artist* (presumably the picture in the Tate Gallery now called *Miss Lloyd* or *The Visit*; Pl. 126)
19. *The Gallery of H.M.S. 'Calcutta' (Portsmouth); lent by J. Robertson Reid, Esq.* (Tate Gallery, London; Pl. 124)
20. *The Widower; lent by J. P. Davis, Esq.* (Art Gallery of New South Wales; Pl. 122)
21. *Meditation; lent by the artist* (unlocated; presumably Pl. 5, 6, or 7)
22. *The Triumph of Will* (*Poem in Five Parts*)
     I. The Challenge; lent by the artist (Private Collection, Besançon)
     The Will, attended by two pages, Audacity (active) and Silence (passive), triumphs over Vice and Temptation
     II. The Temptation
     III. The Rescue
     IV. The Victory
     V. The Reward
     (*The last four pictures are not yet completed*)
23. *Holyday; lent by James Taylor, Esq.* (Tate Gallery, London, now called *The Picnic*; Pl. 123)
24. *Chrysanthemums; lent by E. Hermon, Esq., M.P.* (unlocated)
25. *Portsmouth Dockyard; lent by the artist* (Tate Gallery, London, now also called *Entre les deux mon cœur balance* or *How Happy I could be with Either* after the etching after the picture; Pl. 125)
26. *Gossiping; lent by the artist* (unlocated)

1878

31. *Spring* (*Specimen of a Portrait*) (Stair-Sainty Fine Arts Ltd., New York; Pl. 131, but see chap. V, n. 51)
32. *Croquet* (Art Gallery of Hamilton, Ontario; Pl. 142)
33. *Evening* (presumably the picture in the Musée d'Orsay, Paris; see chap. V, n. 23)
34. *July* (*Specimen of a Portrait*) (Private Collection, New York; Pl. 132)
35. *A Study* (unlocated; described, 'The Grosvenor Gallery', *The Times*, 2 May 1878, p. 7, as a '"study" of which only a pretty simple head is finished')
155. *October, etching* (T. 29; B. 26; W. 33, repro.; see Pl. 130)
156. *Mavourneen, etching* (Pl. 129)

157. *The Bow Window, etching* (presumably *Histoire ennuyeuse*, T. 28; B. 25; W. 32, repro.; see Pl. 80)

158. *Spring, etching* (T. 30; B. 27; W. 34; see Pl. 131)

1879

93. *Under the Chestnut Tree* (unlocated)

94. *Emigrants* (Private Collection, USA; Pl. 83)

95. *Rivals* (unlocated; Pl. 159)

96. *Orphan* (Private Collection; Pl. 138)

97. *A Quiet Afternoon* (unlocated; Pl. 144)

98. *Going to Business* (unlocated; Pl. 151; but see chap. V, n. 18)

99. *The Hammock* (unlocated; described, 'The Grosvenor Gallery', *The Times*, 2 May 1879, p. 3, and 'The Grosvenor Gallery', *Athenaeum*, no. 2689 (10 May 1879), pp. 607–8, as a lady in a Brazilian hammock under a Japanese sunshade of black and yellow; and clearly related to an etching of 1880 of the same title, repro., Wentworth, *Catalogue Raisonné of Prints*, no. 46)

100. *Crossing the Channel* (unlocated; Pl. 146)

281. *Trafalgar Tavern, Greenhithe, etching* (T. 31, 32; B. 28; W. 36, repro.)

282. *Summer, etching* (T. 39; B. 35, W. 43, repro.)

283. *Portico of the National Gallery*, etching (T. 36; B. 32; W. 40, repro.)

284. *A Garden, etching* (T. 35; B. 35; W. 39, repro.)

Appendix IV.   Pictures by Tissot exhibited at the Dudley Gallery, 1882

1–4.   *The Prodigal Son in Modern Life* (Musée de Nantes)
The Departure; In Foreign Climes; The Return; The Fatted Calf. each 85.09 × 114.3 cm.; replicas in water-colour, 31.12 × 37.47 cm. were also exhibited (Private Collection, Besançon)

5.   *Summer Evening*, 34.29 × 58.42 cm. (presumably the picture *Soirée d'été* in the Musée du Louvre, Paris; Pl. 170)

6.   *The Elder Sister*, 88.9 × 49.53 cm. (unlocated; see Pl. 163 for a replica or a related version)

7.   *By Land*, 63.5 × 27.94 cm. (unlocated)*

8.   *By Water*, 63.5 × 27.94 cm. (unlocated)*

9.   *Love at First Sight*, 22.86 × 30.48 cm. (unlocated)

10.   *Leaving Old England* (Gravesend), 22.86 × 34.29 cm. (unlocated)

11.   *Children's Party*, 21.59 × 29.21 cm. (unlocated)

12.   *Children's Picnic*, 19.69 × 26.67 cm. (presumably the picture in the Musée de Dijon; Pl. 166)

* Considering Tissot's penchant for making water-colour replicas of his major pictures and the sequence of photographs in his Albums, it seems probable that the compositions of *By Land* and *By Water* are preserved in the gouache repro. Laver, *Vulgar Society*, Pl. 21, as *Victoria Station*, and in the water-colour *Waiting at Dockside* (Pl. 149).

Appendix V.   La Femme à Paris

Pictures are listed in order of their exhibition at the Galerie Sedelmeyer, Paris, *Exposition J.-J. Tissot: Quinze Tableaux sur la Femme à Paris* (19 April–15 June 1885); followed in parenthesis by their numbers and titles in the exhibition at Arthur Tooth and Sons, London, *Pictures of Parisian Life by J. J. Tissot* (1886); followed by the authors for the accompanying literary texts for the abandoned publication of etchings after the pictures, as given in 'Tissot's Novel Art Work', *New York Times* (10 May 1885), p. 4; followed by the present location of the pictures, and plate references to the present work.

1. *L'Ambitieuse* (3. *Political Woman*), Jules Claretie (Albright–Knox Art Gallery, Buffalo; Pl. 178)

2. *Ces dames des chars* (11. *The Ladies of the Cars*), Théodore de Banville (Museum of Art, Rhode Island School of Design, Providence; Pl. 179)

3. *Sans dot* (2. *Without Dowry*), Georges Ohnet (Mr and Mrs Joseph M. Tanenbaum, Toronto; Pl. 180)

4. *La Mystérieuse* (12. *The Mystery*), Henri Meilhac (unlocated; Pl. 181)

5. *La Plus Jolie Femme de Paris* (1. *The Fashionable Beauty*), Ludovic Halévy (Private Collection, Switzerland; Pl. 182)

6. *L'Acrobate* (16. *The Tight-Rope Dancer*), Aurélien Scholl (unlocated; Pl. 183)

7. *La Menteuse* (10. *The Gossip*), Alphonse Daudet (unlocated; Pl. 184)

8. *La Mondaine* (6. *The Woman of Fashion*), Sully-Prudhomme (Mr and Mrs Joseph M. Tanenbaum, Toronto; Pl. 185)

9. *La Demoiselle d'honneur* (13. *The Bridesmaid*), François Coppée (City Art Gallery, Leeds; Pl. 186)

10. *Les Femmes d'artiste* (9. *Painters and their Wives*), Albert Wolff (The Union League, Philadelphia; Pl. 187)

11. *Les Femmes de sport* (7. *The Amateur Circus*), Charles Yriarte (Museum of Fine Arts, Boston; Pl. 188)

12. *Les Demoiselles de province* (14. *Provincial Women*), Guy de Maupassant (unlocated; Pl. 189)

13. *Le Sphinx* (8. *The Sphinx*), Paul Bourget (unlocated; Pl. 190)

14. *La Demoiselle de magasin* (5. *The 'Young Lady' of the Shop*), Émile Zola (Art Gallery of Ontario, Toronto; Pl. 191)

15. *Musique sacrée* (not exhibited in London), Charles Gounod (unlocated)

L'ÉTRANGÈRE

21.   *L'Esthétique* (4. *Aesthetic Woman*) (Museo de Arte de Ponce, Puerto Rico; see Pl. 193)
22.   *La Voyageuse* (15. *The Traveller*) (Koninklijk Museum voor Schone Kunsten, Antwerp; Pl. 192)

Appendix VI.   Pictures by Tissot exhibited at the International Exhibitions, 1862–1900

1862. International Exhibition, London

197. *Promenade dans la neige* (Paul Touzet; Pl. 1, but see also chap. IV, n. 4)

1867. Exposition Universelle, Paris

588. *Le Rendez-vous* (whereabouts unknown)

589. *Portrait de Mme la marquise de M . . .* (*The Marquise de Miramon*, Marquis de Miramon; Pl. 40)

1871. Weltaustellung, Vienna

(?). *Vive la République!* (Museum and Picture Gallery, Baroda, India)

1872. International Exhibition, London

1176. *The Thames* (unlocated, Pl. 75)

1181. *Bad News* (National Museum of Wales, Cardiff, now called *The Parting*; Pl. 78)

1219b. *M. le Capitaine * * ** (Worcester Art Museum, Worcester, now called *Gentleman in a Railway Carriage*; Pl. 72)

1282. *M. le Colonel * * ** (*Frederick Augustus Burnaby*, National Portrait Gallery, London; Pl. 71)

1888. International Exhibition, Glasgow

860. *Visit to a Ship in the Docks, lent by the artist* (whereabouts unknown)

2447. *The Widower (drawing), lent by John H. Downes* (whereabouts unknown, presumably related to the painting of the same title, Pl. 122)

2448. *Portrait (drawing), lent by John H. Downes* (whereabouts unknown)

1889. Exposition Universelle, Paris

1309. *Portrait du R. P. B . . .* (presumably the *Portrait du Révérend Père B . . . . missionnaire au Gabon* exhibited at the Galerie Sedelmeyer with the *Femme à Paris* series in 1885, no. 31, which is now in the Musée de Nantes; Père Bichet was a connection of the artist's through his brother Marcel–Affricani's wife, Claire Bichet, to whom the painting is inscribed)

1310. *L'Enfant Prodigue; le départ* (Musée de Nantes)

1311. *L'Enfant Prodigue; en pays lointains* (Musée de Nantes)

1312. *L'Enfant Prodigue; le retour* (Musée de Nantes)

1313. *L'Enfant Prodigue; le veau gras* (Musée de Nantes)

1893. World's Columbian Exposition, Chicago

703.   *The Prodigal Son; The Departure* (Musée de Nantes)
703a. *The Prodigal Son; In a Strange Land* (Musée de Nantes)
704.   *The Prodigal Son; The Return* (Musée de Nantes)
704a. *The Prodigal Son; The Fatted Calf* (Musée de Nantes)
859.   *The Prodigal Son: The Departure; In a Foreign Land; The Return; The Fatted Calf,*
       (etchings; W. 58–61)
989.   *Portrait of Miss C.* (pastel; whereabouts unknown)

Bibliography

MULTIPLE entries are arranged in chronological order. Anonymous newspaper and magazine articles are alphabetized under the name of the publication in which they appeared. Anonymous material, such as exhibitions and sales directly related to Tissot, is alphabetized under (Tissot) in chronological order; exhibitions and sales with texts by known authors are alphabetized by author and cross-referenced under (Tissot).

Abdy, Jane, *J. J. Tissot: Etchings, Drypoints and Mezzotints*. London: Lumley Cazalet Gallery, 1978.

About, Edmond, *Salon de 1864*. Paris: L. Hachette, 1864.

Amaya, Mario, 'The Painter of La Mysterieuse', *Apollo*, no. 77 (August 1962), 472–4.

Ames, Winslow, *Prince Albert and Victorian Taste*. New York: Viking, 1968.

d'Argencourt, Louise, and Druick, Douglas, *The Other Nineteenth Century: Paintings and Sculpture in the Collection of Mr. and Mrs. Joseph M. Tanenbaum*. Ottawa: National Gallery of Canada, 1978.

(*Art Journal*), 'The Royal Academy: Part II', *Art Journal*, NS 127 (July 1872), 181–6.

—, 'Exhibition of the Royal Academy', *Art Journal*, NS 138 (June 1873), 165–79.

—, 'Exhibition of the Royal Academy', *Art Journal*, NS 140 (August 1873), 236–41.

—, 'The Royal Academy', *Art Journal*, NS 150 (June 1874), 161–4.

—, 'The Royal Academy: Second Notice', *Art Journal*, NS 151 (July 1874), 197–201.

—, 'The Royal Academy: Concluding Notice', *Art Journal*, NS 152 (August 1874), 225–9.

—, 'The Royal Academy: Second Notice', *Art Journal*, NS 176 (August 1876), 229–32.

—, 'The Grosvenor Gallery', *Art Journal*, NS 188 (August 1877), 244.

Astruc, Zacharie, *Les Quatorze Stations du Salon*. Paris: Poulet-Malassis et de Broise, 1859.

—, 'Le Japon chez nous', *L'Etendard*, 26 May, 1868, p. 2.

(*Athenaeum*), 'Fine Arts: Society of British Artists', *Athenaeum*, no. 1902 (9 April 1864), 513.

—, 'The Royal Academy', *Athenaeum*, no. 1907 (14 May 1864), 682–4.

—, 'The Royal Academy (Concluding Notice)', *Athenaeum*, no. 2326 (25 May 1872), 657–62.

—, 'The London International Exhibition: Foreign Pictures', *Athenaeum*, no. 2332 (6 July 1872), 21–2.

—, 'The Royal Academy (Second Notice)', *Athenaeum*, no. 2376 (10 May 1873), 603–5.

—, 'Fine Arts Gossip', *Athenaeum*, no. 2409 (27 December 1873), 875.

—, 'Fine Arts Gossip', *Athenaeum*, no. 2423 (4 April 1874), 467.

—, 'The Royal Academy (Fourth Notice)', *Athenaeum*, no. 2431 (30 May 1874), 738–40.

—, 'The Royal Academy (Third Notice)', *Athenaeum*, no. 2533 (13 May 1876), 669–72.

—, 'Exhibition of Works in Black and White —Dudley Gallery', *Athenaeum*, no. 2538 (17 June 1876), 836–7.

—, 'The Grosvenor Gallery Exhibition (Second Notice)', *Athenaeum*, no. 2689 (10 May 1879), 606–8.

—, 'Fine Arts', *Athenaeum*, no. 3657 (27 November 1897), 754.

—, 'M. James Tissot', *Athenaeum*, no. 3903 (16 August 1902), 229.

Aubert, Maurice, *Souvenirs du Salon de 1859*. Paris: Tardieu, 1859.

Auvray, Louis, 'Salon de 1869: promenade à travers l'exposition', *Revue artistique et littéraire*, 17 (1869), 5–15.

Baldick, Robert, *The Siege of Paris*. New York: Macmillan, 1964.

Baldry, Alfred Lys, *Albert Moore: His Life and Work*. London: G. Bell & Son, 1892.

—, *Sir John Everett Millais: His Art and Influence*. London: G. Bell & Son, 1899.

de Banville, Théodore, *Esquisses parisiennes: croquis de femmes et de comédiennes*. Paris: Charpentier, 1876.

Bastard, George, 'James Tissot', *Revue de Bretagne*, 2nd ser. 36 (November 1906), 253–78.

Bate, Percy H., *The English Pre-Raphaelite Painters: Their Associates and Successors*. London: G. Bell & Sons, 1899.

Battersby, Martin, *The Decorative Thirties*. New York: Walker and Co., 1971.

Baudelaire, Charles, *Art in Paris: 1845–1862*, ed. and tr. Jonathan Mayne. London: Phaidon, 1965.

Beerbohm, Max, 'The Spirit of Caricature', in *A Variety of Things* (1953), repr. *The Incomparable Max*. New York: Dodd, Mead & Co., 1962, pp. 94–103.

Bell, Mrs Arthur (N. d'Anvers), *Representative Painters of the XIX Century*. London: Sampson Low, Marston and Co., 1899.

Bell, Quentin, *Victorian Artists*. London: Routledge & Kegan Paul, 1967.

Béraldi, Henri, *Les Graveurs du XIXe siècle: guide de l'amateur d'estampes modernes*, vol. 12, s.v. 'Tissot', pp. 125–34. Paris: L. Conquet, 1892.

Bertrand, Karl, 'Salon de 1870. Peinture II', *L'Artiste*, 9 (June 1870), 293–320.

Blanc, Charles, 'Salon de 1866', *Gazette des beaux-arts*, 21 (1866), 28–71.

Blanche, Jacques-Émile, *Portraits of a Lifetime*, ed. and tr. Walter Clement. New York: Coward-McCann, 1938.

—, *More Portraits of a Lifetime*. London: J. M. Dent & Sons, 1939.

Boggs, Jean Sutherland, *Portraits by Degas*. Berkeley and Los Angeles: University of California Press, 1962.

Boime, Albert, *The Academy and French Painting in the Nineteenth Century*. London: Phaidon, 1971.

Boucher, François, *Alfred Stevens*. Paris: Rieder, 1930.

Bourgeat, Fernand, *Salon de 1894: Société des Artistes Française et Société Nationale des Beaux-Arts*. Paris: Ludovic Baschet, 1894.

Bowles, Thomas Gibson, *The Defence of Paris: Narrated As It Was Seen*. London: Sampson Low, Son, and Marston, 1871.

Brooke, David S.; Wentworth, Michael; and Zerner, Henri, *James Jacques Joseph Tissot: A Retrospective Exhibition*. Providence: Museum of Art, Rhode Island School of Design, and Toronto: Art Gallery of Ontario, 1968.

Brooke, David S., 'James Tissot and the "Ravissante Irlandaise"', *Connoisseur*, 168 (May 1968), 55–9.

—, 'Le Monde idéal et intime de James Tissot', *Vie des arts*, no. 50 (Spring 1968), 12–17.

—, 'Tissot's "The Parting"', *Amgueddfa: Bulletin of the National Museum of Wales*, 2 (Summer–Autumn 1969), 22–6.

—, 'James Tissot's Amateur Circus', *Boston Museum Bulletin*, 67 (1969), 4–17.

—, '"An Interesting Story" by James Tissot', *Art Bulletin of Victoria* (1969–70), 22–9.

Burne-Jones, Georgiana, *Memorials of Edward Burne-Jones*, 2 vols. London: Macmillan, 1904.

Burty, Philippe, 'Les Eaux-Fortes de M. Henri Leys', *Gazette des beaux-arts*, 20 (1866), 467–77.

—, 'Exposition de la Royal Academy', *Gazette des beaux-arts*, 25 (1868), 56–73.

—, *Les Émaux cloisonnés anciens et modernes*. Paris: Martz, 1868.

de Callias, Hector, 'Salon de 1861, XVII. Les Lettres Q. R. S. T. V. Y. Z.', *L'Artiste*, 12 (15 July, 1861), 25–32.

—, 'Salon de 1863, XIII', *L'Artiste*, 8 (June 1863), 233–9.

du Camp, Maxime, *Les Beaux-Arts à l'Exposition Universelle et aux Salons de 1863, 1864, 1865, 1866 & 1867*. Paris: Jules Renouard, 1867.

Cantaloube, A., *Lettre sur les expositions et le Salon de 1861*. Paris: E. Dentu, 1861.

Carr, Alice Vansittart (Mrs J. Comyns Carr), *J. Comyns Carr: Stray Memories*. London: Macmillan, 1920.

Carr, J. Comyns, 'Lettres anglaises', *L'Art*, 9 (1877), 120.

—, 'La Saison d'art à Londres, II: la "Grosvenor Gallery"', *L'Art*, 9 (1877), 265–73.

—, *Coasting Bohemia*. London: Macmillan, 1914.

Castagnary, Jules, *Salons (1857–1870)*, 2 vols. Paris: Charpentier, 1892.

Čelebonović, Aleksa, *Some Call it Kitsch: Masterpieces of Bourgeoise Realism*, tr. Peter Willis. New York: Harry Abrams, 1974.

Cham (Noé, Amédée-Charles-Henri, comte de), *Cham au Salon de 1863: deuxième promenade*. Paris: Maison Martinet, n.d.

—, *Cham au Salon de 1867*. Paris: Arnauld de Vresse, 1867.

Champa, Kermit S., *Studies in Early Impressionism*. New Haven: Yale University Press, 1973.

Champfleury, Jules (Jules Fleury), *Les Chats: histoire, mœurs, observations, anecdotes*. Paris: J. Rothschild, 1869.

—, 'La Mode des japoniaiseries', *La Vie parisienne*, 21 November, 1868, pp. 862–3, repr. in *Champfleury: le, Réalisme*, texts selected and annotated by Geneviève and Jean Lacambre. Paris: Hermann, 1973, pp. 143–5.

Chantrel, Émile, 'Salon de 1863: L'art; la critique; les sculpteurs; les peintres', *L'Artiste*, vol. 1 (1 May, 1863), 185–204.

Chesneau, Ernest, *L'Art japonais: conférence fait à l'Union Centrale des Beaux-Arts Appliqués à l'Industrie*. Paris: A. Morel, 1869.

—, 'Exposition Universelle: le Japon à Paris', *Gazette des beaux-arts*, 2nd pér. 18 (1878), 385–97.

Claretie, Jules, 'M. James Tissot', *Peintres et sculpteurs contemporains*. Paris: Charpentier, 1873.

—, *La Vie à Paris: 1883*. Paris: Victor Havard, 1883.

Coles, William A., *Alfred Stevens*. Ann Arbor: University of Michigan Museum of Art, 1977.

Cook, Clarence, *Art and Artists of Our Time*, 3 vols. New York: Selmar Hess, 1888.

Crespelle, J.-P., *Les Maîtres de la Belle Époque*. Paris: Hachette, 1966.

Cummings, Frederick; Staley, Allen; and Rosenblum, Robert, *Romantic Art in Britain: Paintings and Drawings 1760–1860*. Detroit: Institute of Arts, and Philadelphia: Museum of Art, 1968.

Darcel, Alfred, 'Les Musées, les arts, les artistes pendant le siège de Paris', *Gazette des beaux-arts* 2nd pér. 4 (1870), 285–306, 414–29.

Daudet, Mme Alphonse (Julia Rosalie Célestine Allard), *Souvenirs autour d'un groupe littéraire*. Paris: E. Fasquelle, 1910.

Degas, Edgar, *Degas Letters*, ed. Marcel Guerin and tr. Marguerite Kay. Oxford: Bruno Cassirer, 1948.

Domergue, Jean-Gabriel, *Le Second Empire: de Winterhalter à Renoir*. Paris: Musée Jacquemart-André, 1957.

Doyle, Arthur Conan, *The History of Spiritualism* (2 vols., 1926). Facsimile (2 vols. in 1). New York: Arno Press, 1975.

Dumesnil, M. H., *Le Salon de 1859*. Paris: Renouard, 1859.

Duncan, Carol, *The Pursuit of Pleasure: The Rococo Revival in French Romantic Art*. New York: Garland Publishing, 1976.

Duquet, Alfred, *Guerre de 1871: Paris, La Malmaison, Le Bourget et le Trent et un Octobre*. Paris: Charpentier, 1893.

Duranty, Paul, 'Exposition de la Royal Academy et de la Grosvenor Gallery', *Gazette des beaux-arts*, 2nd pér. 20 (1 July, 1879), 366–76.

Farmer, John S., *'Twixt Two Worlds: A Narrative of the Life of William Eglinton*. London: The Psychological Press, 1886.

Finke, Ulrich, ed., *French 19th Century Painting and Literature: With Special Reference to the Relevance of Literary Subject-Matter to French Painting*. New York: Harper & Row, 1972.

Forbes, Christopher, *The Royal Academy (1837–1901) Revisited: Victorian Paintings from the Forbes Magazine Collection*. New York: Forbes Magazine, 1975.

Fricker, Elsa, *Alphonse Daudet et la société du Second Empire*. Paris: E. de Boccard, 1937.

Galimard, Auguste, *Les Peintures murales de l'église Saint-Germain des Prés par M. Hippolyte Flandrin*. Paris: E. Dentu, 1864.

Gautier, Théophile, *Les Beaux-Arts en Europe: 1855*. Paris: Michel Lévy Frères, 1856.

—, *Abécédaire du Salon de 1861*. Paris: E. Dentu, 1861.

—, *Tableaux de Siège de Paris 1870–1871*. Paris: Charpentier, 1886.

Gettings, Fred, *Ghosts in Photographs*. New York: Harmony Books, 1978.

van Gogh, Vincent, *The Complete Letters of Vincent van Gogh,* 2 vols. tr. Mrs J. van Gogh-Bonger. New York: New York Graphic Society, 1959.

de Goncourt, Edmond and Jules, *Histoire de la société française pendant le Directoire.* Paris: Dentu, 1855.

—, *Renée Mauperin: édition ornée de dix compositions à l'eau-forte par James Tissot.* Paris: Charpentier, 1884.

—, *Journal: mémories de la vie littéraire.* Paris: Flammarion, 1956.

Gonse, Louis, 'Les Aquarelles, dessins et gravures au Salon de 1876', *Gazette des beaux-arts,* 2nd pér. 14 (1 July 1876), 145.

—, 'L'Art japonais et son influence sur le goût européen', *Revue des arts décoratifs,* 18 (April 1898), 97–116.

Gourley, Hugh J., 'Tissots in the Museum's Collection', *Bulletin of The Museum of Art, Rhode Island School of Design,* 50 (March 1964), 1–4.

Gowans, Alan, *The Unchanging Arts.* Philadelphia: Lippincott, 1971.

Grangedor, J., 'Salon de 1868', *Gazette des beaux-arts,* 25 (1868), 5–30.

(*Graphic*), 'The Thames—From the Picture by J. J. Tissot', *Graphic,* 7 (8 February 1873), 119, illus. following p. 128.

—, 'The Royal Academy I', *Graphic,* 7 (3 May 1873), 411.

—, 'The Royal Academy II', *Graphic,* 7 (7 June 1873), 539.

—, 'The Royal Academy III', *Graphic,* 11 (8 May 1875), 447.

—, 'The Royal Academy and the Paris Salon Contrasted', *Graphic,* 11 (15 May 1875), 475.

—, 'Exhibition of the Royal Academy III', *Graphic,* 13 (13 May 1876), 471.

—, 'Exhibition of the Royal Academy V', *Graphic,* 13 (27 May 1876), 523.

—, 'Exhibition of Black and White at the Dudley Gallery', *Graphic,* 13 (17 June 1876), 598.

—, 'Exhibition in Black and White', *Graphic,* 15 (23 June 1877), 594.

—, 'The Gallery of H.M.S. "Calcutta" at Portsmouth', *Graphic,* 16 (18 August 1877), 150, illus. following p. 168.

Graves, Algernon, *The Royal Academy of Arts: A Complete Dictionary of Contributors and their Work from its Foundation in 1769 to 1904,* 8 vols. London: Henry Graves, 1906.

—, *A Century of Loan Exhibitions 1813–1912,* 5 vols. London: Algernon Graves, 1914.

Grieve, Alastair, 'Whistler and the Pre-Raphaelites', *Art Quarterly,* 34 (Summer 1971), 219–28.

Griffiths, Richard, *The Reactionary Revolution: The Catholic Revival in French Literature 1870–1914.* New York: Frederick Ungar, 1965.

Gueullette, Charles, *Les Peintres de genre au Salon de 1863.* Paris: Gay, 1863.

(Hale, Philip Leslie), 'Alfred Stevens', *Masters in Art: A Series of Illustrated Monographs,* 10, part 109 (January 1910).

Halévy, Daniel, *My Friend Degas,* ed. and tr. Mina Curtis. Middletown, Conn.: Wesleyan University Press, 1964.

Halévy, Ludovic, *Parisian Points of View,* tr. Edith V. B. Matthews. New York: Harper and Brothers, 1894.

Hamerton, Philip Gilbert, *Painting in France After the Decline of Classicism.* London: Seeley, Jackson and Halliday, 1869.

Hanson, Ann Coffin, *Manet.* Philadelphia: Museum of Art, and Chicago: Art Institute, 1966.

—, *Manet and the Modern Tradition.* New Haven: Yale University Press, 1977.

Harris, Eileen, intro., *Vanity Fair: An Exhibition of Original Cartoons.* London: National Portrait Gallery, 1976.

Hofmann, Werner, *The Earthly Paradise: Art in the Nineteenth Century,* tr. Brian Battershaw. New York: Braziller, 1961.

Holman-Hunt, William, *Pre-Raphaelitism and the Pre-Raphaelite Brotherhood,* 2 vols. London: Macmillan and Co., 1905.

Ikegami, Chuji, 'James Tissot, "Drawing Master" to Tokugawa Akitake', in *Japonisme in Art: An International Symposium,* gen. ed. Chisaburo Yamada. Tokyo: Committee for the Year 2001, 1980, pp. 147–55.

(*Illustrated London News*), 'The Royal Academy Exhibition', *Illustrated London News,* 60 (25 May 1872), 502.

—, 'Fine Arts Exhibition of the Royal Academy (Third Notice)', *Illustrated London News,* 64 (16 May 1874), 470.

—, 'Fine Arts', *Illustrated London News,* 65 (19 December 1874), 590.

—, 'Royal Academy Exhibition: Fourth

Notice', *Illustrated London News*, 66 (22 May 1875), 486.

—, 'Royal Academy Exhibition: Third Notice', *Illustrated London News*, 68 (13 May 1876), 475.

—, 'Dudley Gallery Exhibition', *Illustrated London News*, 80 (27 May 1882), 522.

Ironside, Robin, *Pre-Raphaelite Painters*. London: Phaidon, 1948.

Jahyer, Félix, *Salon de 1865*. Paris: Dentu, 1865.

James, Henry, 'The Picture Season in London, 1877', *Galaxy* (August 1877), repr. in *The Painter's Eye: Notes and Essays on the Pictorial Arts by Henry James*, sel. and ed. with an introd. by John L. Sweeney. Cambridge: Harvard University Press, 1956, pp. 130-51.

Johnson, Jane, comp., *Works Exhibited at the Royal Society of British Artists 1824–1893*, 2 vols. Woodbridge, Suffolk: Baron, 1975.

Jopling, Louise (Mrs Jopling-Rowe), *Twenty Years of My Life*. London: John Lane, 1925.

Jourdan, Louis, *Salon de 1859*. Paris: Librairie Nouvelle, 1859.

Jullian, Philippe, *Dreamers of Decadence: Symbolist Painters of the 1890's*, tr. Robert Baldick. New York: Praeger, 1971.

—, *The Symbolists*, tr. Mary Anne Stevens. New York: Phaidon, 1973.

—, *The Triumph of Art Nouveau: Paris Exhibition 1900*, tr. Stephen Hardman. New York: Larousse, 1974.

Knoblock, Edward, 'James Tissot and the Seventies', *Apollo*, 7 (June 1933), 255-8.

—, 'The Whimsical Seventies', *Country Life*, 80 (26 December 1936), 678-9.

Lacambre, Geneviève, *Le Musée du Luxembourg en 1874*, with the collaboration of Jacqueline de Rohan-Chabot. Paris: éditions des Musées Nationaux, 1974.

LaGrange, Léon, 'Salon de 1861', *Gazette des beaux-arts*, 10 (1861), 321-47.

—, 'Le Salon de 1864', *Gazette des beaux-arts*, 16 (1864), 501-36.

—, 'Exposition de l'Union Artistique', *Gazette des beaux-arts*, 20 (1866), 398-400.

Lambotte, Paul, 'Alfred Stevens', *L'Art flamand et hollandais*, 7 (1907), 153-80.

Laver, James, *Vulgar Society: The Romantic Career of James Tissot*. London: Constable 1936.

—, introd., *Paintings, Drawings, and Etchings by James Tissot Selected from an Exhibition Arranged by the Graves Art Gallery, Sheffield*. London: The Arts Council, 1955.

—, *Museum Piece: or The Education of an Iconographer*. Boston: Houghton Mifflin, 1964.

Lemoisne, P.-A. *Degas et son œuvre*, 4 vols. Paris: Paul Brame et C. M. de Hauke, 1946.

Lemonnier, Camille, *Alfred Stevens et son œuvre, suivi des impressions sur la peinture par Alfred Stevens*. Brussels: G. van Oest, 1906.

Leroi, Paul, 'Sixième Exposition de la Société d'Aquarellistes Française', *L'Art*, 36 (1 January 1884), 91-100.

Lethève, Jacques, *Daily Life of French Artists in the Nineteenth Century*, tr. Hilary E. Paddon. New York: Praeger, 1972.

Levy, Clifton Harby, 'J. James Tissot and his Work', *New Outlook*, 60 (1898), 954-64.

de Lostalot, Alfred, 'James Tissot', *Society of French Aquarellists*. Paris: Goupil, 1883.

—, 'Le Musée des Arts Décoratifs: exposition de MM. le Comte Lepic et James Tissot', *Gazette des beaux-arts*, 2nd pér. 27 (1883), 445-56.

Louvrier de Lajolais, A., 'Société des Amis des Arts du Limousin', *Gazette des beaux-arts*, 17 (1864), 174-83.

de Lurion, Roger, *Nobiliaire de Franche-Comté*, new edn. Besançon: Paul Jacquin, 1894.

Maas, Jeremy, *Victorian Painters*. New York: G. P. Putnam's Sons, 1969.

—, *Gambart: Prince of the Victorian Art World*. London: Barrie and Jenkins, 1975.

MacBeth, George, 'Subliminal Dreams', *Art News Annual*, 36 (1970), 28-39.

McCabe, James D., *Paris by Sunlight and Gaslight*. Philadelphia: National Publishing, 1869.

(*Magazine of Art*), 'The Grosvenor Gallery', *Magazine of Art* (1878), 82.

Mantz, Paul, 'Salon de 1859', *Gazette des beaux-arts*, 2 (1859), 272.

—, 'Salon de 1863', *Gazette des beaux-arts*, 14 (1863), 481-506.

—, 'Salon de 1865', *Gazette des beaux-arts*, 19 (1865), 5-42.

—, 'Artistes Contemporains: M. Henri Leys', *Gazette des beaux-arts*, 20 (1866), 297-317.

Marillier, Henry Currie, *Dante Gabriel Rossetti: An Illustrated Memorial of his Art and Life*. London: G. Bell & Son, 1889.

Ménard, Réné, 'Cercle de l'Union Artistique', *Gazette des beaux-arts*, 2nd pér. 1 (1869), 552-5.

—, 'Salon de 1870', *Gazette des beaux-arts*, 2nd pér. 4 (1870), 38-71.

Millais, Geoffroy, *Sir John Everett Millais*. London: Academy Editions, 1979.

Millais, John Guille, *The Life and Letters of Sir John Everett Millais*, 2 vols. London: Methuen, 1899.

Milsand, Joseph, *L'Esthétique anglaise: étude sur M. John Ruskin*. Paris: Germer Baillière, 1864.

Misfeldt, Willard, E., *James Jacques Joseph Tissot: A Bio-Critical Study*. Ann Arbor: University Microfilms, 1971.

Mitchell, Peter, 'The Success of Alfred Stevens at the Exposition Universelle of 1867', *Connoisseur*, 173 (April 1970), 263-4.

—, *Alfred Émile Leopold Stevens*. London: John Mitchell and Sons, 1973.

Moffett, Cleveland, 'J. J. Tissot and his Paintings of the Life of Christ', *McClure's Magazine*, 12 (March 1899), 386-96.

Monkhouse, Cosmo, *British Contemporary Artists*. New York: Charles Scribner's Sons, 1899.

de Montrond, Maxime, *Hippolyte Flandrin: étude biographique et historique*. Lille: J. Lefort, 1869.

Moreau-Nélaton, Etienne, *Manet raconté par lui-même*. Paris: Henri Laurens, 1926.

Morisot, Berthe, *Correspondence de Berthe Morisot*, ed. Denis Rouart. Paris: Quatre-Chemins-Editart, 1950.

Moulin, Jean-Marie, introd., *The Second Empire 1852-1870: Art in France Under Napoleon III*. Philadelphia: Museum of Art, 1978.

Muther, Richard, *The History of Modern Painting*, 4 vols. London: J. M. Dent, 1907.

de Navery, Raoul, *Le Salon de 1868*. Paris: Librairie Centrale, 1868.

Naylor, Leonard, *The Irrepressible Victorian: The Story of Thomas Gibson Bowles*. London: Macdonald, 1965.

(*New York Times*), 'Tissot's Novel Art Works', *New York Times*, 10 May 1885, p. 4.

—, 'The Week in the Art World', *New York Times: Saturday Review*, 26 February 1898, p. 130.

—, 'The Tissot Pictures and Drawings', *New York Times*, 15 November 1898, p. 6.

—, 'Accident to J. James Tissot', *New York Times*, 19 November 1898, p. 12.

—, 'To Buy Tissot's Paintings. Brooklyn Institute Secures Option on the Collection', *New York Times*, 7 January 1900, p. 7.

—, 'Tissot's Christ. Steps to secure the Paintings for the Brooklyn Institute', *New York Times: Saturday Review*, 17 February 1900, p. 101.

de Nittis, Giuseppe, *Taccuino 1870-1884*, pref. by Emilio Cecchi. Bari: Leonardo da Vinci, 1964.

Ohmori, Tatsuji, *Ukiyo-e Prints and the Impressionist Painters: Meeting of East and West*, 2nd rev. and enlarged edition. Tokyo: Sunshine City Museum; Osaka, Municipal Museum of Fine Arts; and Fukuoka, Fukuoka Art Museum, 1980.

North Peat, Anthony, *Gossip from Paris During the Second Empire*. Sel. and arr. A. R. Waller. New York: D. Appleton and Co., 1903.

Paris, Salon, *Catalogue officiel*. Paris, 1859, 1861, 1862, 1863-70, 1876.

Pennell, Elizabeth R. and Joseph, *The Life of James McNeill Whistler*, 2 vols. in 1. London: William Heinemann, 1902.

Perret, Paul, *Physionomies parisiennes*. Paris: A. le Chevalier, 1868.

Persall, Ronald, *The Table Rappers*. New York: St. Martin's Press, 1972.

Pica, Vittorio, *Giuseppe de Nittis: l'uomo e l'artista*. Milan: Alferi e Lacroix, 1914.

Pickvance, Ronald, *Degas 1879*. An Exhibition Organized by the National Galleries of Scotland and the Edinburgh Festival Society, in Collaboration with the Glasgow Museums and Art Galleries. Edinburgh: The National Gallery of Scotland, 1979.

Pictures of Society Grave and Gay from the Pencils of Celebrated Artists and the Pens of Popular Authors. London: Sampson Low, Son, and Marston, 1866.

Pittaluga, Mary; and Piceni, Enrico, *Giuseppe de Nittis*. Milan: Bramante, 1963.

Poole, Phoebe, 'Some Early Friends of Degas',

Apollo, 79 (May 1964), 391–4.

(*Portfolio*), 'Art Chronicle', *The Portfolio*, no. 193 (January 1886), 143–4.

Privat, Gonzague, *Place aux jeunes! Causeries critiques sur le Salon de 1865*. Paris: F. Cournol, 1865.

(*Punch*), 'The Gay Grosvenor Gallery Guide (A Personally Conducted Tour Through the Collection of Curiosities)', *Punch* (21 June 1879), 285–7.

Redford, George, *Art Sales: A History of Sales of Pictures and Other Works of Art*, 2 vols. London: Bradbury, Agnew & Co., The 'Whitefriars' Press, 1888.

Reff, Theodore, 'Copyists in the Louvre, 1850–1870', *Art Bulletin*, 46 (December 1964), 552–9.

—, 'The Pictures Within Degas's Pictures', *Metropolitan Museum Journal*, 1 (1968), 125–6.

—, 'Degas's "Tableau de Genre"', *Art Bulletin*, 45 (Summer 1972), 316–37.

—, *The Notebooks of Edgar Degas*, 2 vols. Oxford: Clarendon Press, 1976.

Reitlinger, Gerald, *The Economics of Taste: The Rise and Fall of the Picture Market 1760–1960*. New York: Holt, Rinehart and Winston, 1965.

Renan, Ary, 'Une nouvelle illustration des Évangiles par M. James Tissot', *Gazette des beaux-arts*, 3rd pér. 17 (1897), 421–8; 3rd pér. 18 (1897), 61–8.

Rewald, John, *The History of Impressionism* New York: Museum of Modern Art, 1961.

Reynolds, Graham, *Painters of the Victorian Scene*. London: B. T. Batsford, 1953.

—, *Victorian Painting*. New York: Macmillan, 1966.

Roditi, Édouard, 'Tissot: Revolutionary, Dandy, Realist', *Arts Magazine*, 42 (May 1968), 44–6.

Rosenberg, Pierre, pref.; Cummings, Frederick; Rosenblum, Robert; and Schnapper, Antoine, *French Painting 1774–1830: The Age of Revolution*. Detroit: Wayne State University Press, 1975.

Rosenblum, Robert, *Ingres, The Library of Great Painters*. New York: Harry Abrams, 1967.

Roskill, Mark, 'Early Impressionism and the Fashion Plate', *Burlington Magazine*, 112 (June 1970), 391–5.

Ross, Marita, 'The Truth About Tissot', *Everybody's Weekly*, 15 June 1946, pp. 6–7.

Rossetti, Dante Gabriel, *Letters*, 4 vols. ed. Oswald Doughty and John Robert Wahl. Oxford: Clarendon Press, 1965.

Roy, Élie, 'Salon de 1869. Peinture III', *L'Artiste*, 9 (1 July 1869), 69–95.

Ruskin, John, *Fors Clavigera* (Letter 79, July 1877), repr. in *The Works of John Ruskin*, ed. E. T. Cook and A. Wedderburn. London: Allen, 1907, vol. vii.

Saglio, E., 'Exposition de tableaux modernes dans la Galerie Goupil', *Gazette des beaux-arts*, 7 (1860), 46–52.

Schefer, Gaston, *Le Salon de 1897*. Paris and New York: Goupil, 1897.

Scheyer, Ernst, *The Circle of Henry Adams: Art and Artists*. Detroit: Wayne State University Press, 1970.

Schiff, Gert, 'Tissot's Illustrations for the Hebrew Bible', in *J. James Tissot: Biblical Paintings*, with essays by Yochanan Muffs and Gert Schiff and a chronology by David S. Brooke and Michael Wentworth. New York: The Jewish Museum, 1982.

Sheffield, Graves Art Gallery, *James Tissot: An Exhibition of Paintings, Drawings and Etchings*, 1955.

Sherard, Robert, 'James Tissot and his Life of Christ', *Magazine of Art*, 18 (1895), 1–8.

Signorini, Telemaco, *Caricaturisti e Caricaturati al Caffè "Michelangiolo"*. Florence: Civelli, 1893.

Simches, Seymour O., *Le Romantisme et le goût esthétique du XVIIIe siècle*. Paris: Presses Universitaires de France, 1964.

Sitwell, Sacheverell, *Narrative Pictures: A Survey of English Genre and its Painters*. London: Batsford, 1937.

Société d'Aquarellistes Française, *Cinquième Exposition*. Paris: Jouaust et Sigaux, 1883.

—, *Sixième Exposition*. Paris: Jouaust et Sigaux, 1884.

—, *Huitième Exposition*. Paris: Jouaust et Sigaux, 1886.

Spalding, Frances, *Magnificent Dreams: Burne-Jones and the Late Victorians*. New York: Dutton, 1978.

(*Spectator*), 'Fine Arts: The Gems of the Royal Academy', *Spectator*, 37 (30 April 1864), 505–6.

—, 'The Royal Academy', *Spectator*, 45 (4 May 1872), 561–2.

—, 'The Royal Academy (Second Notice)', *Spectator*, 45 (22 June 1872), 787–8.

—, 'The Royal Academy (Second Notice)', *Spectator* 46 (17 May 1873), 637–8.

—, 'The Royal Academy (Third Notice)', *Spectator*, 47 (30 May 1874), 691–3.

—, 'The Royal Academy (Second Notice)', *Spectator*, 48 (15 May 1875), 626–7.

—, 'The Royal Academy (Fourth Notice)', *Spectator*, 49 (27 May 1876), 681–2.

—, 'Art. Black and White', *Spectator*, 49 (29 July 1876), 950–1.

—, 'The Grosvenor Gallery (Second Notice)', *Spectator*, 50 (26 May 1877), 664–5.

—, 'Art. Black and White Exhibition', *Spectator*, 50 (14 July 1877), 888–9.

—, 'French Art: A Comparative Sketch', *Spectator*, 50 (18 August 1877), 1036–8.

—, 'The Grosvenor Gallery (First Notice)', *Spectator*, 51 (4 May 1878), 567–8.

—, 'The Grosvenor Gallery (Second Notice)', *Spectator*, 52 (31 May 1879), 690–2.

—, 'The "Black and White" Exhibition at the Egyptian Hall (Second Notice)', *Spectator*, 52 (19 July 1879), 915–6.

—, 'The Society of Painter-Etchers (First Exhibition)', *Spectator*, 54 (9 April 1881), 472–3.

Staley, Allen, 'The Condition of Music', *Art News Annual*, 33 (1967), 80–7.

—, introd., *From Realism to Symbolism: Whistler and His World*. New York: Wildenstein and Philadelphia, Museum of Art, 1971.

Stevens, Arthur, *Le Salon de 1863*. Paris: Librairie Centrale, 1866.

Strahan, Edward, *Modern French Art*. New York: Lovering, 1881.

Stranahan, Clara H., *A History of French Painting from its Earliest to its Latest Practice*. New York: Charles Scribner's Sons, 1888.

Sutton, Denys, *Nocturne: The Life of James McNeill Whistler*. New York: Lippincott, 1964.

Taylor, Hilary, *James McNeill Whistler*. New York: Putnam, 1978.

Taylor, Tom, *Ballads and Songs of Brittany*. London: Macmillan, 1865.

Thiébault-Sisson, François, 'J. James Tissot', *Les Arts*, no. 9 (October 1902), 1–8.

Thomson, Ian, 'Tissot and Oxford', *Oxford Art Journal*, no. 2 (April 1979), 53–6.

Thoré, Théophile (W. Bürger), *Salons de W. Bürger 1861 à 1868*. Paris: Veuve Jules Renouard, 1870.

le Tilly, Père Jacques, *Evocations de cent ans: centenaire. 1874–1974 du couvent des dominicains, 222, rue du Faubourg Saint Honoré à Paris*. Mimeographed. Paris: Couvent des Dominicains, 1974.

(*The Times*, London), 'Exhibition of the Royal Academy (Second Notice)', *The Times*, 21 May 1872, p. 7.

—, 'The Royal Academy', *The Times*, 3 May 1873, p. 12.

—, 'The Royal Academy', *The Times*, 2 May 1874, p. 12.

—, 'The Royal Academy', *The Times*, 29 May 1875, p. 6.

—, 'Royal Academy Exhibition', *The Times*, 29 May 1876, p. 6.

—, 'The Grosvenor Gallery', *The Times*, 1 May 1877, p. 10.

—, 'The Grosvenor Gallery', *The Times*, 2 May 1878, p. 7.

—, 'The Grosvenor Gallery', *The Times*, 2 May 1879, p. 3.

Tissot, James, *The Complete Collection of the Artist's Works, Reproduced in a Series of Photographs*; vol. 1, 1859–70; vol. 2, 1870–6; vol. 3, 1876–82. Private collection, United States; exhibited under this title at the Dudley Gallery, London, 1882.

—, *Eaux-Fortes, manière noire, pointes sèches*, 1886. See under Yriarte.

—, *La Vie de Notre Seigneur Jesus-Christ*, 2 vols. Tours: Mame et fils, 1896–7.

—, *The Life of Our Lord Jesus Christ*, 4 vols., tr. Mrs Arthur Bell (N. d'Anvers). New York: McClure–Tissot Company, 1899.

—, *Holy Bible: The Old Testament*. New York: M. de Brunoff, 1904.

(Tissot, James), London, Dudley Gallery, 1882. *J. J. Tissot: An Exhibition of Modern Art*.

(—), Paris, L'Union Centrale des Arts Décoratifs, Palais de l'Industrie, 1883. *Exposition des œuvres de J. J. Tissot*.

(—), Paris, Galerie Sedelmeyer, 1885. *Exposition J.-J. Tissot: quinze tableaux sur la Femme à Paris*.

(—), London, Arthur Tooth and Sons, 1886. *Pictures of Parisian Life by J. J. Tissot*.

(—), New York, M. Knoedler & Co., n.d. (c. 1886–7). *A Painter Etcher: The Etched*

Work of J. J. Tissot at the Galleries of M. Knoedler & Co. With an anonymous translation of Yriarte's intro. to Tissot's 1886 *catalogue raisonné of prints.*

(–), Paris, Hôtel Drouot, 9–10 July, 1903. *L'Atelier de James Tissot.*

(–), Sheffield, Graves Art Gallery, 1955. see under Sheffield.

(–), London, The Arts Council, 1955. see under Laver.

(–), Besançon, MM. Renoud-Grappin, commissaire-priseur, et Randot, notaire, 8–9 November, 14–15, 21–2, 1964. *Importante Vente mobilière au château de Buillon, commune de Chenecey-Buillon après décès de Mlle J. Tissot.* Printed announcement and summary of contents for the estate of Jeanne Tissot.

(–), Providence, Rhode Island, Museum of Art, Rhode Island School of Design, and Toronto, Art Gallery of Ontario, 1968, see under Brooke, David S.; Wentworth, Michael; and Zerner, Henri.

(–), Minneapolis, Institute of Arts, 1978, see under Wentworth, Michael, *Catalogue Raisonné of Prints.*

Uzanne, Octave, *La Femme à Paris. Nos contemporaines, notes successives sur les parisiennes de ce temps dans leurs divers milieux, états et conditions.* Paris: Ancienne Maison Quantin, 1894.

–, *Fashion in Paris: The Various Phases of Feminine Taste and Aesthetics from 1797 to 1897,* tr. Lady Mary Lloyd. London: William Heinemann, 1898.

Vachon, Marius, 'L'Exposition moderne du métal à L'Union Centrale', *Gazette des beaux-arts,* 2nd pér. 22 (July 1880), 424–47.

Vanzype, Gustave, *Henri Leys* (Collection des peintres et sculpteurs belges). Brussels: Nouvelle société d'Editions, 1934.

(*Vie parisienne*), 'La Femme à Paris: Exposition Tissot', *La Vie parisienne,* 23 (2 May 1885), 255.

Ward, Leslie, *Forty Years of 'Spy'.* London: Chatto & Windus, 1915.

Warner, Malcolm, *James Tissot.* London: The Medici Society, forthcoming.

Weisberg, Gabriel P.; Cate, Philip Dennis; Eidelberg, Martin; and Johnson, William R., *Japonisme: Japanese Influence on French Art 1854–1910.* Cleveland: Museum of Art, and Baltimore: Walters Art Gallery (Distributed, Kent, Ohio: Kent State University Press), 1975.

Wentworth, Michael, 'James Tissot—A Retrospective View', *Canadian Antiques Collector,* 3 (April 1968), 10–13.

–, 'Tissot's "On the Thames, A Heron"', *Minneapolis Institute of Arts Bulletin,* 62 (1975), 35–49.

–, *James Tissot: Catalogue Raisonné of his Prints.* Minneapolis: Minneapolis Institute of Arts, 1978.

–, 'Tissot and *Japonisme*'. In *Japonisme in Art: An International Symposium,* gen. ed. Chisaburo Yamada. Tokyo: Committee for the Year 2001, 1980, pp. 127–46.

–, 'Energized Punctuality: James Tissot's *Gentleman in a Railway Carriage*', *Journal of the Worcester Art Museum,* 3 (1979–80), 8–27.

Wilde, Oscar, 'The Grosvenor Gallery, 1877', *Dublin University Magazine* 90 (July 1877) 118, repr. in *The First Collected Edition of the Works of Oscar Wilde,* 15 vols., ed. Robert Ross. London: Dawson's, 1969 (rpt. of the Methuen edition, 1908), vol. 15, pp. 5–23.

Young, G. M., *Victorian England: Portrait of an Age.* Oxford: Oxford University Press, 1936.

Yriarte, Charles, 'Exhibition of the Royal Academy of Arts II', *L'Art,* 2 (1875), 253–6.

–, 'Exhibition of the Royal Academy of Arts III', *L'Art,* 3 (1875), 241–55.

–, introd., *J.-J. Tissot: Eaux-Fortes, manière noire, pointes-sèches.* Paris: 64 avenue du Bois de Boulogne, 1886.

Zerner, Henri, 'The Return of "James" Tissot', *Art News,* 67 (March 1968), 32–5.

–, 'James Tissot', *L'Œil,* no. 160 (April 1968), 22–9.

Index of works by Tissot
Paintings, Pastels, Drawings, and Prints
Cloisonné Enamels

Unless otherwise stated, the medium of the work is oil. The principal or first version of any work is followed by replicas, studies for, and prints after it. References in parentheses refer to pages on which a work is identified by plate number rather than title. Portraits identified only by the initial letters of a sitter's name are indexed together under Portraits d'Initiaux; other portraits appear alphabetically under the sitter's name. Works in Cloisonné enamel are indexed together under Cloisonné.

General Index

PLATES

1. *Promenade dans la neige*, 1858.

2. *Le Rencontre de Faust et de Marguerite*, 1860.

3. Henri Leys, *La Promenade hors des murs*, 1854.

4. *Marguerite à la fontaine*, 1861.

6. *Marguerite à l'église, c. 1860.*

5. *Marguerite à l'office, c.1861.*

7. *Marguerite à l'église*, c.1861.

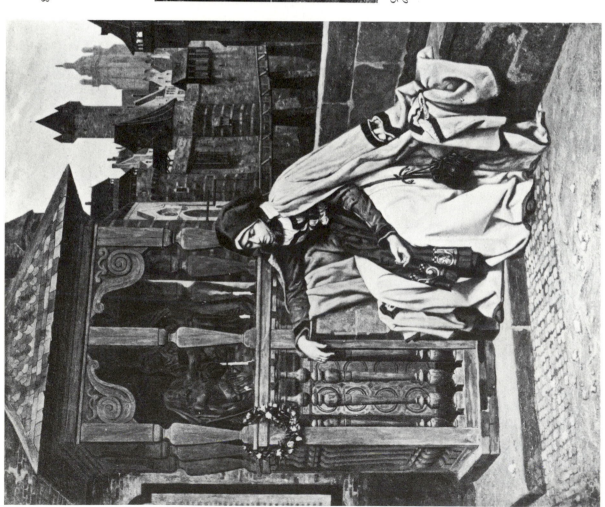

8. *Marguerite au rempart*, 1861.

9. Leys, *Martin Luther enfant chantant dans les rues d'Eisenach*, 1859.

10. *?Pendant l'office (Martin Luther's Doubts)*, 1860.

11. Leys, *La Déclaration*, 1863.

12. *Voie des fleurs, voie des pleurs (The Dance of Death)*, 1860.

13. *Le Départ du fiancé, c.*1863.

14. *Le Retour de l'enfant prodigue*, 1862.

15. Study for *Le Retour de l'enfant prodigue*, c.1862.

16. *Le Départ de l'enfant prodigue à Venise*, c.1863.

17. Study for *Le Départ de l'enfant prodigue à Venise*, c.1862.

18. *Promenade sur les remparts,*
1864.

19. Jean-Léon Gérôme, *Louis
XIV et Molière,* 1862.

20. *Tentative d'enlèvement*, 1865.

21. *L'Enlèvement*, c.1865.

22. *Sur la plage*, c.1864–6.

23. *Portrait de femme*, c.1860–1.

24. *?Mlle M. P . . . (A Girl in Black)*, 1861.

25. Gustave Courbet, *Les Demoiselles des bords de la Seine*, 1856–7.

26. *Mlle L. L . . . (Jeune Femme en veste rouge)*, 1864.

27. Courbet, *Mme Mathilde Cuoq*, 1859.

28. Copy after Jean-Auguste-Dominique Ingres, *Mme de Senonnes*, ?before 1856.

29. *Les Deux Soeurs: portrait*, 1863.

30. *Le Printemps, c.*1865.

31. *La Confidence, c.*1867.

33. *Le Confessionnal*, c.1866.

32. *Le Confessionnal*, 1865.

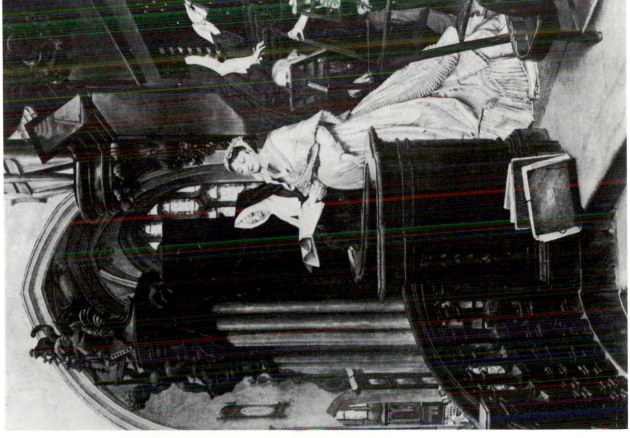

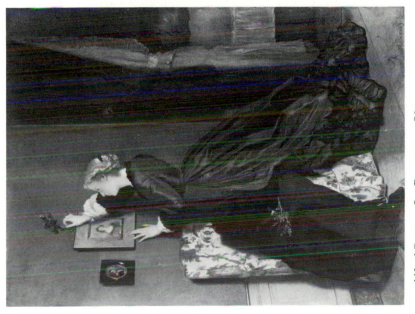

34. Alfred Stevens, *Les Rameaux*, c.1862.

35. *Jeune Femme chantant à l'orgue*, c.1867.

36. *Self-Portrait, c.*1865.

37. Edgar Degas, *James Tissot dans un atelier d'artiste*, c.1868.

38. *The Family of the Marquis de Miramon on the Terrace of the Château de Paulhac*, 1866.

39. *Le Cercle de la rue Royale*, 1868.

40. *The Marquise de Miramon, née Thérèse Feuillant (1840–1912), 1866.*

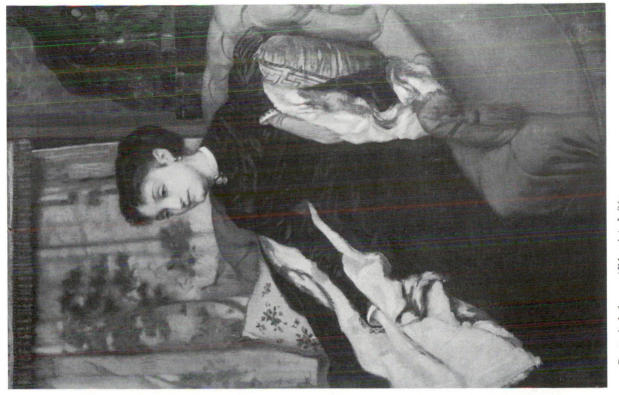

42. *Portrait de femme (Rêverie)*, ?1867.

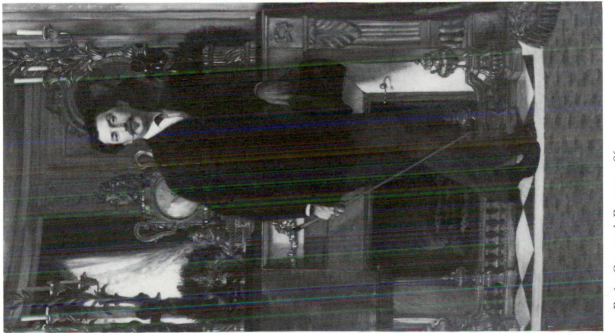

41. *Eugène Coppens de Fontenay*, 1867.

43. *Déjeuner sur l'herbe, c.*1865–8.

44. *La Terrasse du Jeu de Paume, c.*1867.

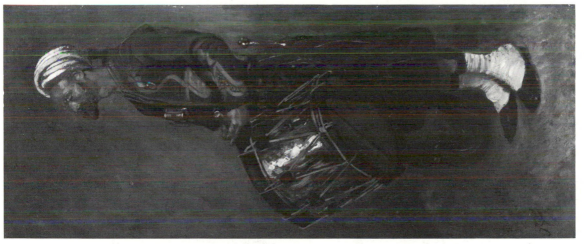

46. Study of a zouave drummer for *Le Retraite dans le jardin des Tuileries, c.1867.*

45. *La Retraite dans le jardin des Tuileries*, 1867.

47. *L'Armoire*, 1867.

48. *Le Gôuter, c.*1869.

49. Stevens, *Fleurs d'automne,* 1867.

50. *Rêverie*, 1869.

51. *Une veuve*, 1868.

52. *L'Escalier*, 1869.

53. Study for *L'Escalier*, *c*.1869.

54. *Prince Akitake Tokugawa*, 1868.

55. *Japonais au bain*, 1864.

56. Jeune Femme tenant des objets japonais, *c*.1864–5.

57. Whistler, *La Princesse du pays de la porcelaine*, 1864.

58. Stevens, *La Dame en rose (Le Bibelot exotique)*, c.1865.

59. *Jeunes Femmes regardant des objets japonais*, 1869.

60. *Un déjeuner, c.*1868.

61. *Partie carrée, c.*1870.

62. J.–M. Moreau le Jeune, *Le Souper fin*, 1789.

64. *La Cheminée, c. 1870.*

63. *Sixième comédien, c. 1869.*

65. *Jeune Femme à l'éventail*, c.1870–1.

66. *A la rivière*, 1871.

67. *Jeune Femme en bateau*, c.1870.

68. *Maison bombardeé pendant le Siège de Paris*, c.1871.

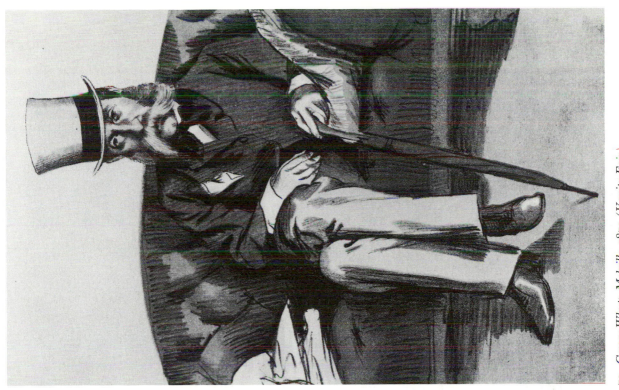

70. *George Whyte-Melville*, 1871 (*Vanity Fair*).

69. *Napoleon III*, 1869 (*Vanity Fair*).

71. *Colonel Frederick Augustus Burnaby*, 1870.

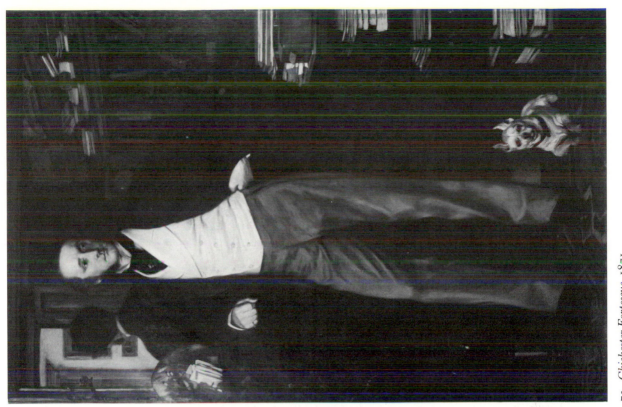

73. *Chichester Fortescue*, 1871.

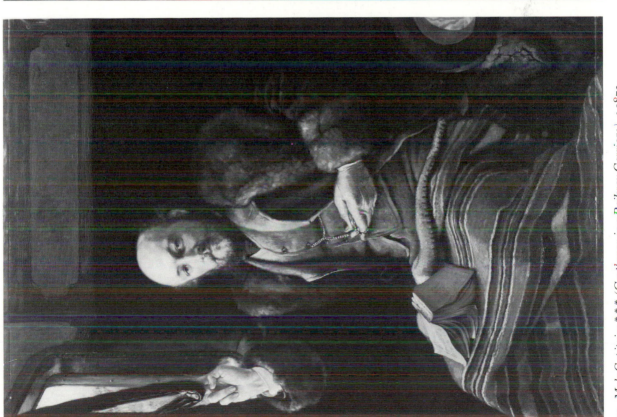

72. *M. le Capitaine* *** (*Gentleman in a Railway Carriage*), c.1872.

74. Whistler, *Wapping*, c.1860–4.

75. *The Thames*, after the picture by Tissot of c.1872, published in the *Graphic*, 1873.

76. *Les Adieux*, 1871.

77. *An Interesting Story, c.*1872.

78. *Bad News (The Parting)*, 1872.

79. *Le Thé*, 1872.

80. *Histoire ennuyeuse, c.*1872.

81. *The Captain's Daughter*, 1873.

82. *The Three Crows Inn, Gravesend, c.*1873.

83. *Emigrants, c.*1873.

84. *The Last Evening*, 1873.

85. Study for *The Last Evening*, c.1873.

86. Study for *The Captain and the Mate*, c.1873.

87. Arthur Hopkins, *The Last Croquet Game of the Season*, published in the *Illustrated London News*, 1872.

88. *Boarding the Yacht*, 1873.

89. John Callcott Horsley, *Showing a Preference*, 1860.

90. *On the Thames, a Heron, c.1871–2.*

92. (Anon.), *Gathering Wood Violets*, published in the *Illustrated London News*, 1872.

91. Sir John Everett Millais, *Autumn Leaves*, 1856.

93. *Autumn on the Thames (Nuneham Courtney)*, c.1871–2.

95. Sidney Hall, *The Autumn Campaign—Caught Between Two Fires*,
published in the *Graphic*, 1871.

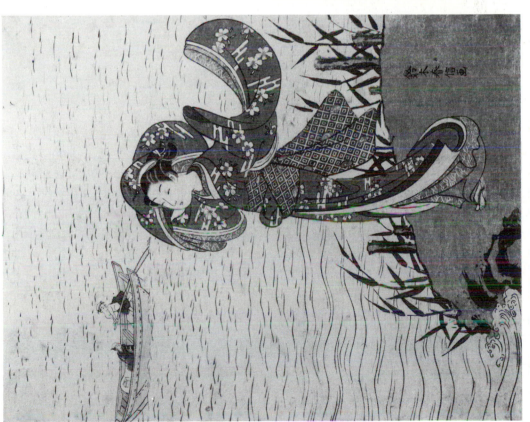

94. Suzuki Harunobo, *A Windy Day by the Riverside*, c.1768.

97. *Quarrelling, c.1874–5.*

96. *At the Rifle Range, 1869.*

98. *Waiting for the Train (Willesden Junction)*, c.1871–3.

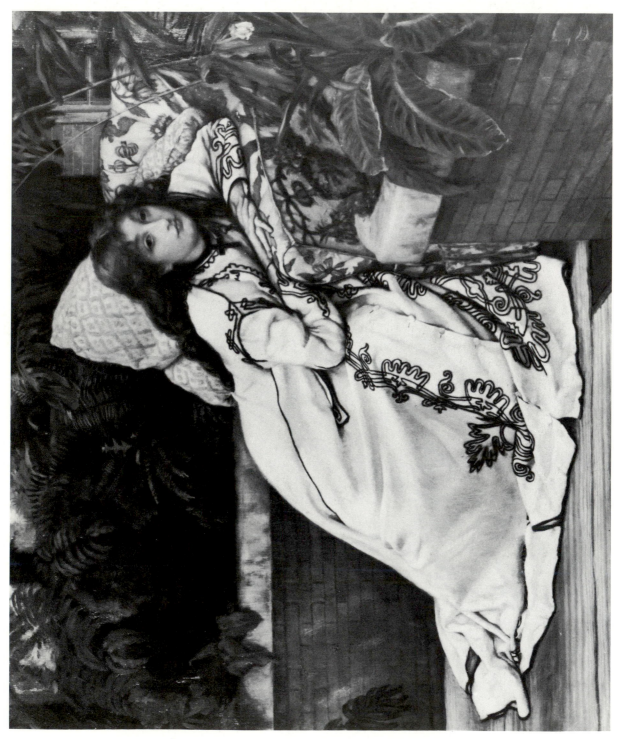

99. *A Girl in an Armchair*, 1872.

100. *A Morning Ride*, c.1872–3.

101. *Too Early*, 1873.

102. *The Ball on Shipboard, c.*1874.

103. *Hush!*, c.1875.

104. (Anon.), *Her Majesty's State Concert at Buckingham Palace*, published in the *Graphic*, 1871.

105. Édouard Manet, *La Musique dans le jardin des Tuileries*, 1862.

106. *London Visitors, c.*1874.

108. *Reading the News*, c.1874.

107. *The Bunch of Lilacs*, c.1875.

110. *A Fête Day at Brighton*, c.1875–8.

109. *Still on Top*, c.1874.

111. *Waiting for the Ferry at the Falcon Tavern*, c.1874.

112. *The Empress Eugénie and the Prince Impérial in the Grounds at Camden Place, Chiselhurst, c.1874.*

113. *A Convalescent, c.*1876.

114. *The Letter, c.*1878.

115. *The Thames, c.*1876.

116. *A Passing Storm, c.*1876.

117. *Ramsgate,* 1876.

118. *Waiting for the Ferry, c.*1878.

119. *Waiting for the Ferry, c.*1878.

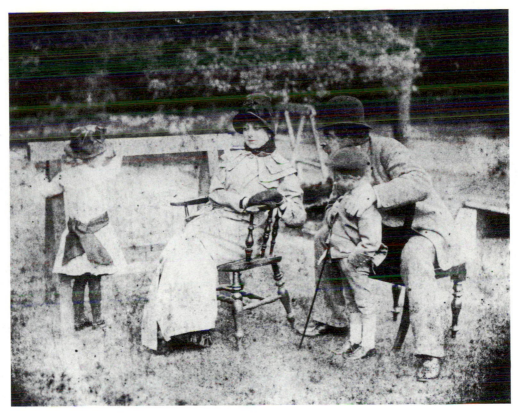

120. Photograph of Tissot with Mrs Newton and her children.

121. *The Terrace of the Trafalgar Tavern, Greenwich, c.1878.*

122. *The Widower, c.*1877.

123. *Holyday (The Picnic)*, c.1877.

124. *The Gallery of H.M.S. Calcutta (Portsmouth)*, c.1877.

125. *Portsmouth Dockyard* (*Entre les deux mon coeur balance*) (*How Happy I could be with Either*), c.1877.

126. *A Portrait (Miss Lloyd)*, 1876.

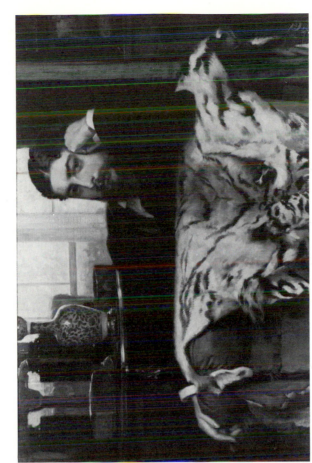

127. *The Chapple-Gill Family of Lower Lea,*
Wooton, 1877.

128. *Algernon Moses Marsden,* 1877.

129. *Mavourneen*, 1877.

130. *October, c.1877.*

131. *Spring (Specimen of a Portrait), 1878.*

132. *July* (*Specimen of a Portrait*) (*Sea-side*), c.1878.

133. Albert Moore, *A Workbasket*, c.1879.

134. *Listening to Music, c.*1878

135. *Mrs Newton with a Child by a Pool, c.*1877–8.

136. *The Henley Regatta of 1877*, 1877.

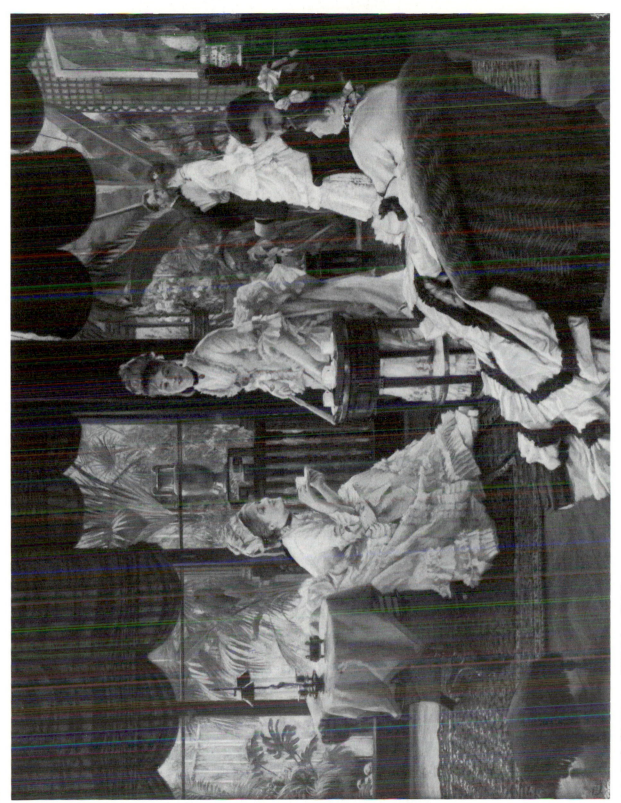

137. *In the Conservatory (Rivals)*, c.1875–8.

139. *The Gardener, c.1879.*

138. *Orphan, c.1879.*

140. *Mme Newton à l'ombrelle, c.* 1879.

141. *Children in a Garden*, quadrilateral vase decorated with figures from *Croquet, c.* 1878–82.

142. *Croquet, c.*1878.

143. *Croquet, c.*1878.

144. *A Quiet Afternoon, c.*1879.

146. *Crossing the Channel, c.*1879.

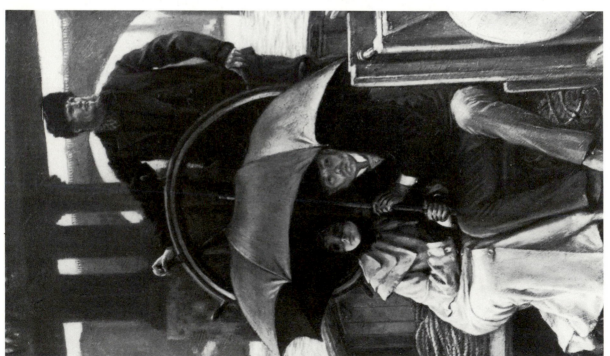

145. *The Ferry, c.*1879.

147. *Goodbye, On the Mersey, c.*1881.

149. *Waiting at Dockside, c.*1881–2.

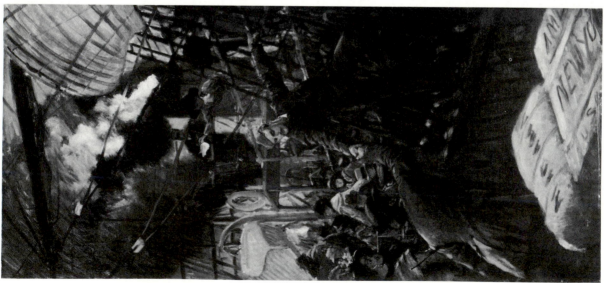

148. *Les Deux Amis, c.*1882.

151. *Going to Business, c.*1879.

150. *The Cabstand, Victoria Station, c.*1881–2.

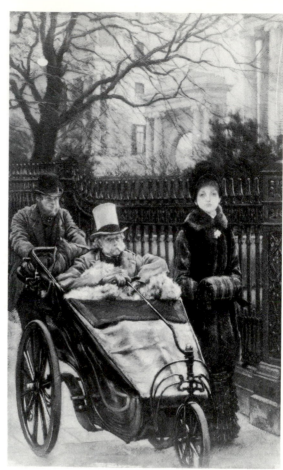

152. *A Convalescent, c.*1878.

153. *Study of Regent's Park, c.*1878.

154. *The Prodigal Son in Modern Life : The Departure*, 1881.

155. *The Prodigal Son in Modern Life : In Foreign Climes*, 1881.

156. *The Prodigal Son in Modern Life : The Return*, 1881.

157. *The Prodigal Son in Modern Life : The Fatted Calf*, 1881.

158. *Fortune*, sculpture, c.1878–82.

160. *Hide and Seek, c.1880–2.*

159. *Rivals, c. 1878–9.*

162. *Rêverie*, c.1881.

161. Photograph of Mrs Newton with an unidentified man.

163. *La Soeur aînée*, c.1881.

164. Photograph of Mrs Newton with her niece.

165. Photograph of Mrs Newton used for the painting *En plein soleil*.

166. *The Picnic, c.*1881–2.

167. *The Park, c.*1881–2.

168. *Le Banc de jardin,* 1883.

169. *Quiet, c.*1881.

170. *Soirée d'été*, c.1881.

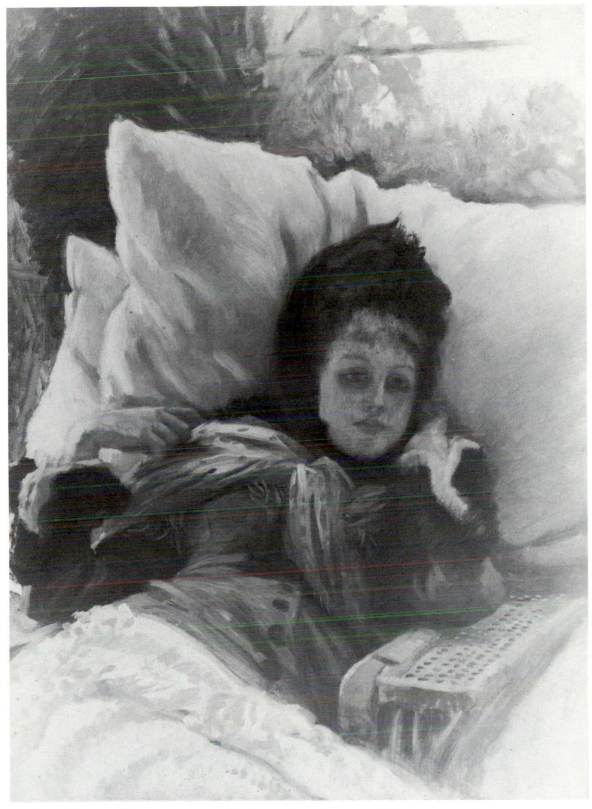

171. *Jeune Femme souffrante (Mrs. Newton Resting on a Chaise Longue)*, *c*.1881–2.

172. Illustration to *Renée Mauperin : Renée and her Father in the Porch of the Church at Morimond.* 1882.

173. Photograph of Tissot and Mrs Newton used for *Renée Mauperin.*

174. *Le Journal*, 1882–3.

175. *Berthe*, 1882–3.

176. *Woman with a Gun, c.*1895.

177. Paul Helleu, *Le Peintre Tissot chez la princesse de Polignac, c.*1895.

178. *L'Ambitieuse (La Femme à Paris)*, 1883–5.

179. *Ces dames des chars (La Femme à Paris)*, 1883–5.

180. *Sans dot (La Femme à Paris)*, 1883–5.

181. *La Mystérieuse (La Femme à Paris)*, 1883–5.

183. *L'Acrobate (La Femme à Paris)*, 1883–5.

182. *La Plus Jolie Femme de Paris (La Femme à Paris)*, 1883–5.

184. *La Menteuse (La Femme à Paris)*, 1883–5.

185. *La Mondaine (La Femme à Paris)*, 1883–5.

186. *La Demoiselle d'honneur (La Femme à Paris)*, 1883–5.

187. *Les Femmes d'artiste (La Femme à Paris)*, 1883–5.

188. *Les Femmes de sport (La Femme à Paris)*, 1883–5.

189. *Les Demoiselles de province (La Femme à Paris)*, 1883–5.

190. *Le Sphinx (La Femme à Paris)*, 1883–5.

191. *Le Demoiselle de magasin (La Femme à Paris)*, 1883–5.

192. *La Voyageuse (L'Étrangère)*, 1883–5.

193. *L'Esthétique (L'Étrangére)*, 1883–5.

195. *Visiteurs étrangers au Louvre, c.*1883–5.

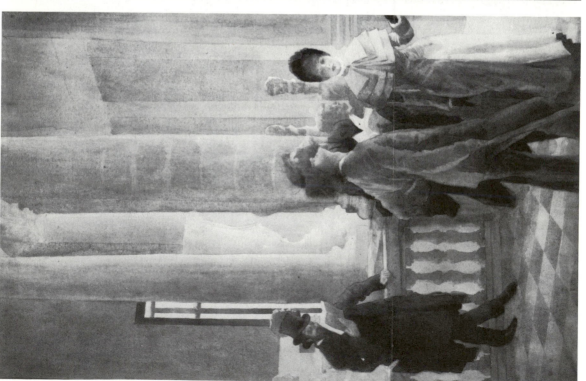

194. *Visiteurs étrangers au Louvre, c.*1883.

196. *The Ruins (Inner Voices)*, 1885.

197. *L'Apparition médiunimique*, 1885.

198. *Behold, He Standeth,* c.1886–94.

199. *The Sojourn in Egypt, c.*1886–94.

200. *The Soul of the Penitent Thief in Paradise, c.*1886–94.

201. *It is Finished, c.*1886–94.

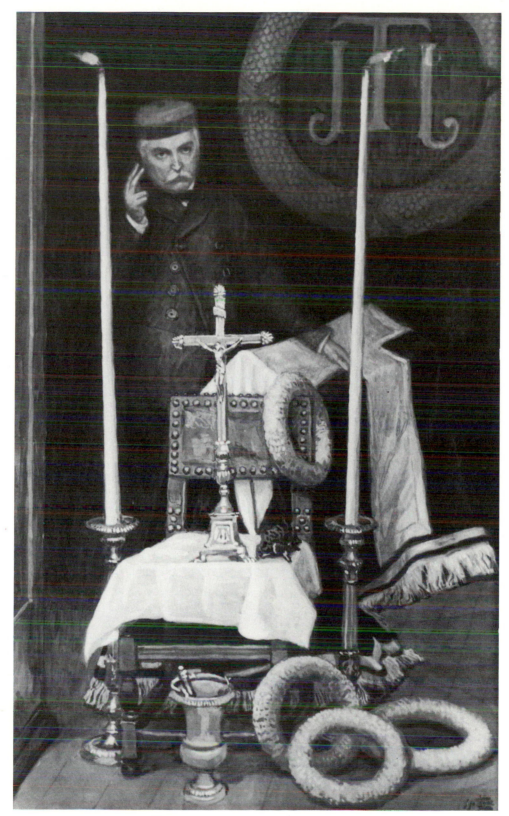

204. *Portrait of the Pilgrim, c.*1886–94.

202. Christ Falls Beneath the Cross, *c.*1886–94.

203. *What Our Saviour Saw from the Cross, c.*1886–94.